SAVING
EUROPE

# SAVING EUROPE

## How National Politics
## Nearly Destroyed the Euro

CARLO BASTASIN

BROOKINGS INSTITUTION PRESS
*Washington, D.C.*

THE BROOKINGS INSTITUTION
1775 Massachusetts Avenue, N.W., Washington, DC 20036
www.brookings.edu

*Library of Congress Cataloging-in-Publication data*

Bastasin, Carlo, 1959–
    Saving Europe : how national politics nearly destroyed the euro / Carlo Bastasin.
        p.    cm.
    Includes bibliographical references and index.
    ISBN 978-0-8157-2196-3 (hardcover : alk. paper)
    1. Monetary policy—European Union countries—History—21st century.  2. Global Financial Crisis, 2008–2009.  3. Euro.  4. Greece—Economic policy—21st century.
I. Title.
    HG930.5.B37  2012
    332.4'94—dc23                                                                            2012005675

9 8 7 6 5 4 3 2 1

Printed on acid-free paper

Typeset in Adobe Garamond

Composition by Cynthia Stock
Silver Spring, Maryland

Printed by R. R. Donnelley
Harrisonburg, Virginia

# Contents

# Acknowledgments

As with all important things in life, it was easier to set a precise starting date for this book than it was to end it. I began the research for the book, collecting information and analyses, in 2009, when I was working at the Peterson Institute for International Economics in Washington and was urged one day to write about the European crisis by the late Michael Mussa. I started the actual writing in 2010, when I was a nonresident senior fellow at the Brookings Institution, dividing my time between Europe and the United States. Until the beginning of 2012, I experienced from a very personal and anxious standpoint the succession of "solutions," "final solutions," and "comprehensive solutions" that have characterized the story of this crisis, whose ramifications in fact are likely to last for many years to come.

I want to thank all of the members of the team at the Brookings Institution Center on the United States and Europe, particularly Fiona Hill and Justin Vaisse for their amazing support and suggestions. For various reasons I am indebted to Franco Bruni, Doug Elliot, Cesare Merlini, Stefano Micossi, and other colleagues at the think tank EuropEos; to Riccardo Perissich, at the Center on the United States and Italy; to Nicolas Veron; and to several colleagues at the Peterson Institute. Several dozen European policymakers, government officials, and analysts, many of them longtime friends, helped me reconstruct the events surrounding the crisis. My gratitude goes to all of them.

Brookings Institution Press offered its valuable services and encouragement in publishing this project. All of the press staff was of great support. In particular, my thanks go to Robert Faherty, director of the press, and to Janet Walker, managing editor. The book benefited decisively from the work of John Felton as editor.

All my back and forth between Europe and the United States, spinning around a continuously changing story, would have not been possible without the firm and loving support of Erica and all my family.

# SAVING
# EUROPE

# Prologue: Other People's Eyes

In a matter of just a few years the euro area has been close to sinking at least three times: in September 2008, in May 2010, and in November 2011. Each time the existential reasons for the euro area have proven stronger than the weaknesses of the ship and the clumsiness of its command.

For a long time the timid solutions to the crisis were dictated mainly by national fears and reciprocal mistrust. Then, by the end of 2011 national politics had reached its limits. European priorities dictated even the change of governments and new common policies prevailed. However, until Europeans emerge with a common—non-national—narrative of the crisis, they will not be able to use the only possible means needed to end it: deeper political integration.

Until then, the crisis may be tamed and even settled temporarily, but it will keep corroding the foundations of the European Union, the world's most advanced attempt to form a human community among different peoples through supranational cooperation and acknowledgment of a common destiny. If the European experiment fails, the world will see national interests resurge in a time when global issues have become vital and cannot be solved by any single nation: social justice as well as freedom, economic cooperation and financial stability, the free circulation of people and of the fruit of their work, the protection of the environment, and peaceful developments in large parts of the emerging world. If there is any hope of a global democratic governance of those issues, it rests on the experience of pooled sovereignty.

The euro is the fragile crown of the European project of shared sovereignty. That is why its survival is so important. The fragility of the monetary union, institutionally and politically, has loomed larger against the backdrop of the power of financial markets whose size and feverish hypochondria are becoming both a guaranty and a pathology for democratic decisions. Under that pressure, European politics have often let mistrust prevail over inspiration. The repatriation of politics and the resurgence of national interests have already infiltrated the European economy. At the end of 2011, the European banking system—the fundamental infrastructure of economic integration—was completely segmented along national borders. The same was true of the financial system. National debts were largely repatriated. Gradually, the national economies were turning back into closed systems. At some point, if this process continues, it might not make much sense to share a common currency, strict fiscal rules, and an onerous system of laws. Since we know that Europe's breakup would hurl it back into obscurity, the search for solutions that do not go in the direction of repatriation must go further.

The reason why this is so difficult is that most of us are still following the wrong explanations of the causes behind the euro crisis. There is no European-wide public discourse, and the narratives are left in the hands of national politicians relating to national public opinions. Inevitably, the story of the euro crisis has become a story of national recriminations prevailing over facts.

I will give one example. On May 6, 2010, the Governing Council of the European Central Bank held an emergency meeting in the restaurant of a fifteenth-century palace in Lisbon. In a dramatic night when the whole world economy seemed to be collapsing, council members made the most unexpected decision in the history of the crisis of the euro area. One of the governors decided to speak the unspeakable and proposed that the ECB buy government bonds of the countries under attack from the markets. His proposal breached a taboo on which the euro had been built. It was a step that would cause the political contamination of the central bank's sacred independence, but it also was the first step into a shared fiscal responsibility among the different countries of the euro area. The shock of all the other bankers around the table could not have been greater because the man who had violated the dogma was Axel Weber, the head of the ultra-orthodox German Bundesbank.

That decision saved the euro, at least temporarily. But the central bankers had just landed back home in Frankfurt the following day when they received an e-mail from Weber saying that he had changed his mind. After a few days, he went public, attacking frontally the very decision he himself had proposed. By hiding the fact that he had been the inspiration for this momentous step, he inadvertently gave reasons for the false myth that Germany had been betrayed by her euro partners. This myth provided an unfounded but powerful narrative that changed Europe, inspiring a sense of mistrust and divisions that hampers the solution and may need decades to be mended.

When three of the participants told me this story—of maybe the single most significant event in the development of the crisis of the euro zone—and when I heard about many other episodes and saw how little-known or even secret they were, I had to accept that economics was not the only tool I could use to understand the amazing sequence of events known as the euro crisis. No matter how much deeper one could go into the study of the databases, that kind of analysis was insufficient and sometimes outright misleading. Unfortunately, the story of the crisis in the euro area had much more to do with politics and human behavior than with predictable statistical models. There was not an invisible hand behind the spiraling events, but rather governments, and private interests, and, above all, people who lost their jobs and safety nets. Finally, I thought that they, too, had remained invisible far too long.

For those reasons, this book is more about politics than about money. Some of the most relevant stories are only apparently financial. In April 2009, for instance, a portfolio constraint was informally imposed on the banks of the euro area that were instructed to channel massive liquidity they had received from the ECB to the states. This mandate to the banks was the first substantial violation of the EU treaty, but it took place in silence because it favored in particular those countries that were considered the bastions of the economic orthodoxy and could, in a system deprived of transparent democratic procedures, exploit their soft power in a hard way. Again, in late May 2010 European banks were told to avoid selling Greek, Irish, or Portuguese bonds because those countries had just been aided by the ECB. In just a few hours, French and Dutch banks started unloading the bonds to the ECB, leaving the burden to the rest of the euro area. The resentment for that imbroglio exploded months later, after German chancellor Angela Merkel and French president Nicolas Sarkozy agreed to impose losses on future investors of euro area bonds. Immediately Germany's banks triggered a sell-off of bonds of the debt-ridden countries, leading to the fateful crisis of 2011.

The story of the euro crisis is a story of developments in politics that raise questions about the pillars of democracy as we know it. Between 2009 and 2011, the crisis was influenced by an irresponsible tug-of-war between the ECB and the national governments. The consequences of the conflict between an unelected body entrusted with the general welfare and the democratically elected governments representing national interests were so grave that they represent a first disquieting test of the contradiction between jealous national powers and a weakly legitimated supranational governance.

Economists do not like to meddle in political analysis for fear of confusing the causes or, as they say, facing problems of reverse causations and of multicollinearity. I thought it was useful to proceed more descriptively, following the chronology and using heterogeneous facts without fear of compromising the analysis. The outcome of this long and tortuous journey is a diagnosis of the European malaise that differs from current public debates that lay the blame on two specific causes. The crisis was neither the fault of a bunch of profligate countries, nor was it caused solely by a group of reckless banks investing the net savings surpluses of their home markets in the bubbles of the European periphery. Those activities contributed, for sure, but the catalyst for the crisis was mainly political: Each country's national political leaders had been unable, since the outset of the euro, to respond to the social costs of globalization once they could no longer resort to the instruments, often delusive and deceitful, of national monetary policy. National politics shoved under the rug the structural changes connected to the new open economic environment, and in order to do that, each country would resort to different tricky stratagems that proved unsustainable once the crisis started. The rest of this prologue explains this interpretation more thoroughly. It concludes that fiscal coordination will not be enough to keep the euro area together and sees a compelling reason for more political integration. My take on events is that once the monopoly of national interpretations is removed, the crisis of the euro may bring a new direction to the history of Europe and beyond, to the role of the state, and to the relationship between public powers and the citizen.

The book is divided by years. It begins arbitrarily with September 2008, at the height of the global financial crisis, when Europe was less than one step away from bringing the world economy to its knees. I am still amazed to see how little understood was the devastating extent of the European banking crisis at that time. In chapter 2, I try to explain the powerful national political interests behind the decision of Chancellor Merkel and many other leaders not to tackle the banking crisis jointly. From that decision, in October 2008, originated the first signs of a sovereign debt problem in Europe, one year before the crisis became public. Political divisions also prevented Europe from taking the lead in shaping a new and fairer world economic and financial system. But the divergent interests among the EU countries were not only due to the inabilities of some leaders and to the pressure of the crisis. The euro countries are still different because of longstanding structural divergences, as explained in chapters 3 and 4, and it was naive to think that national leaders were capable of forgetting their interests by adopting artificially the same policy preferences.

It is surprising how rare the knowledge is that the sovereign debt crisis was evident at the very beginning of 2009 and that very advanced political countermeasures had already been studied (chapter 5). Eurobonds, fiscal union, and other remedies were already on the table. National interests behind the banks, again, were the reason why politics could not agree on actions other than involving the ECB in financing the banks and through the banks finance the governments' public debt (chapters 6 and 7). All this—the first substantial violation of the prohibition of ECB monetary financing of the states—was done in favor of German, Dutch, and French banks, and again it happened by keeping the public unaware. More important, the subterfuge of having the ECB silently finance the purchase of government debt produced the segmentation of sovereign markets, and was a major element of the fight between the ECB and governments in the design of the solution.

Chapter 8 sets the stage for the forthcoming and amazing role of the German Constitutional Court. The crisis cannot be understood without knowing the constraints that the court, at several stages, imposed on Chancellor Merkel. Chapter 9 deals with the discovery of a hidden accumulated deficit on the Greek account books, probably one of the best-known "secrets" of European history. The fact that European institutions had not been able to react earlier to the growing imbalances hidden in Greece led to a breakdown in trust in a common currency.

Dealing with the first half of 2010, chapters 10 to 14 are a central part of the book. They are primarily a chronological tale of the most acute phase of the euro crisis, when a mistaken strategy was adopted, and ending with the first bailout of Greece in May 2010.

Not well known at the time, nor since, the logic behind Merkel's reluctance to intervene was not only electoral, but legal, and she needed to bring the crisis to the point where it affected the whole euro area before she could legitimately intervene in the Greek bailout. Unfortunately, the interaction between politics and finance reached deep into the sentiments of the European peoples, often marring them. The attempts to build a new governance for the euro area were again a test of the conflict between national governments and the ECB (chapter 15). The rest of the story for 2010 is dominated by the shocking decision in Deauville by Merkel and Sarkozy to impose the so-called private sector involvement (that is, losses) in case of future defaults. Market fears took the lead in the crisis. Banks broke the hidden agreement with their governments not to sell the public debt of Greece, Ireland, and Portugal (chapter 16). The landslide began to accelerate.

In 2011 the crisis was marked by a dramatic intensification of the arm twisting between EU governments and the ECB. The acme came in March 2011 when the central bankers voted secretly to suspend the purchase of government securities (chapter 17) of Greece, Ireland, and Portugal. Soon, those countries' bonds became unsellable. Banks trying to deleverage began to sell bonds of the closest proxies: Italy and Spain. In the following months, during the summer, the landslide became unstoppable and extended to the whole euro area while national governments were still trying to buy time before tackling the crisis. In July 2011 (chapter 18), after the contagion went even beyond Italy and Spain, politics became the center of the problem (chapter 19). The insufficient response at national levels—the lack of credibility of the Italian government and the philosophy of "punishment" prevailing in Germany because of mistrust and pigheaded brinksmanship, transformed the crisis from something that directly affected just some countries into one that threatened the entire euro area. Finally, at the end of 2011, the crisis seemed to head toward the break-up of the euro area (chapter 20). This was a dramatic moment that forced national governments, EU institutions, and the ECB to get their act together and design a partial solution: massive liquidity provided by the ECB would facilitate the financing of state debts, but without preventing the markets from continuing to pile pressure on the ailing countries. The goal was to reach 2013 with a euro area turned into a fiscally sterilized zone; in other words, the fiscal problems of any one country could not infect the others. Once public debts were harmless, it would be possible to rearrange some form of economic solidarity and some new kind of economic government. At least, that is the hope.

The lessons of this crisis depend on what we know surrounding the events that led up to and during the crisis, and they will determine the political future of Europe. For this reason I thought it was important to offer a description of the events now, at the beginning of 2012, before the crisis is over, for better or for worse. It will take decades to unravel all the details of the current events, and I am perfectly aware that this book cannot be other than a first contribution. It highlights the mistakes but also the objective difficulties of policymakers in tackling a crisis that could, if handled properly, mark the end of national divisions in a united Europe. In this sense, the euro crisis, after coming close to disrupting the global economy, could still change the world for the better by showing a new sense for human interdependency that speaks the language of solidarity.

In order to overcome the crisis, understanding its causes is indispensable. Two distinct interpretations have dominated discussions of how the crisis matured, and they both begin with the observation that after 1999 there was a significant decline in real interest rates in the so-called peripheral countries within the European Monetary Union: Greece, Ireland, Portugal, Spain, and Italy. According to the first analysis, financial investors from countries that had accumulated excess savings reacted to the absence of devaluation risks in the euro area by moving capital rapidly from the core countries to the periphery, where interest rates were still relatively higher. German and French banks, among others, invested many hundreds of billions of euros in the peripheral countries in a short period of time. The massive inflow of capital led to a sudden and indiscriminate increase in domestic demand, both private and public consumption or investments, in countries like Greece, Ireland, and Spain. The stimulus pushed up the price levels and reduced the competitiveness in those countries, making them even more dependent on foreign capital inflows. That money suddenly disappeared with the financial disruptions of 2008 and the heightened risk aversion caused by the global crisis, and external deficit in the periphery became unsustainable.

The second analysis explains that after the onset of the euro, on the back of lower interest rates, the pressure on government debt service declined in the peripheral countries. Governments abused the fiscal leeway by increasing primary spending. Between 2000 and 2008, Portugal and Ireland both saw annual increases in public expenditure levels of around 6 percent at constant prices, while Greece and Spain averaged around 3.5 percent. Those countries mismanaged the "euro-dividend," that is, the benefit of joining a strong currency with lower interest rates, or they did not take advantage of the new scenario to decisively tackle their public debts. Until 2007 the large increases in public spending were broadly offset by revenue generated from real estate bubbles in Spain and Ireland, also a consequence of low real interest rates. But when financial conditions worsened, the precariousness of fiscal positions in the periphery emerged dramatically.

The first explanation blames the German or French banks for reckless investments, while the second blames the stubborn fiscal profligacy, private indebtedness, low efficiency, and political backwardness of peripheral countries.

Neither of the two explanations cited above is self-sufficient in explaining the crisis without highlighting a significant factor backing both, an understanding of which is required to design a stable solution. And this factor is that the crisis actually was produced by a vast array of short-sighted national policy choices enacted intentionally by all countries for many years since the beginning of the euro in substantial disregard of the consequences for Europe as a whole.

In the 1990s the political meaning of the forthcoming euro was not entirely understood. The common currency was often characterized as an instance of foreign exchange rate integration, one that would reduce exchange rate uncertainties and cut costs for trade. The effect of the monetary union on trade growth within the euro area was overestimated. The overarching effect of globalization changed the expected scenario for European integration, because trade developed more intensely toward other areas (notably Eastern Europe and the new emerging economies), creating more competition than integration among states sharing the same currency. Germany, in particular between the conception of the euro and 2008, became the most trade-oriented country of the G-7 group, almost doubled export and import relative to its GDP, and moved its supply chain for intermediate goods from the south of Europe to the non-euro Visegrad countries (Czech Republic, Hungary, and Poland) and its imports toward products produced most cost effectively by China rather than in Europe. Thus, while German exports (capital goods, intermediate goods, or pharmaceuticals) remained largely insulated from the new global competition, Europe's periphery faced the new reality of global low-wage competition and growing trade imbalances within the euro area.

Also because of the delays in the full implementation of the EU single market, the expected homogeneity induced by internal trade remained only a muted driver of reforms in the euro area. Benign increases in global trade and the toxic stimulus of monetary policy made it easy for governments to hide the need for political action at both the domestic and the European level.

The challenge for politics—in shifting from national frameworks, protected by national monetary policies, to a global open economy—was unprecedented. In the monetary union, governments had to give up a large part of their past policy instruments. While competition increased both within and outside Europe, the countries of the euro area had relinquished the tool of domestic currency devaluation necessary to correct a deficit of competitiveness or an external imbalance. Nor could changes in the money supply and in price levels be used anymore to rebalance the relationship between labor and capital or among sectors of activity. The maneuvering room for fiscal policy also was limited by the strictures of the common fiscal rules. Finally, the old industrial policies, favoring certain sectors of the economy or even specific companies, were limited by the rules of the EU internal market.

In one sense, this was exactly how things were meant to be. European countries needed to embrace stable economic policies and to concentrate on restructuring their economies in an open global market. To do that they committed to apply structural reforms that let capital flow toward the most productive activities and to improve the quality of the labor force. Some countries indeed did this, notably Germany and northern European countries, which started growing at the fastest rates in the western world. Some other countries thought mainly of buying themselves some more time. But all of the euro countries, even the most virtuous, resorted to policies leveraging some form of national opportunism and self-protection that finally produced the crisis.

There is one common rationale in all political systems, however different they may be. Whether in Greece or in Germany or anyplace else, governments prefer policies that allow them to minimize the political cost relative to the result. They do not want to lose the consensus of their voters when they must implement unpopular policies. Hence, they look for "under-the-carpet" strategies. If they have to cut public expenditures, some will opt for shifting the effects onto future generations. If they have to make work more flexible, some prefer to apply it first to migrant workers, who often do not have the right to vote. If national industry has to undergo a painful restructuring, governments will find some kind of financial buffer that will transfer the cost to the future or abroad, in either case again to nonvoters. Each of these is a perfectly rational choice if measured against the political time-horizon of a legislature: the time scale of political costs and elections, four or five years in general. But the kind of economic processes that this behavior helps produce can slip out of control in a matter of a few years and then reveal its real face: political opportunism based on subconscious nationalism and hidden imbalances. In Europe it has been the dark side of the coin, literally, an inglorious national reaction to the visionary choice of creating the euro.

Bogged down by foreign competition, southern European countries have developed a dual market economy where the less vocal or less official part of society—the young, the migrants, the poor—absorbed all the flexibility that was needed to protect the others. The part of the economy that was submerged or even undeclared was also obscured by the political debate. Italy is a good example: it is thought to have lost 30 percent of its competitiveness against Germany in the decade after the onset of the euro, and that is surely so if calculated on the basis of official labor costs. But if one takes the consumer price level as way to compare competitiveness, Italy's competitive loss relative to Germany was almost irrelevant (2–3 percent over ten years). What Italy had done was to compensate for the competitive loss in the regular market by taking advantage of its lowest paid workers, often immigrants, the young, and women, or by abusing tax loopholes through extreme outsourcing, and by sinking part of the country's activity into the black economy. All this allowed Italy to maintain high official wages and at the same time relatively low prices to compete with the other economies. Paradoxically, it also was a politically efficient way to adapt to the monetary union because it ensured to the Italian government the support of a majority of voters. When the crisis broke, however, the underlying fragility of this economy, previously shoved under the carpet, became evident, and Italy had between 2008 and 2011 the worst loss of GDP in the euro area.

Every country reacted with its own tricks. France allowed for higher-than-average public deficits and defended national agricultural and industrial champions by any means. In the ten years after the onset of the euro, France six times violated the deficit limits of the Stability and Growth Pact with no economic justification and kept its public debt at a round total of 15–20 percent of GDP above what was justified and had been agreed with its partners. Ireland tapped European savings through a combination of free riding on the European tax regime and of real estate inflation without any sense of the damage it was causing, first, to the other countries and, second, to its own economy. Political opportunism had also a more conventional face. Luxembourg, for example, had exploited its less-than-accessible tax regime to grant its citizens the highest level of income in the EU. But most of the under-the-carpet opportunism had not been consciously conceived before the euro; it was only the fruit of short-sighted political navigation. Spain's system stands out because of the structure of its collective bargaining, which greatly constrains wage flexibility, and the privileges of permanent workers. Flexibility is provided entirely by a minority: 30 percent of the labor force is mostly deprived of the guarantees given to others. Madrid entered the European monetary system with the highest unemployment rate at 24 percent. In the strong growth period that followed, the unemployment fell to 8 percent in 2007. As the global financial crisis struck, unemployment soared back to 20 percent and swathes of the economy bogged down, proving the precariousness of previous reforms. Between 2000 and 2008, Portugal increased its public-sector wage bill to 13 percent of GDP, while Greece, Ireland, and Spain increased public-sector pay to around 11 percent of GDP. Those salary policies provided political consensus, but they also required external indebtedness that at the time seemed cheap. Greece's hidden buffer for absorbing the competitive pressures was more extreme and pervasive; as noted, the financial reality was hidden and statistics obfuscated.

Even Germany had a secret that allowed it to accommodate the challenge of globalization under monetary union, and actually became a primary cause of the crisis. German banks could get money at the lowest rates in the euro zone and invest it for a decade in higher yielding assets: for much of the 2000s, those were not only American toxic assets but the sovereign bonds of Greece, Ireland, Portugal, Spain, and Italy. For ten years this German version of the carry trade brought substantial profits to the German banks—on the order of hundreds of billions of euros—that did not show up on their balance sheets because the money was transferred to German firms as low-cost loans or to the German political system in the form of abundant financing for regional projects such as infrastructure development. Those profits, paid by other countries' taxpayers, enabled Germany to master, like no other, its restructuring for the global challenge. The relevance of this source of profit is amazingly neglected, although between 1997 and 2008 Germany exported two-thirds of its substantial domestic savings. The total amount of German capital exported between 2002 and 2010 was above €1 trillion, which, thanks to the euro, could be rewarded at rates far higher than the cost of provision and without currency risk. The German advantage, relative to all other countries in terms of cost of funding, has developed into an exorbitant privilege. French banks exploited a similar advantage, given their major role as financial intermediaries between AAA-rated countries and higher yielding debtors in the euro area. The substantial resulting profits often were transferred into assistance for French national firms.

All those policy choices were abused as substitutes for structural reforms and for the elimination of remaining barriers within the EU single market. These choices contributed in different and substantial ways to the building up of divergences and imbalances that came close to destroying the euro area. When the crisis broke, the euro area economy was strained exactly in those points: German banks, Italy's growth, France's public finance, and so on.

The crisis in the euro zone is not a story, certainly not only a story, of delinquency in Greek government statistics. Neither is it a story of irreducible differences in national cultures that will forever separate a selfish but reliable North and an irresponsible and easygoing South. These are catchy suggestions ingrained in a corner of our experience, in our need for categories and clichés, and also in our complacency with prejudices.

It would be unjust to put all countries on the same level, but the crisis was caused by a collective exercise of political illusionism, based on a deliberate choice not to see the euro as a common responsibility and the euro area as a new political dimension. Our political traditions based on partisanship in closed economies provided a justification not to adopt structural economic policymaking consistent with an open political and economic space.

Governments defend their "absurd monopoly," as German finance minister Wolfgang Schäuble called it. But the worst monopoly is the one that concerns the misleading communication by national governments to their electorates. Contrary to the simplistic and self-serving explanations offered in the various capitals, the euro crisis is a multifaceted problem of fiscal crisis in Greece; competitiveness deficits in the southern periphery; a banking crisis in Germany, France, Benelux, Ireland, Spain, and elsewhere; a flawed initial design of the institution presiding over the euro area; and most of all a failure in national politics. If these problems are not tackled together, the crisis will resurface regularly. The lack of a common "European narrative" makes it easier for the national political monopolies to deny the need for further transfers of sovereignty and ultimately solve the crisis.

I do not underestimate the difficulties faced by policymakers during the crisis. The events show that the pressure of financial markets, particularly when they are led by their most speculative avant garde, can be an enormous ballast for policymakers who need to design a long-term strategy allowing savings to flow again from one country to another of the euro area as requested by the inevitable current account imbalances. The euro market for interest rates swap, for instance, is twenty-five times larger than the total amount of government debt in the euro area. A shiver on its spine can break a country in a matter of hours.

Governments are accountable foremost to their national democratic systems. Merkel and the leaders of the German opposition, for instance, have carried the public opinion a very long way beyond where it started. At moments, the nationalistic resurgence in the German public state of mind has been strong and disturbing. More radical feelings surfaced uncontrolled in many other countries, and it was crucial that the German Parliament kept them at bay by consistently

repulsing populist temptations. Merkel has left her fingerprints on some fundamental mistakes—hiding the vices of German banks, dragging the Greek crisis
on far too long, and imposing losses for private investors—but she found little cooperation from the other heads of governments of the euro area when she
sought for a strategy beyond the short term. Merkel is actually unique in building
an ambitious strategy that leads Europe to the Political Union. Sarkozy had the
right intuitions at the beginning but then retreated into national thinking. New
actors like Mario Monti can be the harbingers of a new generation of European-
national policymakers. Others were pathetic and dangerous. Nevertheless, it must
be acknowledged that even during the deepest recession in the history of the EU,
the leaders did not unwind the rules and the laws presiding over the Union.

Unfortunately, Greece's discovery of a shocking fiscal deficit in 2009 was seen
as the "proton pseudos," the original lie, that eroded trust and solidarity. Most
countries resorted to minor accounting tricks—as shown by the discrepancies
between the levels of public debt and the sums of the yearly deficits—but discovering that the Greek deficit was reported at 3 percent of GDP when it actually was 15 percent appeared such a blatant fraud that the smaller fudges across
the euro area disappeared and moral judgment adhered to national characterizations edging on racism. It was not important that Germany and France, with
the active support of Italy, had violated and changed the rules of the Stability
and Growth Pact and that they had prevented the European Commission from
gaining the powers to control national accounts. It came all too naturally that, at
a moment when national governments had to counter the effects of the crisis on
their electorates, the political rhetoric allowed national identity to prevail over
integration. It was a major political mistake. So we are now inclined to think
that we have to disentangle the virtuous and the vicious along national borders.

Identity means also that the euro area has now adopted one single reading
of the crisis, according to which its sole cause was the fiscal profligacy in the
periphery. It is a simple, single, and wrong explanation. Once this "linear" interpretation prevails, we give up the task of understanding that all the mechanisms
of the crisis are actually "nonlinear": contagion, multiple equilibria, sudden
stops, changes of regime, risk correlation, self-fulfilling expectations, and so on.
All of these financial phenomena would require a "nonlinear" political response
or, more simply, an assumption of common political responsibility for the euro
area as a whole.

Moreover, identity is simply the wrong approach for an economic integrated
area. Although Germany is showing the most encouraging model for single
economies in a global context, all countries cannot be equal. On the contrary,
an integrated area thrives from the various specialties of its regions or states.
Inevitably each region will have different productivity levels, and each state's

balance of payments does not have to be on par with the rest to coexist. But if integration must prevail on identity, there is no alternative: some form of solidarity is intrinsic to integration. Eventually, since different economic structures create different political preferences in each country, a democratic system of decisionmaking must emerge and political union must follow.

Political responsibility is needed to develop the strategy of fiscal consolidation into a real fiscal union. The process is already pointing in this direction. National budgetary rules are being strengthened all across the euro area, in part through the adoption of constitutional obligations to keep budgets balanced. Reciprocal control will be enhanced and centralized surveillance will be strengthened. The new legal procedure to prevent excessive imbalances and the European Systemic Risk Board should prevent the buildup of excessive private indebtedness, and further improvements are in the pipeline. The ECB surveillance of countries that receive aid proves that all major domains in economic policy will be kept under scrutiny, including productivity developments and wage-setting agreements. Mutual assistance will be accompanied by comprehensive macroeconomic adjustment programs, which will be discussed and voted on together. National policies will be confronted and discussed in Brussels before even being presented to the national parliaments.

Even if the root causes of the crisis were not fiscal in nature, all its remedies have a fiscal character, representing a transfer of aid from one country to another. So it is important to proceed with fiscal stabilization that can offer guarantees on the future to the creditor countries. From this perspective, 2013 should be the turning point of the crisis. In order to get there, the euro area must undergo a number of severe tests, whose outcomes are far from certain; first of all, it will have to avoid a debt-deflation spiral. Two years later, in 2015, all countries will have a balanced budget, and political cooperation will be possible. The crisis itself has produced the pillars of fiscal federalism and of political cooperation, as explained in the last pages of this book. On its face, this framework promises to make the euro area a more "optimal" currency area. But is democracy so easy to put aside? Or shall we not discover one day that European rules will be circumvented again if they are not discussed and voted on by the citizens? The new institutional framework creates a problem of political legitimacy. As Kant said, the citizen's juridical liberty is the faculty not to obey external laws but rather those to which he has been able to give his consent. A political dimension at the euro level seems inescapable.

The amazing structural changes happening in all euro area countries as a consequence of the crisis, although obscured by the drama of the daily emergency, show that if it manages to endure its painful transition, the euro area soon could be quite a different place, more homogeneous than ever, both in economic and in sociopolitical terms. As in all homogeneous societies, solidarity will find an easier terrain. Guaranteed by reciprocal fiscal control, common initiatives to promote growth on the continent might find solid ground. Pooling resources to build up European research, infrastructures, and welfare will be a rational development. Eventually a common public discourse might see citizens of different countries discuss and decide together their common future in a real federal union and maybe even discover a new non-national meaning for the old aspiration of brotherhood, equality, and liberty.

The aim of this book is not to find solutions, but to offer a mirror to European citizens, so that they could see themselves through the eyes of others. And to show to the American observer how critical interdependency will be in the future. In this sense, the European crisis provides for a formidable challenge for the rethinking of national democracy, also from the American side.

The European crisis had the potential to be the "worst" economic crisis in the history of Europe. It has also the potential to be the "best" political crisis. But to finally approach Ithaca, Ulysses had to cross Scylla and Charybdis. It was never meant to be easy. It may even be a sign of destiny. In ancient times, the Italian strait between Scylla and Charybdis was especially dangerous because of its troubled waters. And because of the harsh mythological wind blowing from Greece. Whose name was Euro.

# 1

## The Origin of Mistrust

### "Chacun Sa Merde"

It did not either knock on the door, or crash the gate. In September 2008, the global financial crisis entered in Europe in silence and brought it to the brink of collapse in a surreal obscurity.

While all the lights were focused on Wall Street's bankruptcies shaking the world, Chancellor Angela Merkel entrenched herself behind a wall of silence as she saw Germany, hidden from public awareness, head toward the same financial meltdown, as one bank after the other risked crumbling before her eyes.

On October 4, 2008, on the stairway of the Elysée Palais in the heart of Paris, she did not even want to pay heed to Nicolas Sarkozy, the French president, who was asking for an immediate, coordinated European reaction. Turning away from her and from the microphones, the French president confessed to his advisers: "If we cannot cobble together a European solution then it will be a debacle. But it will not be my debacle; it will be Angela's. You know what she said to me? 'Chacun sa merde!' (To each his own *merde*)."

Actually, according to an aide of hers, Merkel had quoted a proverb taken from a work written by a monumental figure of German culture, Johann Wolfgang Goethe: "Ein jeder kehr' vor seiner Tür, und rein ist jedes Stadtquartier" (Everyone should sweep in front of his door and every city quarter will be clean).[1] To make the disagreement between the two leaders more ironic, Sarkozy turned back to the press and uttered: "It is absolutely obvious that there are differences between our cultures. . . ."

The reason why Merkel was so opposed to putting on the table "some money," as Sarkozy called it, and backing up the dramatically endangered

European banking system, was indeed also a matter of cultural differences in the heart of Europe. Merkel was shocked by the amount of incalculable risks that she was discovering in her own country and who knows what was hidden in the other countries: homework had to come first. Sarkozy, in that moment of need, had the intuition instead that he could solve the French banks' problems by leveraging a European common response.

It was also a typical Sarkozy-Merkel confrontation: the former's politics by instinct versus the latter's politics by program. "You do not have a real plan," Merkel said to Sarkozy at the Elysée. She did not consider Sarkozy's proposal a credible course of action. Setting up a common fund, mainly financed by Germany, that could become a self-service stash for any country trying to rescue its own banks was a non-starter in her eyes. In a government meeting in Berlin, Merkel had just reckoned that the European bank–umbrella plan that Sarkozy was demanding would make Germany contribute €75 billion, without knowing precisely for what use. Although the French president was urging the move as matter of survival for Europe, Merkel maintained that putting together a common fund would require months of preparations and preliminary negotiations. It was impossible in a few days to arrange a proper legal framework, even only at the national levels. And Merkel did need to make each step legally watertight and she needed also to know how to involve the German Parliament: "They would not understand." She was not le Président, she was die Kanzlerin in a federal, democratic system. Moreover, a common teller open to each and every bank would confuse the responsibilities. Any bank, from any country, could help itself, tap the common resources, and maybe even remain unknown. Finally, and most important, she had learned that it was not a matter of just "some money." It was hundreds and hundreds of billions of euros.

That first disagreement at the Elysée was a milestone in a long story of national interests, political hesitations, and half-hearted reciprocal trust that would make Merkel, Sarkozy, and the other leaders of the euro area accompany the euro to the brink of collapse several times in the following years. It was indeed a crucial moment for the destiny of the euro. National leaders—driven foremost by local economic and political interests—denied that Europe was on the brink. They succeeded in keeping the reality temporarily hidden from the public, but from that very moment they undermined the possibility of a common European response to the crisis. Ever since, the financial threat hitting some banks—particularly in Germany, France, the Netherlands, and Ireland—willingly neglected, mystified, or downplayed, grew larger month by month. In the following years, it became almost impossible to recover the road to unity. Eventually, the seams of the euro area were torn by the consequences of that initial division.

In fact, before coming back at the end of the next chapter to this eventful meeting at the Elysée at the beginning of October, it is necessary to look in some depth at the dramatic events of the weeks and even of the years before-hand and to see at work the powerful factors that made a European response impossible when it was most needed: the fact that the original responsibility for the crisis was primarily American; the hidden problems of the European banks; the national political interests behind the banks; and the conflict between the governments' interests and the action of the European institutions, first among them the European central bank. This is a combination that will be determinant for the rest of the crisis.

On September 15, 2008, three weeks before the Elysée meeting, the U.S. secretary of the Treasury had decided to let the investment bank Lehman Brothers go bankrupt, creating the biggest financial crisis in recent memory anywhere in the world. European leaders were growing aware that the Wall Street crisis, "the American mess" as they called it, was about to haunt them with equal vehemence. The initial, underlying feeling of relief that the difficulties of the "Anglo-Saxons" (as some Europeans sometimes referred to the Americans and the British) were not being visited upon the Europeans and that the speculators in the United States had gotten their just desserts was rapidly fading. The sense of immunity was unraveling, and with good reason: American toxic securities, including the infamous subprime mortgage assets, had been massively absorbed by European banks, and contagion was spreading fast, all the more so because financial interconnections among the twenty-seven European Union countries had grown inextricable in the previous years. Although practically no one was aware of it at the time, Germany had in fact been less than one step away from launching itself and the rest of Europe into a catastrophic crisis triggered by the near-collapse of a German bank. "A few days before, we had just defused the nuclear meltdown," a central banker remembered. "Nobody had understood how close we were."

This is what Merkel knew, and she was particularly worried about the political consequences of what was happening around the world and in her country. A financial crisis was almost inexplicable to European citizens who, all of a sudden, had to be told that they were losing their jobs because some highly paid bankers somewhere in the universe had taken too many risks using their money. The chancellor had seen that people in her country were growing disgruntled with the symbols of power, notably bankers and politicians. She was not going to throw the money of German taxpayers at irresponsible and wretched bankers in her own country, let alone in others. Eventually this whole story was a matter of democracy, not of instinct.

In fact, uncertain over the extent of the crisis, and certain of popular discontent, most European leaders remained hesitant and wary of each other. Just a few days before the October meeting at the Elysée, the Irish government had broken ranks with the rest of Europe. In sheer panic, Dublin announced that it would guarantee all deposits in its six biggest financial institutions for the next two years. If any of the national banks got into difficulties, Irish savers would be sure to get their money back. What would happen to the foreign depositors at the same banks? Or to the foreign banks in Ireland? "Chacun sa merde!" Not one word had been offered to coordinate or even prepare other governments. The decision was aimed at avoiding bank runs and was thus rational from a purely Irish political perspective. However, if other EU countries had attempted to do the same, savers would naturally have withdrawn their savings from banks in countries where these were not guaranteed by the state and channelled them to banks in countries where they were.

Had this spiral of "beggar-thy-neighbor" measures escalated, the integrated financial market would have been shattered and renationalized into domestic markets. The rights of foreigners would be denied and, step by step, legal and political conflicts would have erupted among the EU countries for the first time since 1957 and the Treaty of Rome establishing the predecessor body to the EU. Chancellor Merkel was on a flight to St. Petersburg when she was informed from the news wires of Dublin's decisions. Her reaction was blunt: If requested, the Germans would not bail out any ailing Irish banks, even though she knew that German banks, the public-owned Landesbanken in particular, were among the biggest creditors of Irish financial institutions. It would have been the perfect moment for the European Commission to take the initiative. This supranational institution in Brussels is the executive arm of the EU and is expected to put the interests of the citizens above those of single states. The commission could impose the priority of the common European interest over any uncoordinated initiative. But instead there was no protest against Dublin from Brussels. Not incidentally, the member of the EU Commission responsible for financial services was an Irishman. That was a fateful and telling sign: since the beginning, the European story of the crisis was being told as much by silences as by shouts.

## Good-Bye to American Capitalism: Europe's Turn to Lead

The financial crisis had severely damaged American credibility. From a European perspective, Wall Street was the epicenter of greedy speculations that had triggered an unprecedented global shock. But while the United States was the largest net debtor in the world—reflecting its large current account deficits during the previous decade—the euro area was the world's largest holder of external assets and liabilities. The rapid spread of the crisis globally had highlighted the exorbitant role of finance that, superficially, seemed to distinguish the American from the continental economic models, but actually linked the two worlds. The shock originating in the U.S. financial system had led to disruption in the banking systems in Europe and around the world. In turn, the financial collapse gradually transmitted to the "real" economy (that is, the non-financial sector), as was more and more evident in the United States. Even the impressive growth of the past decade in America—on average 1 point of GDP each year greater than in the euro area—proved misleading once one took into account that the American growth had been inflated by extensive debt creation in the private sector.

But financial integration, promoted by the new, adventurous capitalism imported from Wall Street, had created also a strong interdependence around the world. The American problem was not a problem for America alone. The wealth of European citizens, and their capacity to consume and invest, were influenced by rapid swings in the prices of foreign assets. In part, this was because banks had put a great deal of foreign bonds and stocks into the port-folios of European households and firms. The volatility of foreign asset prices also had large consequences across borders. For all of its suspicion about inter-national finance, Europe had a 50 percent larger amount of foreign assets than the United States relative to the GDP—even without taking into account the intra-EU allocations. Finally, when risk aversion or outright panic emerged in the United States, it rapidly spread throughout the world, changing the invest-ment climate everywhere. Europe discovered it was by no means isolated from the U.S. financial excesses. Its banks had willingly participated in the go-go years of easy finance, maintaining later that it was an Anglo-Saxon manipula-tion of the European virtues of saving and restraint. Criticism of the influence of Wall Street and of the City of London in spreading toxic financial assets in Europe was not unfounded: for instance, two-thirds of the European holdings of U.S. toxic assets par excellence—long-term corporate mortgage-backed secu-rities, the infamous subprimes—were traded through the Cayman Islands, the City of London, and Ireland. American insurance giant AIG alone sold from its London subsidiary $500 billion of credit default swaps to European counter-parts, making them the final victims of the securitization "global food chain." Entire real estate markets, like the Spanish, had been transformed into specula-tive "bubbles" through the supply of cheap mortgages by the British banks that pushed the debts of households sky-high.

In an atmosphere that seemed to represent the twilight of global capitalism surrounding the crisis, "leading the world" became more than just a slogan for European politicians. Europe had long preserved a certain skepticism toward the primacy of the economy and the rightfulness of markets. A culture of politi-cal morality had produced both devastating wars and their antidotes: democ-racy and the separation of powers. The welfare state embodied in European social programs had become the only way to reconstruct a collective sense of positive patriotism after the annihilating experiences of the totalitarian regimes of the first half of the twentieth century. The same historical motivation had led peoples and states to choose the way of the integration of nations and had generated the project of European-wide institutions after World War II. The

EU itself was also an attempt to rise to the global challenge. Taken together, the EU's twenty-seven countries are the largest economic block of the world, and their combined population of around 500 million is the third-largest after China and India. The euro area alone has a larger population than the United States. The EU countries accounted in 2008 for just more than 28 percent of global GDP, greater than the United States (25 percent) and the single largest block in the world.

Their unique form of both supranational and intergovernmental cooperation relies on a new and untested form of power, where leadership derives from consent, and diversity leads to dialogue. In principle, national sovereignty gives way to the will of the majority among European citizens. This was intended to be a pattern that, in the spirit of the founders, could be extended to peaceful cooperation in the world, offering a model for the new emerging powers and, finally, giving a sense of destiny and goodness to Europe's history and thus solving the Schuldfrage, the guilt question, of a continent tarnished by wars and atrocity during the twentieth century. But beneath the grandeur of the European dream remain national interests, personal ambitions, and politics. If "leading" is still a nontranslatable word for Germans, it persists as an oneiric temptation that leaders of these ancient and aging countries, trapped between symbols and traditions of their nineteenth-century sovereignties, cannot resist. Most of them are still governing from within ancient palaces among baroque mirrors that deform the present. They breed fictions of sovereignty and fight deadly domestic political battles while actually yielding power month by month to the global markets or to supranational institutions. Eventually, if they could not find a way to govern globalization, their national powers would be based on denying reality.

In fact, above European citizens hovers a sense of incipient decline, as China, India, Russia, and Brazil appear to be on the rise. Hegel's prophecy—whereby the spirit of the world moves from east to west ("following the movement of the sun")—seems relevant now, and the circle is closing as it approaches Asia. Europeans seem intimidated by the growing social complexity of a globalized world, between changing local conditions and irresistible external pressures. Individuals grope for orientation in increasingly overheated political competitions at national levels, where it is difficult for them to distinguish between action and empty communication. The sense of becoming negligible manifests itself in the spasms of populist politics or in a last nationalistic gasp of its leaders. In a debate at the British Parliament in December 2008, Gordon Brown argued that he had "saved the world," provoking such an outburst of derision from the ranks of the opposition that he strived to regain control, groped awkwardly, and repeated the phrase several times—that he actually had "saved the world . . . banks." At the IMF meetings in Washington, just five days after the fateful summit of October 4, German finance minister Peer Steinbrück attacked the hegemony of the

Americans and the British who "through financial domination had brought the world on the brink of collapse" instead of accepting the wisdom of the German Sozialmarktwirtschaft (social market economy), a sentiment that was widely shared in Berlin. During the previous months, Steinbrück had a number of frontal clashes with the Bush administration. He was still furious remembering how his American counterpart had once received him for just eleven minutes, while standing in a hall. Things had changed now. One official in Washington remembers the climate in those days: "Suddenly we were like pariahs; we were not in the condition to even put forward a suggestion. People were yelling at us and we ourselves knew we bore the responsibility."[2]

During the Bush administration, Europe had stepped up its universalist rhetoric. With good reason, Angela Merkel had used the words "to lead the world" while she was fashioning European policies against climate change and pushing to enact substantial initiatives along those guidelines. At a meeting on October 11, 2008, in the salons of the Smithsonian's National Portrait Gallery in Washington, French finance minister Christine Lagarde recalled that one month earlier she had warned her American colleague, Henry Paulson, of "the coming tsunami" if he let Lehman fail: "The situation is so critical," Lagarde said then, "that my take is that the U.S. has listened, is listening, and will continue to listen to the advice and recommendations of the Europeans. . . . For decades, Europe has been forced to run after the United States, and what is abusively called the Anglo-Saxon world, regarding finance. Now we are clearly seeing a changeover."[3]

In Italy, Silvio Berlusconi boasted offhandedly that he had convinced the American president of the need to bail out the U.S. banks, and had avoided a return to the cold war after Russia invaded Georgia by making a few persuasive calls to his personal friend Vladimir Putin. In fact, the European ambition to "lead the world" became intellectually and politically more compelling with the diplomatic maneuvers of Nicolas Sarkozy, who had assumed the rotating presidency of the European Council (the EU's top policy body composed of heads of state and government) in July 2008, just as the Georgian crisis was coming to a head. With a string of visits and timely and well-aimed initiatives, Sarkozy won the signatures of Moscow and Tbilisi for a six-point ceasefire agreement prepared by French diplomats. "We talk a lot of the importance of a global role for the European Union; we now have an opportunity to prove it," he said to his European colleagues shortly thereafter, according to a participant.

And Sarkozy certainly did not mean to confine European leadership to the diplomatic realm. America in late 2008 was mired in the shocks and controversies of the waning Bush administration. An election would bring a new U.S. president, who would take office the following January. In the meantime, Sarkozy argued, Europe had the opportunity and the duty to lead the world away from the kind of "free-wheeling capitalism" that had taken it to the verge of collapse. Sarkozy called instead for a "new world," in an address to the United Nations General Assembly on September 23, shortly after the collapse of Lehman Brothers. "Let us rebuild together a regulated capitalism in which whole swathes of financial activity are not left to the sole judgment of market operators, in which banks do their job, which is to finance economic development rather than engage in speculation, in which prudential rules apply to all and serve to avert and soften shocks instead of exacerbating them, in which credit agencies are controlled, in which transparency replaces opacity, in which modes of remuneration do not drive people to take unreasonable risks, in which those who jeopardize people's savings are punished."[4]

Sarkozy is the kind of energetic person who can enter a revolving door behind you and unmistakably get out before you. Elected to the French presidency in May 2007 at age 52, he had been considered predestined for the job for a decade. "What made me who I am now is the sum of all the humiliations suffered during childhood," he said once. But he had regularly managed to convert his frustrations into new ambitions. On that October 4, for instance, he had gathered in Paris the heads of government of the four European countries belonging to the Group of Seven (G-7). The idea of the summit had emerged in the previous week, during Sarkozy's daily telephone contacts with Angela Merkel. Besides himself and Merkel, there were also prime ministers Gordon Brown of Britain and Silvio Berlusconi of Italy. They were then joined by the president of the European Commission, José-Manuel Barroso; the president of the European Central Bank, Jean-Claude Trichet; and by Jean-Claude Juncker, the chairman of the group of the finance ministers of the euro area (Eurogroup). The EU needed to find a common position ahead of a meeting of the full G-7 to be held in Washington just six days later on October 10, and which was supposed to offer a remedy to the crisis of capitalism. Sarkozy wanted to show that Europe was capable of reacting to the crisis better than the United States. He had planned to set up a common European fund to rescue the banks, more effective than the one created in America after the Lehman Brothers disaster, the crisis of American Insurance Group (AIG), the U.S. government–sponsored enterprises, Freddie Mac and Fanny Mae, and dozens of other smaller financial institutions. Finally, he wanted to convince the United States to take part in a summit of the world's leading economies and at that event to "recast capitalism in a way to allow European ideas to flourish." In simple terms, he sensed that it was the time for Europe to lead the world.

### The European Bad Conscience about the American Financial Pest

German and French naïve innocence in the face of the world's financial alchemies probably represented more a consequence of ignorance and misunderstanding than chutzpah. Sarkozy and Merkel had simply not taken the measure of the financial interconnectedness that had developed since the origin of the euro area in the 1990s. Germany's massive savings were being regularly channelled to the United Kingdom, Spain, Ireland, and the United States, although often in the form of credits and loans. France's financial role was more similar to that of the United Kingdom—as a financial intermediary in the heart of Europe. Paris received financing from other financial centers, including from the United States, largely in the form of deposits and loans to its financial institutions, and invested them in debt bonds of other euro area countries and extended loans to Spain and Italy.

The analogy with the United Kingdom is not casual; the French authorities had been trying since 1998 to supplant London as the financial center for Europe—based partly on the fact that the British government had stayed outside the euro zone. This effort had met with little success, however. In 2008 London was still ranked as the most important global financial center and Paris was not even in the top ten, while Frankfurt was aiming at developing a global trading platform.[5] The financial services business was the largest positive contributor to the UK balance of payments. The yearly net value was understandably coveted by the French because it was equivalent to an added 2 percent of the French GDP. Paris therefore supported the French banks in conquering the business of traditional intermediation at the core of the euro area. French rhetoric resembled that of an ideological battle against finance, while it concealed strong national economic interests. But, as so often is the case, the two—ideology and interests—were not in contradiction. In the wake of the crisis, Sarkozy saw renewed importance for the role of the state, with a duty to bridle competition and free movement of goods, especially money.

There is an obvious contradiction between advocating the role of national states and invoking Europe's unity, but European culture is also intrinsically plural, and the French president was confident he could create a consensus around a revision of the free-market doctrine. Victim of a frequent French misunderstanding of German capitalism—where market forces are tempered by social concerns and by the centrality of banks, but actually are less directly under the influence of the state than in France—Sarkozy called on Germany to act together with France, decisively and fast. "Europe hit by the unprecedented crisis that is shaking the world," Sarkozy said, "will be able to intervene only if France and Germany will work together in the utmost reciprocal trust and in the most exemplar friendship."[6] He was leading the way, but stubbornly, and to his eyes, inexplicably the Berlin government was blocking the road.

In fact, there was an even deeper problem preventing Sarkozy and Europe from leading the world: an outright denial of reality. The "merde" of which Merkel had spoken had been kept hidden by everybody. In spring 2007, Deutsche Bank suddenly cut its credit lines to a small German bank, IKB

Deutsche Industriebank, which then asked the German public authorities for a bailout. IKB was over-invested in U.S. subprime securities, which, according to the German government, had been sold by Deutsche Bank itself, by Goldman Sachs, Morgan Stanley, and Lehman Brothers. The full details of Deutsche Bank's involvement have never been made public. On August 9, 2007, BNP-Paribas, a leading French bank, had suspended the reimbursement of three investment funds (in effect, freezing their activity), claiming to be unable to give a market valuation for certain derivatives and other structured products contained in their portfolios. During a meeting in Brussels, EU finance ministers discussed a report of an American bank estimating that 40 percent of all the risky assets sold by American counterparts had ended up in Europe. But in the run-up to the October 4 summit, each country, and each national regulatory authority, was still pretending that the European financial system was in good health. On the morning of October 2, Jean-Claude Juncker, who was both head of the Luxembourg government and president of the Eurogroup (the finance ministers of the euro area), said: "European banks are healthy and Europe does not need plans to support them." Irish Central Bank governor Patrick Honohan acknowledged later that in the weeks leading up to the summit, the magnitude of the challenge had not been properly measured: "At no point in the period was it thought by the authorities that any of the banks was facing imminent underlying solvency risks."[7]

## A Good Time to Cry Wolf

National interests in protecting their governments and the financial industry were so strong that they silenced the few European officials who were not blind to reality and urged common responses to the risks of a financial crisis. Starting in 2002, Tommaso Padoa-Schioppa, the intellectual force behind the birth of the euro, had alerted the European Central Bank of his concerns while he was serving as a member of its board. He had set up simulation tests in the event of a major failure of the financial system, which he saw as likely. That silent work had allowed the ECB to react promptly in August 2007, by pumping liquidity into the markets, at the first sign of the crisis. Immediately afterward, in September 2007, the European Financial Committee, a technical group of EU financial officials, approved a confidential report calling on all member countries to consider the crisis in European financial institutions as a matter of common interest and not solely of national importance. In October 2007, the Economic and Financial Affairs Council (ECOFIN), the council of the twenty-seven European finance ministers, pledged to respect the logic of the common interest, but in fact did not introduce any of the incentives to banks or to the authorities that were needed to make the formal appeals concrete.

Padoa-Schioppa, who at that time had become the Italian finance minister, tried to break the gridlock created by the other governments and circulated among his colleagues a letter proposing the urgent commitment to "two limited and specific goals: a common handbook for the rules of financial supervision and the sharing of all information about the largest European banking groups."[8] London moved immediately to undermine Padoa-Schioppa's proposal. It was no surprise. "London is jealous of its prerogatives and has been consistently blocking any common initiative on financial regulation whenever it could," confessed Barroso, the European Commission president. In order to force the governments to meet their responsibilities, the Italian called for a vote of the ECOFIN. The result was that a number of governments large enough to form a blocking minority sided with London, thus preventing action. The political logic of preserving domestic interests and national prerogatives prevailed, and the vote remained secret since the ECOFIN minutes are not transparent enough to report the voting decisions. As a result, until the spring of 2008, nothing changed: the EU formal recommendations against the eventuality of a banking crisis were minimal and practically identical to those made seven years earlier in the so-called Brouwer Report, at a time when the euro was not even adopted as a currency in circulation.[9]

On May 14, 2008, the European Council endorsed the proposals of a committee headed by the former general manager of the Bank for International Settlements, Alexandre Lamfalussy, providing an ambitious framework to improve common controls and exchanges of information, particularly concerning the multinational banking groups. But to complete a process that in some cases began in 2004, the council set the target date of late 2008 or mid-2009. Three action plans were prepared and a crisis simulation was in the works for spring 2009, but this just proved to be too late.

The delay was particularly unfortunate because the crisis that eventually struck was so violent. While its origins will remain a matter of controversy, there is little doubt that financial transactions were the transmission channel of the crisis from one side of the Atlantic to the other. A protracted period of accommodative U.S. monetary policy by Alan Greenspan's Federal Reserve from the 1990s through the early 2000s and of massive capital inflows from China had allowed both an unprecedented increase of bank credits and a greatly reduced perception of risk. Even in Europe the more prudent European Central Bank had not reacted to years of increased volumes of credit, especially in countries where real estate bubbles had developed. Total credit to the nonfinancial private sector from euro area monetary financial institutions increased in real terms by around 40 percent between 2003 and 2007. The growth of credit was facilitated by easier lending conditions and increased leverage among large cross-border financial banks. The low yield in the money markets had been an incentive to take ever-greater risks or increase the profitability of firms and banks through leverage, that is, through debt often re-invested in riskier but more profitable assets. The volumes of credit invested in securities or property had generated the so-called bubbles, thus creating spiraling increases in values of shares and houses. In Spain, for example, the price of real estate had tripled in ten years. Between 1997 and 2007, Spanish households had been massively assuming mortgages at interest rates that were barely above the inflation rate. Money seemed to be free.

For banks that participated in this dangerous game, the risks were greater because of the nature of their business, which was based on a continuous daily refinancing. Bank capital was directly dependent on the value of the securities and was used to borrow huge amounts of money for the short term. Banks renewed their own debts every few hours or days, while providing loans on much longer maturities. Furthermore, since the 1980s, financial deregulation had created a burgeoning shadow banking system outside the radar of regulators. A young American presidential candidate, Barack Obama, called it "an age of greed and irresponsibility in New York and in Washington."

When the first crises broke in the United States in the summer of 2007, banks became aware that many institutions were heavily invested in complex financial instruments whose real value was obscure. The financial system had become an insecure place and banks began to question the creditworthiness of other banks. They stopped trading loans to each other and the interbank market virtually shut down while risk premiums soared to unprecedented levels. Banks were facing severe liquidity shortages. It became ever more difficult to roll over the short-term debt. In this case, the interbank markets acted like a double-edged sword. On the one hand, interbank markets play a very important role in providing liquidity among banks. On the other hand, if a bank fails, or simply risks failing, the interbank market transmits the shock through "contagion." As a consequence, the fear of interbank contagion may reduce interbank lending, creating a credit crunch for firms and households. The simple risk of a bank failure is enough to affect the real (nonfinancial) economy, unless bank surveillance worldwide is so effective as to give transparency to every corner of a financial system. The exchange of information would have been the most effective weapon against the banking crisis, but regulations mandating disclosure were segmented along national lines and nobody wanted to be singled out as a candidate for bankruptcy. As a result, regulators and governments had an incentive to withhold data and even to forge fake information.

## The Worst Crisis since 1931

Policymakers thought that European banks were facing nothing more than a liquidity problem that would inevitably normalize. In the years leading to fall 2008, the European economy was thriving and beating expectations. Germany, in particular, had staged a fantastic recovery and overcame the hurdles caused by

its reunification in the early 1990s. Reforms in several countries were finally paying off. In 2008 the confidence index of firms and households in Germany and
France had reached their highest historical levels. In some cases banks might face
a solvency problem, but nobody considered the possibility of contagion and systemic collapse. In fact, once the situation of the American banks became unsustainable, it should not have been a surprise that the sizable European financial
industry also was at risk: the European Union boasts the largest banking sector,
the largest insurance industry, and the largest payments system in the world. The
EU also has the largest private market for fixed-rate securities, and its derivatives
and equity markets are comparable to those of the United States.

As noted earlier, the first dramatic alarm bell rang in Europe on July 28, 2007,
when IKB Deutsche Industriebank had to be rescued after reckless investments
in American subprime assets. The goal then was to avoid what Jochen Sanjo,
president of the German Federal Office for Financial Surveillance (Bundesanstalt
fuer Finanzdienstleistungsaufsicht [BaFin]), defined at the time as "the worst
banking crisis after 1931." Sanjo's mention of the years between the two world
wars should have been a shocking alarm for everybody in Europe: it evoked the
ghost of the monetary disruption that played a prominent role in enabling the
subsequent rise to power of Adolph Hitler's Nazi regime. "Nine days before the
intervention of the government," then Finance Minister Peer Steinbrück said,
"the chairman of the board of directors of the IKB, Stefan Ortseifen, released a
press communiqué that the bank was expecting to close the year with a positive
operative margin of 280 million euro, while the problems on the mortgage market in the United States would have had practically no effect on the institute."
But the reality was completely different. "It was my first sad experience," Steinbrück observed later, "with the incompetence, risk denial, and disinformation
played out by bank managers."[10] The surveillance board of IKB was kind of a
"Who's Who" of the German economy. The minister raised the possibility of
letting the bank go bust, but he was convinced that this would be followed by a
domino effect and that Germany's role as a financial center would gravely suffer
if the first European bank to fail was German.

Then in mid-February 2008, almost exactly one week after the G-7 summit in Tokyo where Hank Paulson, U.S. secretary of the Treasury, informed his
European colleagues that the situation was under control, Europe saw the first
run on a bank, the United Kingdom's Northern Rock, in many decades. On
March 16, 2008, one of America's oldest investment banks, Bear Stearns, went
belly up. Then it was the turn of problems at the Dutch bank ABN-Amro and
at three German banks: Westdeutsche Landesbank, BayernLB, and SachsenLB.

But the bankruptcy of Lehman Brothers was the real trigger for European
banks. The tipping point—according to the Bank for International Settlements—came on Monday, September 15, 2008, when Lehman Brothers

Holdings filed for Chapter 11 bankruptcy protection: what many had hoped would be merely a year of manageable market turmoil then escalated into a full-fledged global crisis. The previous weekend, at the headquarters of the European Central Bank on the Kaiserstrasse in Frankfurt, had been spent in a sense of extreme alert. The ECB board felt unanimously that Paulson was making a lethal mistake by letting Lehman fail. One of the ECB top bankers tells of frantic calls day and night to Washington to stop Paulson. The bankers knew very well that the failure of a bank as large as Lehman could also tip the European banking system over the edge. But pressures from countries of the euro area were not really taken into consideration in Washington. Paulson was dealing primarily with Gordon Brown, hoping to secure the intervention of Barclays Bank as a rescuer for Lehman. After that last attempt failed, Paulson did not even bother to communicate personally with his colleagues in Europe. Informed of Lehman's failure only after the fact, French finance minister Christine Lagarde reacted wryly: "What I said? I said 'Holy cow!' " At the Berlin Chancellery, the same opinion prevailed: "When I was informed I remained speechless," Merkel's economic adviser, Jens Weidmann, revealed. "Lehman was turning a U.S. crisis into a global one."

European banks dealing with Lehman—most of them in London—saw their assets disappear overnight. There were immediate knock-on effects on other banks. The European and the global financial system froze in a matter of hours. The whole commercial paper market, which many European companies depended on for the funding of their operating expenses, collapsed at once. Stock plunges stopped any firm's plan for capital increases. Corporate growth forecasts were slashed downward. Even so, in the following week European governments behaved as if the problem was not of their concern. The mess was American-made, and it was up to Washington to clean it up. "Europe should not change its policy and in no way imitate the U.S. while dealing with the international financial crisis," Luxembourg prime minister Jean-Claude Juncker advised on September 17. He strongly rejected U.S.-style fiscal stimulus packages aimed at reviving growth. Juncker, who had recently been re-elected for the third time as Eurogroup president, explicitly denied that Europe was in recession: "The main worry we have is inflation." The Budget Law discussion at the German Parliament demonstrates how unaware and uninformed the governments were. According to a German minister, "None of us knew what a CDO or a CDS was," referring to two types of the financial instruments that had gotten Lehman and companies into trouble: collateralized debt obligations and credit default swaps. While Paulson, a former boss of Goldman Sachs, was contributing to the crisis as U.S. Treasury head in Washington, at the German finance ministry in Berlin, perhaps only two officials had a real understanding of how the financial markets worked.

But day after day, a different reality began to emerge. ECB president Trichet began to make the rounds of European chancelleries to sound the alarm. Mario Draghi, head of the Italian Central Bank and also of the G-7's Financial Stability Forum, accompanied by other national bank governors, visited as many finance ministers as possible to explain clearly the drama they were observing. One after the other, European banks were also sending alarms and calling for financial aid—among them the United Kingdom's Bradford & Bingley, France's Dexia, and Belgium's Fortis. The case of Fortis highlighted a unique aspect of the European crisis hitherto little considered: The size of the Belgian bank's liabilities was in fact several times greater than the entire gross domestic product of Belgium. For some individual states, such as Belgium, it thus would be impossible to intervene and absorb the losses of individual institutions. In the 1990s and 2000s, many European banks had grown far too big to be saved by the single countries hosting them. According to statistics provided by the Bank for International Settlements (BIS), the combined assets of the three largest banks of each country were equivalent in 2009 to 118 percent of German GDP (compared to only 38 percent in 1990), 250 percent of French GDP (70 percent in 1990), and 406 percent in the Netherlands (154 percent in 1990).[11] As the governor of the Bank of England remarked, "These banks are global in life, but national in death."[12] Indeed, the typical large European bank conducts less than half its activity in its home country (in contrast to American banks, which do more than 75 percent of their business in the United States).[13] The need for a common European fund intervention seemed compelling.

Suddenly, with markets increasingly in disarray, a growing number of financial institutions faced the risk of default. Rumors of increasing problems spread around the Landesbanken, the powerful German regional state-owned banks, linked to the capillary system of the saving banks (Sparkassen). The German government, whose participation is essential to any common initiative in the EU, had some solid reasons to oppose a common European fund. The first and most conventional was that Berlin was afraid to pay an over-proportional share of the banking bailouts in other countries. The second reason was its inability to ascertain the status of financial institutions due to a lack of transparency across Europe—a problem for which Berlin itself had major responsibilities. But the third and most important reason was that Berlin knew quite well that several unexploded bombs were buried under the European financial ground, and one of them was sitting squarely in German territory.

On Monday, September 22, 2008, the heads of the G-7 governments held a crucial teleconference where they committed not to replicate the Lehman mistake of allowing any bank to fail, no matter how big. But on that very same day, the German government was officially informed of a liquidity problem hitting another German bank: Hypo Real Estate. It was this bank that really brought

Europe to the brink of a financial meltdown. The story of Hypo, shrouded from public view in those days, is key to understanding the uncooperative reaction of the German government to Sarkozy's initiative during the October 4 summit, and Merkel's behavior during the whole development of the European crisis.

### "Worse than Lehman": The Last-Minute Rescue of Hypo Real Estate

The story began in Munich, the beautiful Bavarian capital and a fateful city for German history. While the drama of Hypo Real Estate was unfolding, Bavarian citizens were called to the polls to vote for the renewal of the regional parliament, the Landtag. It was the most important electoral appointment before the German federal election, scheduled almost exactly one year later. A popular citizen's movement that had been relatively uninfluential until now, the Freie Wähler (FW), the Free Voters, was capturing the limelight, sending shockwaves around the political establishment. FW was a protest movement, defending the rights of the "simple people of Bavaria" to such things as kindergartens, low local taxes, and the environment. Its leader, Hubert Aiwanger, then 37, was a farmer from a small village. His rhetoric, in a strong southern Bavarian accent, had nothing of the dreary tones of the beer houses of the 1930s that saw Adolph Hitler rise to power from his original base in Bavaria. But among the ranks of the movement, some more populist and extremist exponents also existed. As with similar movements in other European quarters, members of Freie Wähler used strong words against immigrants and most of all against "corrupt and decadent" politicians. Indeed, according to the latest polls, the movement was eroding the consensus of the traditional parties that had been the pillars of German democracy since 1948. By 2008 Germany was the only country in Europe that had been spared insidious populist movements, but the fears of the political establishment were not paranoid: In thirty years support for the old parties had almost halved. This vacuum could give way to political unknowns. The center-right Christian Social Union, which had governed Bavaria with an absolute majority for fifty years, knew that the global crisis was playing into the hands of the Freie Wähler and feeding into the discontent of citizens against the elites, the politicians, and most of all against the bankers. Not incidentally, in the last weekend of September, tension at the Kanzleramt (Chancellery) in Berlin was heightened in the wait for the outcome of the vote for the Bavarian Landtag.

Just north of Munich is the seat of Hypo Real Estate Holding AG (known as HRE), a holding company composed of a group of mortgage banks. Despite being one of the thirty major German industrial or financial firms, it was founded only in 2003 as an offspring of the crisis-stricken Bavarian banking group Hypovereinsbank. In 2007 HRE bought Depfa, a financial group that had moved its headquarters to Ireland to exploit the lax regulation and taxation regime. Depfa had built up massive debt in the short term through which it could finance its long-term investments. The failure of Lehman and the suspension of activity on the interbank market made it impossible for Depfa to refinance, and so the company faced a crisis. HRE sent out a liquidity alarm the week after the Lehman bankruptcy, alerting the German government and the chancellor herself. At first, it looked like a solvable problem: the German central bank, the Bundesbank, might have opened a credit line and supported the group until market conditions could return to normal. But the reality proved to be quite different. HRE was hiding the biggest black hole in Europe's financial history. A confidential memorandum of October 9, 2008, by BaFin, the German banking supervisory board, recorded in detail the dramatic meetings on September 26–29, a few days after the failure of Lehman, when Merkel was called on to save Hypo Real Estate from collapse, and with it the entire financial system in Germany and Europe. HRE was a listed company—legally bound to communicate to the authorities any relevant information and especially any shortcomings that could influence its price. Therefore it would have to announce publicly the real status of its finances by Monday, September 29, at 1 a.m., as soon as the Japanese markets were to open.[14]

The story began less than sixty hours earlier. On September 26, 2008, at 2:30 p.m., an emergency meeting took place at the modern quarters of the banking regulator, BaFin, in the Lurgiallee, in the northern outskirts of Frankfurt. The three top managers of Hypo Real Estate, led by President Georg Funke, were present and accompanied by six legal experts, representatives of the three major private banks, four representatives of the Bundesbank led by President Axel Weber and later also by his vice president, Franz-Christian Zeitler. Finally, five top managers of BaFin sat around BaFin president Jochen Sanjo, who led the meeting.

Funke, president of Hypo Real Estate, gave a very reassuring representation of the situation: Granted, HRE was in the red, but the problems were confined to its Depfa subsidiary and were purely related to the lack of liquidity in the market. It would suffice to open a credit line of €24 billion in 2008 and another €9 billion in 2009 to solve the problem. Sanjo argued, to the contrary, that the situation was so severe that no temporary solution was acceptable: If anybody were to learn the bank's real situation, no one would lend anything to Hypo Real Estate. It was vital to involve in the rescue the whole German banking system. The heads of the big German banks had to be invited, along with the government, for a meeting the next day.

At 3:05 p.m. on Saturday, September 27, the meeting resumed in the presence of the president of the Deutsche Bank, Josef Ackermann—probably the most important figure in European finance—and of Commerzbank's Martin Blessing. Axel Weber, president of the Bundesbank, announced that the government had refused the invitation to participate in the negotiations. In the United States, the Federal Reserve had been able to inject liquidity of $87 billion into the markets, but this was not doable in Europe. Weber had consulted with ECB president Trichet: European rules are such that the ECB cannot save a single bank from bankruptcy. It can only finance the system, that is, help solvent institutions that request funds through the regular repurchase agreements. "So either we heal HRE now and make it possible to access the ECB financing facility, or the other German banks must secure funding and channel it to HRE," Weber said. The plan was for the Bundesbank to present to Trichet a "national solution." Then the ECB would create on Monday morning an Emergency Liquidity Action that would finance the German banks and let them turn the money over to Hypo Real Estate. "We will have only that cartridge to shoot," the president of the Bundesbank warned. "It is therefore essential that the calculations we're doing are the right ones." HRE apparently needed €35 billion, of which €15 billion could be recouped by selling the assets of the bank. The rest, €20 billion, had to be found. "The government," Weber said, "can do its part."

Weber appealed to the celebrated system-solidarity in Germany, where all powers, political and financial, close ranks to solve national problems. The Bundesbank itself, for all its vaunted independence, plays the same tune. According to documents revealed during the subsequent judicial process involving Hypo Real Estate, it appeared that the German Central Bank had been aware of the bank's problems since February 2008.[15] In that same year, two other banking crises—involving Commerzbank and Salomon Oppenheimer—had been solved over the phone by Merkel and Ackermann. But this time, the government resisted action, and the banks also refused to put up the necessary money. The HRE crisis, the bankers said, was simply too big to be handled. According to the head of Commerzbank, "HRE would be just the beginning." In a matter of weeks, the spiral could sink the most important country in Europe.

Saturday night, with the reopening of the markets fast approaching, a meeting was called again for 9 p.m. Around 11 p.m. Ackermann estimated that HRE had "€185 billion in securities of dubious quality." Bundesbank's Weber called harshly, demanding that the banks put up the money needed to save HRE. He described a dramatic scenario: on Monday endless lines of depositors would be at the doors of German banks across the country withdrawing their savings. Letting HRE fail would be the death of the entire German banking system.[16]

### "I Cannot Use Citizens' Money to Help the Banks"

On Sunday morning, while Bavarian citizens flocked to the polls, a top-level group resumed at the BaFin building in Frankfurt. Finally, private banks put down money: Ackermann's Deutsche Bank committed €5 billion; Martin Blessing promised €2.5 billion from Commerzbank and Dresdner Bank; Wolfgang Sprissler for HypoVereinsbank (UniCredit) brought to the table another €2.5 billion; Postbank offered €1 billion; and a few hundred million euro came from smaller institutions. The package seemed ready: €15 billion of liquidity would be provided by private groups, buying assets or securities owned by Hypo estimated at €42 billion. The remaining €20 billion would come in the form of loans from the ECB against collateral guarantees offered by the Berlin government (which still had not seen the proposal). Half of any losses would end up with the banks (but not more than €2 billion) and half with the federal government.

Finally the government stepped in. Joerg Asmussen, state secretary at the finance ministry, arrived at 5:05 p.m. at BaFin's headquarters. Weber explained to him that in those same hours, the French government was extending a full guarantee for a bank and the Benelux governments were doing the same thing: "You cannot let HRE fail," he told Asmussen. But Asmussen quoted the text of the law dictating the rules for the federal budget. The government could offer guarantees only in case the risk of suffering losses was not greater than 50 percent. It would, in any event, require a parliamentary decision and even the reopening of the budget law: "I must speak with Minister Steinbrück and until Monday that will not be possible." The tension escalated, the chairman of Deutsche Bank accused the ministry of being informed of the situation for four days, then stood up and announced he would leave in order to get to the Deutsche Bank headquarters, the two twin towers that dominate the Opernplatz; he had to prepare his institution for the collapse of the interbank market that would occur in the next hours as soon as the news of HRE's failure triggered panic around the world. All the bankers, indeed, then left the premises.

Meanwhile, at 6 p.m. that Sunday, the German television channels ARD and ZDF released the first forecast on the Bavarian vote: for the CSU, Merkel's ally, it was a catastrophe. The party scored its poorest result since 1954 and lost its majority in the Bavarian Landtag for the first time in forty-six years. It was a stinging defeat for Chancellor Merkel, especially in light of the upcoming federal election in 2009. The grassroots movement of Freie Wähler gained seats in the Landtag for the first time; with more than 10 percent of the votes, it was to be the Landtag's third largest party. Merkel was profoundly upset by the results and appeared, to her aides, to be in a state of shock. While the Hypo Real Estate drama was unfolding, Merkel was in the midst of her worst political moment.

In that state of mind, Merkel received a desperate call for action from ECB president Jean-Claude Trichet, who was in Brussels helping to solve the crisis of the Fortis bank. But Trichet's pleas were rebuffed: Merkel insisted she could never throw the taxpayers' money at the banks. Trichet insisted as persistently as he could, explaining how dramatic for all of Europe the situation might become. But Merkel was resolute: no public money for HRE. Trichet grasped exactly the sense of catastrophe: "We are finished," he confessed to his interlocutors. He tried time and again to call Merkel and convince her, but she seemed not to share his alarm.

In the BaFin building, Asmussen had been left alone. Finally, a telephone call from the finance minister urged him to resume the talks. At 10:45 p.m., the meeting was again convened. The session opened with an ultimatum from the government that the bankers had to come to an agreement within twenty minutes: the losses emerging from an HRE bailout must be shared, 45 percent to the government and 55 percent to the banks with no cap on the losses for the banks. Ackermann stood up again, yelling: "This is the death of the German banking system!" The potential losses, estimated at €17 billion, would put at risk the credit ratings of the private banks and their ability to refinance in already difficult market conditions. The whole system would become fragile, undercapitalized, and vulnerable to any change of wind. At 10:55 p.m., two hours from the opening of the Japanese markets, Ackermann again threatened to scupper the whole deal.

At 11:30 p.m. Asmussen made a last offer. The losses would be divided evenly between the government and the banks, but without caps. These terms had been dictated not only by Finance Minister Steinbrück but also personally by the chancellor herself. The bankers refused and abandoned the meeting. The negotiation had failed. Asmussen and Weber immediately informed the Irish government, which was responsible for the surveillance of Depfa, and ECB president Trichet. In the room, only Sanjo and his team were left, in despair, with memories of the German crisis between the two world wars that ushered the country into the biggest tragedy of the twentieth century.

But the door reopened surprisingly at 11:57 p.m. Ackermann announced that the bankers wanted to resume the negotiations and had their own proposal. He had called Steinbrück trying to spell out clearly the size of the problem if he did not agree: "Herr Minister, you will have to hold a press conference tomorrow around ten o'clock and explain to the world that the German financial industry will have more or less to be nationalized." Steinbrück immediately called the chancellor. Five minutes after midnight, Asmussen returned to the room. During the next forty minutes, the negotiation was intertwined with a stream of phone calls. Imagine the iconic film scene of a countdown before a nuclear explosion as an apt metaphor here. But, again, at 12:48 a.m. Asmussen announced that Chancellor Merkel would not accept Ackermann's proposal.

The opening of the Japanese markets was only twelve minutes away. When the clock struck 1 a.m., Merkel threw on the table a last counterproposal: 60 percent of the losses to be borne by the banks, 40 percent by the government, and a cap on maximum losses for the banks at €8.5 billion. Almost immediately, Ackermann announced agreement. The Japanese markets were already open, but in five minutes a press conference was hastily called to communicate the success: Hypo Real Estate is safe.[17]

## A €100 Billion Bailout and Zero Trust

Little will leak outside the walls surrounding that absurd waltz danced in the northern periphery of Frankfurt by political and financial powers of the leading European country. "If Lehman was a tsunami," said Wolfgang Sprissler, the head of Hypovereinsbank, to an inquiry commission of the German Parliament, "then HRE should be described as Armageddon." The official total asset balance of the bank was €400 billion, but its off-balance activity reached €1 trillion, larger than the average GDP of a European state. Eventually, the German government would have to pour more than €100 billion of taxpayer money into the bank. The ECB also lent at least €90 billion to that single bank, more than it would lend to entire states. A member of the Financial Market Stabilization Fund, established the following month, admitted that what happened before and even after September 2008 was out of control.

There was a reason why global markets were paying no attention to the "European Lehman" going bust in Frankfurt. On September 29, just hours after German bankers and the government reached their agreement, the U.S. House of Representatives voted to reject the first version of the Treasury's proposed $700 billion plan to rescue the U.S. financial industry (it was passed into law in revised form at the end of the week). The Washington debacle was a shock that made it all too evident how difficult it was for democracy and markets to manage the same priorities. The consequences of the rejection by the House were immediately visible in U.S. equity markets, which suffered steep declines in a matter of minutes and continued to sell off during the day. The S&P 500 fell 8.8 percent, led by financial shares.

The Hypo Real Estate drama also showed how difficult it was for Berlin to understand the depth of the financial crisis and the risks of inaction. The political agenda was dictated by popular sentiments—understandable and legitimate as they were—and by the unrelenting cycle of electoral appointments in the German political system. Focused on Bavaria, the government, the parties, indeed all the political system, did not understand that they had to rise to a different kind of democratic challenge, one forged by a complex and interdependent world.

Instead, few self-critical feelings emerged among German government officials, even though a commission that investigated the Hypo Real Estate debacle later discovered that BaFin had alerted the government eight times between January and August 2008 about HRE's situation, without getting a reaction.[18] Even the Bundesbank had sent alarms about Depfa in February and March that year after a special test of the bank. What remained in Merkel's mind, for all the shortcomings of her ministers and of her private and public advisers, was mainly a sense of mistrust. The fact that the crisis occurred out of public view allowed her coalition government to develop a self-indulgent and even dangerous explanation of the events. The government's analysis was simple: Very well-hidden risks and unreliable information on the state of the banks had obscured the problem, nobody could trust anyone, and even the damages caused by medium-sized institutions could be enormous. As demonstrated in the negotiations on HRE, the government could influence the solutions with extreme difficulty and behind closed doors, but only within the national borders where it could still flex its muscles.

An empirical study conducted by the ECB later suggested that bond yield spreads across Europe started to open markedly just after the Lehman crisis on the basis of fiscal imbalances—not of the banking systems predicaments.[19] In fact, keeping the banking mess under cover helped Germany to profit from its emerging privileged fiscal position. Just when Germany's banking system was in shambles, and thanks to that problem having been kept quiet, German government bonds—the benchmark in the euro-denominated bond market—assumed a safe-haven investment status. This was the kind of role that they had never had and to such an extent.[20] The bottom line in Berlin was that everybody was to take care of his own junk. This code of survival was hidden in one single word: mistrust.[21] Exactly one year later, news coming from Greece would sadly provide additional reasons for this feeling.

# 2

## The Secrets behind the Banks

### The ECB and the Denial by the National States

For Jean-Claude Trichet, a lifelong experienced public official, the Lehman and the Hypo Real Estate events had been incredibly demanding. Although the U.S. financial system was the epicenter of the crisis, the European Central Bank (ECB) president knew that banks played a much more crucial role in the European economy than in the United States because they provided a much larger slice of credit to the economy. Moreover, he knew that banks were central to the web of national systems of power in the euro area member states, as the drama around HRE had shown. Still, Trichet was watching with increasing unease how all national authorities tried to hide from their partners the real state of their banks, while pretending they had no problems and raising fences around the national controls on the financial systems. A bigger threat could arise from the governments' behavior: that national bailouts of the banks, burdening the fiscal position of single states, could degenerate into default on national sovereign debts. As a matter of fact, a large part of the entire story of the crisis in the euro area could be told from the perspective of a protracted tug-of-war between the ECB and the national governments, with the former asking the latter to acknowledge their common responsibility in the face of the crisis, without shifting the burden onto the central bank. In order to understand that, it is necessary to consider what those actors were thinking and doing in the face of the banking turmoil in September and October 2008.

Wise and balanced, the president of the European Central Bank had some hours of despair in those days. There were at least two moments when he confessed to his colleagues in Frankfurt the fear that the European economy was damned. Each time he managed to bounce back, finding solutions and uncharacteristically producing a sense of drama in his political interlocutors' mind. Central bankers are not expected to be popular figures who kiss flags or hail the crowds. But less obviously, their decisions may save or damn the world. They must live in balance between their policy decisions and their autonomy from politics. Explaining to the heads of government the devastating potential of the crisis was difficult even for somebody like Trichet, who had a strong grasp of the nuts and bolts of democratic procedures. National politicians were still thinking in compartments, and denial of their larger global responsibility was instrumental to their power based on local consensus.

In fact, Wall Street's shockwaves were received in the European chancelleries with a mix of angry reprimand and creeping fright. On the one hand, European leaders were publicly blaming the Americans for the dissemination of the financial virus, while still considering the continental economy as basically more sound. On the other hand, they saw clear signs of financial instability at home as well, and a few economists also saw the need for a systemic answer.[1] Very disturbing questions were lining up. If the banks were in real trouble, would states have to bail them out? Would they even be in a position to do so? Would the resulting public debt be too large to be sustainable? What would happen if one single state was to accumulate more debt than it could repay? Would its obligations denominated in euro become claims on that country, or on the euro area as a whole? Would the political fabric behind the euro then be strong enough to withstand those unprecedented challenges?

At the beginning, many governments in Europe resorted to forms of denial. The Spanish leader José Luis Zapatero refused to use the word "crisis" because it was "inelegant and unpatriotic." The Italian leader Silvio Berlusconi blamed the press for being at the origin of the crisis. Closing one's eyes to the international nature of the crisis was one of those stratagems. The rescue of Hypo Real Estate or the Fortis bailout really seemed to prove that the authorities were caught completely unprepared to consider the predicament of these banks not as isolated, singular phenomena, but as symptoms of a wider systemic problem. The difficulty of coping with a crisis of unknown scale showed even in the behavior of Trichet's ECB, the most respected among the European-wide institutions and the one technically best positioned to understand the scope and depth of the events. The reaction of the governments, each of them retrenching inside its national borders, made the ECB the only institution acting for the euro area as a whole. Inevitably the ECB, and Trichet, assumed increasingly—and unusually—a primary political role.

The 1992 Maastricht Treaty had shaped the ECB on the model of the Bundesbank, the German central bank established in 1957 that reconstructed the German monetary reputation after the hyperinflation between the two wars. The

Bundesbank was built on the concept of autonomy from politics. Consequently, fighting inflation and maintaining independence were the dominant priorities for the ECB. In a common, but partial, explanation of German historical drama during the Weimar Republic in the 1920s, the direct financing of governments by the central bank was the cradle of a disaster that, with Adolph Hitler coming into power, had become the most terrible tragedy in modern European history. As part of this dramatic heritage the ECB also assumed a severe detachment from national fiscal policies. Nevertheless, since the very first signs of financial instability in Europe in the summer of 2007, the ECB understood immediately that the old orthodoxy was not sufficient. The bank had to actively face the crisis at the cost of becoming more "political" practically overnight. The shocking news of August 9, 2007, when the French bank BNP Paribas announced the suspension of three of its investment funds, had caught even the ECB by surprise. However, in a matter of hours, between the closing of the markets in the Far East and their opening in Europe on August 9, the ECB decided to flush the market with cash. With an unprecedented immediate "auction" of unlimited liquidity—or, in the jargon, a "full allotment"—it ensured that banks could receive almost €100 billion in a few hours. That was vital because as the credit quality of certain financial assets drastically deteriorated, market liquidity had dried up. Banks were unwilling to lend to each other because of the fear of not getting their money back, and they lacked hard information about the soundness of their counterparts (other banks). The risk of complete gridlock of the money market and of the payment system was quickly spotted by the so-called blue collars at the dealing room of the ECB in Frankfurt, where the officials in charge of implementing monetary policy are in regular contact with market operators. In the following weeks the ECB seemed to consolidate its new emergency strategy: it postponed planned interest rate hikes and put additional amounts of liquidity at the disposal of the banks.

Actually, Trichet and his colleagues were not thinking that the strategy of the bank had to change fundamentally. The ECB's idea was still that keeping inflation under control was the best possible contribution to fight financial instability. The dynamics of the financial systems had grown disproportionately in recent years, and it had been difficult to incorporate them in the macroeconomic models.[2] As a matter of fact, during the winter and spring 2008, the financial shock of summer 2007 seemed just an episode and was almost forgotten. The European economy had continued to grow at a brisk pace, so price levels and inflation expectations had increased, and the rhetoric of the European Central Bank had returned to an increasingly hawkish tone. On July 9, 2008, to the amazement of most of the world, the ECB followed "hard talk" on inflation fears with a 25 basis-point rate hike of its reference rate to 4.25 percent. The rate hike virtually coincided with the peak in inflation and was followed immediately by one of the sharpest contractions in quarterly GDP in decades.[3] If the bank's action was a miscalculation, it was not corrected quickly. After the collapse of Lehman Brothers on September 15, an interest rate cut was discussed at the October 2, 2008, meeting of the Governing Council of the bank in Frankfurt, and President Trichet acknowledged, "The situation is clearly absolutely exceptional in terms of the level of uncertainty." Still, the ECB president observed that "we have seen a reduction in the upside risks for inflation but, in the judgment of the Governing Council, while they have diminished, they have not disappeared." Hence, there was no reduction of the reference rates. The global financial system was experiencing a devastating heart attack, but the doctor was still worried that the patient might be too lively.

The ECB interest rate policy had to achieve its inflation target (the "one needle in our compass") and was signalling that "all was normal," while the liquidity management policies aimed instead at securing a well-functioning money market in exceptional and dire straits. The decision to separate the two policies probably forced the ECB to keep the interest rates higher than was reasonable. The necessity to provide an extremely generous supply of liquidity put the ECB in serious embarrassment: on the one hand it was indispensable to keeping the credit flow in the economy, but on the other it entailed a risk of losing control of inflation, the holy grail of the central bank. A simple technical description makes it easy to understand how it could happen. Through market operations, central banks control a short-term interbank interest rate. The target level of that interest rate is determined within a macroeconomic model considering the ultimate target of monetary policy: price stability. Before the collapse of Lehman, the ECB offered to the banks both a borrowing and a deposit facility and set the rate of the two facilities symmetrically around the target interest rate, thus steering accordingly the quantity of reserves needed by the banking system through its open market operations.[4] In the "full allotment" system, chosen in October 2008, the open market operations were conducted so as to satisfy entirely the quantity of liquidity banks were asking for at a fixed rate. In practice, the quantity of money was decided by banks rather than by the European Central Bank. As the quantity of money requested by the banks affects credit flows, economic activity, and ultimately the level of inflation, the ECB was accepting a relevant risk of losing control of the level of prices: its primary objective.

In reality, the ECB had no choice: it had to take over the role of providing liquidity that the interbank market was not able to do anymore. All of a sudden, it had to intermediate large flows of gross funds, in different maturities, in a number of currencies, and to target specific market segments. This produced the "literal explosion of central bank balance sheets."[5] Again, it was not a neutral choice. In such circumstances, a central bank has to take credit of unknown magnitude onto its balance sheet and to make explicit judgments about the creditworthiness of single banks or countries. But, as economist Willem Buiter observed, "Without taking these risks, the central banks will be financially and reputationally safe, but poor servants of the public interest."[6] Basically, the traditional distance of the ECB from the political choices had shrunk dramatically since the first events of the crisis.

The ECB found itself involved directly in the daily management of the crisis. Famous for having the best liquidity crisis-management operation among any of the major central banks, the ECB provided liquidity much more actively than ever.[7] Following the Lehman failure, the ECB recognized the collapse in what economists call "the velocity of money." Worried by the credit crisis and by risk aversion, firms, households, or banks needed more money to respond to the same level of income. Only a strong increase in money supply could avert the risk of a collapse in the economy. Indeed, since mid-September 2008, the ECB had expanded its balance sheet by 35 percent, while the printing of bank notes—a rather suggestive image—increased by an impressive 13 percent.

Inevitably, while governments were prone to deny the reality of the financial crisis and the responsibilities of their national banks, the ECB became—willingly or not—the main policy actor in the euro zone. This role was particularly difficult to acknowledge for an institution protective of its distance from politics. But at that time both the ECB and the governments hoped that the crisis was temporary. They all resisted accepting that the "American crisis" was corroding the well-ordered, quiet life of the continental economy. Was this unwillingness to accept reality due to lack of information, or misjudgment, or a strategy of denial waiting to postpone a more reasoned assessment? In all likelihood, it was a cocktail of these three. After all, the world was facing its first widespread crisis in the age of global finance, and the predicaments of banking and financial institutions in Europe were still dealt with secretively within national borders and artfully played down by the national authorities. In 2009 a high-level report ascertained that since 2007, the European Central Bank had to make decisions in real time on providing liquidity to individual banks, having no access to the data from the supervisory agencies of the countries where the banks operated.[8] Financial obscurity offered the perfect environment for the silent spreading of the virus.

## Ireland, the First Blip on the Seismograph of the Sovereign Earthquake

It fell to Ireland to expose the first signs that, if managed nationally, the banking crisis could develop into something even more dangerous. It started on September 29, 2008, when Dublin introduced the first measures to defend its national banks, extending guarantees to the six largest size ones, without any consultation with its EU partners. Prior to the extension of guarantees, the price level of the credit default swaps (CDS—equivalent to insurance policies against the default of a company or an institution) for the large Irish commercial banks was very high. It declined sharply as soon as public guarantees were in place. At the same time, the Irish sovereign debt spread (the spread between government bonds' yields issued in different states) increased, as well as the CDS on the sovereign bonds, revealing for the first time that markets saw a very clear danger in the sustainability of the public debts as a consequence of the national banking bailout. It was a first blip on the seismograph, showing the way to a much broader sovereign debt crisis in the making.

The consequences of the segmented responsibility for the banking systems along national lines were much worse than imagined at the time. Until the crisis, it was generally taken for granted that financial supervision had to remain at the national level. The rationale for this was apparently very solid: the consequences of a bank's failure ultimately would fall on the taxpayers of the country where the bank resides. To align incentives and ensure appropriate accountability, the reliance on nationally defined tax bases also implies nationally defined financial supervisory institutions. It was only when contagion was spreading before the eyes of powerless regulators that financial borders appeared for what they were—fictitious political projections. Finally, banks were specializing in segments of activities on a global scale, more than in purely national markets. More ominously, they were also outgrowing the capacity of national taxpayers to support them in case of need. But in 2008 the understanding of those changes was still limited. The problems of German and French banks were kept hidden from other countries, and the same happened in the case of Spanish, Greek, British, and Irish banks. As a result, in a matter of two weeks, between the end of September and the beginning of October 2008, the rescue of failing banks on a state-by-state basis and the reluctance to embrace a common solution for the European banking system created a much more profound crisis, one that reached the core of European politics: it was a crisis of sovereign debts and even of the monetary union itself.

In fact, politics on a national level was far from understanding how much the economies of the European Union had grown closely related to each other. The liberalization of capital movements in the early 1990s, the introduction of the euro in 1999, and the extension of market practices around the globe significantly changed the interconnections among economies. The most surprising aspect of the crisis was probably the extreme degree to which all asset prices and all indexes of real activity moved together around the world. In contrast to the 1930s, which witnessed the slow transmission of the Great Depression across countries, in 2008 all firms reacted almost simultaneously and identically. Trade and investment collapsed at the same time around the Western world. For all these reasons, more so than in the past, the instability of one major bank could impact almost instantaneously banks in foreign countries. And it was not a problem limited only to the financial system: what was also stunning was the rapidity of the transmission of financial instability to the real economy, to the macroeconomic imbalances, to private debt, and finally to public finances. The short circuiting could happen in a matter of days, even hours. Contagion became a new political category in Europe in the months following Lehman's bankruptcy—a disease for which nobody was fully prepared.

European financial authorities were no better prepared than were their counterparts elsewhere. The fragmented European national system of banking supervision had never wanted to make way for a common supranational mechanism. In two reports in 2006 and 2007, the European Commission had noted the growing internationalization of European banks.[9] After a series of mergers among domestic institutions, the consolidation process also had taken hold among banks of different countries. The European Central Bank in 2008 had identified forty-six banking groups "systemically important," given their size, which together represented 68 percent of total bank assets in Europe.[10] Half of these groups had significant operations in countries other than where they were based. In Eastern Europe, foreign banking groups covered up to 70 percent of the market. Although banks became more and more European, supervision remained stubbornly national.[11] A major report prepared in 2009 under the guidance of former IMF executive director Jacques de Larosière was critical of national banking supervisors who "did not seem to share their information properly with their counterparts in other Member States or with the US." In too many instances "they were not prepared to discuss with appropriate frankness and at an early stage the vulnerabilities of financial institutions that they supervised. The flow of information was far from optimal, leading to an erosion of mutual trust among supervisors" when the crisis became more acute.[12]

National supervisors had a vested interest in hiding the problems of the banks they should have supervised. Many also were prone to kicking the can down the road, hoping that the massive liquidity provided at low cost by the ECB would be sufficient to allow banks to recover profitability and thus rebuild their capital, using the ECB liquidity support as a shadow grant.[13] National responsibility on financial stability was often used as a pretext to protect national champions, and hiding domestic problems was also useful to protect the banks from becoming easy prey for foreign acquisitions.[14]

Most government interventions were directly aimed at defending primarily national interests. A defensive reaction in some countries was to "ring-fence" assets in their jurisdictions when cross-border entities showed signs of failing, thus reflecting the absence of clear burden-sharing mechanisms for international banks. Supervisors in the United Kingdom, for instance, fearing an imminent collapse of Icelandic bank branches (under the authority of Icelandic supervisors, who did not provide a commitment to fulfil UK bank liabilities), resorted to the UK's Anti-terrorism, Crime, and Security Act to ring-fence Icelandic bank assets within Great Britain. Similarly, German authorities froze Lehman's assets to ensure the availability of cash to satisfy German depositors before all the funds could be used in the U.S. bankruptcy proceedings.

By reacting piecemeal and contingently to each single manifestation of financial instability, national and European Union authorities sometimes simply shifted instability around instead of bringing it under control. In shifting financial problems from one area to another, Europeans (as well as Americans) thought they were controlling risks, while in fact they stoked uncertainty. As Frank Knight, a Chicago economist in the 1920s, had expressed it, uncertainty is an immeasurable kind of risk, and therefore a very dangerous one. But the most significant of these shifts induced by the Irish initiative (and others thereafter) was between banks and states: the CDS price spreads for many banks fell as governments provided guarantees for them, while many sovereign CDS spreads increased. Letting a bank fail was more than a national problem—it was truly a systemic European one—but so, it turned out, was bailing it out.

## Financial Nationalism: The Misleading Model of the Fortis Rescue

Somewhat paradoxically, the introduction of the euro as a single currency in most of the EU first resulted in the creation of larger national banking groups rather than in cross-border mergers, as governments wanted stronger national champions to be ready for what they saw as a forthcoming increase in cross-border competition.[15] Defense of national interests was once more the prime mover.[16] Only the more assertive intervention of the European Commission from 1999 onward, combined with the practical limits reached by intracountry consolidation, led to a development of cross-border banking mergers and acquisitions in the 2000s. This in turn led to the emergence of a handful of truly "pan-European" groups (such as BNP Paribas, Santander, and UniCredit) and culminated in the ill-fated hostile takeover of ABN Amro in 2007 by a consortium of Royal Bank of Scotland (RBS), Fortis, and Santander, a step that contributed to the downfall of the former two.

The rescue of Fortis at the end of September 2008 was interpreted as a successful supranational intervention by the Benelux and the French governments, a template for governments across the euro area and a good omen for the common destination in the coming years. In the same hours when Hypo Real Estate was silently threatening to tip Europe over the edge, a positive European answer seemed instead to come just across the western borders. Unfortunately, even this story had an unmistakable nationalistic streak.

Established in the 1990s as a result of the merger between a Dutch bank and insurance company and another Belgian company, Fortis was an example of the promising process of European consolidation in the financial industry. The process of internationalization was intended to intensify, and in 2007 Fortis had in fact been one of the banks participating in the consortium that engaged in a badly conceived acquisition of Dutch giant ABN-Amro. At that time, Fortis became the twentieth largest business in the world in terms of revenues. Soon afterward, in the spring 2008, Fortis began to show signs of crisis. In June a capital increase went partially unsubscribed because some shareholders declared they did not trust the official accounts. The difficulties became public on Thursday, September 25, 2008, when the rumor spread that Dutch bank Rabobank had made an offer to rescue Fortis. In downtown Brussels, outside the Fortis branches, worried savers started to form lines eager to withdraw their deposits. The next day, Fortis confirmed that 3 percent of deposits had been withdrawn by individual customers, while firms and other banks started to withdraw €20 billion. Up to €30 billion was expected to be withdrawn on the following Monday. The bank was evidently unable to provide such a huge amount of liquidity to repay its depositors.

On Friday afternoon, governments stepped into the Fortis crisis. The Belgian and the Dutch central banks started playing a poker game over which should help fill Fortis's liquidity hole. In the preceding days, the Belgians had already provided €60 billion of the €100 billion that would be necessary to keep the bank afloat. The Dutch had contributed only €10 billion but were balking at providing more. Just fifteen minutes before the end of the daily settlement process, the Belgian Central Bank finally gave in and forked over more money. The European Central Bank was very concerned about the reopening on Monday, and president Trichet decided to rush to Brussels to follow the case personally.

On Saturday morning, negotiations opened with banks interested in buying Fortis, but they failed soon after disappointing details of the securities in the bank's portfolio were made public. The only thing Fortis could do was to ask for a new loan of €50 billion from the Belgian Central Bank. But Belgian prime minister Yves Leterme was rightly worried: if the loan could not be repaid and if the bank's collateralized securities proved to have no market value, it would not just be the bank that would fail, but the whole country.

On Saturday night, resurrecting a plan that had been studied before the summer, the Luxembourg government proposed to the Belgians that Belgium and the Netherlands each acquire a 49 percent share in the capital of any Fortis company or bank headquartered in its own country. The Belgians scheduled a meeting for the following day to discuss this proposal, but the Dutch government was kept in the dark until the last minute. Dutch finance minister Wouter Bos learned of the project only on Sunday at his planned meeting with the Belgian delegation. Opening the office door of his Belgian colleague Didier Reynders, he saw to his amazement that Belgian prime minister Leterme, ECB president Trichet, and French finance minister Christine Lagarde were also present. The plan was presented as a fait accompli. The Belgians would invest €4.7 billion.

The Dutch were expected to commit €4 billion. Bos protested vehemently, but eventually conceded with a verbal agreement. On their return to Amsterdam, the Dutch were convinced that the terms were particularly disadvantageous and decided to call into question the entire agreement.

In the first days of October, while publicly the two governments were proudly boasting about their exemplary cooperation, behind the scenes a furious renegotiation was under way. It rapidly became public: Belgian newspapers were blaming the Dutch government for not transferring the promised €4 billion and for orchestrating the withdrawal of funds by Dutch firms at the Fortis bank, thus forcing the Belgian Central Bank to transfer €50 billion in emergency funds to keep the bank liquid. The Dutch replied that these were only defensive measures because they had been kept in the dark by their Brussels colleagues. The level of animosity between the two countries showed how dangerous it was to rely on intergovernmental agreement without a preordained, common supranational framework. In the end—despite being cited by the French and Benelux governments as examples of harmonious supranational cooperation—both Fortis and Dexia (another Belgian bank rescued temporarily through a similar multinational deal) ended up fragmented along their national lines, the exact opposite of a pan-European solution.

## Banks at the Core of the European National Social Models

Nobody can be expected to be naïve or generous when dealing with financial interests, but financial patriotism also has reasonable historical and even social justifications. Banks and credit play a special role in national economic systems, whereby they often absorb both political and economic shocks, especially in Europe where politics and the economy are more closely interconnected within each country than in the United States. Furthermore, U.S. banks account for only 24 percent of credit intermediation in the country, versus 53 percent in Japan and as much as 74 percent in the euro area. So, because of their relevance for the economy, European banks play an almost public role. Sometimes this is a meaningful role that has wide social implications—like financing social housing or helping households through facilitated credit access. In other cases, proximity to politics means that banks provide parties with financial means or even bend their lending criteria to favor political priorities. In the German case both roles—the social one and the industrial-political one—are extremely important. They represent a core element of German public policy and are key to understanding the government's reluctance to disseminate information to European partners. But at a certain moment a short circuit had occurred: while Germany generates about 29 percent of the euro zone's economic output, German banks accounted for nearly half of the euro zone absorption of U.S. toxic assets and the main problem rested with the stated-owned Landesbanken.

Outright government ownership of banks used to be widespread, but largely disappeared from the EU with the large-scale privatizations of the 1980s and 1990s. The main exceptions are Germany's seven Landesbanken, generally jointly owned by local governments (Länder) and local savings banks in varying proportions. The European Commission, as stated in the various treaties, is indifferent to public or private ownership, but had correctly identified the German Landesbanken as violators of the Single Market rules, that is, the principles of unrestricted freedom of movement for goods and services within the EU. Using public guarantees provided by the German Bund, they were able to tap financial resources at the lowest cost, with a clear competitive advantage. The Landesbanken in particular were intimately tied to local political powers and the German economy. Their profits were a necessary provision of money for politics, and it is no big surprise that national supervisors for years had turned a blind eye to their practices.

It was EU commissioner Mario Monti, one of the most highly esteemed figures in European politics, who spotted the danger in advance. Monti took issue with the privileges and malpractices of the Landesbanken that were harming the European Single Market and also German economic dynamism. The German establishment responded vehemently. It took years of hard-nosed negotiations between Monti and the German government before Peer Steinbrück, then finance minister of North Rhine-Westphalia and representative of the German Laender, agreed to abolish the public guarantees granting the triple-A ratings for all the Landesbanken. But Steinbrück did so only after obtaining a four-year transition period. During the years 2001 to 2004, the Landesbanken exploited fully all the benefits of their triple-A status by raising funds at low cost. They raised around €300 billion, in addition to their current resources, that they reinvested in high-yielding securities. It was also during this period that they accumulated risky assets issued abroad without caring about the consequences. Steinbrück now admits:

> I failed to exert the necessary pressure to induce the Landesbanken to restructure and consolidate. The transition period ended in July 2005 without even the slightest sign of the overdue reordering of the sector: the governments of the German Laender and the directors of the banks completely misinterpreted the role of their regional capitals as financial centres and underwent an absurd megalomania copying the activity of the major international investment banks as a model for their institutes.[17]

The local banks became addicted to this investment behavior. Bundesbank president Axel Weber remarked, unfortunately too late, that in the period between 2004 and 2006—the go-go years of global finance—German "banks increased loans to the national industry only by 0.8 percent," while they preferred investing in exotic new securities.

## Direct Political Interests: The Case of the German Landesbanken

Political interest in using the banking systems to support local activities—and sometimes politicians' own agendas—is a decisive factor behind financial nationalism. State-owned Landesbanken, for instance, have been found to grant loans to corporations with lower creditworthiness than the private banks.[18] Moreover, the probability of granting a loan increases in relation to the local unemployment rate and whether the borrower is headquartered in the same state as the bank. Both attitudes provide evidence that these banks fulfil their objective to support the local economy and also the local political agenda. The likelihood of granting a loan increases significantly the longer the state government has held power but decreases if the state-owned bank is owned by more than one state. The probability that savings banks will lay off some employees drops during election years, while the probability of hiring new personnel increases by 25 percent during election periods, on average, while state-owned banks tend to grant more loans around elections, to both corporate and private clients.[19]

Political influence on banks is not confined to the domain of public banks. In the case of Deutsche Bank, probably the most powerful private European financial institution, one could even say the opposite and speak of the bank's influence on the government ever since the end of the Second World War. In 2008 the crisis of Dresdner Bank was managed by the German government, which engineered the takeover by Commerzbank in agreement with Deutsche Bank. Later, Deutsche Bank was driven by the government to take over Postbank. Starting with the Dresdner crisis in 2008, the riskiness of German banks—as measured by the spreads in credit default swaps—has been consistently higher than the European average.[20]

The influence of politics is surely not only a German problem. In the United States, the announcement of a politically connected new board member yields abnormal returns for the shares of a firm. Furthermore, shares of firms with predominantly Republican members generated abnormal returns following the 2000 election victory of the Republican Party. Politically connected corporations in France tend to employ more people and lay off fewer employees during election years, and this effect is particularly pronounced in highly contested elections. But as a study by the Center for Financial Studies reports, in Germany 87 percent of the system (market shares as accounted by the Deutsche Bundesbank) falls into the category of politically influenced ownerships, either because the public administration owns the banks or because local governments can put their appointees at the helm of the banks.[21]

The case of German savings banks is revealing. The governance structure of savings banks consists of three main entities: the managing board running the day-to-day business; the supervisory board (Verwaltungsrat) controlling the management and deciding on key personnel and major strategic matters; and the credit committee approving individual loans exceeding a certain volume. Two-thirds of the members of the supervisory board are representatives of the bank's government owner, for example, the local county or city. In most cases, these are politicians in the local parliaments. By law, the chair of the supervisory board is held by the head of the local government, that is, the mayor or the head of the county. As the supervisory board not only controls but also appoints the management, there is a very close link between politics and the bank's management.

Political influence is by no means a synonym for wrong policies. Even though a string of corruption cases in German public banks has come to light in the last decade, the efficiency of the German industrial structure can be cited as proving the opposite. Banking support and assistance to medium-sized enterprises—the Mittelstand—has allowed hundreds of firms to restructure in the last decade and withstand the financial crisis. The interaction among industry, banks, and politics in Germany—referred to as Sozialmarktwirtschaft—represents a powerful success story that undermines the common narrative about liberal market economies where the state sets the rules and the market operates as freely as possible, thereby achieving the best possible resource allocation. The German success story highlights that economics is strictly intertwined with politics and the qualities of democracy—responsibility, transparency, openness, honesty—that provide an economic matrix for success. Obviously, if the market is far less perfect than our model representations, the social market, for all its elusive but powerful virtues, is even more imperfect.

In fact, the professional level of political personnel at the helm of German public banks—"bankers in Lederhosen" as they are ridiculed abroad—can be very modest. Moreover, state ownership was responsible for such problems as the low level of capital of the Landesbanken. When state budgets were cut severely, it was painful for policymakers to recapitalize public banks. Banks are supposed to keep minimum levels of capital—roughly speaking, the difference between bank assets (loans) and liabilities (deposits and other funding sources)—for security reasons. A reasonable level of the ratio between capital and assets should provide a cushion if the bank suffers losses. However, capital adequacy ratios are weighted on the riskiness of each asset category. Banks reluctant to increase capital could circumvent the regulatory requirements by buying insurance for their riskier assets, making them less risky from the point of view of the bank's balance sheet. For instance, this step allowed the Landesbanken to reduce the risk weighting on investments, such as subprime related assets, and extend more loans with less capital. The typical insurance contract was the credit default swap (CDS). By using those CDS contracts, risk was transferred from the banks to an insurance company eager to sell them; particularly active was the American Insurance Group (AIG). When default rates on subprime loans began to increase, investors started to cash in their credit default swaps. But AIG did not have the financial reserves to pay off the losses from the largest housing bubble in the American history and had to be bailed out by the U.S. government.

European banks buying insurance contracts were less concerned about the riskiness of their investments. In fact, given the low profitability of the regular credit activity—in some cases determined by the statute of the state-owned banks—German financial institutes had to resort to new sources of income, namely financial investments in higher yielding assets. These were synthetic assets generally sold by American intermediaries or by large German private commercial banks—first of all the Deutsche Bank—and obviously non-German euro area sovereign bonds. Even though private banks had already begun to reduce their holdings of foreign assets in mid-2007, after the first signs of financial crisis, the Landesbanken increased their holdings until well into 2008.

The story of the public banks is indeed symmetric to that of the German private banks. According to the data released by AIG, it was the private banks, first of all Deutsche Bank, that were counterparties in the credit default swaps. Of all European entities, the Frankfurt-based bank was second only to the French Société Générale. A high official of the German finance ministry maintains that "at the start of the crisis, Deutsche Bank was perfectly hedged, they were risking nothing," as far as American toxic assets were concerned. In fact, most of the bank's contracts were sold to the local public banks. Even in the case of Hypo Real Estate, it is still not clear which role Deutsche Bank had been playing. An array of legal hurdles has made it difficult for those who want to understand the structure of creditors of the plagued Hypo Real Estate and the transactions that made it possible in 2009 for HRE to increase its holdings in Greek sovereign bonds, while private banks were clearly cutting them symmetrically. In these circumstances, it is not surprising that the low profitability of the public sector was matched by the high returns on capital obtained by Deutsche Bank even in the middle of the crisis. The full circle of public-private connivance is completed by a disturbing consideration: how could the Bundesbank be so blind to the protracted and massive operations of regulatory circumvention executed a few blocks from its main seat in Dornbusch in the outskirts of Frankfurt? In 2008 the Bundesbank, for some reason, decided not to publish its regular—and compulsory—report on German financial stability during the year 2007.

After the 2001 Enron scandal in the United States, the European Parliament approved a norm that forced banks to consolidate all their off-balance conduits and publish those holdings on their balance sheets by 2005. The German government lobbied hard in Brussels to get a special exception that allowed Landesbanken to do this consolidation with a substantial delay of three years; this made it possible for them to keep these holdings under cover until they published the May 2009 balance sheet.[22] For many of them, it turned out to be too late.

Almost a decade, punctuated by numerous financial disasters, had passed since Mario Monti had tried in Brussels to shed a European limelight on the cracks at the core of the European economy.

## Behind Germany's Success: A Eurozone ATM

For a long time, investing in high yielding paper was a very convenient business for any French or German financial institution. Statistics available at the Bank for International Settlements and other data on banking profits show that after 1996, the fixing of the exchange rate, and the establishment of the euro, the profits of German banks derived from securities intermediation became four times higher.[23] A rough-and-ready estimate of well above €1 trillion invested by German banks in non-German bonds of euro area countries over twelve years—since the exchange rates in the euro area became fixed—gives a total yield above basic financing costs for the German banks of above €200 billion, a sum that corresponds roughly to the total profits of the German banks over that period. That extraordinary amount constitutes a transfer of money from the other euro area countries to the German banks and from them to the German firms and governments. It is reasonable to consider that this untold story represents a substantial part of the success of the German economy since the beginning of the euro.

The specific reason why German banks were invested so extensively in financial assets abroad—compared to those in other European countries—has wider implications for the story of the euro crisis, and it has to do with the country's unbalanced national economic development. Germany's high export surpluses mean that domestic savings are invested abroad (as net capital exports), and capital exports have traditionally been handled through the banking system. In 2008, the peak year for German bank assets, German banks held net foreign assets totalling roughly €1.5 trillion (approximately 60 percent of GDP). Persistently high net capital exports entail a growing risk that German savings can no longer find sustainable real economic investment options abroad and will increasingly flow into assets of questionable value, as happened when German banks invested roughly €300 billion in U.S. subprime securitizations, becoming one of the biggest buyers of such products worldwide. The perceived risk was very weak. European banks were particularly at risk from an AIG bankruptcy because they owned three-quarters of the $441 billion in unregulated complex security instruments supposedly protected by AIG and that were tied to the collapsing subprime mortgage market.

Even the IKB story mentioned in the first chapter—the Düsseldorf bank that was compared to the trigger of a crisis comparable to that of 1931—had an American seal on it. Goldman Sachs was sued by American regulators for selling to IKB and others collateralized debt obligations (CDOs)—structured asset-backed securities that are collateralized by debt obligations tied to subprime mortgages—in early 2007, as the U.S. housing market faltered, without disclosing that the hedge fund Paulson & Co. helped pick the underlying securities so it could bet against them. According to the SEC, "Goldman wrongly permitted a client that was betting against the mortgage market to heavily influence which mortgage securities to include in an investment portfolio, while telling other investors that the securities were selected by an independent, objective third party."[24]

In 2008 SachsenLB, one of the smallest Landesbanken, required support with public money with a credit line of €17.8 billion, even though its capital was only €1.5 billion. The president of the surveillance board of the bank was also the finance minister of the Land and its next president. SachsenLB had hidden in its balance sheet—and therefore hidden from its owner, that is, the state—a Dublin affiliate that had invested €17 billion in mostly toxic assets. Overall, the bank's off-balance investments were close to €28 billion, an amount comparable to those of Citigroup or UBS, which were among the largest—and most troubled—banks of the world. However, in mid-September, trying to soothe nerves, the Bundesbank was still repeating, "The German financial system is stable and its resistance to adverse shocks has markedly improved in the past few years."

In other European countries, national politics were no less involved with the financial system. French banks indeed were as exposed as the German banks to risky assets. They could fund at the lowest cost, thanks to the triple-A quality granted to France, and reinvest in higher yielding paper at the periphery of the euro area without any currency risk. After ten years of such a dolce vita, French portfolios were burdened with assets that all of a sudden became of lower quality. Banking responsiveness to political objectives cannot be defined as a violation of good market principles. A developed market economy is more complicated than described in textbooks. Political and economic behaviors cannot be easily disentangled. One reason why French banks had been investing massively and consistently in Greece was probably the fact that Greece used to invest around 5 to 6 percent of its GDP in military expenses, buying arms and defense equipment, much of it from French firms. None of these priorities is really public in the European discourse. Relying on mutual trust in such an environment was not an easy task.

### A Plan for the European Banks

National interests and political and banking lobbying ensured immobility even while the heat of the crisis was growing. Finally in September 2008, when problems became acute and undeniable, European institutions and governments realized it was high time to bring a political response to the threatening turmoil.

The original initiative for a common European response to the banking crisis came from a small technical institution in Brussels, the EU's Financial Services Committee, that studied what Europe could do in the likely event that a fund for rescuing banks at the European level would become necessary. In response, a plan that planted the seeds of a common response was circulated by Dutch officials on September 27 envisioning a "European Recapitalization Fund." The proposal read as follows:

> All member states could commit a fixed percentage, say 3 percent of GDP (equivalent to approximately €300 billion for the entire EU). The committed amount would be reserved for the exclusive use of that member state. The fund would in effect consist of 27 separate funds, at each member state's sole disposal, but the funds would be operated along the same lines. The main purpose of the fund would be to provide extra capital to—in itself—solid financial institutions in exchange for preferential shares, where in the present market circumstances an emission would be difficult.

The response of the German finance minister, Peer Steinbrück, was unequivocal:

> I don't see any need for Germany to put 3 or 4 percent of its GDP in such a package without knowing what this German money will actually achieve and whether we'll solve concrete problems with it. The individual banking cases in Europe can have very different causes. In some cases we are dealing with a bank that has a solvency problem. In other cases like Hypo Real Estate we're dealing with a liquidity problem. Such a supranational umbrella might not be helpful in these specific cases. To put it mildly, Germany is highly cautious about such grand designs for Europe.[25]

Steinbrück's words were surprising in light of the Hypo Real Estate case that was also, but by no means only, a liquidity problem to be solved only by resorting to a supranational institution, the ECB. His denial is even more extraordinary in light of what he himself admitted later: "The enormous danger connected to the lack of transparency [in the banking shadow system], became clear to me only when the earthquake reached IKB in summer 2007 and I heard of the existence of a conduit, a special purpose company, named Rhineland Funding Capital Corporation, which presided over the purchase of another company named Lorelei. This company had a turnover of about €12 billion in securities that will require years to be disentangled and properly valued."[26] Notwithstanding the dire picture of the German financial situation, or maybe because of it, Berlin was opposing any opening to international controls and regulation.

But the Dutch government was very determined. Prime Minister Jan Peter Balkenende himself took an updated version to President Sarkozy at the Elysée on October 2. The following day, senior Dutch government officials visited Jens Weidmann, Angela Merkel's economic policy adviser in Berlin, as well as Jon Cunliffe, his counterpart in London. A new version of the Dutch plan, with its significantly explicit title "A European Coordinated Recapitalization Approach:

27 Commitments under an EU Framework," was then circulated to members of the European Financial Committee.

According to the text, the twenty-seven member countries would commit themselves to recapitalizing the systemically important banks "in need of additional capital," either directly by injecting capital themselves, or by facilitating solutions from private investors through guarantees or other means. The funds of each country would be used exclusively by that state, based on its independent decisions on which banks would qualify for the aid and on the size of the aid. "Legal frameworks differ, banks differ and policy preferences differ country by country, so there needs to be flexibility regarding the modalities," the plan said.

The European character of the initiative would be guaranteed only by a joint announcement, by the simultaneous availability of funds in the context of this initiative, and by the respect of commonly agreed principles.

The plan remained almost unknown to the public, but the nature of the Dutch proposal was embraced by the national governments. Since guarantees offered by the state to the banks represent a contingent liability, they do not appear on the government's balance sheet. Only if and when the guarantee is called, would the payments under the guarantee show up in the national budget. Obviously, it is bad for taxpayers not to be fully in control of the potential cost of the guarantee. That cost, instead, should be borne by the shareholders and the unsecured creditors of the bank who made the wrong investment decisions and who—if not forced to pay a penalty—will be inclined to repeat the same mistakes in what is normally called a case for moral hazard. But governments were mightily happy to hide the problem under the carpet.

### Elysée Summit of October 4, 2008: The Plan Is Rejected

Finally, after this long detour into the intricacies of European financial and political reality, we are back on the stairway of the Elysée on October 4, where we started. Arriving by late afternoon, Merkel was greeted in front of the Elysée by Sarkozy, who was visibly excited. Before entering, she released a prepared statement: "Policymakers will make up to their responsibility in a dire situation and those who originated it will contribute to the solution."

"Take Angela Merkel's words," Sarkozy said, "translate them in French and you have exactly my thought."

In fact, the two leaders went on bickering for hours and, as we know, the summit failed. The body language of the two leaders at the customary press conference afterward has already become a European classic: Sarkozy animatedly gesticulating around Merkel, while she raised a single finger clearly mimicking a no. That was the genesis of the "chacun sa merde" sentence. The press conference was an embarrassment: "We had a meeting that was necessary and maybe constructive," Sarkozy said with no sign of the usual excitement in his voice.

However, there was more to the story of the failed meeting. Toward the end of the working dinner on the evening of October 4, Merkel was given a message saying she had to rush back to Berlin in the early morning to rearrange a new rescue package for Hypo Real Estate within twenty-four hours.[27]

As Merkel arrived at the Chancellery, her economic adviser, Jens Weidmann, reported that the Bundesbank was tracking movements whereby more and more Germans seemed to be drawing cash from their deposits. The demand for €500 banknotes had increased remarkably. Some savers were asking to move money from one deposit account to another just to check whether the money was still there. If one ATM of the thousands in the country broke, for any technical reason, people might suddenly panic. Weidmann feared that the German public was preparing for a run on the banks and Merkel needed to appear on TV to reassure them. In retrospect, Steinbrück deemed the broadcast to be "legendary." "Merkel and I were perfectly aware we were dancing on the edge of a razor," he said. The two politicians appeared together in front of cameras standing in the sky-lobby on the same floor as Merkel's office in the Chancellery in Berlin. In the background was the painting "Nach dem Knall," a German landscape. In a later interview with German broadcaster ZDF, Steinbrück revealed the real strategy, referring in this case to Hypo Real Estate: "We expect and hope that especially the European Central Bank . . . is helpful by opening a security window which further secures the liquidity of this bank." This call for action by the ECB was to become a crucial feature in the rest of the European crisis.[28]

## A Solution that Creates Bigger Troubles Ahead

The situation of the banking systems across Europe was nearing standstill. The signals became unmistakable for the ECB, too. In fact, monetary assessments changed radically between Thursday, October 2, and Wednesday, October 8, convincing the ECB that the upside risk to inflation—deemed visible just six days earlier—had now disappeared and that participation in the first major rate cut coordinated with all the other central banks of the world was due.

The urgency to act could not be denied. The Dutch plan was sent to the council of European finance ministers (ECOFIN) meeting on October 6 and 7, only two days after the failed Elysée summit—and it was this group that made the important decisions. In the twelve pages of the final document adopted by the council, the finance ministers agreed to "support any systemic financial institutions, defending the stability and health" (of those institutions) and to "protect the deposits of individual savers." The protection of investors was ensured by the promise to intervene "even, among other things, with recapitalization of vulnerable systemically relevant financial institutions." The statement concluded: "We will be prepared to intervene in a coordinated manner."

Finally on October 9, Sarkozy agreed with Merkel to convene a new meeting at the Elysée on October 12. For this occasion, Sarkozy introduced a new twist: he would summon only the seventeen euro area countries. It was the first time that these countries would meet not just at the level of finance ministers, but at that of heads of state and government. They would become the Eurosummit, a super-Eurogroup. However, Sarkozy invited also to the summit Gordon Brown, the only non-euro head of government, who in the past weeks had become his constant interlocutor.

Unfortunately, the Dutch plan, despite its realism and timeliness, was a typical second-best solution: a compromise with far-reaching unintended consequences. The subsequent months showed that the announcement by most governments of substantial rescue packages, differentiated nation by nation, caused an adverse shift in market sentiments toward sovereign borrowers. Instead of considering the euro area as a whole, markets started dissecting it along national borders. This caused sovereign credit default swap (CDS) premiums for euro area countries to increase sharply, whereas the CDS premiums for European financial corporations started to decline. Interest rate premiums on sovereign bonds themselves started inevitably to differentiate, opening a fault line that would explode in the coming months—something that would not have happened if there had been a common solution. The banking crisis had given Europe its first test for stronger cooperation, and it had flunked it. The cost of this failure would become immense when the sovereign debt crisis emerged.

# 3

## Europe's Awkward Ambitions to Change the World

### Vanity and Power among European Leaders

The onset of the financial crisis in the United States offered a wonderful chance for the Europeans to change the financial system, to regulate globalization, and finally to make the world economy more respectful of the principles that they chose as basis for the European society: "pluralism, non-discrimination, tolerance, justice, solidarity" (as in article 2 of the Treaty on European Union). However, instead of promoting unity in Europe, the initial phase of the U.S.-induced crisis offered national leaders the best chance in decades to vaunt their personal primacy on the world stage and praise the nature of their national models. The heads of government spoiled their chance to change the world by engaging instead in a personality competition that reached just short of comical levels.

In the midst of the crisis, narcissism was in vogue. Coming out of the October 2008 European Council meeting, Italian premier Silvio Berlusconi watched with some scorn Nicolas Sarkozy and José Manuel Barroso running toward the TV cameras before the other leaders to communicate the EU's decisions to the world. "They are amateurs," said the French-speaking media-tycoon to a colleague. "You should never go in front of a camera to convey optimism without before making up properly." To the surprise of his interlocutor, the Italian leader drew out of his pocket a cotton disc prepared with the right masking color. A couple of weeks later, a note was found in a London cab with the instructions for a proper make-up delivered to British prime minister Gordon Brown by one of his aides. Personalities play a crucial role in international diplomacy, where negotiations are often held face-to-face among national leaders. The ubiquitous visibility offered by the non-stop media cycle enhances the personification of politics. It is especially relevant for a national leader to communicate continuously and capture the collective imagination in a world were national politics can be less relevant than ever. "Daily and hourly, the politician inwardly has to overcome a quite trivial and all-too-human enemy: a quite vulgar vanity," said Max Weber, the great German sociologist who had a special disrespect for egotistic politicians. He would have been amazed by the events at the beginning of October 2008.

### Gordon, the Savior of the Universe

Gordon Brown sensed instinctively his role as pivotal in Europe and in the world.[1] In fact, his energetic actions in the financial crisis reflected this perspective, which he later explained: "We were days away from a complete banking collapse: companies not being able to pay their creditors, workers not being able to draw their wages, and families finding that the ATM had no cash to give to them." However, he did not have much respect for a potential European response. While he urged the European Union to act together, he said, "it was clear now that Britain had to act first."[2]

On October 7 the situation at the financial houses in the City of London was out of control. In the morning hours, the shares of Royal Bank of Scotland, overextended by an ambitious acquisition in 2007, and of HBOS tumbled by around 40 percent. The Bank of England estimated that capital losses for six of the largest U.K. banks were likely to be in excess of £100 billion, threatening the solvency of individual institutions and the collapse of the entire banking system.[3] (Losses would eventually be at least double that estimate.) It was necessary to tackle the concerns about capital, liquidity, and funding that had eroded confidence in the banking system. London, which had remained outside the euro zone and was diffident toward any European common initiative, was ready to pre-empt the action of its partners. At the same time, the British authorities had to grapple with the domestic effects of the failures of Icelandic banks, where billions of pounds of British savers' money was trapped, and the sudden flight of funds to Irish banks, which were now protected by a state deposit guarantee issued by the Irish authorities. The British government, hitherto the European standard-bearer of privatization and free markets, was ready to step in to support its banks with state capital and public guarantees. Brown, who had been a finance minister himself for many years, was well aware of the risk: If we do not intervene, he explained to the French president, the whole British financial system will be wiped out in a matter of hours.

The British Treasury offered to inject up to £50 billion ($87 billion) into British banks to buttress the capital they needed to support their businesses; in return it would get preference shares. Second, the Bank of England's "special liquidity scheme" would double in size, making at least £200 billion of readily cashable Treasury bills available for banks to swap for their less liquid assets. And third, the Treasury would guarantee as much as £250 billion of new wholesale funding obtained by banks.

The sheer size of the plan and the U.K. government's influence on the news media resulted in the plan being hailed as a triumph for Gordon Brown, who claimed repeatedly he had "led the world." In some British press reports Brown was even described, with well-hidden irony if ever, as the "savior of the universe." This instant legend reverberated through the continental press, often uncritical of British reporting. But beyond its size, what made Brown's plan so seductive was that it contemplated the nationalization of ailing banks. It was an act of courage that the U.S. administration had not been able to take for ideological reasons. In fact, Brown's was a bold and comprehensive plan, but it was hardly original, was not among the first conceived in Europe, and for sure was never the template that Brown pretended it was for other countries. But it was particularly less helpful than other plans because it did not take into consideration the many coordination problems created by the interconnection of the European banking systems. Indeed, as the ECB noticed: the non-negligible possibility of some banks ultimately being nationalized forced (European) banks' credit default swaps (CDS) spreads to increase further, reflecting the fact that nationalization is considered a so-called credit event in standard CDS contracts.[4] In late 2008 the equity prices of large and complex banks fell below the levels last seen in 2003.

## Partisan Protectionism

The left-right ideological cleavage, another intrinsic reason for political disunity among European governments, also was at work during the banking crisis. While Gordon Brown's Labor Party was ready to propose the nationalization of British banks, Sarkozy's and Merkel's center-right parties were much more reluctant. The political distance between left and right responded to a pattern of "partisan protectionism," whereby right-wing parties reacted to the opening of the global economy by protecting firms and capital ownership while liberalizing the labor markets and unloading the costs of adjustment on the opposite political constituency (while obviously left-wing parties had the opposite strategy). However, the divisions among governments with different political orientations had historical roots, which were linked expressly to the role of the modern nation state. The moral critiques of the differences of wealth and social status are connected in Europe with the death of feudalism and its system of privileged inheritance and the rise of nation states. The urge for equal treatment among citizens, which emerged across Europe in the eighteenth and nineteenth centuries, changed the grid of social organization according to two principles: the market, which in theory provided equal opportunity for participation in the production of wealth, and the nation state, which in theory protected individual rights and liberty. The market and the state became instrumental in the development of civil rights, with the market more on the side of individual freedom and the state as the defender of social justice. Therefore, appealing to the state in the midst of an economic crisis, which had been caused by the markets and resulted in a great deal of social injustice, seemed all too natural. National leaders felt as justified as ever to implement national policies without being too concerned about Europe as a whole or the reciprocal positions in other countries.

While Brown was capturing the limelight, the French press reported Sarkozy's growing irritation. But the French leader, who held the rotating EU presidency, could not afford to open an internal rift in the EU. The plan for a new summit at the Elysée in Paris on October 12 took shape in a matter of a few days. It was not possible to summon an extraordinary European Council just one month after the previous one, so Sarkozy suggested a meeting limited to only those countries belonging to the euro area.[5] Usually, such a meeting involved a group of countries that regularly convenes at the level of finance ministers, in the so-called Eurogroup. This time, it was to be the heads of state and government, a "Eurosummit." That meeting will be remembered as the decisive event of the initial leg of the European crisis. For Sarkozy, the first step was to bring the German position closer to his.

After the long negotiations in Brussels on the plan for separate but concerted support to the banks, agreement on the document for the summit was almost a done deal when, the day before the summit, Sarkozy invited Merkel to celebrate the fiftieth anniversary of a historic meeting between two giants of recent Franco-German history: Charles de Gaulle and Konrad Adenauer. The Sarkozy-Merkel meeting, in diplomatic language a Blaesheim-meeting, was held in Colombey-les-deux-Eglises, the birthplace of General de Gaulle.[6] The atmosphere was embued with historical significance, and the two leaders made gracious statements. Sarkozy hailed Merkel with a "Vive l'Allemagne, vive la France."

## The Elysée October 12 Agreement

On the morning of October 12, Sarkozy met for more than an hour with Brown, ECB president Jean-Claude Trichet, and Eurogroup chairman Jean-Claude Juncker for a common assessment of the situation in the financial markets. At the commencement of the full meeting, which was to last almost three hours, Brown, the only head of a non-euro government, was invited to explain the British plan for twenty minutes. After that it was agreed he should leave. The final declaration was agreed to without him and was not even discussed in his presence. Nevertheless, after leaving the meeting, the British prime minister summoned reporters and announced that the Europeans had adopted the British plan. According to one of the participants to the summit, the German distance from Brown's plan had been clearly expressed by Merkel during the meeting:

"We need to provide banks with the sufficient capital so that they are able to handle consciously. . . . [W]e provide support, we do not nationalize banks. What we are doing is helping them through the State."

The final summit statement ("A Concerted European Action Plan for the Member Countries of the Euro Area"), although signed only by members of the euro area, appeared to have committed the entire EU:

> As members of the euro area, we share a common responsibility and must contribute to a common European approach. We invite our partners to adopt the following principles so that the European Union as a whole can act in a unified manner and avoid that national measures negatively influence the functioning of the single market and could affect the partner countries.

The principles were indeed later agreed to at the meetings of the twenty-seven finance ministers.[7]

The details of individual national plans were to be announced simultaneously the next day. In fact, as requested by the Germans, there would be fifteen distinct European funds—one for each country then using the euro—whose responsibility would rest with each country but following shared principles. Merkel had introduced the concept of a "common toolbox" to be used by each country in keeping with its specific needs. Berlin also succeeded in passing a change in the accounting rules for the banks' balance sheets that would exempt them from the application of the "market value rule"—accounting for assets according to their current market price—as requested by Deutsche Bank boss Josef Ackermann to the chancellor personally. The fall in the market value of most assets would endanger many institutions with risky assets in their portfolios; thanks to the new provision Ackermann could announce that his bank would post a profit in the third quarter of the year, propping up confidence.[8] However, the choice of that accounting method had dramatic consequences in the following years. German and French banks no longer had an incentive to clean up their balance sheets, and they actually kept most of the toxic assets on their books, thus maintaining themselves in a fragile state for years.

## Embarrassment in Brussels: What Are EU Institutions For?

The European Commission and other EU institutions tried to reinforce the October 12 commitments of the heads of governments. But the reputation of the commission suffered severely at that crucial moment and was tarnished by allegations of ineffectiveness. The European Parliament, in particular, was enraged by the commission's lack of initiative. Steps on financial regulation were left in the hands of the governments, and the commissioner in charge, the Irishman Charlie McCreevy, was particularly criticized. His credibility had suffered because he had spent a large part of his mandate rejecting proposals for stronger vigilance on the banking industry.[9] Commission president Barroso himself was accused of acting only as a mediator, being too servile toward Sarkozy and Berlusconi, and of trying only to win further approval from Brown and Merkel, who were crucial for his own future reelection. Monetary Affairs Commissioner Joaquin Almunia tried to convince Barroso that this was the ultimate moment to take the initiative, but the president probably had less political courage than his predecessors, Romano Prodi and Jacques Delors, and instead dug in his heels. Barroso's defense was that London would block any initiative because it was protective of its dominance as a financial center, so therefore "one needs to be pragmatic." Gordon Brown's persistent opposition to the commission and to its head had turned into a personal burden for Barroso, who could not count on Sarkozy, either. The Portuguese's strategy was not to provide leadership, and not to encumber the individual governments, either.

One by one, the EU institutions and officials were folding under the pressure of markets and of national governments. Monetary Affairs Commissioner Almunia, for instance, promised to apply the exemptions related to "exceptional circumstances" reasonably when judging forthcoming excessive public deficits. Neelie Kroes, the antitrust commissioner, was instructed, by France in particular, to give the green light to banking recapitalizations with state money. The commission's Directorate General for Competition had to rule on the acceptability of state aid to the banking system as well as bank mergers; while it did not seriously attempt to resist the scale of assistance for the banks, it did try to modulate the distortive consequences. It published a set of guidelines on October 13 (and a second on December 5) noting that Article 107 of the EU Treaty (TFEU, the Treaty on the Functioning of the European Union) provided that the commission may allow state aid "to remedy a serious disturbance in the economy of a Member State."[10] The directorate sought to insist that such aid respected key conditions, such as non-discrimination, and did not place aided banks at an undue advantage. This judgment from Brussels was probably very generous. Press reports, for instance, suggested that the French plan at first was to be rejected because it proposed an 8 percent coupon, but in the end it was allowed. When the U.K. authorities reviewed the merger among Lloyds-TSB and HBOS and decided that, despite competition concerns, it was in the public interest, the commission's competition office did not object. The timidity of the European Commission in the wake of real emergencies in national capitals accelerated the "repatriation" of European politics.

For all the efforts in Brussels, Frankfurt, and in the national capitals, the first euphoric reaction of the markets petered out rapidly.[11] Financial indexes fell back sharply a few days after the summit as fears of recession grew. A new challenge was looming large on the agenda of the European leaders: how to rescue the economy from a steep fall in growth and employment. Again, the action taken was another step toward decentralizing the decisions on the political economy back to the national level.

## Sarkozy à la Conquête de l'Europe

On October 21, Sarkozy spoke to the European Parliament in Strasbourg, trying to maintain the momentum of his leadership, keeping in mind that he would soon be dealing face-to-face with the American president. He had the ambition to show the European way to reform world capitalism. How has all this been possible? he asked the parliament. How can we avoid this happening again? Has Europe its own ideas to defend? A policy to propose?

> In this context . . . I proposed, on Europe's behalf, that we hold an international summit to lay the groundwork for a new Bretton Woods, in reference to what happened in the aftermath of World War Two, to promote a new global financial system. This idea is gaining ground. What should Europe's objective be for this summit? Europe must promote the idea of a radical reform of global capitalism. What happened was a betrayal of capitalism's values. It didn't call into question the market economy. No rules, speculators being rewarded to the detriment of entrepreneurs. . . . We must promote the idea of a new regulatory system. Europe must propose these ideas, and it will do so. First, that no bank working with State money should be able to work with tax havens. No financial institution must be able to operate without being subject to financial regulation.

But Sarkozy made two other more interesting points to the Parliament.

> Stock markets are at a historically low level. I wouldn't like European citizens to wake up in a few months' time and discover that European companies belong to non-European investors who purchased them for next to nothing when share prices were at rock bottom, with European citizens left asking: what have you done? I ask each of us to think about whether it might be opportune for us too to create sovereign wealth funds in each of our countries and perhaps whether these national sovereign wealth funds could, from time to time, be coordinated to provide an industrial response to the crisis. I might add that I noted with great interest the American plan for the automobile industry—$25 billion at unbeatably low interest rates to save the three American automobile manufacturers from bankruptcy.
> Can we leave the European automobile industry in a market where there is a serious distortion of competition with its US rivals without looking at the possibility of a European sectoral policy to defend the European industry? This doesn't mean us calling the single market into question. It

doesn't mean us undermining the principle of competition. It doesn't mean undermining the principles governing State aid. It means that Europe must put forward a united response, one which mustn't be naïve, in the face of the competition from the other major world regions. Our duty is to ensure that, in Europe, we can go on building planes, ships, trains and cars because Europe needs a robust industry. The presidency will fight for this policy.

Sarkozy added one last thing:

It isn't possible for the Euro Area to go on without a clearly identified economic government. We can no longer go on like this. I want to pay tribute to the action of the ECB, I want to say that I firmly believe the ECB has to be independent, but for the ECB's action to be fully effective, it must be able to discuss with an economic government. That was the spirit of the treaty. The spirit of the treaty is to foster dialogue, democracy and reciprocal independence. And also to my mind, the Eurogroup's real government is a Eurogroup which meets at head of State and government level. And I was absolutely amazed to learn, when I requested this meeting, that it's the first time since the euro's creation that there's been one. Honestly: we create a currency, we give ourselves a central bank, we have a single currency policy and we haven't got an economic government worthy of the name![12]

## Beethoven's Bonaparte Reminiscence

Sarkozy envisioned EU institutions as being second in line behind heads of governments, so he was determined not to return the power of the Eurogroup to the finance ministers and to keep the European Commission limited to its role as guardian of the EU treaties.[13] Leadership of the Eurogroup, in Sarkozy's view, should be left to the president of the European Council, representing the heads of governments. His goal was to establish the Eurosummit as the new protagonist for the economic governance of the euro area. Incidentally Sarkozy was planning to head the Eurosummit for the coming fourteen months by leveraging on the fact that the countries holding the two forthcoming rotating presidencies of the EU were the Czech Republic and Sweden, neither of which was a member of the euro zone. Sarkozy saw a strong opportunity to establish himself as the leader of Europe.

Berlin's first reaction to the French president's plans was an icy silence. Merkel appeared to have legitimate fears that Sarkozy's strategy would lead to an overturning of the EU's fundamental principles: the primacy of the treaties and of the common rules on national political agendas. Moreover, Berlin was clearly concerned about the risk of a loss of discipline on the economic policies requiring fiscal rigor, the single market, and the stability of the euro: in other words, the economic foundations of Europe. Soon the silence was followed by the economics minister's terse remark that the French proposal contradicted "all successful principles of our economic policy."

*Der Spiegel* reported: "The problem with Sarkozy, from the Chancellery's standpoint, is that he cannot be trusted. When he speaks of a 'European economic government,' his listeners in Berlin translate this to mean 'economic government under French leadership.' When he calls for state-run economic programs, they interpret his words as an attack on the European Union's Maastricht Treaty, which sets clear debt limits for countries. As the Germans see it, the thrust coming from Paris marks the beginning of a conflict over which model is to dominate Europe in the future, that of the social market economy, which keeps the government out of the business of running companies to the greatest extent possible, or the French model of a government-controlled economy. An adviser to Chancellor Merkel said, 'Sarkozy wants to seize the opportunity to shift the economic and political balance in Europe.'"[14]

Confronted with the reactions in Berlin, Sarkozy had to take his rhetoric down a notch. He actually went out of his way to deny that he wanted more protectionism or a wider margin to spend public money. But on October 23 in Argonay in the department of Haute Savoie, speaking to an audience of entrepreneurs, he maintained that "politics was back" and that "the ideology of the dictatorship of the markets and the powerlessness of government is dead." He then advocated the establishment of a fund worth €175 billion to defend "key industries," wishing that other national states in the EU would do the same. And indeed they did. "Without me Europe would be in a sorry state" was how the satirical newspaper *Le Canard enchaîné* interpreted his remarks. Probably stretching its interpretation a bit, the paper also noted this: "Bush is finished, Blair is no longer in office, and Merkel, well, she too isn't the right one. I am the only one." When Merkel read the sentence, she couldn't resist remarking sarcastically: "Some have smaller egos, while others happen to have bigger ones."[15]

Ever since Ludwig van Beethoven changed the name of his "Bonaparte Symphony" to "Eroica," rejecting Napoleon's self-crowning as the act of a tyrant, French personal ambitions have always gone down badly among Germans. But what made suspicions reach the alarm level in Berlin was hearing the details of a very interesting strategy that "sources close to the president" circulated in France. Sarkozy, faced with the need to relinquish the rotating presidency of the European Council on December 31, 2008, wanted to make the presidency of the new Eurogroup summit (among leaders of the euro area countries) a personal power base until the end of 2009. His reported reasoning was that neither the Czech nor the Swedish prime ministers (who were due to hold the rotating presidency of the European Council in 2009 after France) could also head the

Eurogroup summit because their countries were outside the euro area. Sarkozy aimed to establish his power over the euro area for the next fifteen months, setting a precedent. Some newspapers used the word "coup" to describe his attempt to grab power in Europe.

## Europe Challenges U.S. Leadership

Before jetting off to Camp David to meet with President George W. Bush, Sarkozy told the other European leaders that he hoped "literally to rebuild the foundations of the financial systems."

Sarkozy's assertiveness played to the moral high ground that he thought Europe had gained in the aftermath of the appalling status of the U.S. economy. Moreover, he sensed that everybody had to admit that under the surface of globalization—a regular issue in French rhetoric against the "Anglo-Saxons"—deep fault lines were appearing. At the end of October the American stock market was collapsing and seemed to have no chance to rebound in the foreseeable future. Indeed, it would lose $3.9 trillion in value, almost a third, after the U.S. presidential election in November 2008 until hitting bottom at the end of March 2009. Global trade was spiralling downward; it would fall 12.2 percent in 2009. At their worst, said Larry Summers, chief economics adviser to the new U.S. president, Barack Obama, these declines exceeded the initial drops of the 1930s. "Companies fired millions of workers. Fear and hysteria abounded. What we know of that period is that during that time the stock market fell more sharply than in the six months after Black Tuesday in 1929, that global trade declined more rapidly than in the first year of the Great Depression, that the economy was not self equilibrating and that a variety of vicious cycles were pulling it down even deeper, at a rate of 700,000 jobs a month at the worst of it."

The French president arrived at Camp David, the official weekend resort of American presidents, on October 18 on the heels of a new awareness in the United States that Europe could not be dismissed as an economic museum—"a place for languorous meals and vacations, not economic innovation," as the *New York Times* put it. During the previous ten days Europeans had proved more nimble than Americans at getting to the root of the global financial crisis. After initially dithering, Europe's leaders came up with a financial bailout plan that "has now set the pace for Washington, not the other way around, as had been customary for decades."[16]

With the American economy in its deepest crisis since the Great Depression, President Bush had been under intense pressure from European leaders to take steps to tighten financial oversight and better coordinate financial market regulation around the world. But any discussion of international oversight of financial markets was, in the view of the White House, problematic. As the *New*

*York Times* noted, "American officials do not want other nations to control this country's banking system." Just hours before the joint statement at Camp David, President Bush, in his appearance with Sarkozy and Barroso, warned that any effort to overhaul the international financial system must "preserve the foundations of democratic capitalism—a commitment to free markets, free enterprise and free trade." The Europeans had been pressing for a meeting of the Group of Eight industrialized nations, but Bush went one step further, calling for a broader global conference that would include "developed and developing nations"—among them China and India.[17]

At Camp David, Sarkozy tried to stand his ground: "This may be a great opportunity if we do not fall back into the hateful practices of the past, practices that have led us exactly where we are right now." Bush's offer to hold a summit meeting in the United States appeared to be an effort by the administration to wrest control of the proceedings from Sarkozy, who favoured a "G-8 plus 5" format under the aegis of the United Nations. Earlier, Sarkozy had secured the agreement of the UN secretary general, Ban Ki-Moon, to host a meeting in December in New York to mark symbolically where the crisis originated. But a senior White House official said that offer was moot. "We appreciate the suggestion by the secretary general, but the United States has committed to hosting the summit," the official said. "There's lots of force out there coming from the Europeans for ideas on what ought to be on the agenda, but there are lots of very important countries in the world that have a stake in this, and they have their views, and we have our own views."[18]

The statement issued after the private dinner at Camp David was also much less than what Sarkozy had wanted. Bush had kept for the United States both the political and the material organization of the planned meeting. Instead of a more restricted group where Europe had a larger slice of the cake, Bush arranged for a summit of the G-20 countries.[19] Sarkozy and Brown were no longer at the center of the stage lecturing the old colony. The European Commission was not even invited to participate in the G-20 meeting until later, after some awkward negotiation ratcheted up a personal invitation for Barroso.

Sarkozy had one more ace up his sleeve. In his European Council capacity, he was going to meet with the leaders of Asia in Beijing on October 24–25. It was an opportunity for the French president to rake in the support of the powerful new protagonists on the world scene. Actually, the motto of the seventh Asia-Europe meeting was "toward a win-win solution," but in the end, the final statement was at most bland: "Leaders. . . agreed that long-term stability of the global and regional financial markets is key to sustainable economic growth of both regions."[20]

Chinese premier Wen Jiabao was more blunt:

The present crisis has laid bare the weaknesses in the existing international financial system and governance structure. The international community is calling for accelerated reform and the establishment of a fair, just, and effective international financial system. I deem it important to do three things in this regard: first, increase the say and representation of developing countries in international financial organizations; second, expand the scope of the regulation of the international financial system, with particular emphasis on strengthening the supervision of the major reserve currency countries; and third, establish a reasonable global financial rescue mechanism.

Europe was not mentioned directly, the United States was to be put under security checks, and eventually both Europe and the United States were to provide more room for Asian countries in international institutions. It was the first signal that the Western crisis would lead to a reshuffling of international power.[21]

## Paris-Berlin: The Divorce and the British Lover

During the Asia-Europe summit in Beijing, Sarkozy asked Merkel to discuss a new initiative to support the European economy in Paris on November 7. The French president's analysis was simple: The disruption of the global economy was much more profound than imagined hitherto. A fiscal initiative must be undertaken collectively. The euro area countries have a chance to integrate voluntarily their fiscal policies without need for a change in the European Union rules. Merkel's response was as clear: The heads of state and government should continue to shape the basic elements of economic policy for the EU, while all questions relating to the currency union should be addressed in informal meetings of the finance ministers from the euro zone countries. This had been the policy since the European Council resolution of December 1997, and this is how she wanted it to remain.

Sarkozy's strategy was crumbling: divisions were weakening him in the EU and his global initiatives were losing impact once confronted directly by Washington or Beijing. For all his hubris, the French president was still paying the price for the internal divisions in Europe. Without working to develop a preliminary consensus, Sarkozy found himself with little leverage other than his ideas and personal energy in an arena where balance of powers and arm twisting were much more clearly understood.

Berlin at this stage did not share Sarkozy's fears of a recession or his expressed need to launch a new initiative to support the European economy. The analysis of the crisis in Berlin was in fact much different from that in France. Germany relied on the capacity of its economy to react, thanks to the recently upgraded flexibility of its firms and the strength of its welfare provisions. The majority of the economic think tanks were estimating flat growth for the next year. From

Berlin's perspective, this would be a tolerable pause given the extreme conditions. No cyclical policy was particularly useful, and, in fact, public expenditure would imply more taxes in the future and would hinder private investments. A first hint of a "conjunctural program" was made by Angela Merkel in her weekly podcast on November 1. She was wearing a red blazer in the small Kabinettsaal in the Chancellery, without reading the few pages prepared by the staff. In that circumstance she mentioned she would prepare "a comprehensive investment package." But two days later during her government's coalition meeting, the reaction was less than favorable. The sixteen measures that she wanted to discuss were opposed firmly by her CDU party representatives. Most of them did not want to endanger the goal of a balanced budget. Nominally the package amounted to €50 billion, although the real sum was probably one-third that much.

Confronted once again with Berlin's "nein," Sarkozy opted for the British card and invited Gordon Brown as a new favorite partner for Paris. It was a desperate attempt to sideline Merkel. The first meeting was held in Versailles on October 28, and Sarkozy used no caution in pointing out that a new powers-equilibrium was about to see the daylight in Europe: "I'd like to tell you how happy I am to be having a meeting with Gordon Brown, the British Prime Minister, with whom, I must say, we've been working hand in hand since well before the start of the crisis. . . . I told him that the entente cordiale between the British and the French wasn't enough. I proposed an entente amicale and Gordon talked about the entente formidable."[22]

There was still a huge opportunity for Sarkozy to lead the world: the G-20 meeting on November 14–15 in Washington to lay the foundation of the "new Bretton Woods," for which Gordon Brown showed a similar sensitivity. In fact, and unfortunately for Sarkozy, Brown had already agreed with Bush to convene the G-20 again in London in 2009, when the G-20 presidency would be under Brown's leadership and responsibility, thus undermining Sarkozy.

Sarkozy wanted to use the EU Council on November 7 to get an official endorsement giving him the authority to deal on behalf of Europe. The French president proposed to his European colleagues a document entitled "Terms of Reference," which called for more effective coordination among the member states and issued an invitation to ECOFIN and the European Commission to "submit to the next European Council a European strategy comprising principles for action and specific measures to cope with the economic slowdown and maintain economic growth and employment."

Most member state delegations were taken by surprise by a document clearly inspired by Sarkozy's desire to obtain a personal mandate to effectively assert Europe's—or maybe France's—position on the reform of global capitalism. Once more, Berlin was especially alerted and Merkel soon played her cards in the course of a bilateral meeting before the European Council. It was a defining moment for both Merkel and for Sarkozy, who came to recognize that Germany could play a stronger hand in bilateral negotiations. The title of the document was changed from "Terms of Reference," which implied a mandate to Sarkozy, to "Agreed Language," pre-empting any individual intiative by the French president. Merkel made Sarkozy add a new phrase stressing that the EU strategy would build on the existing ones: the "Lisbon Strategy" of 2000 (to boost Europe's competitiveness) and on the 1997 Stability and Growth Pact (intended to keep fiscal deficits under control), thus limiting the margin for Sarkozy's hypothetical ideas of a new economic government for the euro area. A phrase calling for "the promotion of free trade" was added, to avoid any temptation of protectionism. Finally, the IMF was called on to exercise its role of macroeconomic surveillance fully.[23] Sarkozy had been reined in.

### The G-20 Meeting, November 14–15: No French Revolution

The spirit of the G-20 meeting of mid-November 2008 in Washington was evidently different from what was planned by the French president. George W. Bush was still in charge, and President-elect Obama didn't show up. Mario Draghi, Italy's central bank governor, was the first of the representatives to arrive at the White House for a state dinner on November 14. He was also there in his capacity as president of the Financial Stability Forum, the institution that was to propose new regulations for the global financial markets. The issue was central, as many emerging countries were asking the more advanced countries to admit their responsibility in originating the crisis. But the official answer from the White House the next day was that the meeting was not about discussing the causes, but the cures. In the relatively small State Dining Room at the White House, around an oval mahogany table, the U.S. president seemed in control of the situation. At his sides were sitting King Abdullah of Saudi Arabia and President Luiz Inácio Lula da Silva of Brazil. The closest European was Gordon Brown, who was sitting in front of the American president. Bush opened the dinner remarking that "free capitalism was the engine of wealth, progress, and social improvements around the globe."

The meeting was historic, mainly because it marked a major shift in the global balance of power by bringing to the fore all the largest emerging economies. The final communiqué recognized not just the failures of the financial system itself, but also the underlying mistakes in macroeconomic policies. It also stressed two imperatives: strong and cooperative action to stimulate the world economy and maintenance of the open economy on which all depend. The very fact that the rhetoric of coordination had come through so vividly was a success. Furthermore, the leaders gave their finance ministers a set of tough objectives to be carried out by the end of March 2009. These included a set of Common Principles for regulating the financial systems that rewarded the European efforts.

We will strengthen financial market transparency, including by enhancing required disclosure on complex financial products and ensuring complete and accurate disclosure by firms of their financial conditions. Incentives should be aligned to avoid excessive risk-taking. . . . We pledge to strengthen our regulatory regimes, prudential oversight, and risk management, and ensure that all financial markets, products and participants are regulated or subject to oversight. . . . We will also promote information sharing, including with respect to jurisdictions that have yet to commit to international standards with respect to bank secrecy and transparency. . . . Regulators should enhance their coordination and cooperation across all segments of financial markets, including with respect to cross-border capital flows. Regulators and other relevant authorities as a matter of priority should strengthen cooperation on crisis prevention, management, and resolution . . . We are committed to advancing the reform of the Bretton Woods Institutions so that they can more adequately reflect changing economic weights in the world economy in order to increase their legitimacy and effectiveness. In this respect, emerging and developing economies, including the poorest countries, should have greater voice and representation.[24]

The meeting was actually a step toward a period of better international coordination. However, the intellectual ambitions of the Europeans definitely conflicted with the interests of the Americans to preserve the capitalist system to the extent possible in the form they had created. European ambitions also posed conflicts with the emerging countries, which were eager to maintain the economic infrastructure (notably free trade) that had been conducive to their formidable emergence from poverty. Finally, Europeans were too divided to express a credible alternative model for the rest of the world.

## Sarkozy's Visions Unsettling German Europe

Personal agendas of national leaders were too divergent and the sense of a common endeavor was too far removed from the political interests of the individual governments. The limited role of the European Commission during the crisis left the field free to conflict among national priorities. A well-informed news analysis published by the French daily *Le Monde* gave a vivid insight into the agenda of the French president. This useful testimony revealed how national leaderships were destined to be counterproductive, exacerbating European divisions.[25]

According to the analysis, which credited the Elysée as the source reflecting the personal vision of the president, Sarkozy claimed he had won a power struggle against Chancellor Merkel and the German immobility she represented. Merkel had profited in the past from the decline of Sarkozy's predecessor,

Jacques Chirac, and had gained the upper hand in the EU—strengthening her grip thanks to the usual support of smaller countries traditionally allied with Germany. Sarkozy had won to his cause, beyond Spain and Belgium, some of the smaller countries like Greece, Portugal, and the Netherlands. If it could overturn the balance of power, Paris was sure it could change forever the inertia of Europe. Even Merkel's opposition to a regular Eurosummit (convening the head of states and governments of the euro area) was because Berlin feared it could not maintain its blocking power in a new institutional environment.

The French president shared what he described as the British vision in which politics was the domain of the governments coordinated by the European Council, and he believed that London would eventually adopt the single currency. "You think it is fun to have the pound in this state?" was the question raised at the Elysée, showing a surprising lack of insight into the British position. Paradoxically, if Sarkozy wanted to change the world, Gordon Brown preferred to save it as much as possible. To repress the financial sector would hit the industry that generated in 2007—thanks mostly to the international activity of the City of London—40 percent of all the profits of the British economy. The collaborative spirit of the British should have aroused French suspicions, considering that London had decided to free-ride on the other European countries by jumping the monetary gun and letting the pound devalue brutally.[26] The euro rose to a record high of 0.98 against the pound on December 30, 2008, up from 0.73 the year before (+34 percent).[27] In scale, the British devaluation was similar to a "default", but of the kind that is made to be paid over the years by the trade partners and by the foreign creditors. An opportunism that represented exactly the opposite of the reasons of peaceful cooperation behind the euro.

Nevertheless, the new alliance with London and the temporary break-up of the Franco-German axis were celebrated on December 8, when Sarkozy visited Brown (together with Barroso and Juncker) for a widely publicized preparatory meeting before the last European Council summit of the year. It was the first time that any such restricted and high-level European meeting had been held without the presence of the German chancellor.

# 4

## Too Different for One Policy

*Fiscal Stimulus? "France Is Working on It, Germany Is Thinking about It"*

The inability of European leaders to offer a collective answer to the crisis was not just a function of their competition to lead Europe, or the world. As the events at the end of 2008 show, it was also a consequence of the deep underlying differences in economic structure among their countries—differences that the introduction of the euro had magnified rather than narrowed. Differences among regions of an integrated area are not only normal, but even desirable, because they reflect the necessary specialization of each area. Inevitably the different activitites result in different levels of productivity and trade imbalances, as happens regularly among different states in the United States. If there is no political union or some form of fiscal compensation, the structural differences create not only deeper economic imbalances among the countries, but also different economic policy preferences.

Political priorities became even harder to reconcile when, at the end of 2008, the focus of the crisis moved from rescuing the banks to reviving the flagging economies. Paris and Berlin, in particular, were at loggerheads on the need for economic and fiscal stimulus. The public evidence of the policy distances came to light at the end of November, during a meeting between Merkel and Sarkozy that was intended to be a display of unity and friendship.

The invitation to Paris for the tenth Franco-German consultation in November was particularly well-received by Angela Merkel. President Sarkozy had taken the opportunity to invite the chancellor for lunch in the private apartment of his second wife, the famous model-turned-singer Carla Bruni. Merkel had an overall good personal relationship with the French president. Although she was not always sure of the reliability of French politicians, she admired Sarkozy's energy. He had caught her eye at one of their first meetings in Kiel (the capital of Schleswig-Holstein) in 2005 during an otherwise boring Christian Democratic Union (CDU) party convention that Sarkozy had turned into a lively and optimistic debate on conservative policies. Merkel also liked Carla Bruni, the glamorous Italian hostess, who sometimes acted as a translator in such gatherings. On this occasion in November, Merkel and the Sarkozys were to have lunch together by themselves. The atmosphere would be predictably cheerful. Unfortunately, the idyllic scene was marred even before it could occur. During a joint press conference before lunch, the chancellor stressed the "strong agreement" of both countries and highlighted that both were enacting a number of economic measures that would not burden their budgets, for example, by cutting red tape. She clearly minimized the differences in the volume of public expenditures that the two governments wanted to use to fight the slowdown of the economy. But all of a sudden, sitting next to Merkel in front of the journalists, Sarkozy completely changed the tenor and called out straightforwardly for Germany to do more to support its economy through a second stimulus package. "As far as coordination is concerned, we are in agreement. As far as more stimulus is concerned, we are also in agreement," he said. But then, referring to further stimulus, the French president let fall a sentence that would become a hit in newspapers around the world: "France is working on it, Germany is thinking about it."

The reluctance of Germany to throw money at the crisis was, at that time, almost unique among the advanced economies. There are historical and structural reasons for the German attitude. Merkel, for instance, has a clear picture of the long-term problems that Germany has to face. First of all, the demographic trend is dire: The population, now at 81 million, could decrease by 10–20 million within a generation. Absent significant new immigration (which is deeply controversial), economic growth will inevitably decline, strongly affected by the diminished labor force. The aging of the German population is particularly worrisome for its impact on fiscal stability, since welfare expenditures will increase due to the weight of pensions and health care. Germany should be saving money right now to prevent future public deficits; this can be done either through maintaining a budget surplus or by continuing to hold a constant surplus in the balance of payments (at the cost of deficits elsewhere in the world and in particular in Europe, where trade is especially intense). But a symmetrical problem concerns Germany's younger workers who, in the future, will have to be sufficiently qualified to sustain the activity of high value-added sectors, which are the only ones that can provide incomes sufficient to support an ailing welfare system. Unfortunately, German schools and universities are not top quality and they need to become better able to help the integration of the high share of young immigrant students (more than half of the schools' population in cities like Berlin or Frankfurt), upon whom the labor market will depend. These are among the reasons why Chancellor Merkel wanted to cut as much as possible from all items of the federal budget except for education, which she wanted to increase with full force.

But an even deeper structural reality is behind the differences among European countries, which leads to divergent economic policies. Germany, for instance, has a number of industrial giants that respond to the well-organized social structure of the country and have reaped the benefits of the boom in global trade. Italy hosts in its northern regions more than 30 percent of all the small to medium-size enterprises of the euro zone, responding more to the impulses of the global market than to the country's disorderly national politics. In 2008, 40 percent of Britain's overall profits were produced by the financial industry, while the country's formerly powerful manufacturing sector played a negligible role. Portugal's major enterprises are domestic energy providers, and Greek exports stand out in the EU as negligible relative to the country's GDP. In short, Europe's national economic structures are derived from a past when national borders had greater meaning and from country-specific social models.

While Europe was struggling in late 2008 to respond to the crisis, policy divergences became a major factor in hampering a common strategy. The political divide among the United Kingdom, France, and Germany, in particular, had its roots in different economic philosophies that had remained insufficiently discussed even when the Maastricht Treaty—establishing the common currency—was negotiated in 1991–92 and later ratified by national parliaments. After the European monetary union was conceived, there was a general understanding that it had to follow some kind of German preference for stability, which had proven its merits in the monetary excellence of the deutsche mark. However, the political class throughout the continent appeared not to fully grasp what this general understanding really meant or how it could be made to work. The 2008 crisis destroyed the silent compromise that had permitted most countries to pretend for an entire decade that their national priorities had changed little even though they had relinquished their currency and their monetary policy. In this sense, the crisis that began in 2008 was mainly a crisis rooted in national politics, as well as in finance.

## Anglos and Saxons: Structural Divergences

The divergence in economic and political cultures became clearly visible in December 2008 when European governments discussed their strategies to counteract the slump: did Europe need to boost public expenditure as the United States was doing and as the G-20 had called for? When economic activity falls so steeply, economists agree that government intervention is necessary to keep production and consumption at a level to prevent unemployment from becoming structural—that is, a point when jobless workers grow disillusioned, turn away from the labor market, and may not be able to return even when the recovery begins. This permanent damage is equivalent to a structural loss of potential growth for the national economy. Government intervention means, in plain terms, some form of public deficit, either through public consumption and investments—generally income support for households or some kind of new construction program—or through lower taxes or more credit. The resulting government deficit must be financed by the central bank or by the markets. With the financial system almost paralyzed, the role of the central banks becomes crucial. While bending monetary policy to fiscal purpose is anathema for the German economic culture, it became the first resort for the United Kingdom, which had 85 percent of its public deficit financed by the Bank of England in 2009.

The differing choices for use of a central bank during a recession can explain why Germany and the United Kingdom were on opposite fronts at the end of 2008, with Germany resisting the calls for monetary, as well as fiscal, stimulus strongly urged by the United States and Britain. A central bank can support fiscal stimulus by purchasing government securities on the open market. By doing so it triggers an increase in money supply and in the available funds for banks, and makes interest rates fall. Once short-term interest rates tend to zero, a central bank can maintain monetary stimulus through a process known as "quantitative easing": by acquiring longer-term government securities and financing these purchases by again expanding the money supply, in other words, monetizing the public debt. While quantitative easing belonged in the toolboxes of the Bank of England and other central banks, it was banned by the German Bundesbank because the policy holds an implicit inflationary danger.

Once the economy recovers, the central bank should sell back the government securities and demonetize the public debt. However, the markets might reasonably demand higher interest rates to absorb a public debt that might have grown substantially during the recession. A central bank controlled by or beholden to the government might then be forced to keep on buying treasury securities, again expanding the monetary base, at the cost of creating more inflation. The higher the inflation in respect to otherwise-expected price levels, the higher the benefit for the state, which will see a reduction in the real level of its debt (as a kind of inflation tax). In theory, a government-influenced central bank would try to constantly beat inflation expectations, and in the remote case that it can do that even in the context of sophisticated financial markets, the result can be hyperinflation. In case of a deep recession like the one that was confronting Europe, potentially leading to deflation, quantitative easing could be taken into account because it might be the only policy that draws the economy away from a "liquidity trap" where no interest rate can be set low enough to spur the private demand. Unfortunately this extreme form of monetary accommodation, advocated then by many in the United States and the United Kingdom, embodies practically everything that can create distrust in a German policymaker: the risk of hyperinflation as a consequence of the direct purchase of government bonds ( as happened in the 1930s); a politically dependent central bank that cannot resist the pressure to finance debts; an instability scenario for long-term investments in industrial activities; and a sense of risky uncertainty for households that rely on their savings. Looking beneath the economic language used at the end of 2008, the issue between London and Berlin was also a conflict between protecting the British model based on the financial system (which therefore benefits from easy credit provided by a politically sensitive central bank) and on a flexible exchange rate, versus the German model based on large industrial structures and jobs oriented toward exports and, therefore, in need of long-term stability and low inflation.

### German Fiscal Rigor or a Relaxed French Approach

If that was the policy rift between Berlin and London, a different gap was making difficult the political coordination between Berlin and Paris at the end of 2008, particularly as far as fiscal discipline was concerned. In this case, too, behind the different approaches there are structural reasons that influence the functioning of the monetary union. Because they shared the common currency under the European Central Bank, France and Germany could not resort to central bank financing of debts and had to rely on borrowing from the markets. In order to do that, governments are subject to a permanent budget constraint: they must remain solvent. To do this, governments cannot allow the value of their net stock of outstanding debt to exceed the discounted value of their future primary surpluses (the difference between total current revenues from all kind of taxes and current expenditures). When the primary surpluses are too low to reassure markets, a government has to cut current or future public spending, or raise current or future taxes. If it fails to do either (or both) of these things, markets can doubt the future solvency of the state and demand higher premiums on interest rates paid on sovereign debt, thus aggravating the burden of the debt and possibly even forcing the state into default. This is what West Germany experienced in 1948, before a monetary reform gave birth to a deeply engrained stability culture, to the deutsche mark, and later to the Bundesbank.

To appease markets, governments—when they increase their debts to counteract a recession—have to provide assurance that they will cut spending or raise taxes as soon as the economy can recover. Alternatively, governments can tie their hands through long-term irrevocable commitments to cut their debt. Unfortunately, since the introduction of the euro, France had failed to eliminate its budget deficit even in years of good economic growth and successfully resisted the resulting penalties that should have been imposed against it under the terms of the 1997 Stability and Growth Pact (under which euro zone countries pledged to keep annual budgets close to balance). From the German point of view, most euro area partners did not have credible plans for eventually reducing the debts that they were eager to contract. The German and French governments had themselves set a bad example in 2003 when, against the recommendations of the EU Commission, they were allowed by their fellow governments to violate the budget rules.[1] It was a clear abuse of power by the two largest euro zone economies.

The signal throughout the euro zone was that rules were less stringent than previously thought, especially since the country that insisted on them (Germany) was one of the first to violate them and get away with it.[2] The effect of that decision went even deeper than was publicly perceived at the time. Starting in 2004, fiscal policies changed in many countries—probably also a reaction to fiscal fatigue of the previous decade. Governments could have used the more porous debt ceilings to pay the cost of structural reforms.[3] Instead, many governments used it to appease their electorates. Wages were allowed to rise for public workers or taxes were reduced for some parts of the electorate. Had Berlin offered a green light to its partners again in 2009, the situation in the euro area might have turned rapidly critical and eventually resulted in countries resorting to the common central bank as the unique source of financing. But again, behind the cultural divides, there was a divergent political interest between Germany, which starting in 1998 had staged an impressive shift from public to private job creation, and France, which preferred that the state—and therefore the state's money—help national industry.

The recent mistrust on fiscal policy between Germany and France had originated in 2007 when Sarkozy publicly and unilaterally gave up a commitment to bring the French deficit into equilibrium—close to zero—by 2010 and even hinted at delaying the adjustment to 2012 or probably 2013. He needed some room to allow for tax cuts that he had promised in his presidential campaign. Berlin vehemently protested, and the showdown occurred in the most surprising way. After the first signs of financial instability in the summer of 2007, when French bank BNP-Paribas froze three of its money market funds, Sarkozy, at his own initiative, took the opportunity to participate in the meeting of the Eurogroup. It was absolutely exceptional for a head of state or government to take part in the assembly formed only of finance ministers. Sarkozy was convinced that his position as head of state would allow him to impose his priorities on those of the ministers. He was immediately at loggerheads, however, with German finance minister Peer Steinbrück, who was feeling not a pinch of intimidation and attacked Sarkozy frontally. The episode led to quite a disconcerted sense of disappointment and mistrust of the French president in the German establishment. Paris was the indispensable partner for Berlin. It was vital to have a reliable partnership with a political player who could bring southern Europe closer to the mainstream European mentality without the contentious intolerance that some northern Europeans exhibited. Even so, it seemed to the Germans that Sarkozy could not be the partner for this task. On December 12, 2008, a similar problem appeared during the EU Council when Merkel asked that the final document of the summit called to return "as soon as possible" to the medium-term objective of balanced budgets, while Sarkozy opted for a milder "swiftly."

Monetary union was built on the assumption that fiscal rules, strictly applied, would be enough to isolate countries that were not playing the game rigorously. But things were not going that way. States wiggled out of the Stability and Growth Pact's strictures—including France and Germany in 2003, as noted. Greece started fudging the rules even before its entrance into the euro zone in 2001 and never respected the limits even with the help of faked accounting. Peripheral countries were not the only regular violators of the limits. France and Germany did as badly as Portugal, only marginally better than Italy, and much worse than Ireland and Spain. Before 2011, no fewer than sixty-five to seventy violations of the 3 percent deficit threshold had occurred that were not justified by the economic downturn.[4] Finance ministers recoiled from punishing one of their own. They humbled and dismantled the European Commission's authority to enforce the rules, then they blamed the commission for not controlling their own misbehavior. When the economic cycle improved, most countries deliberately missed the opportunity to reduce their debts. In a number of cases annual deficits were below the limits, but mysteriously the long-term debt increased by more than the deficits implied, mostly due to "creative" accounting. The pressure for restraint came mainly from the ECB and was exerted as a ritual without much substance, although Trichet did manage to convince the French of the need for more fiscal discipline.

## Divergences Caused by Euro-Optimism

A key problem that the crisis painfully revealed was the unintended consequences of the euro for some national economies. After losing a critical instrument of adjustment—their national currencies—governments did not adapt their policies to the new realities of open economies in a global market. The euro zone is an imperfect currency area because the economic structures of the member states are different, labor and capital are not sufficiently mobile from one country to the other, and "sticky" domestic prices and wages can fail to reflect true market conditions.

Actually, it was expected that the monetary union itself would smooth some of the problems. But contrary to the expected outcome, fiscal, financial, and economic imbalances became more extreme during the run-up to monetary union and especially in its first decade. Germany's export-led economy created excess net savings that had to be invested abroad; the United Kingdom's financial dominance had crowded out industry, encouraged a risk-taking mentality in the banking system, and supported deregulation at any cost through all sectors of the economy; and Spain's process of catching up with the higher income countries of the euro zone had led to negligence of bubbles inflated by huge capital inflows invested in real estate.

Problems of this kind are well known to any economist familiar with standard theories and models: when nominal exchange rates are fixed and capital mobility is perfect, a change in nominal consumption or investments in one country has a large impact on the economy because interest rates are determined at the euro area level and do not rise in response to the higher consumption.[5] But higher consumption still creates inflationary pressures that hit particularly the prices of nontradable goods and later transmit to the prices of tradable goods (items and services that can be traded across borders), thus eroding the overall competitiveness of the economy and creating a current account deficit. When domestic prices increase, consumers purchase more imported than domestic products. So trade imbalances become a crucial element of economic integration. In this process real interest rates act as an amplifying and destabilizing force: countries with higher consumption rates—and higher inflation—will enjoy a relatively lower level of real interest rates (that is, after deducting for inflation) and an additional stimulus to their demand.[6]

Silently, the external imbalances built up a potential to destabilize the euro area. Excess saving in surplus countries like Germany was channelled through capital markets into countries with external deficits like Spain or Greece in massive amounts. While in principle this flow of money could facilitate the catch-up of less-developed economies, in reality it happened much too fast: there was a clear misallocation of capital due to weaknesses in financial regulation and expectations that turned out to be too optimistic. Spain was a clear example of how difficult it was—even with the best intentions—to deal with what seemed a benevolent flow of capital toward economies that were catching up. Spain, in fact, had low levels of public debt and deficit, but still received lots of capital, especially through the U.K. banks. Madrid—to the extent it was aware of the problem—could not adjust in a few years its industrial structure to employ productively the capital blindly thrown into the country by European banks. Theoretically, it should have reacted by dampening its own growth and increasing the budget surplus by 4-6 percent of its GDP. At the same time, the real estate boom was inflating fiscal revenues up to 2.9 percent of GDP yearly.[7] But how was it politically possible for any government to explain to its citizens that taxes had to be increased by 20 percent to stem the flood of foreign capital being invested in their country?

All in all, the external position of the euro area as a whole (its aggregate current account) was close to balance. But especially after 2004, the differences among countries reached unusual levels: From 2002 to 2007, the current account deficits in Greece, Portugal, and Spain averaged more than 7 percent of national GDP. By contrast, Finland, Germany, and the Netherlands ran average surpluses of more than 5 percent of GDP. The scale and persistence of the imbalances was greater than during earlier decades. At the onset of the common currency, current account imbalances in the euro area countries ranged from −5 percent to +7 percent of GDP. By 2007 the range had widened to −14 percent to +8 percent of GDP.[8]

Since the beginning of the euro, Greece, Portugal, and Spain had accumulated net inflows of capital from other countries equal to more than 70 percent of their national GDPs by 2008. This degree of external indebtedness was among the highest of all thirty-four countries belonging to the Organization for Economic Cooperation and Development (OECD). Only Finland had previously experienced a similar situation, following the collapse of the Soviet Union. On the flip side, creditor countries also reached near-record levels: Germany had a net external position of 20 percent of GDP, and the same measure topped 40 percent in Belgium and Luxembourg. According to OECD calculations, between 2004 and 2008, both the large current account surpluses of Germany and the Netherlands and the major deficits in Greece, Portugal, and Spain showed an unexplained component, not related to the positive effects of economic real integration.[9] One possible reason, often raised by IMF analysts, was stronger financial market integration: in other words, speculative financial investments amplified the underlying economic imbalances.

## The EU Commission Tries to Catch Up

While Germany was resisting—although isolated—the pressure from other European countries and from the United States for a major impulse to the economy, on November 26, 2008, the European Commission launched its initiative for growth in the EU. It was the European Economic Recovery Plan (EERP), with the aim of providing a coordinated short-term budgetary stimulus to demand as well as reinforcing competitiveness and potential growth. The total package amounted to €200 billion (representing 1.5 percent of EU GDP), of which member states were called on to contribute around €170 billion (1.2 percent of EU GDP), with the remaining €30 billion (0.3 percent of EU GDP) coming from EU and European Investment Bank (EIB) budgets. "The stimulus measures," the commission announced, "would come in addition to the role of automatic fiscal stabilizers and should be consistent with the Stability and Growth Pact and the Lisbon Strategy for Growth and Jobs." The commission's document backing up this plan gave a description of a very severe situation:

The euro area and several member states are already in recession. The risk is that this situation will worsen still further: that investment and consumer purchases will be put off, sparking a vicious cycle of falling demand, downsized business plans, reduced innovation, and job cuts. This could push the EU into a deep and longer-lasting recession: the economy contracting further next year, and unemployment could rise by several million people. Quick and decisive action is needed to stop this downward spiral.[10]

The Recovery Plan was based on two mutually reinforcing elements. First, short-term measures were intended to boost demand, save jobs, and help restore confidence. Second, "smart investment" was to yield higher growth and sustainable prosperity in the longer term. There was an evident lack of focus in the plan, which mentioned, for instance, "efforts to tackle climate change" as an orientation for jobs policies. In reality, the EU common budget was limited in amount and was already allocated. Furthermore, the modest influence of the commission on member states' plans was demonstrated by the absence of a clear timeline detailing which part of the stimulus had to be delivered and by when—a crucial aspect of coordination. In fact, for all the usual rhetoric on coordination, what became evident was that it would be the national governments, not the EU as a body, that were to activate the resources called for in the plan. Even so, the president of the commission, José Manuel Barroso, desperately needed to give visibility to the EU executive. It was evident that the plan did not represent a genuine EU response and was simply a case of the EU coordinating national responses.

The prominent role of national states was no surprise. Article 121 of the EU treaty (ex art.103 of the Maastricht Treaty), designing the pillars of the euro area economic policies, left to member states the main role of managing fiscal policy:

> Member States shall regard their economic policies as a matter of common concern and shall co-ordinate them within the Council. The Council shall, acting by a qualified majority on a recommendation from the Commission, formulate a draft for the broad guidelines of the economic policies of the Member States and of the Community, and shall report its findings to the European Council.

The possible coexistence of a centralized monetary policy and a decentralized fiscal policy in fifteen member states of the euro zone (as of late 2008) had been questioned ever since Maastricht, even in times of benign economic conditions. During a deep crisis, the commitment of the member states to "conduct their economic policies with a view to contributing to the achievement of the objectives of the Community" was increasingly difficult. The possibility that the European Commission would step forward and take the reins of coordination from the hands of states was daring at best. Indeed, the recovery plan document of the commission backfired in some European quarters. The estimate of spending 1.5 percent of EU GDP was either too large for the real common commitment or too small for the real amount of resources deployed by the states. Some governments blamed the commission for not having stressed even more the major role that automatic stabilizers (such as social welfare programs) play in the European economies. As a result, both the markets and the international partners of the G-20 had an easy game pointing out what appeared to be an insufficient effort by the Europeans.

While states played their cards, only one common policy instrument offered a point of leverage for intervention at the European level—the common currency: "The euro, in particular," remarked the commission in the recovery plan, "has proved to be an invaluable asset for the EU economies and an essential element of stability. Supported by the strong role played by the independent European Central Bank, the euro protects against destabilising exchange rate movements, which would have greatly complicated the national responses to the crisis."[11]

Indeed, the weakest EU countries in that period were Iceland, Hungary, Latvia, Bulgaria, Estonia, Lithuania, Romania, and the United Kingdom, the last of which resorted to a massive devaluation of the pound during the second half of 2008, by about 20 percent against the euro and 30 percent against the dollar. Eastern European countries not belonging to the euro area were so severely exposed to financial instability that they were considered candidate for default, and the EU and the IMF had to intervene with financial aid. Doubts were rising about Austria, reflecting the exposure of its banking system to other non-euro countries in eastern Europe. The contrast between the solidity of Slovakia and Slovenia—both members of the euro area—and the impact of the crisis on non-euro countries seemed a striking confirmation of the virtues of the euro that had brought Sarkozy to make the bold forecast that even London would come to accept the common currency. Denmark, too, in those weeks floated the idea that it was considering joining the euro. The countries that did not fit neatly into this picture were Greece and Ireland, whose interest rates had begun to spike because investors considered both of them increasingly risky. Credit default swaps (CDS), which offered insurance against the risk of default, were being actively used by investors to take into account the eventuality of a country's default. On December 5, Ireland's CDS premium reached its highest historical level of around 220 basis points.

## A New German Weapon: The Schwaebische Hausfrau

Angela Merkel had been under pressure for weeks and reacted by attacking easy spending in many countries, which, according to her Chancellery's analysis, could inflate new bubbles around the world. At a meeting of her party in

Stuttgart, the capital of the Land Baden-Wuerttemberg known for the thrifty attitude of its schwäbische inhabitants, the chancellor coined her own new nickname: "Here in Stuttgart, one should simply ask a schwäbische housewife for the right and wise answer: you cannot live a long time beyond your means."[12]

Berlin's strategy was a mix of orthodox rhetoric and silent pragmatism. Beyond the substantial and cultural refusal to engage in fiscal activism, tactical reasons also lay behind Berlin's resistance to acknowledging a need to spend public money for economic stimulus. The first reason was the fear of giving the green light to other euro partners, who were less inclined to fiscal discipline and could patently violate the limits fixed by the Stability and Growth Pact. This would jeopardize the stability of the euro area and potentially pave the way for Germany to step in with financial aid. The second reason was that any common initiative through supranational bodies, especially through the European Commission, would imply a larger-than-proportional financial contribution from Germany—with most of the benefits flowing to weaker countries. Hans Werner Sinn, the economist who played a prominent role during that period as an adviser to Chancellor Merkel, plainly explained this reluctance. Germany's hesitancy, he said, is due to a

> suspicion of the European Union's redistribution machinery. When Sarkozy and other EU leaders demand Germany's participation in an economic stimulus and rescue package, one reason is that they expect Germany to again bear the lion's share of the costs. For example, of the €5 billion extension of the Cohesion Funds [EU aid to states for environmental and transportation projects] approved by the European Parliament in December 2007, Germany received nothing, but it bears 20 percent of the costs. Germans have always been enthusiastic proponents of the EU, not least because they hoped that a European identity would help compensate for their damaged national identity. So, whenever it came to restructuring the EU, they always accepted a level of influence that was small relative to their country's size. Although Germany's share of the EU population is 17 percent, it receives 13 percent of the voting rights in the EU Parliament. . . . Former French President Jacques Chirac did not hesitate to justify this imbalance with a reference to World War II, which the Germans accepted. But their enthusiasm has limits.[13]

Public spending has regularly proven to be unpopular with the German electorate. In the early 1980s a relatively modest—by current standards—fiscal slippage was the key driver in the collapse of Helmut Schmidt's government. Germany's 2002–04 overrun of the Stability and Growth Pact ceiling similarly contributed to a massive loss in government popularity. Even the presence of the Social Democratic Party in Merkel's governing Grand Coalition was not facilitating Keynesian policies.[14] The reluctance of the German public to acknowledge any merit to spending public money easily hampers the effect of fiscal policy and delays its effects.[15] The German spirit of "fiscal solidarity" began to lose its appeal with unification when all Germans had to pay a very high additional tax (named "Soli") in order to help integrate the east with the west. In addition, the openness of the German economy to global markets argued against public expenditures. With exports accounting for up to 52 percent of GDP and imports at 45 percent of GDP, half of any fiscal stimulus would benefit imports and therefore leak abroad.

## The National Consensus Government of the German Economy

A change of German sentiments started in Frankfurt, where the banking system was feeling the harshest winds of the crisis. Notwithstanding €400 billion in state guarantees and €80 billion in capital transfers, the German banks were perfectly aware that they would not be able to resist any major accident along the road. A visitor in the capital of Hessen, the financial center of Germany, at the end of 2008 was struck by the gloomy climate. But it was an isolated case. Most of the country's other regions were still enjoying the tailwinds of the recent industrial and export successes. Moreover, Berlin, the federal capital, with only a trivial minority of its population actively employed in the private economy, was shielded from the crisis, and there was even a sense of Schadenfreude about the doldrums of western capitalism. But the influence of Frankfurt's banking lobbies was powerful, in particular because the German government relied on advice from Deutsche Bank. The bank's experts envisaged a scenario were the real economy went downhill in the wake of the financial crisis with a recession to follow.[16]

Finally on December 14, a Sunday evening, Merkel convened a high-profile consulting group. Sitting next to each other were the most important bankers, trade union leaders, industrialists, and economists of the country. At the gathering in the Kabinettsaal on the fifth floor of the Chancellery, Merkel asked the thirty-two participants to sketch the state of the economy from their points of view. The economists in the room spoke of an unprecedented decline in global demand that was bound to plunge all Europe, Germany included, into a full-blown recession. Deutsche Bank's head, Josef Ackermann, had a colorful description of the situation: "It looks like a protracted earthquake with changing epicenters." After three hours, Merkel was convinced that a second fiscal stimulus was indispensable.

As a German journalist revealed in a book on Angela Merkel, after dinner, Peter Loescher, the president and chief executive officer of Siemens AG, surprised everybody by announcing that he would not resort to firing workers. Merkel asked if others could promise the same. A number of leaders of some of the largest industrial firms, which normally manage labor relations in close agreement with the unions, appeared willing to do so.[17]

Merkel told the group of a letter that she had received from the director of Trumpf, a smaller machinery firm. In the letter the industrialist said he had decided to introduce retraining courses for workers whose hours would be cut (rather than laying them off) as part of government programs to reduce the impact of the crisis on employment. The idea of using non-worked hours for the retraining of employees was very much appreciated by the chancellor, and Labor Minister Olaf Scholz was given the task of developing a proposal along these lines. In a matter of days Scholz organized a new meeting with the labor relations managers of the thirty largest firms in Germany to ensure their support for the initiative. In the week before Christmas, Chancellor Merkel met the presidents of the Laender to urge them to orientate their investments toward the requalification of workers. The well-known German system of solidarity was demonstrating its potential. A broader deal between government, industry, and trade unions also was feasible. Within weeks, a fiscal package bringing stimulus for 2009 at 1.5 percent of GDP (double than in France and slightly higher than in the UK) was prepared, putting Berlin in the position of economic leadership in Europe.[18]

# 5

## First Doubts about the Euro

### The Crisis Moves from Banks to the States

By the beginning of 2009, evidence had emerged that the financial crisis was bound to become a sovereign debt crisis—with all the implications that would have had for the integrity of the euro area. Only an astonishing case of selective distraction can explain why this development was lost in the public debate at the time, and then forgotten. The repatriation of both politics and policies that we saw in the last chapters was probably responsible.

It should have been obvious that the problems of the banks were becoming a huge burden for some states. But banks were dealt with nationally, so the overall consequences would be tragic for the euro: on the one hand, no common response was developed for the banks, and on the other, no common fiscal policy was provided for the region as a whole. As a result, the cost of bailing out the banks created strong differences in the sustainability of each state's public debt within the euro area. It was as if a large amount of explosives was deposited beneath the monetary union.

As explained in the previous chapter, some important economic divergences among the countries of the euro area were structural in nature and were ingrained in the historical experience of each national society. But in the events beginning with the first days of 2009, it appears unequivocal that a dynamic set in that exacerbated the divergences among euro zone countries, based primarily on the interaction between the debts of the banks and those of the states. Unfortunately, in a matter of the first few weeks of 2009 and in the exceptional circumstances of the crisis, the euro was no longer a part of the solution, but instead became a central piece of the problem.

Behind closed doors, shielded from public scrutiny, EU governments and institutions actually started very early to prepare countermeasures to deal with a sovereign debt crisis. During the first two months of 2009, the policy proposals put before the EU governments were amazingly advanced. They were, in fact, even daring in terms of political integration—so much so that they frightened the heads of government, who were paralyzed by the shocking uncertainty around their banking and economic systems. In reality, banks were in much worse shape than they were ready to admit. The inertia and silence of the banks proved to be fatal. Without clarity on the situation in the financial industry, the markets eventually saw a bigger problem in the euro area, where each country was building up its public debt and had problems in funding its economy. Suddenly, the fundamental nature of the euro—its capacity to build a single economic and financial area where national real economic divergences would diminish with time and external imbalances would decline or be harmless—was less convincing than in the past. Now, economic variations between countries seemed destined to grow wider rather than narrower. For the first time, the future of the euro seemed in doubt.

The first alarm rang very early in 2009. On January 7, Germany attempted to auction off €6 billion worth of ten-year bonds, but investors bought only 87 percent of them. Seven other European countries had faced difficulties in issuing government bonds in the previous few months, but this was the first time in eight years that a German auction technically "failed" to such an extent. It was a shock because the German bond market had been very liquid, and Germany was seen as the safest sovereign in the euro zone, if not in the world. The failed auction triggered an alarm among sovereign bond investors across Europe. The yields of highly indebted countries, in particular Greece and Italy, started to diverge from those of countries with sounder fiscal positions.

Between January 9 and 23, Standard & Poor's, the American rating agency influencing the opinions of the markets, announced a hail of six downgrades or outlook revisions against Ireland, Spain, Portugal, and Greece. This news came as a bolt out of the blue. Every day investors feared further worrying announcements from the rating agencies, creating an incredible amount of anxiety. The S&P action was a game-changer for the markets, which had trusted blindly the successful development of the euro since its onset.

### A Young and Fragile Currency: The Beginning of the Separation

The euro area was especially fragile under the blows of the rating agencies because it was a youthful currency and a unique case of a "currency without a state." In less than ten years it had not been established as a real reserve currency. This meant that the majority of the investors holding the debt of euro area member states were private investors, as opposed to U.S. sovereign debt, which is mainly held by public investors, other states, and central banks. Private investors are much more prone than public institutions to run for cover at the first sign of reversals and as soon as the balance of risks changes, particularly so if they are foreign investors. Private nonresident investors held only one-seventh of U.S. debt, private residents held one third of it, with the rest in the hands of stable investors, notably central banks and sovereign wealth funds.[1] The U.S. Federal Reserve, for example, held 18 percent of the U.S. debt and was actively engaged in a massive purchase of American securities. The European Central Bank (ECB), by contrast, was limited in its purchase of European government bonds. Private nonresidents held on average more than 50 percent of national debts of the euro area countries, with levels ranging from 42 percent in Belgium to 85 percent in Ireland. So, without steady hands behind the euro, private investors moved rapidly from one country debt to another, even within the euro area, each time that bad news or a revision by the rating agencies changed the mood of the markets.

The extent and complexity of global financial markets as they have developed recently are such that, for instance, the market for euro-denominated interest rate swaps, one of the financial instruments most commonly used by professional investors, reaches volumes of €211 trillion and can change direction swiftly, provoking irresistible movement in government bond prices, particularly for a currency area with no central political authority and no central bank deputed to the defense of financial stability. The amounts outstanding of CDS on sovereign bonds is not even known, but it is estimated to have doubled between 2005 and 2009. The volume of sovereign CDS is still very small relative to the underlying government bonds, but when tensions in the market increase, it is the CDS market—mostly speculative—that leads the bond market, not the reverse. The euro offered numberless opportunities for arbitrage for professional investors among fifteen national markets without even bearing a currency risk. So paradoxically, as soon as other risks increased on the market, more speculative investors found an ideal environment in the European securities, moving for instance from Greek to German bonds—a deal they would have hardly even thought of in the past. For the same reasons long-term investors were much less at ease. As a matter of fact, each time market sentiments turn, they can easily build a new rationale and, all of a sudden, analysts were asking if the monetary union had been a failure in disguise. A growing sense of instability grew over the European currency early in 2009.

Paradoxically the first years after the introduction of the euro in 1999 had seen a very substantial success in terms of monetary stability. Inflation in the euro area had been, on average, lower than during the previous decade. The shared currency had led to a sharp fall in real interest rates, especially in the so-called peripheral countries of the euro area, as nominal interest rates converged toward the lower German levels.[2] Growth outlook had greatly benefited from the relatively low cost of money and from the opening of new markets around the world that—together with the completion and deepening of the EU single market—had moved governments to enact structural reforms underpinning national competitiveness. Countries that had been historical laggards suddenly became the fastest growing: Greece had the highest growth rate in the euro area, followed by Ireland and Spain. These countries seemed not only to catch up with the rest of the EU in terms of growth, but to lead the others and to hold the promise for permanent growth. As a consequence, demand for credit expanded rapidly. Households and firms in the periphery sought to borrow so they could reap the available growth opportunities via investment and enjoy immediately the benefits of prospective wealth gains.

As real interest rates fell, financing conditions eased markedly, and banks and investors relaxed their standards. There seemed to be less reason to differentiate among countries, so spreads between government bond yields narrowed to very low levels. Part of the rapid expansion of credit was justified on grounds of market fundamentals. But, as a board member of the ECB put it, "In an environment of large-scale structural change in peripheral economies and their financial systems, distinguishing the impact of improved fundamentals from that of 'bubble-like' behaviour proved a formidable challenge."[3] Little noticed, part of the credit growth served to create and nourish financial and economic imbalances that ultimately would prove unsustainable, especially in the housing market. Where mortgages had once been scarce or expensive, they became cheap and readily available. House prices boomed as "institutional and psychological factors fuelled an asset price bubble in real estate."[4] The dynamism in construction and financial services supported high levels of overall growth, drained resources from other sectors, and increased the vulnerability of some economies to shocks in finance and in the real estate market. Furthermore, high growth increased imports, pushed wages up all across the economy, and, with time, reduced competitiveness, resulting in large deficits on the current account of the balance of payments. This required inflows of financial capital from abroad. Furthermore, high growth and the inflows of capital hid the weaknesses in fiscal policy through higher tax revenues.

The global financial crisis triggered a complete reversal of these trends: housing markets collapsed, credit became problematic, growth rates plummeted, and so did tax revenues. Major fiscal deficits emerged just when banks looked increasingly shaky as a result of the implicit liabilities that ultimately would burden the accounts of states to which the banks had been loaning money. At the beginning of 2009, a vicious cycle between state problems and banking crises built up very rapidly. Since both problems, fiscal and banking, were governed at the national level, and no common European pool of resources was available to deal with them, sovereign debts became the epicenter of the new crisis. Spreads—interest rate differentials—among bonds issued by euro area governments started to diverge markedly. Rates went up especially for Greece, Ireland, Spain, Portugal, Italy, and even Austria—whose banks' exposure to eastern Europe was higher than 80 percent of its GDP—relative to Germany.

According to a Bank for International Settlements (BIS) quarterly review, "Investors' confidence was rattled when, despite a combined $925 billion of private and government capital injected into the global banking sector since the third quarter of 2007, further signs of banking problems emerged in both Europe and the United States."[5] Those problems defeated the view that large-scale government support in the third and fourth quarters of 2008 had restored sustainably the banking sector's stability. The dates show the amazing connection between the banks and debt problems: On January 8, almost coincident with the failed German bond auction, losses at Dresdner Bank had to be backstopped by a state bailout package for Commerzbank, which had recently acquired its former rival. BIS's account read, "The stream of bad banking news accelerated as similar news involving other major banks aired during the following week."[6] On January 15 the Irish authorities seized control of Anglo-Irish Bank. Though it was a small bank in global terms, the failure of Anglo-Irish was key in changing the mood of the markets globally. Viewed by the Irish authorities as systemically important to the country's financial system, the beleaguered bank was nationalized late on the evening of Thursday, January 15. On Friday morning, the share prices of the other major Irish banks—Allied Irish Banks and the Bank of Ireland—fell sharply, by 12.9 and 13.3 percent, respectively. This was the trigger for a new burst of anxiety as financial stocks got hammered and sovereign spreads soared, in Ireland and elsewhere in the euro zone. In the week after January 16, Irish sovereign spreads jumped by 20 percent over the previous week's average of 142 basis points. During the following week, the sovereign spreads rose a stunning 80 basis points to 260 basis points, almost 50 percent over the previous week's average. The connection between financial rescue interventions and government bond risk premium became the hallmark of future events.[7]

Having no common fiscal policy, nor a common fund to back up the banks, Europe saw large discrepancies in how the financial shockwaves hit national public debts. The rescue packages adopted by governments in favor of national banking were of unprecedented size. For instance, the Irish government issued guarantees covering liabilities equivalent to more than 200 percent of GDP. In its Global Financial Stability Report covering 2009, the International Monetary Fund (IMF) published estimates of the expected order of magnitude of the costs related to the support operations including three elements: the net costs of direct support to banks; the expected eventual costs of guarantees; and the costs, net of recoveries, of central bank liquidity provision. The outcomes were mind-boggling figures.[8] The IMF estimated that credit writedowns on U.S.-originated assets by all holders since the start of the crisis would total $2.7 trillion. Including assets originated in other mature market economies, total write-downs could reach $4 trillion over the period between 2009 and 2011, approximately two-thirds of which might be taken by banks. The European Central Bank soon acknowledged the direct consequences for sovereign debts and the potential effects on the integrity of the euro area: "It is reasonable to assume that the capital injections and guarantees provided by governments to the financial sector, coupled with the adverse effects of the economic downturn on their fiscal positions, prompted investors to discriminate among sovereign borrowers on the basis of the soundness of their public finances."[9]

In terms of economic efficiency, decentralizing fiscal decisions normally is desirable, even in a federal system. However, a shock like the one caused by the global financial crisis on a group of countries sharing the same currency and the same monetary policy loaded all the cost of adjustment onto national fiscal policies. National governments felt ever more called on to respond to their taxpayers. For some countries, the burden on the public debts of bailing out banks was huge, erasing all efforts during the previous ten years to cut public budgets. The problems caused by finance were showing up in the form of higher debts and unemployment and lower incomes for the citizens. It became evident that a justice problem was arising in national democracies. The grave consequence was a further repatriation to individual governments of relevant policy decisions—a back-pedalling toward the past. It also became clearer than before that Europe faced a profound dilemma of having a common currency but without a common fiscal policy to ensure its stability. Ultimately, the "soul" of the euro, that is, the political will behind it, was challenged.

## Is the Euro Becoming the Problem?

Since the moment when the euro was conceived, it was accompanied by skepticism on the part of non-European observers. Over the years political and nationalist overtones have characterized various attacks on the project, but economic concerns about the common currency ultimately were based on the lack of political unity within the euro area. An easy way to grasp the issue is to take into account the differences between a euro area country and another country with its own currency, when both are under the threat of a default. For a country like the United Kingdom, for instance, which does not belong to the euro area, a risk of default would prompt many investors to sell both U.K. government bonds and pounds. While this would force interest rates up in Britain, the largest effect would be the rapid depreciation of the pound—as happened in the second half of 2008—until it reached a level where the number of buyers equalled the number of sellers. As economist Paul de Grauwe put it, "The pounds would remain bottled in the UK" and the quantity of pounds would be unaltered.[10] The loss in the value of the currency would reflect the lack of confidence in the economy, or in the government, or in the prospects for payment of the public debt. If the depreciation were not enough to attract enough buyers to roll over the public debt, the Bank of England would be forced to step into the market for government securities and ensure that—provided the run from the U.K. assets does not become colossal—the government avoided a liquidity crisis and bankruptcy.

A country belonging to the euro area is in a much different situation. Once investors run from such a country and sell its government bonds, they can invest their euros in other, supposedly safer, countries in the euro area. The stock of euros in the ailing country thus shrinks. Its government experiences a liquidity crisis and may find it more and more difficult to obtain funds to roll over its debt at reasonable interest rates. In this case, the country's central bank cannot step in and finance the government—and the central bank for the entire euro area, the ECB, has a clear mandate not to do so. Knowing this, the financial markets become more worried and ask for higher and higher risk premiums on the government's bonds. Eventually, the markets self-fulfil a default when the country's liquidity crisis becomes an even more serious crisis of solvency. Once the global crisis had triggered risk aversion, the euro countries appeared more vulnerable than others when the political will to defend the integrity of the euro area as a whole was put in question.

In fact, the mistrust of the markets mirrored a recurrent underestimation of the political will behind the European project. This is particularly the case in the United States and the United Kingdom, where many economists, investors, and political analysts apply to the euro project the same simple cost-benefit logic prevailing in financial analyses and view it with skepticism, ignoring its meaning for the European aspiration to a common political destiny.

The first reason for the change of sentiment in the markets toward the euro was the heightened risk aversion set off by the global financial crisis. Ever since the first shock on Wall Street, investors had kept a much sharper focus on credit risks in many asset classes, including sovereign securities, that once were considered almost entirely risk free. Wider sovereign debt yield spreads were just another consequence of the sudden flight from risky investments.[11] A second reason involved debt dynamics and their sustainability: the recession and the measures enacted by governments led to a substantial worsening of public accounts, so investors were assessing the ability of single national governments to impose fiscal consolidation. The fiscal costs of the banking crisis, which hit each country differently, played a major role in differentiation. According to market analysts, at the beginning of 2009 the risk of the European Monetary Union breakup was only a fourth and last motivation for the markets' more skeptical attitude toward the euro.

*A Special Case of Blindness: An Atlantis of the Twenty-First Century*

Another case of selective blindness, primarily on the part of the markets, was the fiscal state of Greece. Kostas Karamanlis, prime minister in 2009, and a stocky 53-year-old conservative, had come to power in 2004 when he shocked his countrymen by stating that Greece was "effectively run by five davatzides [pimps]." He pointed his finger at a group of businessmen whose cozy relationship with the previous Socialist government and local media bosses had given them an edge in winning public contracts in the run-up to the 2004 Olympics in Athens. A few years later Karamanlis found himself in a similar political situation, defending himself during a corruption scandal that had involved members of his own conservative party, the Nea Dimokratia (New Democracy).

The markets' blindness to the true fiscal status of the Greek public budget was particularly ironic because the two major parties governing the country alternatively—Nea Dimokratia and the rival Panhellenic Socialist Movement (PASOK)—had been accusing each other of false fiscal accounting for years and with some reason. Eurostat, the EU statistical department, had refused to validate Greece's public accounts at several stages. In 2002 a review by Eurostat (the EU's data-collection agency) changed the government's budget balance from a surplus to a deficit. In 2004, Eurostat refused to validate the fiscal data transmitted by the Greek government to Brussels and asked for a revision. On that occasion the European Commission harshly accused Greece of "imprudent" and "sloppy" fiscal policies. The EU Council started to discuss at that time how to give to Eurostat more powers to control the national accounts, but that crucial decision was vetoed by France and Germany.

The audit conducted in Greece after the change of government in 2004 discovered that Athens had falsified Greece's macroeconomic statistics, and it had been on this basis that Greece had been accepted into the euro zone. "Our duty is to tell the truth to the citizens," Karamanlis promised at the beginning of 2009. "What is at stake is not the government or only one political party, but the course of the country, the future of the young generation." This was a remark that history will remember with bitter irony.

*Rating Agencies Bringing PIGS to the Slaughter*

Once the financial crisis hit in 2008, the American rating agencies had a wide berth in leading market expectations. The wake-up call was abrupt. Standard & Poor's, Moody's, and Fitch were still embarrassed by their failure to spot the trends leading to the financial crisis; for example, they had granted Lehman Brothers and AIG very high levels of rating (AA and AAA respectively) when the firms were already broken. Fannie Mae and Freddie Mac each had an AAA rating when the U.S. government took them over on September 7, 2008. The number of security issuances labelled AAA had increased by a factor of 200 in the previous ten years. Now, those same rating agencies were eager to ring the bell as often and loudly as possible. Europe offered them the perfect showcase.[12] As a paper published by the IMF reported, "Rating agencies have not antici- pated the macroeconomic weaknesses of European economies consecutive to the financial crisis."[13] After three revised outlooks for Spain, Portugal, and Ireland were published in early January 2009, Standard & Poor's announced on January 14 it would downgrade Greek debt from A to A–.

The widely read financial blog of the *Financial Times* commented: "In the euro zone, there has always been a quartet of nations with a somewhat unsta- ble rating position: the PIGS. That is, Portugal, Italy, Greece and Spain. Rating agency S&P though, in a slew of rating announcements this week, has affirmed Italy's A+. So we need a new vulnerable I on the cusp of downgrade. Step in, Ireland. With a AAA rating." In this psychological game of "group dynamics," there was an unconscious need to blame, isolate, and shame the weakest. The "PIGS" brand, born in the 1990s, was a suitable tool.[14]

After Spain and Portugal were downgraded, interest rates became more and more divergent: Greece was paying 5.8 percent on its ten-year government bonds and Ireland 5.5 percent, against 3.8 percent for France and 3.3 percent for Ger- many. These were differences not seen since the creation of the euro.[15] Ireland was forced to deny reports that it might seek help from the IMF. Nevertheless, the price of its credit default swaps (the cost of protection in derivatives mar- kets against a default by the country) edged close to the record high reached on December 5, 2008, on the heels of the fuller disclosure of the Irish bank- ing problems. Spain's long-term debt was stripped of its AAA rating because of deteriorating public finances. But S&P also pointed specifically to the weakness derived from belonging to the euro zone: Spain had no independent monetary or exchange rate policy. Euro zone membership thus protected Spain from exchange rate crises, S&P said, "but also puts greater onus on microeconomic and fiscal policies." Although also detailed analysis of the rating agencies' behaviors were conducted, their announcements were regularly accompanied by outrage in the affected countries, as well as widespread indignation that the same institutions had been blinded by problems in American firms.[16] Moreover, the tone used by the agencies in their reporting was rough: PIGS were taken to the slaughter.

## Secretly Searching for a Plan against Defaults

The first alarms about fiscal instability in the euro area were aggravated by the fact that Europe's institutional framework could not contemplate financial assis- tance to governments in distress as laid out by the 1992 Maastricht Treaty. This was not a design fault of the Economic and Monetary Union but rather the result of an explicit request by the most fiscally virtuous countries during the

1990s that enabled the less virtuous to join the monetary union. The treaty required national parliaments to give up their sovereign right to issue currency. But the governments' rights to collect taxes, borrow, spend, and redistribute income remained very much at the national level, each government being wholly responsible for the debt it issued.

In fact, the Maastricht system was based on other principles—amounting to fiscal policy—that had never before been tested by international federations. The first was the "rules-based" character of the regime, represented most clearly by the criteria that the treaty requires would-be members of the monetary union to satisfy before entry and by the provisions of the Stability and Growth Pact. The supposedly automatic nature of this nonpolitical, nondiscretionary system was based on the right of the European Commission to impose sanctions on countries that breached the rules. Ultimately, however, the system really relied on mutual surveillance in the hands of the governments, which had the power to overrule the commission in that regard; thus, the arrangement was indeed political and far from automatic. The system's poor transparency—and the lack of credibility of the rules—clashed with the Maastricht Treaty's no-bailout rule in the event that the markets decided that a country, for whatever reason, was on an unsustainable path. The obvious alternative to such a rules-based regime (where the rules proved elastic) was a fiscal union with a federal budget. But that was beyond the limits of the possible in the building of the Maastricht Treaty between 1989 and 1991, when the fiscal positions of European states were even more differentiated. As a matter of fact, between 1992 and 1996, the future euro area had to live through enormous currency fluctuations. At that time, a common fiscal policy was unthinkable. Jacques Delors, who was then president of the European Commission, had to struggle enormously to persuade Helmut Kohl and François Mitterrand to agree to a common EU budget of only approximately 1 percent of the GDP of the European Union.

Inspired by the Zeitgeist of the early 1990s, the Maastricht Treaty embraced a strict definition of fiscal solidarity along national lines, ensuring that one country would never need to bear another's fiscal costs. Without such a stricture, the monetary union (and thus the euro) would have never seen the light of day. Other rules were designed to prevent countries from needing to be bailed out in the first place. Even so, the text of the treaty did not explicitly rule out the possibility of fiscal assistance. Paradoxically, the European Commission could provide financial assistance, but only to countries outside the euro area, for example Hungary and Latvia, which had borrowed through the so-called medium-term financial assistance, a facility, worth €25 billion, that could be used to assist EU members undergoing balance of payments difficulties (the risk of government default would qualify as such). At the beginning of 2009, a discussion opened on the possibility of applying Article 122 of the Maastricht

Treaty, which envisaged financial assistance to any EU member "seriously threatened with severe difficulties caused by natural disasters or exceptional occurrences beyond its control." The EU Council could approve that assistance rather swiftly, acting by qualified majority rather than by negotiated consensus, which was its usual, laborious procedure. However, without a mandate for setting up a crisis mechanism for the euro area, the debate stoked further uncertainty instead of damping it.

The lack of a clear system for a debt crisis resolution had set off alarms in Brussels, Paris, and Berlin in 2009. But to publicly engage the heads of government was problematic, so behind the scenes a number of subministerial groups of experts were silently put to work early in the year, one of which became known as the "group that does not exist." German and French high-level officials of the respective finance ministries, joined by Eurogroup head Jean-Claude Juncker and by EU officials, the head of the Economic and Financial Committee (then Xavier Musca), and a representative of the European Commission began to meet regularly. Most of these gatherings were meant to remain top-secret because of the intractable issues being discussed. Among such issues was what would happen if one country hit the wall and could not pay its debts? How could the European Union react in the face of a major financial calamity in one country that might have a reactive effect and endanger all the others? The first secret working group focused on the Hungarian problems, which had to be solved through the IMF. In the meantime, the Baltic countries also had to seek help, mainly from the IMF. In the specific circumstance of Latvia, the European Commission discovered that it had neither the necessary information nor the technical capacity to enact a plan for bailing out even this small European country. Nevertheless, together with the ECB, it succeeded in convincing Latvia not to abandon its currency peg to the euro—against the advice of the IMF—helping to stabilize the medium term prospects for the economy.

Those involved in these clandestine meetings first had to study the legal foundations for an eventual crisis mechanism. This was a matter of understanding how much leeway the EU treaty offered for hypothetical interventions similar to those enacted by the IMF. According to a 2010 report in the *Wall Street Journal,* "Membership of the Task Force was limited to senior policy makers—usually just below ministerial level—from France, Germany, the European Commission, Europe's central bank and the office of Jean-Claude Juncker. . . .The task force met in the shadows of the EU's many councils and summits in Brussels, Luxembourg, and other capitals, often gathering at 6 a.m. or huddling over sandwiches late at night. Participants kept colleagues in their own governments in the dark, for fear leaks would trigger rampant speculation in financial markets."[17]

An internal document of the German finance ministry gives details of the depth of the discussions that went on in Brussels at the EU Commission, in several policy and finance committees of the EU, and in bilateral Franco-German forums. In crisis cases, the confidential document reported, the payment problems of ailing countries could be solved if the euro partners with safe credit ratings raised money for them by issuing their own bonds. One version mulled in Berlin actually would have guaranteed only the first few years' coupon payments, therefore addressing the issue of moral hazard for the longer duration and hence facilitating the attachment of conditionality. This method was particularly attractive for Berlin because it was legally unproblematic and did not need the establishment of a new institution that would smack of an economic government for the euro area. Nevertheless, it would also place the burden of bailing countries out on a few major EU states, Germany most of all. Moreover, if the crisis expanded, it would not be possible for single countries, especially the smaller ones, to keep up with their commitments to help the others.

Alternatively, a group of several member states could collectively float a bond. Berlin was opposed to that option because the cost (in interest yields) for the pooled bond would be higher than if Berlin were to go it alone. In practice, this would have led to a fiscal transfer from Germany to the weaker countries and thus laid the basis for a euro zone bond that could be instrumental in advancing by stealth the agenda of those who sought deeper European integration. Another possibility was direct aid by the EU. Although the European treaties did not include provisions that would allow Brussels to undertake aid measures at the EU level, the German finance ministry concluded it would be legal for the EU to do it. According to the ministry's legal analysis, the EU could provide aid if a member state faced extraordinary circumstances. An informed analysis by the German magazine *Der Spiegel* reported that this procedure "would come with complications, since it would represent the first time that the EU would fund its loans on the capital markets."[18]

A possible alternative was to use the European Investment Bank (EIB), which has a well-established function of borrowing in the markets for investment projects in the EU and beyond. According to its Corporate Operational Plan from December 2008, it was set to increase its lending by about 30 percent, or €15 billion, in 2009 and 2010. However, while the EIB's overall mandate includes contributions to the integration, balanced development, and economic and social cohesion of the EU member states, its function has traditionally been to lend to small and medium-sized enterprises.

The final possibility was an aid package provided by the International Monetary Fund. Normally, the IMF can issue loans under far stricter conditions than would be possible for the EU or member states. The involvement of the IMF was considered problematic because it would imply interference from Washington on the whole set of economic policies concerning the affected country, potentially including the European Central Bank's monetary policy. The credibility of the euro area and of Europe as a whole would be diminished by resorting to policy remedies from outside.

With hindsight it is impressive to see how close Europe was in early 2009 to providing for the instruments that might have prevented future disruptive events. While there was plenty of time to enact the proposals, all options remained suspended in the air without a solid institutional framework, which made it difficult to absorb into national and European legislation. Moreover, the options posed problems related to political responsibilities and accountability. Nevertheless, the European Commission put on the table and supported the most far-reaching proposals. But all these proposals ultimately fell by the wayside because Berlin blocked the road, arguing that most of them could bring hard-to-measure political and financial consequences or were legally ungrounded. Then, one year later, the Greek crisis hit the markets in the euro area.

# 6

## The American Crisis Becomes
## the European Crisis

### Sarkozy Tries a Second Conquest of Europe

The dispute between Germany and France on the management of the euro zone dated from the first concepts of deeper economic integration in Europe. In the January 1991 French draft of what was to become the Maastricht Treaty, a proposal for an economic government parallel to the ECB was clearly stated. Such a proposal could not survive the opposition of the Bundesbank, which saw the need for a full-fledged political union if the euro zone countries were to share fiscal responsibilities. However, French diplomats considered it a national victory that they managed six years later, in 1997, to achieve agreement that finance ministers of the euro zone would meet regularly in what became the Eurogroup. Now, Paris wanted to move that a notch higher to the level of heads of state or government.[1]

Germany was even more suspicious of any step that appeared to pool the fiscal policies of euro countries now, in 2009, when their weaknesses were emerging. However, Sarkozy's diagnosis was very clear: Europe was not controlling its decisionmaking process during a phase when the financial crisis was blowing hard and threatening the cohesion of the euro zone. The French president wanted to organize an extraordinary meeting of heads of state and government of the euro area in February 2009, without waiting for the traditional spring European Council in March, to show the solidarity of the monetary union and commit to a minimum of fiscal discipline to dissuade financial markets from attacking the weaker states, as they had done the previous fall in the cases of Iceland and Hungary. An article by the French daily Le Monde, describing the Elysée's vision, observed that "one month after the end of his [European Council] presidency, Sarkozy finds that the European Union (EU) has become invisible. The Czech presidency is considered passive, like the European Commission. . . . Mr. Sarkozy has emerged very concerned about his telephone conversation with Barack Obama, Monday, Jan. 26. The next day, before the leaders of his party, Sarkozy explained that the U.S. banking crisis was in its infancy more than at the end. He expressed also his concerns about the vulnerability of the weakest countries in the euro zone, explicitly mentioning Greece."[2]

During the previous October, Hungary, the country of origin of Sarkozy's family, had been a powerful example of the crisis hitting single states, with Europe being caught off-guard and forced to surrender the initiative to the IMF. French government officials saw the intervention of the IMF as the first step toward the disintegration of the euro area. Furthermore, continued IMF intervention in Europe would imply the arrival of Sarkozy's political rival Dominique Strauss-Kahn on the European political turf that Sarkozy hoped to continue dominating. (Until he was caught in a sex scandal in the United States in 2011, Strauss-Kahn was widely considered the leading Socialist candidate to oppose Sarkozy in the 2012 French presidential elections). To avoid resorting to the IMF, two options were available. The first, representing Germany's preference, was leaving it mainly to the state in question to recover by self-imposing a draconian austerity plan. The alternative was to organize a European rescue package, which raised serious legal and political problems. Article 101 of the Maastricht Treaty explicitly forbids central banks from coming to the aid of states. However, a French minister said, "If we stick to the letter of treaties, it goes in the wall."[3]

Sarkozy indeed seemed to be feverishly considering a number of proposals that were floating in Brussels and among European analysts. Among these were the direct involvement of the ECB in providing liquidity to states; a common European debt agency that might manage the sovereign debts of the countries of the euro area by sharing risks but also reducing the interest rate spreads on the debt of weaker states; and even a recently refashioned old proposal of issuing a common European bond. The French president was in close contact with the president of the European Central Bank, Jean-Claude Trichet, who was determined to lead his institution exclusively under the treaties—in other words, avoiding any steps not expressly outlined by Maastricht and other treaties.[4] Furthermore, none of those proposals was to the liking of Germany. In Berlin, a spokesman for the government dismissed the proposals Sarkozy was considering as not necessary in the short term and, in any event, not to be discussed in public.[5]

Sarkozy was well aware that, before formally proposing anything, he needed to reach a prior agreement with German chancellor Angela Merkel, whom he was going to meet in Munich on Saturday, February 7, during an annual conference on security issues known as Wehrkunde. The story of this meeting between the two leaders of the largest European countries is a grand piece in the European theatrical tradition. Apparently Sarkozy kept the chancellor waiting for forty-five minutes, worsening the personal chemistry between the two of them. When they finally met, Merkel rejected with the harshest tones Sarkozy's proposal for a summit of the heads of state and governments of the Eurogroup on the basis that none of the topics was specific to the euro area and to convene the sixteen countries would imply a divisive act that would undermine the Czech presidency. As usual, Sarkozy had to concede.

## And the Second Guillotine

The Czech government took over the presidency of the European Council for the first half of 2009, but its inexperience in EU matters (the Czech Republic had joined the EU only in 2004) had induced Prague to rely heavily on the Brussels institutions, mainly the European Commission and the Council Secretariat. Prime Minister Mirek Topolanek also decided to open a permanent channel with the German Chancellery. Berlin agreed with Prague that they had to launch a special initiative to put a damper on Sarkozy's ambitions. With the chancellor's assent, Topolanek convened a special meeting at the beginning of March for the twenty-seven EU countries, just a few weeks before the regular spring meeting of the EU Council and ten days after a special meeting in Berlin (February 22) of the EU leaders who were to attend the G-20 summit in London at the beginning of April. The main purpose was to cut the ground from under Sarkozy's feet and kill his proposed Super Eurogroup in the bud.

This new relationship with the former Eastern bloc nation was crucial for Berlin. Two other recent entrants into the EU, Hungary and Latvia, were managing to weather the financial crisis only with help from the EU and a major contribution from the International Monetary Fund. This was exactly the kind of configuration that appealed to the German government. In effect, Sarkozy's strategy, for all his understanding of the danger, was backfiring as a consequence of his failure to reach agreement with Berlin and of his overlooking the importance of the new EU member states. Sarkozy and Merkel appeared to be opening the way to a new polarization of Europe, again divided between West and East, in which Berlin was at ease drawing consensus from the new member states in compensation for France attracting support instead from the southern European countries.

In this context, the issue of protectionism suddenly emerged to heighten the polarization. On February 8, 2009, Sarkozy said France would move to provide government-backed, five-year loans at favorable interest rates to national carmakers Renault and PSA Peugeot Citroen of €6 billion each, as well as €500 million for Renault Truck. Unfortunately, Sarkozy made things much worse when he stated during an interview on French television that "it is justifiable if a Renault factory is built in India so that Renault cars may be sold to the Indians . . . but it is not justifiable if a factory of a certain producer, without citing anyone, is built in the Czech Republic and its cars are sold in France." His comments were an indirect reference to PSA Peugeot Citroen, which has a plant in the Czech city of Kolin. Immediately, the Czech government said it would call on EU member states to address the issue of protectionism at a special summit in February. Far from being the only country mulling protectionist measures, France stood out as defending it publicly, rather than working in the dark. The same accusation of protectionism was levelled against Merkel for her mishandling of a crisis involving Opel, the beleaguered car maker that U.S. owner GM wanted to close or sell but that was kept alive in Germany through state-aid to which the EU Commission turned a blind eye. A similar case involved the Swedish government when it promised Swedish automakers Saab and Volvo government subsidies if they agreed to shift production away from Germany and Belgium and back to Sweden. Berlin's economics minister Karl-Theodor Guttenberg also made it clear that he planned to stimulate "jobs in Germany, not in the Far East."

But for the moment Sarkozy was in a corner surrounded by French discontent that overtook the country during "Black Thursday" on January 29, when a general strike lambasted the popularity of the president and of the government, hours before a fiscal package was approved in Paris. To put the pieces back together, the French president had to give up his plans for the new and enhanced role of the Eurogroup. It was a significant trade-off: the sacrifice of what he saw as institutional improvements to compensate for the defense of national interests.

## The Unexpected Debate on Fiscal Union

It was only on February 25, 2009, that German finance minister Peer Steinbrück chose to speak about the unspeakable. "We have a few countries in the euro zone which are getting into difficulties with their payments," Steinbrück told a crowd at an event of his center-left party, the Social Democrats (SPD). He described a gloomy prospect for the coming years, at least for some members of the euro zone. "Ireland, especially, is currently in a very difficult situation," Steinbrück said, and then elaborated further: "If one country of the euro zone gets into trouble, then collectively we will have to be helpful. The euro-region treaties don't foresee any help for insolvent countries, but in reality the other states would have to rescue those running into difficulty." This statement, observed *Der Spiegel,* "was tantamount to a complete reversal."[6] Until that point, not a single representative of the German government had been willing to discuss the possibility of aid measures for countries in financial straits. Instead, they had kept pointing to the Maastricht Treaty, which prohibits the community of states from bearing the debt burden of individual euro zone members.

Hardliners, such as ECB chief economist Jürgen Stark, didn't want to hear anything about proposals for a bailout. "The ban preventing the EU and its member states from taking responsibility for the debts of partner countries is an important foundation for the currency union to function," he said.[7] Stark's fear was grounded on the typical "moral hazard" argument: additional member states would abandon their fiscal discipline if they knew others would bail them out.

A part of the German press was taken aback by Steinbrück's statements and preferred to line up with the popular diffidence toward solidarity with the European partners. The conservative *Frankfurter Allgemeine Zeitung,* for example, undertook a hard line with populist overtones:

> The crisis has relentlessly exposed the weaknesses of Europe's monetary union. Small countries on the edge of the EU have lived beyond their means and failed to get their welfare systems and national budgets in order in time. Under the cover of a unified currency, they continued with their same bad habits. So it's natural that investors are now demanding higher risk premiums from these weakened countries when they borrow money by issuing bonds. These countries may soon be faced with the choice of either forfeiting their deficit policies or giving up the euro. The apparently comfortable option of falling back on Germany won't bring about a rescue—it would instead result in rapid inflation for everyone. And if Germany, as Europe's most reliable bond issuer, loses the trust of its investors, the euro will collapse, too. That's why the promised community of stability cannot become a union of unlimited liabilities.[8]

The German public debate in February 2009 was more lively and varied than generally assumed. But the reason why it developed into a defining moment of the euro-crisis was that it introduced the concept of Transferunion in the European context, a concept so powerful as to overwhelm an honest search for the causes behind the crisis. Transferunion is a mechanism ingrained in the fiscal federal system in Germany, whereby each year wealthier regions are called to transfer income to the poorer ones. It is a constant and regulated yearly procedure that has turned very expensive for the citizens of the former West Germany because the internal income divergences among the Laender had dramatically increased after German reunification. Germany had struggled since 1989 to keep under control the financial and social consequences of reunification. The specter of a larger Transferunion on a European scale was appalling to German citizens and politicians. The analogy, however, did not really fit the current situation if one considered the financial crisis as the consequence of a unique shock. But if the underlying assumption was that poorer European countries would have to be helped permanently year after year in the future, then the parallel was disquieting. An aide to Chancellor Merkel offered a revealing explanation: "German citizens—and the German government as a consequence—would have no problem in lending a lot of money in one shot to a partner. Even knowing that the money would not come back easily. What citizens do not want is the syndrome of the Fass ohne Boden [the bottomless pit]: year after year a flow of money to no avail. This would tear nerves and erode the European commitment of this country."[9]

It was not easy to introduce a debate on fiscal solidarity in the middle of a crisis. Ever since the meetings in the 1990s to prepare for the Economic and Monetary Union, proposals for a greater fiscal integration, as well as of financial solidarity, had been advocated by many economic policy analysts. But European governments claimed that coordination was adequately addressed via the Stability and Growth Pact, with its limits on fiscal deficits, as well as by the no-bailout clause of the Maastricht Treaty.[10] However, while the treaty prescribes that "the Community shall not be liable for or assume the commitments of central governments" and that "a Member State shall not be liable for or assume the commitments of central governments, regional, local or other public authorities," it also says: "Where a Member State is in difficulties or is seriously threatened with severe difficulties caused by exceptional occurrences beyond its control, the [European] Council may, acting unanimously on a proposal from the Commission, grant, under certain conditions, Community financial assistance to the Member State concerned."

The question presented to policymakers was whether to follow the original script for the monetary union, that is, to allow interest rate spreads on sovereign debt to widen with the anticipation that this, in turn, would encourage the exposed governments to tighten their fiscal stances to restore credibility. The alternatives were to allow debt restructuring to take place, or to invoke the "exceptional occurrences" clause of the treaty and establish some form of fiscal solidarity. While policymakers were hesitating and working on proposals for solidarity behind the scenes, market analysts were receiving a rather different message on a worsening of the crisis. Faced with the prevailing political mantra of fiscal tightening or default, the markets seemed to have no doubt that a bailout was not in the cards. Vastly wider spreads in borrowing costs illustrated the market's conclusion that the political and social fabric in the peripheral member states (Greece, Portugal, and Spain, for example) would not withstand the necessary fiscal tightening in the midst of recession, making a debt restructuring the more likely outcome. Some analysts argued as early as February 2009 that the tensions in the euro area would lead to one or two of the peripheral member states' imminent exit from the euro zone, which would almost certainly lead to their defaulting on debts. Goldman Sachs, in a timely analysis, commented:

> The German government may have realized that it may face one of two evils: participating in pre-emptive community organised support for a Euro-zone sovereign debtor, or a later rescue operation (by the German

government alone) of domestic creditors. And, between the two, the former would appear to be the better option, particularly as stating such willingness might just do the trick in itself.[11]

At the same time, experts at the finance ministry in Berlin were becoming aware that the exposure of German banks to the debt of the six other largest euro zone members was equivalent to more than one-third of German GDP.

## Banking Ground Still Shaking

The weeks between the end of February and the end of March 2009 turned out to be a seminal moment in the developing crisis in the euro zone. Finance ministers, meeting in the ECOFIN Council or in the Eurogroup, had to choose between hanging together or not. On the one hand, the path to more integration was difficult because of the lack of an adequate institutional framework for taking decisions and for regulating the policy responsibilities. It was outright impossible to set up a single fiscal authority for the euro area in a few weeks, but it was not easy, either, to design an emergency mechanism endowed with enough money to assist the countries facing fiscal problems. On the other hand, the chacun sa merde—way seemed to be understood by the markets as the fastest route to the end of the euro.

The decisive factor behind the choice facing governments was the worrisome status of the European financial system and in particular the incidents that kept happening in the German banking landscape. An open discussion on fiscal solidarity would require a transparent disclosure of the fragility of the banking situation, but in that regard Berlin preferred a strategy of denial when dealing with its European partners. To keep the reality of the banks' accounts covered, Steinbrück fought hard to avoid a common regulation imposed by Brussels. The European Commission was trying to introduce stricter regulations and to enforce respect for the competition rules and antitrust principles. Brussels wanted national governments to facilitate the build-up of additional capital in the national banks. Moreover, to get more transparency, EU monetary affairs commissioner Joaquin Almunia wanted countries to adopt "uniform methods of asset valuation and the account of capital values." But Steinbrück staunchly opposed a rapid introduction of the new measures. "I think it is unreal to introduce the new directives at the next EU Council at the end of February," he said. "It is more important to avoid the failure of any systemic-relevant institute."

Soon it became clear where Steinbrück's worries were coming from: politicians of the north-western Land Schleswig-Holstein admitted that it would face inescapable bankruptcy if requested to bail out the Hamburg HDH Nordbank with €3 billion. The German paper *Bild Zeitung* branded Schleswig-Holstein as "quasi-bankrupt." The Land had no political room to maneuver, a member of the government in Kiel admitted: "A bankruptcy was likely in the same way as in Iceland."[12] The Hamburg Landesbank had lost around €2.8 billion in badly conceived speculations. It had already received guarantees for €30 billion in November from the public fund for the German banks, SoFFin, but this had proven to be insufficient to return the bank to a sound position. Steinbrück had been asked to intervene personally to solve an impasse that threatened to create the first (regional) state bankruptcy in Europe—and the first German bailout. At the same time, attempts to rescue the much bigger and politically relevant Westdeutsche Landesbank were tottering.

Guenter Verheugen, the German vice president of the European Commission, commented bluntly on the state of the German Landesbanken, saying they were "world champions in risky banking transactions."[13] Indeed, the IMF had spoken of "imprudent ventures" by the German public banks. The *Financial Times* quoted an unnamed international policymaker saying that "large German banks could lose up to three quarters of their total equity," making them unable to continue unless quick action was taken to purge bad assets from their balance sheets and to take on capital.[14]

The symptomatic reaction in Berlin to the risk of bankruptcy in Schleswig-Holstein was to accelerate the introduction of a "debt brake" in the German constitution, according to which the sixteen German Laender would need to run a balanced budget from 2016 onward and the federal government deficit would be capped at 0.35 percent of GDP. Instead of tackling the bank problem at HDH Nordbank, Berlin imposed fiscal austerity on all of its Laender. This was a paradoxical knee-jerk reaction that in the following months was to become a footprint for the euro zone countries facing crisis.

For many EU member states, torn between the need to restructure their banks and the desire to protect them, misrepresentation became the name of the game. In the case of France, national regulators allowed banks to move away from "fair-value" accounting of bad quality assets, thus shifting the scrutiny from individual bank balance sheets to a far more damaging general air of uncertainty over the entire financial system. But while national governments were dithering, they could not hope to do it indefinitely: The balance sheets of banks seemed to deteriorate at breakneck speed, and the IMF estimated that aggregate global bank losses had risen to $4 trillion dollars from "only" $2.2 trillion in January.[15] Of this, less than $1.3 trillion had been disclosed so far by individual banks. European bank losses were to reach $1.4 trillion to $1.6 trillion by November 2009, greater than total previous losses at U.S. banks.[16]

The determination, especially by Berlin and Paris, to withhold the data on their national banking systems reinforced the lack of coordination among European governments. This foggy situation gave a free hand to a flow of news and analyses depicting the European situation as dire. On February 12, for example, a British newspaper reported on a confidential memo distributed among EU finance ministers asserting that the toxic debts of European banks risked overwhelming a number of EU governments and might pose a "systemic" danger to the broader EU banking system.[17] On February 17, Moody's announced it was set to downgrade banks with large eastern European exposure, and more precisely banks from Austria, Italy, France, Belgium, Germany, and Sweden, which accounted for 84 percent of western European bank loans in eastern Europe. In the same period, Goldman Sachs reported that under its baseline scenario, total gross losses (including securities) of euro zone–owned banks were at €915 billion (10 percent of GDP). Goldman said that banks had so far written down the equivalent of 4 percent of EU GDP. In the worst-case scenario, involving a protracted recession and direct consequences on the financial system, the estimated losses would double, Goldman Sachs said. Disguising the reality became awkward in Germany when a newspaper disclosed a confidential document of the financial regulator BaFin, which revealed that the financial crisis had hit German banks significantly harder than was previously known.[18] The paper cited a new measurement date, February 26, by which time German banks faced risks adding to €816 billion, double what had been reckoned previously.[19]

*Keeping the Banks' Problems Under Wraps*

Between February and March 2009, the focus of the markets moved rapidly from the United States—hitherto the epicenter of the financial crisis—to Europe. The interaction of unknown bank problems and growing public debts drew the attention of investors to the capacity of weaker countries to finance themselves without being too dependent on external borrowing. The reason is that three deficits—public, private, and the current account of the balance of payments—are linked by identity. If the state is in massive deficit because of the problems of its banks and if private savings are negative because of the recession, the country will also run a deficit in its external balance; that is, it needs to import foreign capital to finance the state and the economy.

The attention of the markets was catalyzed by the problem of the current account divergences in the euro zone. This was a very unfavorable indicator for the unity of the euro area because discrepancies in competitiveness—in simple terms, the capacity to hold a positive balance in trade—had increased rapidly, reaching an all-time high in 2007. The variations called into question the validity of the core idea of the monetary union: that it would induce increasing convergence among the economies. In reality, the export performances also had been differentiated in the previous ten years. Countries like Germany, Slovakia, Austria, or Luxembourg had benefited from a surge in exports of goods and services, with annual growth averaging 7–8 percent or more. These countries routinely ran current account surpluses all through the 2000s. In contrast, Belgium,

France, Italy, and Portugal had posted dismal export performances, with average annual growth in the 2–4 percent range.[20] These countries generally ran current account deficits. Changes in the prices of goods and of labor—necessary to correct competitiveness gaps—are particularly difficult in the euro area economy, which is characterized by labor and product market rigidity. Inflexible wages and prices make adjustments more costly—reducing employment instead of wages and dismantling industries instead of restructuring them—and more protracted. Gradually, investors started looking at the euro area as less homogeneous than in the past. For the first time, in fact, investors had concrete fears that the basis of the euro area was not solid.

Eventually, the European authorities could not delay designing a plan to react to the alarms of the market. They had to tackle both the problems with the banks and those with the fiscal deficits. But instead of tackling the banks' problems, national politicians in the EU preferred to keep them under wraps and instead debate plans for global financial regulation. They actually launched an ambitious reform of regulatory architecture that would change the European banking landscape only in future years, once it was approved and finally enacted.[21] They also trod a more politically rewarding ground by attacking the outrageous salaries of top bankers and the incredible bonuses that they were still earning, to the bafflement of the population.

In fact, by avoiding a transparent assessment of their banks, governments were only aggravating the crisis. Exactly like the others, the German government clearly wanted to buy time so it could restore bank profitability, mainly thanks to government support and easy financing conditions from the ECB. The Bundesbank's description of the crisis is in itself revealing, indicating it was mainly a problem of waiting for the recovery to take place while the banks reduced holdings of what seemed, from time to time, the most dangerous assets in their portfolio.[22] In the first months of 2009, for instance, they got rid of holdings in eastern Europe and Russia.[23] By August 2009 German banks' total exposure to those countries amounted to €129 billion, or 5.3 percent of the total exposure of all banks. However, exposure to eastern European countries had declined by 10 percent compared with September 2008. It was now necessary to buy the time to extend the same game to the whole euro area.

Several weeks of negotiations were needed between Brussels and Frankfurt—and particularly among the representatives of ECOFIN and the Eurogroup—before a first remedy against the crisis could take shape. It was finally found around mid-March, and it seemed at the time to be the perfect recipe. It would actually push the euro area to the brink of disaster.

# 7

## The European Central Bank's
## First Rescue of the States

### The Hidden Grand Bargain

In the spring of 2009, long before the debates of 2010 about getting the European Central Bank to help struggling governments finance their debts, the ECB actually provided them with indirect help—in a stealth violation of its mandate. The secret deal, call it the "Grand Bargain," was closed behind the scenes and formally respected both the EU treaty and the Statute of the ECB. But the fact is that when, in May 2009, the ECB decided to step in decisively and help the ailing banks through a huge provision of liquidity, these banks were asked by the governments to use the money to buy the public bonds, and the banks complied by purchasing up to 70 percent of the new debt issued by their national states in 2009. This mechanism helped to ease the funding of the states, but further segmented the euro area by concentrating different levels of risks inside the national borders. The Grand Bargain was a short-term, emergency solution, but it also had severe drawbacks, and the ECB wanted it to be temporary and asked, in vain, for a more structural solution for the deleveraging of banks and states. The lack of compliance by the governments marked the beginning of an arm twisting, destined to last years, between the ECB, which was urging an exit strategy from the financial crisis, and the national governments, which were procrastinating on their commitment to tackle the banking predicaments, particularly in light of the severe recession.

During March and April 2009, the top managers of the main banks of the euro area were summoned by their national central banks and by their finance ministers. Frequent meetings regularly occur between the markets and the authorities in all countries, but in those weeks the exercise of "moral suasion" assumed a quite exceptional meaning: national ministers asked the private banks to commit firmly to the purchase of national government bonds. It was a milestone on the road to the Grand Bargain, one that changed the history of the crisis.

Although there never was a deal underwritten more or less formally by anybody, several top bankers concede the huge pressure they received from their national regulators about specifically subscribing national debt. The fact is that in Europe a tripartite game was established in April 2009. The deal entailed three major steps. The first was that governments fighting the recession committed not to expand their fiscal deficits beyond reasonable limits. As a second step, the ECB agreed to provide for a monetary stimulus by offering cheap liquidity directly to the banks. Finally, the banking system reinvested the liquidity received from the ECB, mainly in national sovereign bonds, and got a higher yield in doing so.

It seemed a perfect solution to the problems of the banks and of sovereign debt that were putting the euro in danger. De facto government financing was facilitated by banks in a way that could restore their own profitability through an easy trade: banks received ample liquidity from the ECB at the lowest possible cost and reinvested it in government paper that was still perceived as a risk-free asset but carried a yield certainly higher than what the banks had to pay the ECB. Government and banks both could be shored up this way, and it all came at a very hypothetical cost of future inflationary risks for the excess liquidity provided by the European Central Bank.

In fact, the whole deal amounted to a thinly veiled financing of government debt by the ECB, although indirectly through the banking system. It was evidently a violation of the spirit of the Maastricht Treaty's limits on the role of the ECB in the monetary union. Article 104 explicitly forbids the central bank to finance directly the EU member states:

> Overdraft facilities or any other type of credit facility with the ECB or with the central banks of the Member States in favor of Community [EU] institutions or bodies, central governments, regional, local or other public authorities, other bodies governed by public law, or public undertakings of Member States shall be prohibited, as shall the purchase directly from them by the ECB or national central banks of debt instruments.

The treaty did allow for the ECB to finance the banks, but in this case the hidden arrangement by which the banks financed the states with the same money received from the ECB would raise questions about the legitimacy of the deal. The violation of the spirit of the treaty was the reason why the Grand Bargain had to remain—as it did—secret. Nobody protested, in contrast to what happened later during the crisis, because all countries benefited from the deal. The arrangement was particularly embarrassing for the Bundesbank because that institution, as the purist defender of central banking autonomy from politics, was the first to benefit from the bargain. In the course of 2008–09, for instance, the ECB lent more than €80 billion to the bankrupted Hypo Real Estate bank against a guarantee consisting mainly of German sovereign bonds. The hidden arrangement was the consequence of the German government's resistance to more far-reaching solutions in terms of fiscal integration of euro zone member states. If Berlin did not want to lay bare the accounts of its banks and did not want to advance down the road toward European fiscal solidarity, the only method of fixing the problems of both the banks and the states was to resort to the ECB as a provider of unlimited liquidity.

The ECB had begun providing ample short-term liquidity to the banking system in August 2007 (after BNP Paribas froze three of its hedge funds), and then it did so regularly starting in October 2008.[1] While those emergency actions were dictated by necessity, in May 2009 the central bank changed strategy and provided liquidity on a more stable basis and with a longer duration (one year) to dispel any doubts about the solidity of the banking system; it did so following the criterion of full allotment, that is, all the liquidity requests by banks were satisfied. In the same period, the ECB had adjusted its monetary policy to reflect the collapse of the real economy by cutting gradually the reference interest rates in the euro area from 4.25 percent to 1 percent.[2]

The first one-year liquidity operation by the European Central Bank was conducted in May at particularly low rates; as a result, many banks tapped the facility even if they were not under stress.[3] The operation created the easy and wished-for arbitrage opportunity: banks collected liquidity at low interest rates and immediately reinvested it in higher-yielding sovereign bonds. For this reason a second operation was issued at slightly higher rates.

Interestingly, the third operation in 2009 had rates that limited the easy arbitrage. The ECB had observed with increasing unease the delays of the governments in designing and implementing a fiscal exit strategy as well as plans to recapitalize the banks. In effect, they were free-riding on the monetary financing indirectly provided by the ECB: taking the money but doing nothing to correct their fiscal problems. So, the Central Bank decided it would close the Grand Bargain in the autumn of 2009.

However, the effects of the Grand Bargain were already beyond control. Banks had been accumulating heaps of national sovereign bonds. They could not imagine that the government paper was not going to be as risk free in the future as it had been in the past. Moreover, the European and national authorities—governments or central banks—had not considered a major side effect on the fragmented European regulatory system whereby banks—responding to the explicit requests of their governments— concentrated in their portfolios mainly the government bonds of the countries where they were located. By doing so, they were doubling the risk ingrained in a future crisis in the euro area: once a country got in danger, its government bonds would be a special burden for its domestic national banks. This was a typical case of what economists call a "risk correlation."

The repatriation of capital represented by this trend was a major reversal of what happened earlier in the short history of the euro. Between 2003 and December 2008, for instance, the estimated share of Greek sovereign debt held abroad increased from 48 percent to 66 percent. Ireland's equivalent development was from a share of 54 percent to 64 percent. Portugal went from 60 to 86 percent. Those shares had increased continuously in the years prior to the crisis reaching the peak at the end of 2008. But then, once the crisis struck, the trend started to reverse substantially. In fact, the collapse of cross-border capital flows happened all over the world as a consequence of increased pressure by governments on their domestic banks and other institutional investors to absorb additional domestic public debt. Moreover, repatriation of capital increased as a consequence of fears by banks of default or even expropriation by foreign governments. The situation within the euro area started to diverge markedly. Greek banks held a relatively low share of Greek national public debt (15 percent) compared to Germany, where at least one-third of the domestic debt was in the hands of the German banks. As a consequence, countries like Greece, Ireland, and Portugal looked more exposed to the nervous reactions of markets and to the repatriation of capital than did Germany and others. Eventually, the Grand Bargain helped make some countries in the euro area more unstable than others.

## Central Banks as Lonely Firefighters

The role of the world's central banks, coordinated during the increasingly frequent meetings in Basel at the Bank for International Settlements, was vital in this early phase of the financial crisis. Thanks to the interventions of central banks, events in the global financial system had unexpectedly taken a positive turn in mid-March 2009, despite a still-negative macroeconomic and financial outlook. Signs of dysfunction remained in many markets, but central bankers were more inclined than earlier to provide a backstop for the financial problems. Market volatilities declined, most markets bottomed out in that month, and asset prices began to recover as more determined policy actions induced markets to show some optimism.

The claimed neutrality of the central banks from the arena of public policy decisions was put on hold in the reality of the crisis. Not only did decisions by central banks substantially influence the solutions, but so did their words. A key factor behind improving asset valuations was the confidence effect resulting from the public announcements by the major central banks when they expanded both the range and the amount of assets that they would be prepared to purchase outright. Early in March, the Bank of England announced plans to purchase private sector assets and government bonds. On March 18, the U.S. Federal Reserve followed with news that it would acquire up to $300 billion worth of longer-term Treasury securities. Speculation about the possibility of similar measures being taken by the ECB also affected euro area bond yields. In its 2009 annual report, BIS mentioned "signalling effects" by the central bank that would later be observed in Europe, following an announcement in early May that the ECB would start purchasing euro-denominated covered bonds (derivatives backed by cash flow from the underlying pool of investments).[4]

For the ECB, it was highly unusual to be involved in bailing out the European economy. While the Federal Reserve has a more precise statutory commitment to support the economy and its growth, the dominating goal of monetary policy in the ECB statute is price stability. Support for the economy comes only as a distant second goal, and only if it does not diminish the commitment against inflation. There was a further specific reason why the Grand Bargain put the ECB in a particularly uneasy situation. While the Federal Reserve could provide liquidity to a market-based financial system, the European Central Bank System had to deal individually with single banks. Inevitably, this is a much less neutral and more personal management of the crisis.

Dealing directly with the banks was essential for the crucial role that they have in the European economy. ECB president Jean-Claude Trichet explained it extensively:

> At the end of 2007, the stock of outstanding bank loans to the private sector amounted to around 145 percent of GDP in the euro area. The corresponding proportion of bank loans to GDP in the United States is only 63 percent. This means that the banking sector is more than twice as important in the euro area as it is in the United States. It also means that to be effective, ECB policy must focus first and foremost on the banking sector. Similarly, direct debt securities account for 81 percent of GDP in the euro area. The corresponding proportion in the United States is 168 percent. This means that market-based financing plays a much smaller role in the euro area and is only half as relevant as in the United States . . . . Against this background, it is natural that the Federal Reserve's 'credit easing' policies mainly target markets for debt securities, whereas our policies of 'enhanced credit support' focus on banks.[5]

Another peculiar feature of the European economy that Trichet had to take into account was its modest flexibility. Prices and wages are more sluggish in the euro area than in the United States, due to higher labor-market protections and a lower degree of competition on the product-market. This sluggishness, on the one hand, has drawbacks because it slows down the adjustment of the euro area economy to adverse shocks. At the same time, the social safety nets offer some protection against very bad outcomes and provide an anchor for private sector expectations. "In the euro area," Trichet observed, "the institutional framework provides such an anchor through the medium-term stability orientation of fiscal policies and monetary policy geared toward fiscal sustainability and price stability. In this environment, overly activist policies risk destabilising expectations and, thus, being counterproductive."[6]

The unorthodox policy setting of 2009 not only put strains on the ECB, it also could not be a permanent solution, for an important reason: the bank's indirect lending to governments sharply reduced the incentives for national governments to rein in the bloating debts in both the private and the public sectors. Trichet saw that governments would not resist the temptation to free ride on monetary support and would delay acting on their part of the Grand Bargain: to rein in their fiscal deficits and clean up or recapitalize the banks.

In all respects, the Grand Bargain was, indeed, a very exceptional step for the euro zone. But those were, indeed, exceptional times. The economy was plunging in the first quarter of 2009 and nobody was able to say how much deeper and how much longer it was going to fall. By mid-March the shocking news was that the recession in 2009 was going to be deeper in Europe than in the United States. The financial and global nature of the crisis was making it less predictable, but some economists were reversing the earlier analysis that gave an advantage to the European economy because it could benefit from rigidity of employment as a stabilizer during the slump. Instead, German industrial production fell –7.5 percent in January 2009, against the previous month, which seemed to prove the exposure of the European powerhouse to the collapse of world trade. The March ECB *Monthly Bulletin* published the downward revisions for the euro zone: annual real GDP growth was estimated to be between –3.2 percent and –2.2 percent in 2009, and between –0.7 percent and +0.7 percent in 2010. A joint expected decline in exports (–8.3 percent in 2009) and in domestic demand, in particular investment (–7.2 percent in 2009), was at the root of the weak figures. The slump was so brutal that it risked denting the potential output of the EU, putting workers permanently out of jobs or dimming prospects for investments.[7]

## The EU Council: "The Markets Do Not Yet Believe Us"

When the EU heads of state and governments met on March 19–20 for the European Council, the issue of the integrity of the euro area was not even mentioned in the final communiqué. This was not surprising due to the private character of the negotiations and the sensitivity of the subject. During the general debate on financial stability, Trichet, who increasingly had become the cornerstone of the European gatherings since the crisis broke, stressed that the first priority was to restore confidence in the financial markets. According to data mentioned during the meeting, the authorities had channelled, in the form of capital or guarantees, a great deal of money into the banks, roughly equivalent to 23 percent of cumulative euro zone GDP. "But the markets do not yet believe us," Trichet was reported to say, "partly at any rate because the commitments we have entered into are so far-reaching," while incidents could always be just around a corner. It is extremely important, the ECB president argued, "that we persuade the markets to believe our undertakings."[8] What the president implied was evidently that, for all the aid that the ECB was willing to lend to single banks, it was a temporary solution. Governments had to take over soon the responsibility of cleaning up the credit institutions, and they had to do it transparently.

In fact, the European Council at its March 2009 meeting endorsed a wide-ranging initiative to reform the financial systems, based on the profound and ambitious analysis of the High Level Group on Financial Supervision in the EU, chaired by former IMF managing director Jacques de Larosière, which had presented its final report on February 25.[9] However, the European leaders gave the problems of disclosure of banks' bad assets and of the recapitalization of the weaker institutions only vague deadlines. "Commission proposals on hedge funds and private equity, on executive remunerations and on further strengthening capital requirements" were all part of the same agenda.[10] The fundamental issue of undercapitalization of the banks had been tackled mutely and randomly hitherto. In the maze of national initiatives, European governments' measures in support of the banking sector were not coming across in the market as decisively as they should have.

Beyond the general policy statement that no major financial institution in Europe would be allowed to collapse, the national fiscal authorities had taken impressive steps to safeguard the banking systems. Explicit guarantees of more than €1.5 trillion had been announced and capital injections into banks totaled up to €200 billion. But single incidents were hard to keep under cover: on June 22, 2009, for instance, the shares of Crédit Agricole, one of France largest credit institutions, fell 4.84 percent in a matter of minutes after data from Emporiki, the bank's Greek subsidiary, forced a major revision of the expected income.[11] This was just four months before first revelations of a major debt crisis in Greece.

Not surprisingly, most American analysts continued to consider the situation of the banking system as the "key downside risk" for the European economy.[12] The risk in Europe seemed aggravated in comparison with the American activism on financial disclosure. To increase confidence in the financial system, U.S. regulators in April 2009 conducted "stress tests" on nineteen bank holding companies to ensure that they were sufficiently capitalized under a set of assumptions about losses in various bank assets over the next two years. Following the release of the results in early May, U.S. regulators directed ten of the examined banks to increase their levels of capital or to improve their capital quality by including more common shares. Several banks took advantage of the reduced uncertainty and the increased risk appetite of investors that accompanied the publication of the stress test results to raise equity and issue debt.

## The G-20 in London: A Cornerstone for Global Finance

The preparation of the Group of 20 (G-20) meeting, which was to take place in London on April 2, was a crucial moment for economic diplomacy between Europe and the United States. European leaders needed finally to recover their efforts of coordination in view of a G-20 that was meant to be the cornerstone of the global political response to the crisis. The previous G-20 meeting in Washington in November 2008 had played out in the early days of the financial storm and under the leadership of an outgoing U.S. president. The London summit was to be the crucial test for financial regulation and for stimulus policies. Essentially, the issue was between the United States and the United Kingdom on one side, asking for stronger economic stimulus from China and Germany (the countries posting surpluses in their external balances), and Europe on the other side, asking for more regulation in global finance.

In the run up to the summit, the European governments—and Berlin specifically— were under fire from the United States for refusing to enact larger fiscal stimulus programs. Larry Summers, the chief economic adviser at the White House, was a relentless critic of what in Washington was widely considered "fiscal obsessions" in Germany, and he intensified his efforts just before the London G-20 summit on April 2. Gordon Brown had been the first European leader to meet President Obama in Washington in March, and he tried to pass on the American arguments to the Europeans, but he himself seemed to have lost faith in Keynesian-style stimulus. The estimates of the effects of the American $700-plus billion fiscal package, enacted in February, were really unconvincing. Some of the money was devoted to tax cuts, but a lot was shovelled into projects with low multiplier effects. Jobs were created, but many were of a purely temporary nature and were destined to disappear with the end of the stimulus. In the meanwhile, at least to European eyes, the U.S. fiscal balance was degenerating.

Several G-7 meetings took place at the level of finance ministers, who discussed the need to reconcile the transatlantic positions. Germans replied to Summers's criticisms by noting that the euro area as a whole had a balanced current account, and, therefore, there was no margin for more private or public consumption unless one was willing to accept an external deficit in an uncertain economic environment and in the middle of the worst recession in recent European history. But Summers insisted that in a world where emerging countries could not easily correct their surplus positions and where it was impossible for oil producers to keep their domestic demand at the level of their exports, it was inevitable that other countries—Europe foremost—would need to post deficits, just like the United States had been doing for so long (the world's current account is balanced by definition). In an interview with the *Financial Times,* Summers observed: "There's no place that should be reducing its contribution to global demand right now. It is really the universal demand agenda."[13] His plea fell on deaf ears. Jean-Claude Juncker, chairman of the European finance ministers, rebuked Summers: "The sixteen finance ministers agreed that the recent American appeals insisting Europeans make an added budgetary effort were not of our liking." A columnist of the *Financial Times* described the remark as having "the crotchety air of a dowager duchess sending a substandard amuse-bouche back to the kitchens."[14]

EU leaders had discussed, and rejected, the U.S. pressures during the European Council of March 19–20 in Brussels. José Manuel Barroso was explicit in a statement to the twenty-seven heads of state and governments: "The U.S. wants the EU to do more. The EU benefits from automatic stabilizers, however, which the U.S. does not have. . . . We cannot announce fresh stimulus packages every day. Our priority ought instead to be to make sure that what we have already done actually works."[15] Jean-Claude Trichet added, "We are now at the limits of what is possible." Angela Merkel agreed: "We don't need any further stimulus measures at this stage."[16]

The European Council conclusions of March 20 estimated the existing European fiscal measures totaled more than €400 billion, representing around 3.3 percent of European GDP.[17] However, Merkel insisted that policy must return "to positions consistent with sustainable public finances as soon as possible." The current situation was exceptional, she explained during the meeting, "and the EU must return as rapidly as possible to a fiscal stance that is compatible with the stability and growth pact." For the first time, she tried to pin down an agreed deadline for starting the "exit strategy" from fiscal stimulus.[18]

Merkel held a videoconference with President Obama shortly before the G-20 meeting in London, which followed the meeting of European leaders by less than two weeks. The Chancellery, along with the White House, is one of the few government seats in the world that can safely use video communication instead of the usual "red phone" (the one at the Chancellery is actually black) provided with an encrypted system. They tried to set the main points of the agenda as clearly as possible before the summit. This was important for the chancellor, who had the impression that Obama was inclined to change the agenda during the course of meetings—something that ran against her working methods. For Obama, it was particularly difficult to give the right weight to each European voice. The Lisbon Treaty had yet to be ratified, and so the mechanisms that were supposed to give the EU a single voice were still in the making.

Sarkozy and Merkel sent a letter to the EU leaders before the G-20 stressing the "historical chance" to improve the economic and financial systems and global cooperation.[19] They reckoned that the EU fiscal stimulus amounted to 3.3 percent of EU GDP. The two leaders met just after arriving in London to fine tune a common position. Sarkozy immediately attacked the financial industry, saying the system had turned immoral and needed to be provided with a new sense of morality. Apparently, Sarkozy and Merkel had repeatedly signaled that they did not want to consider financial regulation as a trade-off for economic stimulus. Merkel especially was in a different position at this point because the volume of fiscal stimulus provided to the German economy had been partly acknowledged by other governments: "It cannot be a horse-trading exercise," she was quoted as saying.[20]

The opening reception of the summit was held by Queen Elizabeth at Buckingham Palace, and on that occasion President Obama introduced his wife Michelle to the other heads of state and government. Obama and Merkel had a chance to exchange views while sitting side-by-side around the table at the dinner hosted by Gordon Brown in the evening.

After the work session, at the ExCel conference center in the London Docklands, the final text responded to the European positions on regulation: no sector of the financial system should remain hidden; hedge funds would have to register; rating agencies were dealt with in a half-page of the final text; and remuneration of financial managers was mentioned extensively.

Merkel and Sarkozy thought they had succeeded. Merkel actually sounded quite happy with the outcome: It was a "very, very good, almost historic compromise," she said after the conference. The final declaration was a "document of the trade." There was agreement on the establishment of a "clear financial market architecture" with stronger regulations.[21] German finance minister Peer Steinbrück repeated one of the most innovative sentences in the document: "The era of banking secrecy is over." It is clear that they underestimated the chameleon-like ability of the financial industry to adapt itself in ways that enable it to escape regulation.

The final communiqué of the G-20 indeed took quite a number of innovative steps in the direction of re-regulation of financial systems.[22] The leaders also issued a declaration, "Strengthening the Financial System," saying they had agreed to establish a new Financial Stability Board (FSB) that should collaborate with the IMF to provide early warning of macroeconomic and financial risks and the actions needed to address them. The G-20 leaders also committed to reshape the regulatory systems to take account of macroprudential risks, and to extend regulation and oversight to all systemically important financial institutions, instruments, and markets. This would include, for the first time, systemically important hedge funds. Finally, the G-20 leaders committed to provide $1.1 trillion—most of it to the IMF—for programs designed to improve international finance, credit, trade, and overall economic stability and recovery.

## Hiding the Banks behind the Grand Bargain

All of a sudden, between April and May, a blip resounded on the sonar of the apparently comatose German economy: German industrial giants had started again to increase their exports to the world, proving the benefits of the painful restructuring of the preceding decade. After the modest gain by 0.9 percent in June, the euro area as a whole also saw its exports rebound strongly by 4.1 percent in July. Germany was drawing behind itself the rest of the European economy as the exports among the member countries jumped 7.5 percent in July.

The fact that the economy was finally showing some encouraging signs of recovery was received by the governments as a confirmation of the strategy of the Grand Bargain. In fact, however, under the silent financing provided by the ECB, the situation in the European banking sector was becoming even more obscure. Two important publications from the IMF and the Committee of European Banking Supervisors (CEBS) came out with contradictory results. According to the results of CEBS's EU-wide bank stress test, which looked into the robustness of the twenty-two largest euro area and non–euro area cross-border banks, the European credit institutions did not require additional capital to keep their Tier 1 capital ratios "above 8 percent" (the threshold requested by regulators) even in case of a stress situation. In contrast, the IMF estimated that euro area banks needed $150 billion additional capital to meet the 8 percent Tier 1 capital ratio in its base scenario.[23]

Clarifying the state of the banks was crucial, as the ECB remarked time and again using always the same words: "Concerns remain relating to a stronger or more protracted negative feedback loop between the real economy and the still strained financial markets."[24] It was kind of a code-phrase that started signalling, every month, ECB's growing disappointment with the compliance by the governments with their leg of the Grand Bargain. The ECB knew the risk implicit in providing the liquidity for the purchase of government bonds in the absence of a strategy of fiscal containment and of banks' recapitalization.

Under pressure from the IMF, the European finance ministers in May 2009 mandated that the CEBS coordinate, in cooperation with the European Commission and the ECB, an EU-wide, forward-looking stress test. The stated goal was to measure future vulnerabilities of the banks. Unfortunately, once more national financial protectionism prevailed. Large cross-border financial linkages mean that stress tests must be Europe-wide to be truly accurate. But European governments preferred to implement the commonly defined methodology each its own way. As national authorities cannot be trusted to place the EU common interest above their own, a central body should have been empowered to double-check national assessments and make sure they were genuinely comparable. However, governments again were eager to empower only themselves and then filter the conclusions of the committee managing the supervision exercise.

A presentation of the outcome of the EU-wide stress test on an aggregated basis was held at the ECOFIN meeting at the end of September. No single bank was mentioned, and no specific information was to be found in the official documentation. EU policymakers did not want to explicitly include the possibility of a sovereign default in the stress scenarios of the banks for fear this assumption would become self-fulfilling. Probably, they also did not want to highlight the fiscal problems behind sovereign debt because that would imply naming and shaming the fiscally weaker countries.

The result was so vague and implausible that even the ECOFIN ministers and central bank governors noted that "should economic conditions be more adverse than currently expected, this would have significant impact on the potential losses for the banks concerned. Under such an adverse scenario, the potential credit and trading losses over the years 2009–10 could amount to almost €400 billion." Nevertheless, the official statement concluded, "The financial position and expected results of banks are sufficient to maintain an adequate level of capital also under such negative circumstances."[25]

## ECB Money Directly into National Debts

Without governments taking stock of the banking problems, the financial side of the crisis was entirely left in the hands of the ECB throughout the summer of 2009.[26] The central bank was well aware that banks were not using the liquidity to prop up the economy. According to its November *Monthly Bulletin*, "The annual growth rate of bank loans to the non-financial private sector turned slightly negative in September, with annual loan growth to both non-financial corporations and households declining further and being negative."[27] Indeed, instead of using the additional liquidity to provide new loans to households and companies, banks hoarded a great deal of it at the ECB's deposit facility, which increased from €72 billion on average in August–September 2008 to €121 billion in the same period of 2009. As the ECB observed, the fall in production and trade, coupled with the ongoing uncertainty in business outlook, was dampening firms' demand for financing. Referring once more to the commitment expected by banks and governments, Trichet started using another code phrase that became a regular refrain in the following months: "Against the background of highly demanding challenges, banks should take appropriate measures to strengthen further their capital bases and, where necessary, take full advantage of government measures to support the financial sector, particularly as regards recapitalisation."[28] But, as shown earlier, banks preferred a different way—paradoxically made possible by the ECB and requested by national authorities—to eventually accrue their capital: purchasing government bonds.[29]

In fact, what was interesting was where the ECB money went: basically, government paper. While every other item in balance sheets of banks had been shrinking since the intensification of the crisis, holdings of government securities increased substantially, at an annual pace of 20 percent between July and September.[30] Citigroup estimated that the total amount of government paper held by euro area banks increased by €280 billion between October 2008 and August 2009. The yields of sovereign bonds were on average three times higher than the cost of liquidity at the ECB financing facility. As a result, borrowing from the ECB to invest in government debt was a sure deal to increase short-term profits—and it also helped improve the appearance of the banks' balance sheets through the purchase of supposedly high-quality paper.

The euro area's aggregate net issuance of central government securities from October 2008 up to the end of July 2009 had been around €600 billion. As the increase in net holding of government paper by banks was €280 billion, this meant that nearly half of the expansion of the net supply of government paper was matched by the rise in demand from euro area banks. If the buying of government securities by central banks—of around €90 billion—is also taken into account, more than 60 percent of the net supply of government debt was covered by demand from monetary and financial institutions.

Some analysts found the argument even more compelling when they looked at the situation at the country-by-country level. The breakdown by country of the ECB's provision of liquidity showed that some banking sectors were much more reliant than others on ECB funding. The share of ECB's liquidity obtained by ten euro area countries—via open market operations during the June–August 2008 period compared with the same months in 2009—showed that Greece, Ireland, and, to some extent, Spain were the countries where banks had most increased their reliance on ECB liquidity.[31] Furthermore, banks with the greatest increases in funding from the ECB tended to be those that raised their holdings of government paper the most.

German banks bought the smallest amount (relative to their total assets or relative to German GDP) of national government paper and looked for higher— and apparently safer—yields in other countries in the euro area, as they had been doing for the previous ten years. In some countries, such as Austria, Ireland, Portugal, and Spain, the banks' buying of government securities represented around 60–70 percent of the net issuance by the central governments compared to the previous months. In essence, by concentrating the risks of sovereign debt in the national banks, the Grand Bargain had provided a temporary remedy to the first leg of the euro area crisis—but it was also building up the potential for a more disruptive crisis later on.

# 8

## Karlsruhe, Ruling the World from the Province

### Merkel Intimidated by the Court

After nine months of unprecedented economic troubles and political divergences, Chancellor Merkel's speech on May 27, 2009, at Berlin's Humboldt University was anxiously expected around the world. For Europe, the month and location were highly symbolic. May 9 had been the fifty-ninth anniversary of the declaration by then French foreign minister Robert Schuman that a new form of organization of states in Europe would be formed and called a supranational community. This was the proposal that inaugurated the building of a united Europe. Moreover, Humboldt University was the place where nine years earlier on May 12, 2000, Joschka Fischer, then German foreign minister, launched his famous proposal for a "European Federation" of independent states based on a formal constitution.[1] Fischer's speech set in motion a pro-European debate across the continent that first resulted in a never-adopted constitution for Europe but then produced the more limited Lisbon Treaty of late 2007.

May 2009 was also a crucial moment for the chancellor to make clear her view on where Europe stood. The world was in the middle of the deepest recession in recent history. There was no better opportunity to reinvigorate the desire by many for political solidarity in the euro area. But Merkel declined the opportunity from the start: "I will have to disappoint you on this point," she said, "because I believe that defining long-term goals sometimes makes it more difficult to take the necessary next political steps." The Lisbon Treaty was the "best of our current efforts" in European integration, and "the national states are the masters of the treaties." She added that "we should avoid everything that leads to the transfer of competences through the back door."[2]

The reason for Merkel's cold shower was her concern about a forthcoming ruling by the German Constitutional Court. At the end of June 2009, the court had to release, from its premises in Karlsruhe, a much-awaited assessment of the compatibility of the Lisbon Treaty with German law.

The Lisbon Treaty could have a profound impact on national sovereignty because it strengthened the character of the European Union as a "body in its own right," enhancing its legislative powers, streamlining its decisionmaking, and bolstering its institutions. It implied a quantum leap for the EU in various ways: institutional consolidation,[3] establishing two new top positions within the EU—the president of the European Council, who will preside over the council composed of the heads of state and government, supplanting the previously rotating presidency,[4] and the high representative of foreign and security policy[5]—and extending the powers of the European Commission,[6] the European Parliament,[7] and the European Court of Justice.[8] Furthermore, the European Central Bank and the national banks were explicitly mentioned as executing monetary policy for the EU.

Merkel wanted to see how the Constitutional Court would judge, for instance, the fact that by extending majority votes in most fields of EU responsibility—notably on single-market affairs, on agriculture, and on economic and fiscal policy—the treaty was supposed to facilitate a stronger policy interdependence, affecting the national control over those domains. In these areas, the European Parliament was to have legislative powers equal to the European Council of ministers, which switched to a process of decisionmaking by qualified majority (a system requiring approval by more than 50 percent of votes). By mid-2009 all EU countries except Ireland, Poland, the Czech Republic, and Germany had completed ratification of the Lisbon Treaty.

Merkel was worried that a negative assessment by the high court could impair the European Union and particularly the role of Germany in the community. For that reason, before the ruling, she was eager to play down any expectation of further European integration. Some advisers to the chancellor argued that she did not find this difficult to do. She had doubts about the feasibility of political integration of many countries with different cultures and histories, and the previous months plagued by painful crisis management had not made her more optimistic. She was convinced that her only reasonable choice was to slow down French president Nicolas Sarkozy and other leaders who were pushing for greater shared fiscal responsibility within the euro zone. In this regard, the German Constitutional Court played a crucial role in the management of the whole crisis. Its shadow was to hover over the rest of the financial crisis and become probably the most important factor behind the German management of the Greek debt crisis starting in early 2010.

Furthermore, during 2009 Merkel was at the center of a shift in the constellation of German political forces backing an ever-stronger European integration. The chancellor had resolved to abandon the "Grand Coalition" with the Socialists (the coalition behind her government since 2005) to enter into an alliance with the liberal party, the Free Democrats, whose enthusiasm for European integration was much more tempered even than hers. This shifted the political axis of Germany away from Europe and farther from the domestic political center, and thus altered the political axis of the entire euro area. Together with a ruling by the Constitutional Court—setting legal limits on how far Germany could go in accepting European integration—Merkel's political realignment dramatically reduced the room for her government to maneuver on European turf. Ultimately, these developments also would give Merkel a legal motivation to bring the euro crisis to the brink of disaster in 2010.

On June 30, 2009, the eight judges in Karlsruhe voted almost unanimously. They confirmed the compatibility of the Lisbon Treaty with German fundamental law but also declared that no further progress in European integration and no further delegation of sovereignty to the EU could be made in the context of the current German constitutional framework. Only one judge refused to endorse German acceptance of the Lisbon Treaty. The first reaction throughout Europe was of widespread relief, in particular among the political class. The court had not blocked Germany's adherence to the new, more ambitious Europe as foreseen in the Lisbon Treaty. However, within a matter of days, a closer look at the judgment revealed that the apparently clear "yes" of the court to Germany's involvement in European integration was accompanied by profound and disturbing observations on the shortcomings of European democracy. Informed observers began to deduce that Germany actually was moving away from its traditional pro-European policy. The most direct consequence of the ruling was that any step that the government was expected to take in conjunction with the European partners, in anything affecting the living conditions of German citizens, would have to be submitted to the German Parliament for approval. Moreover, no sovereignty could be shared at the European level on issues such as fiscal policy.[9]

Since the founding of the Federal Republic of Germany in 1949, no other institution had gathered so much credibility among the German public as the Constitutional Court—not even the Bundesbank, the sacred guardian of monetary stability. Defending the law and sticking to principles of order and justice had been essential in the postwar reconstruction of a country that was a morally and physically destroyed land. Appealing to the fruitful tradition of legal philosophy molded by the illuminating works of jurist Hans Kelsen, the German judicial power had established a widely acknowledged role of providing a stable orientation for political debate. Kelsen understood the state's maintaining distance from the common sociological categories of "nation state, territory and sovereignty." He saw it rather in the domain of the legal Sollenssätzen (principal duties). Therefore, the main feature of the state had to be, in line with Immanuel Kant's vision, the existence of an objective legal system. Greek philosopher Heraclitus's appeal—"People ought to fight to keep their law as to defend the city's walls"—was especially embraced after Carl Schmitt's subordination of the law to political power during the Nazi period.[10]

The court's seat in Karlsruhe, near the border with France, also had become a German base for the thoughts of Heraclitus. Symbolically, the rationalistic building housing the court is made mostly of glass walls. Surrounding it is a restricted area and, even more important, a respectful aura. Its prominent role is enshrined in article 31 of the Grundgesetz, the German Fundamental Law, according to which the decisions of the court are binding "for the Constitutional bodies of the Federation and in the Laender as well as for the judicial courts and other authorities." Still, nomination of judges is strongly molded by political affiliation; each and every one of the respected personalities has a political affiliation and is nominated by a party according to the prevailing equilibriums at the Bundestag and the Bundesrat. The judges stay in power for twelve years so that their "independence" transfigures into autonomy. At the end of June 2009, they gave a shocking demonstration of their power.

Based on its self-established theory, under which every German citizen is holder of a democratic right to a legislature that is endowed with substantial powers to determine the destiny of the German people, the court examined the Lisbon Treaty in each and every detail. The claimants who brought suit, especially Peter Gauweiler (a conservative Bavarian politician with strong antipathy for Europe), alleged that this democratic right had been breached by the treaty, but they could not point to any specific injury that they had suffered. The constitutional complaint amounted to an "abstract" review of the treaty, a remedy that the German Fundamental Law reserves for the federal government, any government of a Land, or for a third of the members of the Bundestag. But as a jurist at Humboldt University in Berlin observed, "The Court saw the constitutional complaints, which had been filed by the extreme right and the extreme left of the political spectrum, as a welcome opportunity to define the constitutional limits of the European integration process. Far from reflecting the views of the constitutional framers, the ruling reads like a political manifesto from the judges."[11]

### The Closing of the European Horizon

In fact, by requiring a reform of the law that accompanied the ratification of the Lisbon Treaty, the judges in Karlsruhe—according to a former president of the court—were taking the European integration "to a dead end."[12] The Karlsruhe

Lissabon-Urteil, as the ruling was known, appeared as perhaps the most serious threat ever to the future of the European Union—a threat that was triggered in the union's most crucial country and came at the very moment when the global financial crisis would require even greater political coordination.

Some German ministers had actually worried that the court might reject the Lisbon Treaty in its entirety. In particular, the two most conservative judges were reported to have been tempted along that line. Nevertheless, even in Berlin the first elated reactions to the ruling of the court withered rapidly, and negotiations took place in Berlin and Munich between the Chancellery and the Bavarian party (the Christian Social Union, the local sister party to Merkel's Christian Democratic Union) to moderate the tones of their reaction. In a matter of days, those in the German press who at first were euphoric about the ruling suddenly became cautious. All major parties, except the extreme left (one of the promoters of the constitutional complaints), clearly had in mind the damage to Germany itself if the ruling isolated it in the European political arena. But the genie was out of the bottle.

In fact, the ruling also hid a suggestion: "The Lisbon Treaty, extending the powers of the EU, has increased, not reduced, the democratic deficit. This would justify the construction of a European political system more accountable, a true political union," the text said.[13] But an initial attempt by the government to limit the damage with optimistic interpretations fell rapidly on deaf ears. The German court was pointing its finger at all European decisions not taken unanimously and went further: the overall "structural problem of the European Union is at the center of the review of constitutionality." The rationale was relatively simple. The court stated that in many respects the European Union has the form of a federal state, but its legitimacy is derived from the national states. It does not have the decisionmaking procedures typical of a federal state and does not reflect many characteristics of a full democracy in which the will of equal citizens and of a homogeneous people can find expression. For this reason, the powers and competencies that can be conferred to the European Union at the policy level are those—and only those—that do not substantially affect the lives of citizens, as they are identified by the judges in Karlsruhe.[14]

Anti-European politicians immediately saw an opportunity. Hours after the ruling was released, members of the Bavarian state parliament threatened an appeal to the Karlsruhe court to block Iceland's request to join the EU. It appeared as if Germans suddenly were given a special veto right over European common decisions—a right deriving from and originating in the inalienable right to rule on national issues. That was indeed the core of the ruling. In the 421 paragraphs of the text, the Karlsruhe judges required that if the European Union claimed expanded responsibilities, a test of competence had to be run to ensure that "the untouchable crucial component of the German Constitutional

Law, remains safeguarded." The court claimed the right to determine which powers were within the boundaries of European integration and which could not be surrendered to the EU by the German state. The ruling applied both in general terms and in the details. In the words of one commentator, the court asserted its reservations "in the form of a dynamic and flexible veto right," so as to deny the European Union any delegation of sovereignty that had not been previously and specifically authorized by the German national parliament. It followed, therefore, that the court was asserting for itself the right to determine each step that Berlin could undertake toward forms of European integration. In other words, the court at Karlsruhe was to become the primary site for the assessment of the legality of relations between Berlin and the European Union, and therefore also a crucial actor in the EU.

In this sense, the German court also explicitly attributed to itself powers that exceeded those of the European Court of Justice. This was a showdown between the two courts after a seventeen-year competition, since the German court's judgment on the 1993 Treaty of Maastricht. While the European Union's Court of Justice had the ultimate judgment on the validity and enforcement of European laws, the Karlsruhe court had claimed unequivocally its undisputed competence on constitutional requirements as far as Germany was concerned. Although in a few digressions the German court recognized the superiority of European law over national law and the principle of openness—enshrined in the German Constitutional Law in regard to the international community and Europe in particular—the court placed itself as an indispensable element in any relevant European rulings. In practical terms, the court positioned itself at the end of the judicial process and therefore above the rest. According to the judges, in Germany accession to a European federal state would require the creation of a new constitution, which would go along with the declared waiver of the sovereign statehood safeguarded by the Basic Law. There was no such act yet. The European Union continues to constitute a union of rule (Herrschaftsverband) founded on international law, a union that is permanently supported by the will of the sovereign member states.

The primary responsibility for integration, therefore, is in the hands of the national constitutional bodies that act on behalf of the peoples. With progressing integration, fields of action essential for the development of the member states' democratic opinion-formation must be retained. In particular, it must be guaranteed that the responsibility for integration can be exercised by national bodies of representation of the peoples.

Not even the further development of the powers of the European Parliament could completely fill, according to the German court, "the gap between the extent of the decisionmaking power of the Union's institutions and the citizens' democratic power of action in the Member States."[15]

Measured against requirements placed on national democracy, the court insisted that election of the European Parliament does not take due account of the principle of equality of citizens; therefore, the parliament is not competent to take authoritative decisions on political directions in the context of the supra-national balancing of interests among the states. The court's main objection to the European Parliament lies in the diversified structure of the electoral districts, whereby the vote of an elector in the Luxembourg district (when electing the country's representatives in the European Parliament) weighs a dozen times more than the one cast by a German citizen voting for his representatives. EU parliamentarians are not elected according to the principle of "one man, one vote," but on the basis of "national contingents." This regressive representation is exemplified in the text: every Maltese member of the European Parliament is elected by only 67,000 Maltese citizens, a Swedish member by 455,000 Swedes, and a German by 857,000 Germans.[16]

## There Will Never Be a European State

In the court's view, the European Parliament cannot be considered a truly representative body reflecting the will of the European electorate. Due to this structural democratic deficit, further steps of European integration that go beyond the status quo should not be allowed to undermine the states' political power.

The positive aspects of the ruling, at least for those with pro-Europe views, should not be denied. The court rejected every objection that had challenged the compatibility of the Treaty of Lisbon with German Basic Law.[17]

European unification on the basis of a union of sovereign states under the treaties may, however, not be realized in such a way that the member states do not retain sufficient room for the political formation of the economic, cultural and social circumstances of life. This applies in particular to areas which shape the citizens' circumstances of life, in particular the private space of their own responsibility and of political and social security, which is protected by the fundamental rights, and to political decisions that particularly depend on previous understanding as regards culture, history and language and which unfold in discourses in the space of a political public that is organised by party politics and Parliament. To the extent that in these areas, which are of particular importance for democracy, a transfer of sovereign powers is permitted at all, a narrow interpretation is required. This concerns in particular the administration of criminal law, the police monopoly, and that of the military, on the use of force, the shaping of the circumstances of life by social policy and important decisions on cultural issues such as the school and education system, the provisions governing the media, and dealing with religious communities.[18]

The court's list of powers that cannot be transferred to the European level included "fundamental fiscal decisions on revenue and expenditure." In that one line, the German Constitutional Court struck down the possibility of European fiscal integration—or even forms of shared fiscal responsibility. The day after the publication of the ruling, a former constitutional judge, Paul Kirchhof, expressed his satisfaction: "The European Union is a contract between sovereign states and as such a political space of secondary rank." Fiscal matters, especially, cannot be moved to the European community level or even shared, he said. To him, the meaning of the court's ruling was clear: "There will never be a European state as long as the German constitution has life."[19]

## Germans Taking Distance from Europe

In a matter of hours after the ruling was published, the representatives of the Bavarian Christian Social Union (CSU) party were summoned to draw up a strategy to force a repatriation of crucial EU decisions to Germany, first of all the admission of other countries—especially eastern European candidates. In a closed session of the CSU regional group in Kloster Banz in Bavaria's Oberfranken region, members discussed how to impose strong conditionalities on any decision by the federal government in European matters. Even some representatives of Merkel's own CDU party talked along similar lines, but Merkel moved silently to restrain the Euroskeptics. The SPD—the Social Democratic junior party in the Grand Coalition—closed ranks with the chancellor in a responsible fashion. Some CSU leaders tried again to threaten new constitutional complaints if Germany would not abide by the reservations of the Karlsruhe court, but Merkel could not give in without isolating Germany in the international community. The government decided to obtain the ratification of the Lisbon Treaty by the German Parliament on September 15, twelve days before the German federal elections.

In the 1950s the idea of a "United States of Europe" was supported by 80 percent of the Germans. Between 1953 and 1979 the Institut für Demoskopie in Allensbach seven times polled German citizens on whether they believed that "they would have experienced during their lives that the west European countries would have melded into a United States of Europe." In 1953, 41 percent answered yes while 29 percent answered no. In 1979 the results were reversed: only 31 percent thought that they would ever live in a "USE," while 50 percent thought they would not. By the 1980s the institute no longer asked the question, saying it was not "contemporary" anymore. More recently, the question changed significantly. In May 2008, Germans were asked how they would react if one morning they would hear the news that the European Commission had been cancelled. Twelve percent said they would be happy to hear that news, 43 percent would be sorry, while an upsettingly large share—45 percent—answered they were indifferent or had no opinion. The analysts observe that a feeling of indifference about Europe was sinking into the German population and had already made its way among the younger generation under age thirty. Indeed, 54 percent of younger Germans said they were "not particularly interested" in the European debate, while only 25 percent were "very interested." Most of them seemed to take Europe for granted.[20]

The reason for the growing indifference lies in the identification of the European Union with the idea of peace—die Friedensbotschaft—after the tragedy of the world wars. "Enter a cemetery in any village," said Wolfgang Schuessel, a former Austrian chancellor in 2006, "and look at death caused by the wars and you will know what that means." In the 1980s a majority of Germans wanted a faster run to more integration. In 2004–05 Germans were asked in surveys to define their preference on the admission of new countries into the EU; by a wide majority, they expressed a preference for a smaller, more homogeneous European Union and more "deepening" of the integration among the existing members.

But the nature of the political leadership had been changing even faster than the attitudes of the German population. During his term as chancellor (from 1998 to 2005), Gerhard Schroeder had broken what his predecessor Helmut Kohl had considered a taboo: he had called for a revision of the voting mechanisms inside the European Council so that it would take into account the size of national populations—something that was actually echoed by the new Karlsruhe court ruling. The principle of representation in this case ran against the logic of avoiding a "right to lead" for Germany above any other countries. An old debate on Germany's Sonderweg (special way) was being revived by Schroeder in the tradition of another Social Democratic leader, Kurt Schumacher, who had strived for the reunification of Germany after World War II. The balance for Germany between looking toward its deutsch-deutschen border or its western allies had been clearly identified by "der Alte," Chancellor Konrad Adenauer, who opted for identifying with the rest of Europe. Later, Helmut Kohl had managed to keep the two visions together. In his historical achievement, in 1989, he agreed first on advancing European integration and setting up the monetary union, and shortly after that he succeeded in achieving German reunification— taking both, he said, as two sides of the same coin. But his eventual successor, Angela Merkel, had a different sentiment for Europe relative to Germany. Born in Hamburg, she grew up in East Germany, the product of a German transformation that took precedence over any other global or European development.

## Berlin Turns Away from the Center

"The global crisis will dictate the outcome of the federal election," declared an adamant Angela Merkel. In fact, in September 2009, exactly one year after the implosion of global finance, the German election campaign was molded by a revealing change in the political patterns of popular consensus. It was a reflection—actually a second stage—of a political crisis caused by the fragmentation of the political spectrum once dominated by the two largest popular parties, the center-right Christian Democratic Union and the center-left Social Democratic Party, which had formed the Grand Coalition and governed since 2005. Now, in 2009, at least five parties were contending for dominance as the inevitable consequence of a government that had been formed on the basis of heterogeneous interests. The unlikely coalition formed in 2005 had been a phenomenon that justified an alarm about the "Italianization" of German politics through the formation of inherently unstable coalitions. Then, in 2009, Merkel decided to side instead with the Free Democrats and forge a new alliance more on the right. The results of the election on September 27 indeed marked the birth of the new CDU-FDP coalition. The political character of the new alliance was rather undefined, however, because no precise coalition contract was signed. The really remarkable event, more than the new government, was the end of the Grand Coalition experiment that four years earlier had seemed to herald a new era for European politics, one in which domestic ideological divisions were put aside to cope more efficiently with the new European political divide: not between ideologies of the left and right but between national interests and European ones.

The most recent event at the root of the crisis of German social democracy dated to March 1999 and the striking divorce from the SPD of its charismatic leader Oskar Lafontaine. As former SPD chancellor Helmut Schmidt in the late 1970s could not retain the environmental vote—a spin-off that gave birth to the Green Party—then chancellor Gerhard Schroeder left an opening on the left of the political spectrum through which many voters, disconcerted by the SPD's difficult modernization, moved toward a party, Die Linke, formed by the heirs of communism in East Germany and led by Lafontaine.

The crisis of capitalism since 2008 had made all the large German parties look more like social democratic parties, but this had not benefited the moderate left, as represented by the party carrying that name. Merkel had been swift in replacing the classic leftist themes of "solidarity" and "socialization" with a more ambiguous "common ownership," whereby the state intervenes by helping endangered industries. This was a concept Merkel widely abused in the case of automaker Opel, which received subsidies under a condition protecting only the company's German plants. A threat to social democracy in the wake of a capitalist crisis may sound surprising, but in the 2009 elections the SPD received only 24 percent of the vote, far below the 46 percent that only two decades earlier was considered the goal of each of the two largest parties. In some Laender, the SPD fell below 20 percent of the vote, as the third or even fourth party.[21] If the SPD ceased to be a party that aspires to a majority and if the CDU refused to repeat the experience of the Grand Coalition, then the Social Democrats could be compelled to build new political alliances with the extreme left and with the Greens. An alliance with Die Linke would be a return to the hard left after fifty years, well after the time when former chancellor Willy Brandt had discarded what he called "ideological ballast" of the SPD.[22]

The sense of defeat was hitting the party's goal of solidarity based on the dynamism of social reforms, a more competitive industrial system, strengthening the role of the education system as a social elevator, and even promoting competition among companies as a benefit for the citizens. Since the 1950s, the SPD had grasped the political significance of reforms, of antitrust, and promotion of merit-based policies; giving a "green light to those who are capable" became a party slogan. But the party structure dominated by trade union officials still prevailed. Schroeder aimed to bring to the center of the Social Democratic project a new subject: the skilled and ambitious worker in the context of a knowledge-based society structured according to the forms and rhythms of the market. The centrality of the knowledgeable individual, coupled with rhetoric about innovation and technology, replaced the old focus on social class and strengthened the aspiration of the party to define itself as a new center.

But in a society that had become more complex as a result of the German reunification and globalization, the Social Democratic galaxy was found to rotate too quickly. In the logic of postsocialist "agency of interest" for the new center, as some political scientists were dubbing it, the SPD lost the outlying fringes of consensus. The outcasts searched for a critical anti-capitalist narrative and found it in the person of Lafontaine, a living symbol of those who had fled or been expelled from the SPD paradise.

In some ways, Merkel was facing a similar problem in her new coalition with the Free Democrats. She had hid the idea of such a government from the voters. No ideological campaign—and therefore no clarity—was allowed before the election. In fact, the election campaign had been kept asleep by the two major parties: exciting the minds when a grand coalition is governing means giving a louder voice to the opposition on the extreme fringes of the political spectrum.

The day after her electoral victory, even Merkel was worried about the SPD's setback. The historic reversal of her former coalition partner, now thrown into opposition, could also have consequences for her own party. A wider role for the leftist fringe could force the SPD to forge a new alliance with Die Linke in order to form an effective opposition at the Bundesrat (the chamber of the Laender representatives). The political struggle between left and right would then be more radical, an ideal terrain for populists on both ends of the spectrum, especially for those who were anti-European. Merkel would then have more difficulty managing the reduction of the debt accumulated during the financial crisis, intervening on social spending, and at the same time giving tax cuts to justify the alliance with the Free Democrats. In other words, the end of the Grand Coalition was almost inevitable, because of the crisis of the two major popular parties, but the alternative choice of a polarized majority was very likely to prove to be a severe mistake that would undermine the traditional pro-European line of the two Volksparteien. In a matter of months, this mistake would surface in the sudden turn of the FDP toward a populist, anti-European stance exerting great influence on the behavior of the German government during the Greek crisis.

Furthermore, from a European balance-of-powers perspective, political radicalization in Germany meant the weakening of the country's role as the broker between the left and the right in the European debate. Polarization and ideological confrontation in Europe over the fate of capitalism might have led the right and left in France and Italy to drift away from the political center, just at a moment when the economic crisis seemed to call for more cooperation at the national level to clear the way for more supranational policies. European politics seemed to lose itself in the maze of ideologies even when a consistent European vision of reforming capitalism was required.

As often happens, the internal dynamics of political contention took priority over broader considerations. On the morning after the election, the political focus immediately shifted to a new arena: the scheduled local parliamentary election on May 9, 2010, in North Rhine-Westphalia, the most populous of the German Laender and the one where a pre-election agreement between SPD and Die Linke seemed most likely. It was then very clear that May 2010 would be a defining moment for German politics, but nobody could imagine that it would be even more so for all of the euro area.

# 9

## The Well-Known Secret of the Greek Tragedy

### The Primary Lie

George Papandreou and his Socialist PASOK party had won parliamentary elections just two days earlier, when on October 6, 2009, Bank of Greece governor George Provopoulos reported privately to him that the country's budget deficit was escalating above a shocking 10 percent of GDP. Officially, Greece was still expected to run in 2009 a deficit of only 3.7 percent. In the same hours, the European Commission in Brussels—unaware of the revision in Athens—was presenting its annual report on the euro area, which included the old and much more comforting figure for the Greek deficit. What central banker Provopoulos was envisaging in Athens was the highest deficit ever recorded by any euro area country in two decades, going back to when the euro was still a distant project. Moreover, the new deficit estimate would throw on Greece the suspicion of having committed the biggest fabrication in the history of the European Union.

Europe is conceived as a community of law, "pursuant to the principle of sincere cooperation" among its members and institutions.[1] When the suspicion emerged that Greece could have fudged its fiscal accounts, it was a shock to the fundamental principles of the European Union itself. That Greek governments were prone to some accounting creativity had been common knowledge for years. But the amazing growth of the economy since Greece joined the euro in 2001 had led even the most skeptical observers to believe that after Athens became part of the euro zone and adopted all the required European regulations and procedures, it would change its old habits. On October 6, 2009, that belief appeared delusional.

The day he heard this disturbing news, George Papandreou, son and grand-son of former prime ministers, reminisced. On April 21, 1967, when he was fourteen years old, a gun was put to his temple. Soldiers, under orders from the generals who ruled Greece, had stormed into his family home to arrest his father, Andreas, then a centrist deputy in parliament. The father was hiding on the roof. So, the soldiers took the son onto a terrace and threatened to shoot him until the father showed himself, which he did. Now, forty-two years later, the deficit he inherited was like a different gun pointed at him.

A rumor about the skyrocketing deficit started to leak in Athens, Brussels, and Frankfurt, and still it seemed too unbelievable to be true. After all, between 1996 and 2008 Greece had recorded the highest growth in the euro area. Its average income had grown from 70 percent of the European average to 90 per-cent. Greece was widely considered the greatest single beneficiary of the mon-etary union. How could a government get into so much trouble when its econ-omy was doing so well?

Paradoxically, for a few days the rumors about the Greek debt failed to pro-voke the shockwaves that such an economic bombshell might be expected to unleash—even after the reality behind the rumors was indirectly confirmed to some European governments by sources in Athens. But the real story was that nobody was entirely surprised. Greek policymakers as well as European chancel-leries had just looked elsewhere, considering Greece simply too little and iso-lated to pose an existential problem to the entire euro zone. Papandreou and his finance minister, George Papaconstantinou, were grappling with a reality of which they said they were absolutely not aware. In a private meeting with the German finance minister at the beginning of the year, before the election, Papan-dreou had actually referred to the rumors about the fiscal situation in Greece, say-ing half-jokingly, "I am not sure I really want to win the vote." Papandreou and Papaconstantinou, two respected and mildly-mannered men, probably were not fully informed of the disaster, or maybe they were just hoping that it could not be too bad. Even so, it was undeniable and widely known that the Greek public accounts were unreliable. During the election campaign, while the incumbent prime minister, Kostas Karamanlis, the leader of the conservative Nea Demokra-tia party, had proposed two years of tight fiscal policies—evidently well aware of the fiscal disaster that his government was keeping hidden—Papandreou prom-ised to launch a €2.5 billion stimulus package. "We can't have a recovery if we don't take steps to get the economy moving again," he told his supporters.[2]

But, apart from Karamanlis, who was responsible for the snowballing of pub-lic debt between 2005 and 2009, when his government let the nominal value of public debt increase by 50 percent from €200 billion (100 percent of GDP) to €300 billion, were the socialists really so naive as to ignore the state of Greece? Was Provopoulos not informed? Had the European Central Bank not had a glimpse of the real situation? A primary source reports that already in 2008 two countries, Greece and Ireland, had been warned of their dire fiscal problems in several meetings in the presence of ECB president Jean-Claude Trichet. The European Commission had raised red flags during several meetings of the EU governments. The European finance ministers (in the capacity of ECOFIN) and the ECB had put pressure on Athens, but with bitter disappointment they saw no results. Ireland had implemented several unpopular measures to tackle its problems, first of all by cutting public wages. On the contrary, Karamanlis, obviously for electoral reasons, had never agreed to cave in to European pressure, and public expenditures had dramatically increased in the six months before the vote. A close aid to Papandreou described the events in this way: "In 2004, New Democracy changed the existing law governing the national audit. Previously all military expenditure (reaching up to 5–6 percent of GDP) was assessed in the audit based on when the military equipment was delivered, not when it was ordered. New Democracy changed this to make the deficit under PASOK seem larger. Strangely, the EU Commission accepted this change. But three years later, just before national elections in 2007, New Democracy changed the system back to the old one to make its own deficit seem smaller." Once again Brussels accepted the change as requested by the national government and that was probably the primary source of confusion about Greeks fudging the fiscal deficit.

## Debt as a Mirror of the Society

Papandreou presented his government's policy statement to the parliament on October 9. His priority was clear. "We have reached a point where we either will defeat the deficit, or the deficit will defeat us," Papandreou stressed, reminding Greeks of a phrase his father, as prime minister, had used years before.

It was a moment of despair for Europe, but the climax had yet to come. Nine days later on October 18, the new finance minister, George Papaconstantinou, revealed to his euro zone counterparts that the country's fiscal deficit would reach 12.5 percent of GDP in 2009 (the final revision in late 2010 brought it to 15.8 percent). He attributed the large deviation of fiscal data to three reasons: first, the global recession; second, a set of fiscal problems, including overestimated revenues, excessive public spending, and a collapse of tax collection mechanisms; and third, the lethal one—a conscious misbehavior that he dubbed the "hiding" of significant figures by the former government. In essence, the problem Greece presented for Europe was not only one of the flawed structure of the monetary union: it was the disregard of the principle of honesty and solidarity in European cooperation by a national government and the incapacity of Europe to control the misbehavior. Greece's partners might be able to help solve the country's economic problems, but how—and even why—could they solve a problem of unethical behavior? The EU, as previously noted, rests on the principle of mutual sincere cooperation and is ill-equipped to countenance the possibility of an outright defiance of common rules, in the form of persistent fraudulent accounting and intentionally miscalculated statistics. Did the discovery actually unearth a long-lasting suspicion—unspeakable without being described as racism—about Mediterranean morally lax attitudes? Former German Bundesbank president Hans Tietmeyer used to say that there was a difference among Europeans "due to culture and climate." Was it, in a word, the confirmation that European monetary union had put into the same kettle of fish too many different animals?

Some Mediterranean societies indeed have among their traditions a feudal conception of public life; in other words, power-accountability and transparency sometimes can be less than optimal. Their economic structures often reflect this social characteristic and are matched by the bad quality of public policymaking. Just like Germany, they emerged from fascism or civil wars in the second half of the twentieth century. But while Germany was rebuilt and instructed in the ways of democracy by foreign powers, Greece, Spain, and Portugal experienced dictatorships up until the 1970s.

In Greece the process of building public support for democracy also meant establishing an elaborate system of subsidies and welfare assistance through the political parties. George Papandreou's father, Andreas, for instance, had given pensions to farmers who had never made contributions to support them. The governments established a national health program and a system of education using borrowed money. As the Greek newspaper *Kathimerini* observed, "At last, all those who had been shut out by the right-wing establishment which triumphed in the Civil War in 1946–49—and which was thoroughly discredited by the dictatorship of 1967–74—would get to share in the wealth of the nation. The fact that this new middle class was founded on wealth that the country was not producing meant that the economy broke free from all logic and went into its own orbit."[3]

The overheated competition between left and right, against the backdrop of the human dramas of the civil war and of the military dictatorship, now had the public sector as a bedrock for consensus. People who got jobs in public service were granted lifetime immunity from being fired, and their numbers increased as each successive government took office. The wasteful public sector, in turn, condemned the private sector to inefficiency and lack of competitiveness. As *Kathimerini* commented, "New Democracy [the party of Prime Minister Karamanlis], especially in the 2004–09 period, made the situation worse by doing almost nothing to cut costs and increase revenues, allowing the economy to career out of control."[4] The roots of Greek economic inefficiency were a particularly touchy issue if raised by Germans, who had occupied the country during World War II. The lack of German empathy was a sad discovery for Greeks and particularly so because the European Union was born to reconcile peoples after the tragedy of World War II.[5]

Actually, joining the EU was not, by itself, a guarantee for Greece that its economy and its society would develop more closely along the lines of other EU countries. While joining gave Greece a stronger legal framework and a template for modernization, in some sense the EU also reinforced old vices because it offered a source of huge subsidies that were detached from economic reality. In fact, far from originating internally as a result of its own development, the strong growth recorded in Greece in the previous decade was a direct consequence of its membership, since 1981, in the EU. Greece benefited especially from strong EU support for agriculture, and later from the euro. Interest rates sank rapidly after Greece joined the common currency in 2001, helping the government to rein in the deficit (at least for a while) and keep the public debt relatively stable. Joining the euro zone also gave a strong boost to private investments supported by credit offered by the newly restructured banking system.

Adopting the euro also brought responsibilities. Greece had to rely on its own capacity to reform to make its product and labor markets efficient and flexible enough to compensate for relinquishing the weapon of currency depreciation. Most analysts of Greek affairs accuse unspecified interest groups or powerful lobbies of sabotaging structural reforms: "Structural reforms," writes economist Gikas Hardouvelis, "clashed against a mosaic of different interest groups and against people's lifestyle."[6] When the government led by Costas Simitis tried in 2001 to reform the pension system through just minimal changes, 1 million people—one tenth of the population—took to the streets in protest. Reforms halted rather abruptly and even the new government that took over in March 2004 under Kostas Karamanlis's Nea Demokratia—although enjoying an unusually strong parliamentary majority—refrained from reforming the economy. However, the inflation rate, stoked by closed markets and protected lobbies, was consistently higher than in the rest of the euro area. In September 2007, the political majority behind Nea Demokratia dramatically shrunk, and a second Karamanlis government started an unprecedented increase in public expenditures. Indeed, EU institutions clearly were aware—months before Papandreou received the grim news about the scale of the deficit—that the situation in Greece was getting worse. On March 24, 2009, the European Commission sent a formal notice to the European Council stating that "an excessive deficit existed in Greece." The "Opinion" delivered by the EU Commission reveals the caution of the EU institution in denouncing a violation by one of the governments:

> For 2009, the Commission services' January 2009 interim forecast projects the general government deficit net of one-offs at 4.4 percent of GDP (3.7 percent including one-off revenue) on the basis of a prudent assessment

of the 2009 Budget Law approved by Parliament on December 21. Never-theless, a worse-than-projected budgetary outturn in 2008 should entail, ceteris paribus, a more pronounced negative base effect in 2009. Based on the customary unchanged policy assumption and assuming the discontinu-ation of one-off measures, the 2010 deficit is projected at 4.2 percent of GDP. Therefore, the deficit criterion in the Treaty is not fulfilled.[7]

The European Council endorsed that conclusion a month later, noting that an "excessive deficit" had occurred in both 2007 and 2008. But the pressure of European institutions seemed irrelevant: the Greek fiscal frenzy became a frantic inebriation in the six months before the general elections in October 2008.

## Powerful Lobbies

Greek politicians and European policymakers were not the only ones who were wilfully blind to what was happening in Greece. International investors had remained hypnotized by Greece's growth performance during the preceding ten to fifteen years and had completely lost interest in the underlying imbalances. Actually, Greece was the only country in the euro area having twin large defi-cits—in the public budget and in the balance of payments—revealing an econ-omy that, despite posting a very high level of growth, was not efficient enough to export and to generate the taxable income that would make it possible to service the public debt.

According to many Greek economists, the impressive 4 percent average growth performance of the years between 1994 and 2008 was mainly due to cheap credit, incentives promoting tourism, EU structural funds, a short-term boost from the 2004 Olympic Games and related Athens-area infrastructure, and extensive pub-lic borrowing. None of these increased the efficiency of the economy but instead boosted easier profits for powerful lobbies in a still-underdeveloped industrial landscape. Globalization had led to a boom in shipping, once among the stron-gest industries in Greece, but shipping had mostly relocated to London, where it had its corporate bases and followed the local jurisdiction and tax regime. A common saying among Greek merchant ship owners is that "one should not own even a kiosk (periptero) in Greece." Powerful lobbies were at work in the country resisting its modernization. While trying to fix the tax collection system, Papan-dreou denounced the activities of some Greek banks in the system of tax evasion and mentioned a pan-Balkan fuel-smuggling operation as an example of elusive practices allegedly costing Greece an estimated €3bn annually. In the past, lobbies directly influenced the government, which was sheltered from the check of the parliament. In Greece, two other balancing powers, the judiciary and the media, are often dismissed as hampered or plagued by political influences. According to economists Theodore Pelagidis and Michael Mitsoupoulos:

The slow and malleable proceedings of the judiciary ensure that any unlawful actions usually are not persecuted efficiently. This completes the design of a system in which reform-minded politicians, who threaten the status quo, are easily removed from the political scene. Those politicians who cooperate with the interest groups are rewarded not only with long-lasting political careers, but also with immunity from prosecution against almost any unlawful acts they may engage in, even if such acts are unrelated to their office and if their immunity violated basic human rights.[8]

The result is the handover of unchecked mandates to the winners of elections. Critical observers note, for instance, that not all court decisions are published and offered to the public's scrutiny, together with the fact that the minutes of the committees of the parliament are also unpublished. When obscurity becomes a state of nature for politicians, they can be pretty confident that in the rare case when anybody reports that they broke the law, no punishment or remedy will be enforced in an effective way. That attitude was extended to Greece's reporting to the European Union.

The pervasiveness of the collusive mentality is such that transparency, when it occurs, falls on hostile ground even among sectors of the general public. Everyone participates, more or less willingly, in the shadow economy, sometimes simply because it is difficult or even impossible to comply with the laws. The global anti-corruption organization Transparency International, in its 2010 report on perceived corruption, placed Greece at the bottom among all EU member nations.[9] Transparency International calculated that the average Greek family pays an "average of 1,450 euros [US $1,850] in bribes per family a year."[10]

When the EU reviewed Greek malpractices in the use of EU funds, the discoveries were again unpleasant. The European Anti-Fraud Office (OLAF) presented an internal report documenting that between 2000 and 2006, €925 million had been improperly used in 1,073 cases—some cases involved agricultural subsidy malpractice, others were simply false submissions. The EU asked to be refunded for €955 million in the period 1996–2006 because of malpractices in agricultural subsidies or simply false submissions.[11] EU agricultural subsidies were especially prone to corruption in Greece. For example, farmers would count herds twice in order to receive double subsidies from the EU. Farmers also could receive up to four times the correct amount of aid by giving false statements on the size of their land—statements that were impossible to verify since Greece has almost no land registers. The revenue items in the state budget had been hidden in 385 "off-budget funds." A mix of nationalistic rhetoric and lobbying had bloated military expenditure, especially in the first half of the decade; this often benefited French and German arms industries. In 2007, for example, Athens concluded an agreement with France for the delivery of six multipurpose frigates at a cost of €2.5 billion. The order was suspended when the Greek debt crisis broke in 2009, but Sarkozy engaged personally to "convince" the ailing Greek government to maintain the commitment. Chancellor Merkel did the same when Greek payment for expensive German submarines appeared uncertain.

## A Justification for the Break-Up of the Euro

Anecdotes on Greek disrespect for rules are far from unique in Europe. Especially in parts of the south and the east, but even the core countries report a high share of underground economy equivalent on average to one-sixth of GDP. The strong characteristics of Mediterranean societies make it easy for anyone wanting to resort to Max Weber's kind of cultural distinctions. In *The Protestant Ethic and the Spirit of Capitalism,* Weber put forward the thesis that the Calvinist ethic determined the pronounced development of capitalism in some countries vis-à-vis the Catholic societies. Notoriously, he focused on the shift of Europe's economic center after the Reformation away from Catholic countries such as Italy, France and Spain, and toward Protestant countries such as the Netherlands, England, Scotland, and Germany.[12] Such religiously inspired simplifications, including a metaphor comparing northern ants and southern crickets, did not fit properly with Europe's current difficulties. After all, England and Ireland were among the countries most exposed to indiscipline and financial misbehavior, while German, Dutch, and French banks had originated and provided the excess capital that allowed Greece and Spain to live beyond their means. But in reality, in the context of less regulated societies, the notion of individual responsibility, so crucial for the Protestant ethic, is strongly diminished. On the one hand, this is because the normative framework is weak and always subject to an interpretation that does not necessarily lead to a punishment when one breaks the rules. On the other hand, the arbitrariness of power in such a society means the state is wholly responsible for putting things in order. The marketplace no longer counterbalances political power; the state gives little autonomy to the individual citizen who is also exposed to the abuses of powerful special interests. In fact, the detachment of the individual from the common good was accentuated by the peculiarity of the Greek fiscal system, whereby the average family pays no income tax, and only a very small proportion of the population pays the vast majority of income taxes. Since the average voter is not a taxpayer, politicians have an incentive to misuse tax funds, especially in the above-mentioned context of tolerance of illegal behavior. The political cost of running a higher debt is low because the number of voters who theoretically benefit from public expenditures is higher than the number of voters bearing the cost of it.

Technically the sustainability of public debt is a concept that relates to assumptions about the future—namely the intertemporal budget constraint—that must be grounded on consistency in the past and in the present.

Unfortunately, Greece historically had a bad fiscal record and had already been "bailed out"' by the European Community in December 1985 when it obtained a loan of 1.75 billion ECU (a predecessor to the euro) under the balance-of-payments assistance facility.[13]

## Mistrust: The Ultimate Reason to Be Divided

Greece's longstanding problems illustrated a general unwillingness by the EU to confront wrong political decisions, to double-check information and statistics, and to address in a timely manner any dilemmas arising from the insufficient economic convergence. The power of the EU Commission in this regard was limited by the EU Council, that is, by the heads of governments. As game theorists know very well, in the case of international coordination, the transparent and massive exchange of information is a potential substitute for political intervention or interference. When information is not only missing but falsified, it can lead to extreme solutions: either the delegation of political sovereignty of the country to the partners, or dissolution of the institutionalized cooperation. The prospect of a break-up of the euro area, hitherto implausible in both political and economic terms, suddenly received an ethical and juridical legitimacy.

The reliability of Greek government deficit and debt statistics has been the subject of continuous and unique attention for several years by European institutions. In 2004 Eurostat produced a comprehensive report on the revision of the Greek government deficit and debt figures, showing how the Greek statistical authorities had misreported figures on deficit and debt in the years between 1997 and 2003. And subsequently, Eurostat, on five occasions, has expressed reservations on the Greek data in its biannual press release on deficit and debt data.

Almost all countries, including France and Benelux, showed levels of debt higher than the sum of the deficits. In a January 2010 analysis of the quality of Greek statistics of previous years, the European Commission mentioned a number of disconcerting findings, notably severe irregularities in Greece's "excessive deficit procedure" (EDP) notifications of April and October 2009.[14] A shocking analysis by Gustavo Piga, an Italian economist, revealed similarities in several countries—Greece, Portugal, and Italy, among others—in order to demonstrate compliance with the 3.0 percent annual fiscal deficit limit required by the Growth and Stability Pact for countries in the euro zone. According to Piga, banks like Goldman Sachs, Deutsche Bank, Lehman Brothers, and Morgan Stanley advised some euro area governments on the best methods to hide or postpone fiscal deficits. An interesting method, used by both Italy and Greece, was to issue government bonds denominated in low-interest currencies, yen for instance, but bearing a higher-than-usual yield in favor of the investment bank, which would compensate the government for the differential through a higher payment of the bond price. In this way, a government could post an increase in special incomes in the current year—when it needed to respect the deficit criteria—at the cost of higher interest expenditures in future years (when the politicians in charge might no longer be in power). This was not a story just from the past. As the *New York Times* revealed, at the end of October 2009 a team led by Goldman Sachs's president, Gary D. Cohn, offered the Greek government a financing instrument that would have pushed debt from Greece's health care system far into the future. In the deal, Athens would have been burdened by huge back-payments to Goldman in 2019.[15] In dozens of deals across the continent, banks provided cash upfront in return for government payments in the future, with those liabilities left off the books. Greece, for example, traded away the rights to airport fees and lottery proceeds for years to come. The news was that this time Athens did not pursue the Goldman proposal.

## Yes, a Model for Europe

The first of what would become several showdowns over Greece occurred in Luxembourg at the Eurogroup meeting on October 18. On Monday evening, the new Greek finance minister Papaconstantinou briefed the Eurogroup meeting about developments in the Greek economy. The minister noted a significant worsening in many sectors, mostly an expected shrinking of the GDP by 1.5 percent in the current year, a sharp 20 percent decrease in investments, a 15 percent decline in tourism, and a 20 percent drop in shipping revenue. Papaconstantinou also told his euro zone counterparts that the country's fiscal deficit would reach 12.5 percent of GDP. He attributed the large deviation from previous estimates to the negative economic picture, the overestimation of fiscal revenues, excessive public spending, and a collapse of tax collection mechanisms, and, finally, made a remark that soon became famous about what he called the "hiding" of significant figures.[16] On behalf of the Greek government, he committed to submit an updated three-year stability and growth program to Brussels in January.

The EU partners' reaction was of concern bordering on shock. After Papaconstantinou's presentation on the country's fiscal problems, Eurogroup chairman Jean-Claude Juncker, with a characteristically dry sense of humor, commented, "I have to say that I am very impressed by the difference between the old and the new figures." He added, "It happens occasionally, but if it happens again we risk putting all Eurostat data at risk of credibility."

"We want to know what has happened and why it has happened," the EU's economy commissioner, Joaquin Almunia, said. "Serious discrepancies will require an open and deep investigation."

Papaconstantinou presented to his colleagues a long-term program of economic restructuring and deficit cutting in a period of three to four years. However, Athens resisted pressures by the European partners to enact a radical and immediate fiscal correction. The government was still trying to buy time and, in doing so, probably made the crisis much worse than it might have been. In the following days, Athens published a final budget draft showing the long-term public debt rising to 121 percent of GDP in 2010, from 113.4 percent in 2009. EU forecasts for Greece in 2010 were worse, with the annual deficit at 12.2 percent and the public debt rising to 124.9 percent of GDP. The 2010 draft budget was adopted by the Greek government on November 5, 2009, setting a deficit target of 9.4 percent of GDP. "Under a no-policy-change assumption, the European Commission projects the government deficit to continue to exceed 12 percent of GDP in both 2010 and 2011."[17]

That first decision of the Greek government to proceed more cautiously than was asked for by the partners was to become a ballast in the bailout discussions of the coming months. The probably inevitable stream of continuous revisions of the statistics, month by month, produced a loss of trust in the reliability of Athens. When George Papandreou announced on October 23, 2009, to his PASOK party friends that Greece was going to become a model country for Europe, he probably could not imagine how close he was to reality.[18]

## The Grand Bargain Splinters on Fiscal Indiscipline

An underlying political disagreement made the 2009 revelations of Greece's debt problems enormously dangerous for the equilibrium within the euro area: A rift on fiscal policy had been building up for months between France, Spain, Italy, Portugal, and Greece on the one side, and Germany, Finland, Austria, and the Netherlands on the other.[19] In October 2009, Paris dropped a bombshell when it said it no longer aimed to reduce the French budget deficit to under 3 percent of GDP by 2012. Even on optimistic growth assumptions, France seemed destined not to hit the target until 2015 at the earliest, de facto giving up policy coordination within the euro zone. As we have seen in Chapter 7, the reduction of fiscal deficits was a crucial component of the Grand Bargain with the ECB. In effect, the French deliberately broke with the Grand Bargain and, not incidentally in the same month, the ECB decided to stop providing the liquidity at very low interest rates that had boosted the purchase of the euro area government bonds by the banks.

The French decision came as a proof of divergent paths within the euro area, because Germany, by contrast, had just committed itself to a more virtuous path. Berlin had changed its constitution so that the federal deficit in future years could not exceed 0.35 percent of GDP over the economic cycle.

Paris expected its overall public deficit to reach 8.2 percent of GDP in 2009, rising to 8.5 percent in 2010. Germany expected its deficit to swell from 3.7 percent of GDP in 2009 to 6 percent in 2010. Juncker, from Luxembourg and chairman of the European finance ministers, implicitly going back to the memory of France and Germany conspiring to evade the Stability and Growth

Pact's 3 percent deficit limit in 2003, commented during the October 18 Euro-group meeting: "Smaller member states would have great difficulty in explaining to their citizens why spending cuts and tax rises were needed to bring deficits down, if their bigger neighbors did not take similar action." Fiscal coordination was in shambles.[20]

The final blow came in mid-October. Exactly when the Greek drama was unfolding, Germany was actually preparing an incredible flouting of fiscal rectitude and transparency. During the new government's coalition talks, an idea was floated that would have involved fudging the constitutional deficit limits that Berlin had just proposed. The concept would be offered as a way the rest of Europe could curb the fiscal threat resulting from the financial crisis. The problem for Merkel and her allies was that although the fiscal ceiling of 0.35 percent of GDP for the federal government structural deficit was not to come into force until 2016, reaching that target meant that deficits must start coming down as soon as 2011. That requirement was too tight for Merkel's CDU and her coalition partner the FDP, who together won the September elections on promises of tax cuts. The new coalition invented a new accounting trick: The deficit law seemed to ignore any borrowing before 2011; a special fund could borrow the money today, then fill the gap between revenues and spending after the rules came into effect. It was nothing more than a "shadow budget" that would open the floodgates to any kind of abuse and imitation. What was really paradoxical was that a majority of the German population was against the tax cuts and favored budget restraint.[21] The newly celebrated wedding between Merkel's Christian Democrats and the Free Democrats (Liberals) actually heralded problems for the rest of Europe.

# 10

## Let Greece Default?

### Mistrust in a Political Solution

On January 12, 2010, the European Commission confirmed that Athens had falsified its statistics and that "severe irregularities" had been detected in Greece's accounting of its public deficit. Chancellor Merkel declared instantly that Greece's mounting deficit risked hurting the euro, which was going to face a "very difficult phase" in the coming years. The comment, posted on the German government website, was soon removed. Heated sentiments were breeding on the heels of the Greek shock. Sometimes they translated into public statements made by the highest political representatives of single countries, thus immediately causing extreme reactions in the markets.[1] Three days later Merkel had to backtrack, praising the "Herculean effort" of the Greek government in taming the budget deficit, but there was no mistaking the real feelings beneath the surface.

The beginning of 2010 marked a crucial twist in the whole crisis. The size of the Greek economy was such that a debt restructuring at that point should not have been traumatic for the rest of the euro area. Unfortunately, the financial implications were much more sizable than the purely economic one. Losses of about €100 billion by banks in France and Germany—caused by a potential Greek default and the possible collapse of Greek banks—were not then endurable. From that perspective, it was necessary to restructure the Greek debt at a future time, after the European banks had gained solidity. Or alternatively, Greece and other debt-ridden countries could be bailed out in some manner. The combined public debts of Greece, Portugal, and Ireland, the weakest links in the euro chain, were less than €700 billion—representing roughly 7 percent of total euro zone GDP and less than 9 percent of its average public debt. To deal with the problems caused by their bankers, national governments had already silently increased their debts by much more, on average by 20 percent of GDP, or about three times the total amount of the debt of the peripheral nations. The Greek government by itself owed $435 billion, less than Lehman's $613 billion balance sheet before its failure. Helping Greece, Portugal, and Ireland was therefore a feasible task for the euro area as a whole. But this would have required strong political will to advance the European integration at a time of crisis.

Several reasons account for why political will was lacking: mistrust first of all, then the conflicts among the leaders in earlier stages of the crisis, and finally, but most important, the uncertainty about countries much larger than Greece, such as Italy. But as far as Germany was concerned, other reasons of an ethical, juridical, and cultural nature also came into play. In principle the bailout problem was very simple: Greece had been hit by the international crisis—it could spread contagion to all of Europe—therefore Europeans must help Greece. But was the premise of this syllogism correct? Was the international context the real reason why Greece was rotten? Aristotle defined proton pseudos as the flawed premise that mars a syllogism and produces the wrong conclusion. And the European Commission had certified the false premise when it neither demanded nor received the truth from Greece. The answer was not that of absorbing someone else's debts. "You will not cure an alcoholic with alcohol," German finance minister Peer Steinbrück said, as a modern Martin Luther denouncing the sale of indulgences. Beyond ethics, juridical boundaries were a strong constraint. Jürgen Stark, a German member of the European Central Bank board, had stated these boundaries bluntly on January 7: "Greece is in a very difficult situation. Not just the deficit is at very high levels, but the country has also suffered a serious loss of competitiveness. These problems are not related to the global crisis, but were created in-house. And they must be addressed with appropriate economic measures in the interests of Greek citizens and respecting the responsibilities that the government has toward the euro and its partners. . . . The markets are deluding themselves if they think that at some point the other Member States will put their hands in their pockets to save Greece."[2]

Later in January 2010 Moody's warned that the Greek economy faced a "slow death" from deteriorating finances. Credit default swaps on Greek debt rose 49 basis points to 328 basis points, the biggest one-day rise ever. Angela Merkel, a physicist by education, found herself confronting a financial kind of risk she was not acquainted with. Her approach to politics has always been described as scientific: seeking hard evidence for a solution and then coldly experimenting with ways to reach it. Max Weber described at length the incompatibility between political attitudes and those of a scientist. Acting rationally is different from scientific analysis because you need at the same time a theory of causation and a theory of risk. Politicians need to be able—more than scientists—to take risks in their decisions. Merkel belonged to a different category in shunning risks or not acknowledging them.

## Trichet's Complete Opposition to a Default

The EU institutions and the leaders of the euro area repeatedly discussed the options at hand for Greece at the beginning of January. There were essentially two alternative positions. The first was represented by ECB president Jean-Claude Trichet's complete opposition to any traumatic intervention in the debt problems of the euro area. The second was offered primarily by the experts of the International Monetary Fund, who were much more sceptical about the possibility for Greece to recover without a cut in its debt.

When the idea of Greece's leaving or being pushed out of the euro was put to Trichet at a press conference in Frankfurt on January 14, he declined to comment on what he described as "absurd hypotheses." Still, behind the scenes Trichet had to struggle to suffocate the idea of a default, which was taking hold at the Chancellery in Berlin. Trichet observed that the risk of pressuring Athens to default was incalculable. No developed economy had ever defaulted since 1948. Such an event in the euro zone would undermine the credibility of the monetary union and was likely to affect other countries once their fiscal positions appeared to be less than solid. Confidential econometric tests conducted at the ECB confirmed Trichet's fears. But they were only statistical tests, simulations based on the recent experience of volatility dynamics in the Lehman crisis and based on contagion from the problems with large banks. These tests established only a thin empirical basis for Trichet's towering rhetoric defending the integrity of the European Monetary Union. His fears of contagion effects throughout the euro area were justified by one important element frequently overlooked by non-European economists: the central role of government debt securities in the functioning of the European banking system, which held huge amounts of those assets and used them as guarantees for their funding. Putting in doubt the entire asset class of sovereign securities, even of only one country of the euro area, would have endangered the entire European financial system. The nature of contagion thus became the most important analytical problem in the course of the crisis. The ECB was dreading the direct effect of contagion provoked by a Greek default, while other economists feared the opposite: not letting Greece restructure its debt and not helping it to sort the fiscal problem would create a lengthy phase of uncertainty that might extend to other countries.

The ECB also rejected the pessimistic assessment of the Greek economy that the International Monetary Fund delivered to European policymakers. Greece had been able to grow at 4 percent on average in the past decade. Despite how bad the fiscal situation was, it was simply necessary for Greece to recover the past rhythm of economic growth and abandon bad policy choices that had led to the current problems. The figures provided by the Greek government also showed that revenues from the taxation of personal income amounted to only 9 percent of the national income, including the "black," or informal, economy. It was sufficient to double that share—to a level that would still be lower than the European average—to shore up the state's budget forever. Moreover, if over the preceding ten years Greek public sector wages had only gone up at the same pace as inflation, and public employment had not increased—hardly impossible measures—the Greek budget deficit to GDP ratio in 2010 would have been around 4 percentage points lower and the debt to GDP ratio about 30 percent lower. Finally, Greece had an estimated amount of €300 billion in sellable public ownership, fungible real estate, or commercial enterprises. It would have been enough to privatize one-third of those enterprises to bring the public debt in line with the average of the other euro area countries.

Unfortunately, the economic analysis depended on the kind of policy that had to be implemented, and because of the lack of available financial support for Greece from the EU countries, the ECB had to stick with the so-called Frankfurt-consensus, that is, economic restructuring through fiscal austerity. A lower fiscal deficit would not kill economic growth and would not create a deflation that would increase, rather than decrease, Greece's debt-to-GDP ratio. This adoption of the Frankfurt consensus was a strategy that, in the course of the crisis, proved to be wrong.

## Greece Is Different

There were two fundamental explanations for the mistakes in the assessment of the prospects for Greece. The first was the prevalence of conventional economic policy analysis. The second was a misplaced analogy with the successful experience in Eastern Europe.

Trichet's reading of the internal problems of the countries in the euro area was probably forged by his experiences in the 1980s and in the first half of the 1990s when the degree of openness of the European economy was increasing and fiscal austerity, coupled with structural reforms, could be counterintuitively expansionary in a context of rapidly declining interest rates. As was the case in other countries during the previous two decades, the main cause of Greek uncompetitiveness was identified in the level of labor costs, and a classic way to influence it was by cutting the wages of public employees. By adjusting internal prices, fiscal austerity and wage deflation would be beneficial to the private sector, thus restoring the competitiveness of the whole economy, improving the balance of payments and, eventually, rebalancing the public accounts. More recently, the analysis of competitiveness has become much more articulated and focused on specific characteristics of the local markets or on the efficiency of the micro-structure of single sectors. In Greece, for instance, problems as important as the excessive labor costs actually resulted from the inefficiency of tax collection and of the public administration. The fact that the national system of transportation was hostage to powerful interest groups, and the vast corruption in public procurement, had greater impacts on the potential growth than did labor costs.

In playing a policy role that was unconventional for the ECB, Trichet needed the bank's analysis to be as simple as possible so it could be easily communicated to the policymakers. The ECB had elaborated, for instance, a system of simple indicators of competitiveness, called the "traffic lights," that were easy to read but often sent very controversial—and sometimes plain wrong—policy suggestions. That happened when Trichet charged a relatively young German official, who had little experience in international missions, with the task of designing the strategy for Greece and other ailing countries. The official used a rather limited set of analyses based on the prevailing Bundesbank view that austerity does not depress an economy—along the lines of the so-called "non-Keynesian" effects of fiscal policy that the ECB also applied rather indiscriminately. The ECB officials in charge for Greece seemed not to take into account the fact that the Greek economy was more closed than all the others in the euro area, and that fiscal contraction has stronger effects in a closed economy than in a relatively open one. Taking what sometimes seemed to be an ideological standpoint, the ECB task force on Greece rebuffed the doubts raised by other economists on the self-defeating strategy of enforcing fiscal austerity and prepared for conflicts with the other international institutions involved in the mission.

The other reason for the misunderstanding by European officials of the Greek situation was the analogy with eastern Europe's successful experience in the previous year. Most of the new European countries had managed to recover surprisingly well from the deepest recession since the communist era. Most of them had not touched their exchange rates (which were pegged to the euro), and therefore their monetary policies were exactly like those of a euro area country. They managed to find a sounder path to renewed growth through a painful but fast adjustment. Wages and prices were reduced by up to 20 percent in one year. European officials thought that all Greece had to do was to follow the same policies.

The case of Latvia, in particular, had been the crucial test for the credibility of the European institutions relative to the IMF. In the last quarter of 2008 Latvia's GDP contracted by 10.5 percent, and in February 2009 the government asked the IMF and the European Union for an emergency bailout loan of €7.5 billion. Just like in Greece, Latvian wages were out of line with productivity, and inflation was above 10 percent, so the IMF wanted to make the loan conditional to the devaluation of the currency (the Lat), breaking its peg with the euro. The analyses of the investment banks agreed with the IMF. However, the ECB, the European Commission, and the EU member states were fiercely opposed to the IMF currency policy. The EU institutions were worried that a devaluation would immediately trigger contagion in Lithuania, Estonia, and in the other non-euro European countries, killing their plans to join the euro in the near future and destabilizing the economy of the area and beyond (Sweden and Austria would be drawn in, for example). Even the Latvian government did not want to devalue its currency, knowing how difficult it would be to repay its external debts denominated in euro or dollars.

In the end, the IMF gave in to the conditions of EU commissioner Joaquin Almunia, but observed publicly that it did so only because the EU was the main contributor. The Latvian government started in early 2009 to lower prices and wages by at least 10 percent (20 percent for public employees) in a context of recession and severe unemployment. In a relatively short time the Latvian economy started to export. Growth returned at the beginning of 2010, and internal and external debts declined. The European policies were successful and safeguarded the attractiveness of the euro for the eastern countries. The ECB position on Greece in 2010, therefore, had to be considered as backed by political consensus in the EU and not as a fixation of the central bankers.

Nevertheless, there was a substantial difference in the case of Greece that the ECB failed to point out. The eastern European countries could compensate for the domestic deflation through an increase in external demand. Their economies were extremely well integrated into the western European supply chains; the banking systems were about 70 percent in the hands of foreign banks, and foreign direct investments were a stronger component of demand than domestic investments. Greece was in a completely different situation. For Greek industry in general, 85 percent of profits came from domestic sales, so once the domestic demand was cut through lower wages, expected profits would decline by roughly the same amount. Investments would also be suspended and unemployment worsened, thus starting a deflationary spiral. The ECB insisted that a deflationary adjustment was necessary because the Greek trade deficit had to be brought down, and once the economy was in balance it would find a more solid bedrock for growth. In the high-level meetings in Europe, Trichet could produce European data that were not available to anybody else, so he was able to win his argument and convince most of the heads of government to agree with him in ruling out the possibility of default by any euro area country. The underestimation of Greece's problems was partly due to characteristics of the economy that macrostatistics could hardly reveal, first of all that an inefficient public administration could sabotage the implementation of even the best reform plans. But the main flaw was that the success of the austerity cure depended on the aid provided by the European partners in the form of loans at an affordable cost, that is, at interest rates much lower than those priced by the market. This side of the cure was far from settled.

## Panicking on 2 percent of the EU GDP

Since the beginning of 2010, Prime Minister George Papandreou had to fight off speculation that Greece could be forced out of the euro zone or to seek assistance from the International Monetary Fund to rescue its battered economy. These two hypotheses became a regular matter of contention in the public debate over international economics. The possibility of IMF involvement became increasingly appealing in Washington. The IMF had vast experience in dealing with countries in fiscal distress, especially in Latin America during the 1990s. But of late the IMF had to step in to help Europe, too, and was currently overseeing the recovery programs of three new EU member states: Hungary, Latvia, and Romania. The ECB and the Brussels institutions considered an IMF intervention as an acknowledgment of failure for the political project of the euro zone. However, the option found some support within the broader EU, especially among non–euro area member states, including the United Kingdom and Sweden, where concerns about the credibility of the euro were less important. A March 2010 paper from the Bruegel think tank took most observers by surprise in siding with an IMF intervention:

> Would it be credible for the Commission to monitor progress, which may imply stopping aid payment until corrective action by Greece? The Commission has the technical competence, but it may find it difficult to balance external financing and stability pact requirements against one another. . . . How would the EU react to anger in the streets of Athens? Would all euro zone countries stay on the same line? Or should some be excluded from the rescue because they may be candidates for future operations? Furthermore would the budgetary costs be bearable if similar operations were needed in other larger countries, a risk that would probably increase with the stand-alone solution?[3]

One could easily conclude that Europe was panicking over a country worth only 2 percent of its total GDP, and that the core problem was political rather than fiscal. Although the European Council had called for policy coordination, nobody was ready to invest political credibility in a bailout that would change permanently the interdependency of political decisions by member states.

Since the beginning of 2009, in an environment plagued with fear and protest, government ministers in Athens had blamed market speculators and attacked the credit rating agencies for misinterpreting the actions of the new government and for hurting Greece, seemingly deliberately. Although the frustration in Athens was understandable, this was not the kind of rhetoric that would have helped

Greece in that moment. The euro started to fall day after day to the lowest levels against the dollar in more than four months after Moody's said on January 13 that the success of the Greek budget plan "cannot be taken for granted" and that Athens as well as Lisbon were facing "slow death."[4] After EU monetary affairs commissioner Joaquin Almunia told the first ECOFIN meeting of the year that "the situation in Greece is having effects on other countries," Spain, Italy, and France started discussing among them a proposal for extending loans to Greece.[5] Germany and the Netherlands opposed rewarding Greece's bad behavior, however, and killed the proposal in the bud.

The hypothesis of Greece being banished from the euro started to spread as a simple answer to a much-too-complicated question. The transposition of the problem from Greece to the whole euro area was implicit in the words of Bank of Greece governor George Provopoulos on January 22: "The problems faced by the Greek economy are extremely serious. However, the key question is whether it will be easier to solve them from inside or outside the euro zone. My answer is that it will be unequivocally easier to solve these problems from within the euro area."[6] A confidential presentation prepared by the economists of the EU Commission for the finance ministers of the euro group observed that the difference in competitiveness of member countries and the resulting imbalances "are a cause for serious concern for the euro zone as a whole." The presentation added that divergent developments "weaken the confidence in the euro and endanger the integrity of the monetary union." Until that point, EU leaders had consistently refused to take seriously the possibility of a break-up of the euro area, both in public and in private.

## The New German Consensus

The role of German public opinion proved to be the crucial element in the political aspect of the European crisis. It is not difficult to understand that, in rational terms, bailing out Greece would have been beneficial to German citizens. The absolute cost was limited but the advantages would be huge: benefiting German banks (which held large amounts of Greek debt), avoiding institutional uncertainty at the European level, preventing contagion spreading not only to peripheral countries in the euro area but to Eastern European countries as well, and, most important, keeping the euro stable.

Nevertheless, polls showed that 67 percent of German citizens strongly opposed bailing out Greece.[7] Was there a specific anti-Europe feeling in this massive response? Probably not, as shown by the fact that the share of population calling for a return to the deutsche mark was actually declining. The share that opposed helping Greece was exactly the same share that had opposed bailing out automaker Opel in 2009 and the Karstadt and Hertie department stores.

The apparent change of attitude among Germans toward "conventional solidarity" must not be misinterpreted. Although younger voters are more inclined to individualism, the average German remains in favor of the Sozialmarktwirtschaft and of "efficient solidarity"—mistrusting public bloated expenditure while favoring state intervention with social inclusiveness. A new consensus had been molded by the recent successful experience with structural reforms concerning both a greater flexibility in the labor market and the dynamism in the ownership of industrial firms, derived from the breakup ten years earlier of the protective old habit of cross-shareholding in German capitalism.

Germany's export-oriented model has a greater attraction than is often recognized. Critics of German dependency on the domestic demand of neighboring European countries underrate the transformation derived from the growth of trade on a global scale. The previous ten years had shown that in the new global market, even small comparative advantages were producing much greater increases of export volumes than in the past, thanks to the dimensions of the new emergent markets.

What was happening in Europe—as blatantly demonstrated by the divergence between Greece and Germany—were some of the results of introducing a common currency during a period defined by globalization and trade expansion. Trade flows are directly affected by what economists call the export participation effect: Some firms, formerly unable to export, become active in international markets once their products and services can be paid for with a common, stable currency. Exporters start to serve a larger number of foreign countries and to sell a larger number of products, and more of each product, in foreign markets. Effects on prices are also significant: Through the transaction cost effect, a fall in the costs associated with exporting activities directly translates into lower export prices. Arbitrage opportunities for customers force firms to reduce their markups and limit their ability to extract value by quoting different prices in different countries. All in all, tougher competition enhances a process of selection and restructuring among firms.

If one takes into consideration all these consequences from the increased role of exports, one should reconsider the conventional hypothesis that adoption of the common currency would result in the greatest restructuring of firms in laggard countries—where it was most needed and where the old habit of devaluing currencies to boost exports had to be abandoned. Quite the opposite had been true: the past experience of countries in international competition had paid well in adapting to the global markets. Germany, for example, had spent seven years after its 1992–93 revaluation of the deutsche mark within the ERM (the Exchange Rate Mechanism that prepared the Euro) in the process of recovering competitiveness. German firms in the 1990s moved away from the very difficult internal economic environment and started looking for market shares abroad. In 1991 the sum of import and export relative to the GDP in Germany was 52 percent, lower than in France or Italy. By 2008, the same sum of import and export amounted to 90 percent of Germany's GDP, the highest of all G-7 countries, 50 percent higher than in France or Italy, and three times higher than in the United States.

What had become evident to German citizens was that structural reforms, which increased productivity, were more than proportionally rewarded by increased exports. The resulting growth benefited employment and government revenues, thus creating room for social expenditures and leading to a consensus in public opinion. It was a virtuous circle, whereby the positive attitude of citizens toward structural reforms encouraged more productivity enhancements by German firms and produced more income for everybody. The focus on efficiency and global connections also had political implications that showed clearly in the exporting nations. In Italy, the north-south fault lines grew wider, and there was less tolerance in the more advanced northeastern regions for subsidizing the relatively backward southern regions. Regional distances also grew markedly within Belgium and the Netherlands. In Germany, social solidarity was already strained by the east-west divide. However, the new awareness of the global context led Germans to make only moderate requests for salary increase, thus deferring the benefits of growth. Firms and public opinion even opposed tax cuts proposed by Merkel's new governing coalition. Under this "New Consensus" in German society, there was no cultural room for understanding the Greeks, who were seen as self-indulgent and irresponsible.

For Germans, the priority of competitiveness reached unprecedented levels. The wage agreement for the metallurgical sector, reached on February 18, 2010, provided for an annual medium nominal wage increase of 1.4 percent and introduced groundbreaking elements in terms of giving employers more flexibility to use part-time rather than full-time workers. In some sectors of low value-added services, employers did not even grant the agreed-upon very low wage increases to the 90 percent of workers who did not belong to a trade union. A ruling by the Federal Labor Court encouraged the fragmentation of larger unions in the public sector, while a reform of job-placement centers opened the way to new kinds of flexible employment. Even the latest legislation on unemployment subsidies, while strengthening the system, emphasized the fight against abuses by those who preferred to obtain the subsidies rather than accepting a new job.[8]

If salary increases were excessive relative to productivity in Greece and some other euro zone countries, between 2005 and 2009 Germany had seen wages increase less than productivity. German nominal wages even decreased in 2009, for the first time in the history of the Bundesrepublik. The deficit in the balance of payments would force countries like Greece into many years of slow growth of domestic demand and also affected imports from Germany. But Germany's overall trade is so large that it cannot be seriously impaired by problems in countries like Greece, Ireland, or even Spain. The fastest-growing share of trade now derives from non-European markets. The new emerging markets—China, India, Russia, and Brazil—trade with Germany six times more in volume than they do with France or Italy and twenty times more than they do with Spain.

## The Appearance of a Two-Speed Euro Area

The sudden drama of the Greek crisis shed new light on the external deficits of the euro zone countries. A country's current account balance plays an important role in assessing the fiscal position because it indicates whether the government has to rely on foreign investors to fund its deficit.[9] If the sustainability of public debt does not hang primarily on the decisions of external investors, the state can, up to a certain level, increase taxes on the private sector to fund an unexpected deficit. But if financing the deficit depends on the availability of foreign capital, then to lure those investors it may be necessary to raise interest rates, possibly even to unsustainable levels.

A current account deficit is also a simple indicator of a lack of competitiveness of the economy. In order to reverse such a deficit, it may be necessary to begin a long process of structural reforms that could last for years. In a fiscal crisis situation, simply promising reforms might not be enough to attract the needed financing. A government might be forced to frontload an impressive array of reforms that could prove unpopular with the electorate, surprised by the sudden political change. For all these reasons, a current account deficit is a very critical weak point for indebted countries.

The Greek crisis suddenly opened the way to a simple and catchy distinction between the euro area core countries—although only some of them had a current account surplus—and the "periphery," that is, a neologism for the Mediterranean countries, plus Ireland. Most countries in the euro zone's periphery were indeed not only struggling with the sharp deterioration of their fiscal positions but also with sizeable current account deficits. Although Greece's twin deficits stood out, a closer look at the current accounts in Ireland, Portugal, and Spain in 2009 showed that not only did the governments in those countries need to adjust their budgets, but so did the private sector. Italy enjoyed the benefits of a solid high-saving private sector that could compensate for the huge public debt, but the country was also a clear example of the costs of the burden that the public imbalance laid on the private economy and that had been paid through years of low growth and of crowding-out of private investments. Even an adjustment in the net savings position of a euro zone country would imply that the country's growth was likely to struggle to keep pace with the rest of the euro zone. In other words, the divide between a stronger part of the euro area and a weaker, more indebted, and policy-challenged one would inevitably become deeper.

The trade balance is driven mainly by the strength of internal demand relative to external demand and by the country's relative competitiveness. A key factor in competitiveness is labor costs, which had increased dramatically faster in most other countries than in Germany. There was a kind of a geographical correlation that made the increase in labor costs greater based on the distance from Germany.[10] Since exports to the rest of the euro zone represent a significant share of total exports for the peripheral countries, competitiveness can be restored through relative wage restraint or faster productivity growth. Wage restraint is a painful process of deflation that can initially depress the GDP, thus making the debt-to-GDP ratio even higher. Improving productivity is a long and uncertain process. In the meantime, the key driver of fiscal and external sustainability becomes the net income balance, which is determined to a large extent by the interest rate spreads that these countries need to pay on their new debt issues. Before the crisis started, Europeans often denied the relevance of the intraEuropean trade imbalances. But since these imbalances were compensated by capital flows from surplus countries (mainly Germany) to the others, with the crisis the issue of competitiveness creating trade imbalances became influenced by the strength of the creditor countries relative to the debtors. The symbol of this new balance of powers was the interest rate spread relative to the German bonds; it was a fever indicator of difficult capital flows. Day by day, and then hour by hour, this fickle indicator of national health started to dictate the accelerated beat of the European heart. For a faint-hearted patient, any news can be frightening.

## Berlin's Mistrust of the EU Commission and Call for the IMF

At the beginning of 2010 the euro itself became a catalyst of the crisis; it was considered a strait-jacket by national governments seeking room to maneuver in response to the crisis. Those euro zone governments that were falling under the unfortunate triumvirate of weak growth prospects, financial sector fragility, and an unsustainable trajectory of public debt were increasingly penalized in the bond market. Ireland, Greece, and Spain were the hardest hit. Of the three, only Ireland had designed a credible fiscal plan.

The Greek government had prepared a budget with substantial cuts for 2010 and a goal for the fiscal deficit of 9.1 percent of GDP. However, the European Commission had questioned several of its underlying assumptions and called for clearer measures on the revenues side and for more structural adjustments (instead of one-off measures) to produce sustainable cuts on the expenditure side, including in the public-sector wage bill and pensions. Finance Minister

George Papaconstantinou presented to the European Commission a supplementary budget and a multiyear "stability program" for the period 2010–13, which envisaged reducing the budget deficit by 4 percentage points to 8.7 percent of GDP in 2010 and thereafter to 5.6 percent in 2011, 2.8 percent in 2012, and 2 percent in 2013. The Commission gave a benign assessment: "Overall, on the basis of the detailed information included in the updated stability program, and in spite of several risks, the 2010 budgetary target seems within reach."[11] That was not helpful for the external credibility of Greece and was lethal for the credibility of the EU Commission.

The German government observed the tug-of-war between Athens and the EU institutions with deep mistrust. Both the government and the Bundesbank shared the analysis that the European Commission was not capable of forcing a national government into a decisive policy correction; in other words, no political authority in Europe, with democratic legitimacy, could impose itself on a national government. Paradoxically, there were only two "forces" that could prevail on the national democracies: the markets and their global governance counterpart, that is, the International Monetary Fund.

Germany's new finance minister, Wolfgang Schäuble —like Trichet and French president Nicolas Sarkozy—opposed letting the IMF intervene, so he was attracted to the idea of establishing a European Monetary Fund (EMF). Such a fund would first supply a country with emergency loans, based on strict requirements to cut down its spending. But if it became clear that the country's debt had become unsustainable, the European Monetary Fund would buy up its entire debt, at a maximum cost of 60 percent of the country's GDP. For creditors of a country with a debt load equal to 120 percent of GDP, that would mean a steep loss, or "haircut," of 50 percent of their credit.

The idea of a "Fund" had appeal for Merkel because it made private creditors share the burden of a default instead of just the taxpayers. But in the end, Merkel seemed to prefer a system of bilateral financings that would easily have circumvented the no-bailout clause in the EU treaty. Confronted with what she thought was too complacent an approach by the European Commission, she definitely turned to the idea of directly involving the IMF.

The direct conclusion was that the solution to the crisis could not come from European politics at that stage. Or, eventually a solution could come only to the extent that European political institutions could use the markets to impose their will on countries. In order to do that, it was necessary that any kind of aid, coming from the EU institutions, would not completely resolve the country's problems and would imply a loss on the part of private investors. One way or another, uncertainty had to remain so that the markets would be able to put pressure on the country of concern—Greece in this case. It was a strategy that would have huge consequences for years to come.

# 11

## Bringing the Euro to the Brink, in Order to Save It

*Market Pressure Reality and Conspiracy Theories*

In the late winter of 2010, Europe's rhetoric inclined toward Oswald Spengler's tragic vision of Western decline, plagued by the power of money, the disintegration of communities, and the domination of plutocrats and demagogues. It was an irrational vision but was deeply entrenched in European culture and rooted in the nervous system of societies. While politics struggled to cope with the financial crisis, the "power of money" had emerged out of the metaphor between February and March. With a typical mix of leveraged bets, frantic information, and herd behavior, financial markets interacted with the emotions of public opinion across the continent. On February 5 the popular German newspaper *Bild* published one of the first alarmist headlines that reflected its euroskeptical campaign reaching millions of readers: "Will the crisis-countries destroy the euro?" News about protests in Athens against the government's austerity package made the rounds in Europe and created a picture of Greece as an irredeemable country. Well-informed reports gave details of the huge amount of Greek capital fleeing to Cyprus via banking channels. The impression was that rich Greeks, after avoiding taxes, were managing to avoid the cost of a national failure, leaving Greece even more in need of aid from other countries' taxpayers.

On February 8 the *Financial Times* published a shocking article on its front page: "Traders and hedge funds have bet nearly $8 billion (€5.9 billion) against the euro, amassing the biggest ever short position in the single currency on fears of a euro zone debt crisis."[1] Figures from the Chicago Mercantile Exchange, often used as a proxy of hedge fund activity, showed investors had increased their positions against the euro to record levels in the week to February 2. The price for credit default swaps (CDS) on Greek debt reached 410 basis points—twice as high as at the end of 2009.[2] These trends suggested investors were losing confidence in the single currency's ability to withstand any contagion to other European countries from Greece's budget problems.

The ugly mood was evident in Manhattan, as depicted in a fascinating story in the *Wall Street Journal* that sent shockwaves all across the Atlantic.

> Some heavyweight hedge funds have launched large bearish bets against the euro in moves that are reminiscent of the trading action at the height of the U.S. financial crisis. The big bets are emerging amid gatherings such as an exclusive "idea dinner" earlier this month that included hedge-fund titans SAC Capital Advisors LP and Soros Fund Management LLC. During the dinner, hosted by a boutique investment bank at a private townhouse in Manhattan, a small group of all-star hedge-fund managers argued that the euro is likely to fall to "parity" with the dollar, people close to the situation say.[3]

According to a participant, the "idea dinners" were actually a regular appointment for people who did not need a special opportunity to convene. The dinner referred to by the *Wall Street Journal* was hosted by Monness, Crespi, Hardt & Co., a research and brokerage firm. During the dinner, three portfolio managers spoke about investment themes related to the European debt crisis. A major hedge fund owner, who was represented at the dinner, admitted that the meeting raised serious concerns among the American authorities and that the Department of Justice opened an inquiry pursuing the investment firms that took part.[4]

The presence of the Soros fund management was particularly evocative for Europeans, who still remembered the attack that George Soros successfully launched against the British pound in 1992 breaking the European Monetary System, a precursor of the monetary union. Soros, head of the $27-billion asset fund manager, had just warned publicly that if the European Union did not fix its finances, "the euro may fall apart." The European currency traded above $1.50 in December but had plunged to $1.35 by early February. "With traders using leverage—often borrowing 20 times the size of their bet, accentuating gains and losses—a euro move to $1 could represent a career trade. If investors put up $5 million to make a $100 million trade, a 5 percent price move in the right direction doubles their initial investment," the *Wall Street Journal* commented.[5] That simple example shows how dangerous financial markets can become when they see a one-way bet: once the trend of the markets in univocal, the leverage becomes much more powerful as a speculative tool. In the *Journal's* example, a leveraged investor runs virtually no risk at all of losing the initial capital (the first $5 million of the example) after he has made the first win and can become even more willing to bet on extreme outcomes. Therefore the role of the non-European analysts and media, influential in building the narrative of the markets and inclined to express a longstanding scepticism about the euro, created a powerful self-fulfilling mechanism, further facilitating the speculation.

By the week of the dinner in Manhattan, the size of the bearish bet against the euro had risen to record levels of 60,000 futures contracts—the most recently available data and the highest level since 1999, according to Morgan Stanley. The data represented the volume of futures contracts that would pay off if the euro sank to specific levels in the future. But an especially important remark was made by one of the dinner speakers, Donald Morgan, head of hedge fund Brigade Capital, who told the group he believed Greek debt was an early domino to fall in a contagion that eventually would hit U.S. companies, municipalities, and even Treasury securities.[6]

A few weeks later, the *Financial Times* broke a story that hedge funds were raising "their bets against the euro amid growing fears of a regulatory backlash against their trading positions on the specific sovereign debt of Greece and other weak euro zone economies."[7] An estimated $12.1 billion of short positions were outstanding against the currency, according to the Commodity Futures Trading Commission. At the beginning of February, when markets had first taken the stage on the euro debt, short positions against the euro totaled just over $7 billion. The mechanics of the trade give an interesting insight into the fragility of the euro. Apparently, hedge funds began to buy large amounts of CDS protection against Greek debt in mid-2009, in anticipation that markets would wake up to Greece's debt problems and hence look to the CDS market to hedge the risks. Until 2009, the cost of buying such protection was very cheap because few investors saw a sovereign default as a likely event. Indeed, until the banking crisis hit in 2008, ten-year CDS protection on Greek government debt could be purchased for as little as 20 basis points—0.2 percent of the amount insured—per year. The hedge funds bought up the CDS protection without owning the underlying bonds. This so-called "naked" CDS trading has a particularly bad taste for regulators, who see it as purely speculative. Actually, the CDS became much in demand at the end of 2009 when European banks, with 95 percent of foreign holdings of Greek sovereign bonds, discovered the risk of a Greek default and were worried enough about it to want to hedge their investments. It was mainly bank-run hedging operators, known as credit valuation adjustment (CVA) desks, classed as risk management units rather than proprietary traders, that started to buy credit default swaps from hedge funds, pushing their price sky-high. Since CDS are an indicator of risk, the increase in prices raised red flags all around and turned the fear—that they were supposed to counter—into sheer panic.

## Governments Tempted by Denial

During a bilateral meeting on February 4 at the Elysée Palace, Sarkozy shared his concern with Angela Merkel. Since the end of January the challenge of the markets had grown. Analysts had discounted the austerity plan advanced by the Greek government, which had already been criticized by the EU Commission on February 3. EU economic and finance ministers, meeting as the ECOFIN, had established a technical committee composed of officials from finance ministries, the European Central Bank, and the European Commission, which prepared a number of contingency plans. Still, Merkel wanted to proceed with extreme caution. During the bilateral meeting at the Elysée the chancellor for the first time expressed to Sarkozy her worries about the reaction of the German Constitutional Court to an eventual breach of the EU treaties and explained that she needed to consolidate political support even within her own party. She was actually going to convene the parliamentarians of the CDU-CSU fraction in the coming days to discuss the crisis. During the meeting with the French president, Merkel mentioned the need for an "economic government in Europe," but that seemed a vague reference for the future and offered no comfort to the Greeks. Even as Merkel and Sarkozy were meeting, ECB president Trichet in Frankfurt was working to tamp down expectations of a strong intervention by the bank in favor of Greece: "A lot of people," he said at a press conference after the monthly board meeting, "imagine that you have this kind of sequence: you have problems and you get help, and conditionality comes with the help. This is the normal case for a country which is not in the euro area. In the euro area, the situation is very different: you have ex-ante (not ex-post) help because you are in the euro area, then you have an easy inbuilt financing of the current account deficit."[8]

Even under the heavy storm of attacks against the euro and European sovereign bonds, the attitude of the European authorities was still mostly on the defensive side. On February 5, a confidential memo was prepared for the European Union finance ministers by their deputies at the ECOFIN. Ministers were instructed to skirt questions about a possible bailout of Greece and emphasize instead their support for the government's deficit-cutting measures. If asked about the risk of a Greek default, ministers were advised to say they were "fully confident" that the country "will rise to this challenge," according to the confidential EU memo titled "Elements of External Communication on the Fiscal Situation in Greece."[9] Despite this tone, it was one of the first known EU documents that even contemplated the hypothesis: "Will the euro area (or the EU) provide help to Greece in case of a risk of default?"[10] The note's recommendation on sidestepping such questions was called a "defensive point."

By early 2010, European governments faced a dangerous set of pressures. From below, popular sentiments were building, especially in Germany, against a bailout of Greece. A popular argument was plainly exposed by the newspapers and taken up countless times in TV programs in Germany, as demonstrated by the following example: "The Greeks take to the streets to protest against the postponement of the retirement age from 61 to 63 years. Should the Germans no longer retire at 67 but at 69 to ensure that the Greeks can enjoy early retirement?"[11] The newspaper *Bild* reported on the paradoxical situation in Athens: "Experts maintain that tax evasion ranges yearly around €20 billion."[12] *Bild* quoted the *Frankfurter Allgemeine Zeitung* according to which only 5,000 Greeks out of a population of 11 million pay taxes on incomes higher than €100,000. In Athens, *Bild* continued, "there is the highest concentration of Porsche Cayennes in Europe. And the capital harbors some of the largest yachts of the Mediterranean . . . tax frauds are common in the economic activity. In Europe an average of 10 percent of VAT is evaded, while in Greece the average is 30 percent. State officials' corruption reaches yearly €3.5 billion."

On February 10, *Frankfurter Allgemeine Zeitung* took a hardline stance, airing the idea of going back to the deutsche mark:

> Germany is still hesitating. But pressure is growing. Europe must help the Greeks, is the slogan of the European Commission, launched by French President Sarkozy. In plain language this means that Germany must respond for the debt of Greece. But the pact behind the euro was different for the Germans. Before the farewell ceremony of the German mark, the Maastricht Treaty was signed, which explicitly forbids that a member of the monetary union is liable for the debts of another. If this central precept of fiscal stability is not respected, then the Maastricht Treaty, the Stability and Growth Pact and the debt limit in the constitution are not worth the paper which they are written on. Then the Germans will want the deutsche mark back.[13]

Day by day, characterizations of the crisis grew dimmer. Germany was again associated with the word Zahlmeister (paymaster), while bailing out Greece opened the way to "chain reactions" whereby after Greece would be just the first country in line: "The markets have Portugal, Spain, Ireland, and Italy in their sights."[14] Kurt Lauk, head of the CDU's Economic Council, said on February 15 that Greece would lose voting privileges in the EU in the event of a bailout. A few days later Hans Michelbach, a CSU lawmaker, called on Germany to resist any move to provide financial aid to Greece because any assistance would provoke a "spiral without end."

In the crucial hours of February 2010, two souls were beating inside the German government. Finance Minister Schäuble, who had been the mastermind behind former chancellor Helmut Kohl's push for European integration in the early 1990s, remained sincerely devoted to consolidating the European project and was working for a swifter intervention in the Greek crisis. He envisaged earlier than others that the crisis could open the way to a fiscal union at the euro level. By contrast, Chancellor Merkel was digging in her heels. Merkel had a deep concern about the legal, political, and technical hurdles that she would face in the implementation of a bailout. On February 9, plans of the finance ministry were leaked to a German newspaper. "Berlin wants to save Greece. Spectacular turnaround: Germany will offer help to the strapped Greeks. Finance Minister Wolfgang Schäuble is driving a rescue plan. The capital market responded enthusiastically."[15] The plans were intended to probe different ways for an aid package to Greece, taking into consideration both bilateral aid and internationally coordinated actions at the EU level. However, any form of state aid for Greece required a vote by the Bundestag, and Schäuble struggled to get the necessary parliamentary backing as soon as possible.

Merkel's reaction to the leak from the finance ministry was blunt, and her spokesman Ulrich Wilhelm had to make clear that no decision had yet been taken. The European Council was to meet just two days later on February 11, and Merkel was preparing for a hard-nosed negotiation. She still had to keep in mind popular discontent in Germany about any kind of bailout; the specific reservations that the German Constitutional Court might raise concerning any attempt to violate the no-bailout clause in the Maastricht Treaty; and finally the complexity of negotiations among twenty-seven EU countries, where Germany was maybe the most influential, but surely was also the one that would foot the highest bill.

The relationship between Merkel and Schäuble developed into one of the most important aspects of the crisis. The finance minister was determined to defend the pro-European stance of the CDU tradition and, as already said, was a supporter of the idea of a European Monetary Fund as an embryo of economic government for the euro area. But in February 2010 he fell sick after a routine hospital operation. A wound did not heal and he had to spend two months in bed missing important meetings. Later he confessed that he was feeling so miserable that he offered his resignations twice to Merkel, but she had not accepted them. Schäuble's political problems were mainly with the two smaller parties in the government coalition, the Bavarian CSU and the Free Democrats. "I have accepted that at that time my ideas would have not obtained the majority in the government's coalition," Schäuble explained later. "As a finance minister you can be successful only if you have a relationship of confidence with the head of government. . . . I am so loyal that I do not need to show it."[16] However, gradually his health condition put him on the sidelines and dampened the divergences between his public statements and Merkel's.

## February 11 Meeting: Saving the Euro Area Only "As a Whole"

Shielded from public scrutiny, the Eurogroup ministers met on February 6 to establish the basis for the EU Council's urgent declaration on the Greek crisis, which was expected to be released the following day. Schäuble had prepared for the meeting with his French counterpart, Christine Lagarde. Although relations between the two ministers were good, they could not agree on one of the crucial points. Despite the standard clichéd interpretation of European politics, Lagarde agreed with Merkel on the need for IMF involvement, while Schäuble agreed with Sarkozy on the reasons to oppose such involvement in Europe's troubles. One of the technical implications of involving the IMF had far-reaching political consequences: based on its statute, the IMF can grant loans only to countries that adopt precise commitments and stick to them. If IMF aid was to be provided, a multi-year program had to be prepared. If this was politically unacceptable for the creditor countries that did not want to get bogged down in a long and uncertain commitment, Greece would have to return to the markets for its debt financing within twelve months. Such a schedule was very unrealistic if one took into account the country's macroeconomic imbalances. If one was dealing only with the fiscal side of the Greek economic problem—as the more direct source of spillovers for the euro area—then the therapy would consist of forcing draconian spending cuts and frontloading all the fiscal adjustment into one year, whatever the other social or economic costs might be. That might have appealed to Berlin, but it was not very plausible once subjected to close scrutiny.

The draft text prepared by the Eurogroup ministers, at Schäuble's initiative, blamed the markets "largely driven by speculative behavior," but invited the European Commission to come forward with "proposals to further strengthen the coordination and surveillance of national economic policies within the euro area." The draft added:

> We have also reviewed the situation in Greece and . . . we invite the Council to adopt, on the basis of the Commission's proposals a comprehensive and effective package of recommendations to Greece, including the committed additional measures, to overcome its fiscal problems and economic imbalances. The Commission will design and coordinate such actions, drawing on the expertise of the ECB and the IMF, where relevant.
>
> Eurogroup ministers underline that our economies are closely integrated and linked together by our single currency, the euro. The euro, by its very existence provides an element of stability and protections against market turbulences. The members of the euro area share a common responsibility for the stability in the euro area and our economic policies are a matter of common concern. On the one hand participating member states are required to conduct sound national policies in line with the agreed rules. On the other hand, the euro-area member states will take determined and coordinated action and provide support, if needed, to safeguard financial stability in the euro area as a whole.[17]

A teleconference among the Eurogroup ministers was held on February 10 to finalize the draft while, for the first time, in Brussels officials discussed the option of building a "firewall" in favor of Greece.[18] Chancellor Merkel immediately signaled that she could not accept the text. Guarded though its language was, the document went too far for both public opinion and the constitutional court. Watching from Brussels, analyst Peter Ludlow observed: "Barely twelve hours before the European Council was due to meet, the EU did not therefore have a common line. Given what the markets were expecting, it was a dramatic situation. It was also a serious challenge to Herman Van Rompuy's authority. Having decided to launch his career as president of the European Council with an informal meeting, Van Rompuy was confronted with the prospect of a disaster."[19] Van Rompuy had just been nominated the new president of the European Council at the December 2009 EU summit, a post that was to be the most important new institutional result of the 2009 Lisbon Treaty. Under such pressure, in the early evening of February 10 Van Rompuy took the initiative:

> He asked the Council Secretariat to notify members of the European Council and the media that the meeting on the following day would begin at midday and not, as originally planned, at 10.00. The official reason was that it was snowing heavily in Brussels and that there would almost certainly be delays in incoming flights. The real reason was to allow time for him to broker an agreement and thereby prevent any hint of the breakdown reaching the media. Van Rompuy told Angela Merkel, George Papandreou and Nicolas Sarkozy that he and his staff would begin work immediately on a fresh text, taking account of the various views that he had heard, and that he would like to discuss the document with them at 10.30 on the following morning. He invited Jean-Claude Juncker and Jean-Claude Trichet to join him at a working breakfast which had already been arranged with José Manuel Barroso and José Zapatero, where, he said, they would have an opportunity to review the situation and prepare for the meetings that were to follow. He instructed his staff to work on a draft statement which he would present first to Merkel, Papandreou and Sarkozy, then to the European Council as a whole, and finally to the media.[20]

According to one of the participants, the confrontation between Merkel and Sarkozy was once more the most notable point of the meeting on February 11. The French president urged an immediate decision with all his strength, arguing: "Let us put some billions immediately on the table, then we will fix the details." Merkel reacted with analogous force: "Without a plan the answer is no!" It was reminiscent of the similar fight on October 2008 over the establishment of the common fund for the banks (see chapter 1). According to a witness of the discussion, Merkel said she needed to know exactly "how much money and in which form. It is indispensable to decide whether to stick primarily to the European law or to the national laws. Further I want to know how we will organize the verifications of the conditionality attached to the loans and I want to fix a precise calendar of quarterly revisions of the situation. All this is impossible without a plan. Finally I want the IMF to be involved directly in the operation."

Absent these requirements, she was afraid of being dragged into the usual collusive negotiations among the partners who were ready to give a green light and solve an immediate problem while neglecting the consequences.

Sarkozy argued against the involvement of the IMF, saying such a step would deliver the euro into the hands of the Americans. But Merkel observed that the Americans were influencing the euro anyway, through the exchange rate and through their interest rate policy, which was not independent from political power in Washington. The reaction of Sarkozy was described as rabid. A witness said that the violence of his language was beyond any precedent. But the core of the argument was the same: we need to start immediately, we cannot afford to wait. Merkel's final word was as sharp: "Not without a plan!"

Van Rompuy who had absorbed everybody's observations during the preliminary meetings, submitted a new text to Merkel, Sarkozy, and Papandreou, and it was accepted without amendments. Shortly before 1 p.m., he and his colleagues adjourned from the Justus Lipsius building to the Solvay Library, a few hundred meters away, where the rest of the European Council had already assembled. Papandreou walked between Merkel and Sarkozy. When they saw journalists waiting for them, they stopped and let Van Rompuy alone reach them. He announced that they had a common text to be submitted to the council. According to a French observer, "Merkel and Sarkozy smiled, apparently with no tenseness at all, and not saying a word. Mr. van Rompuy is now Europe's voice."

There was practically no discussion in the meeting among the twenty-seven countries. The text was presented by Van Rompuy and was approved. It was a defining moment. Berlin and Paris had finally taken over the leadership of Europe and they had found in Herman Van Rompuy an institutional counterpart. At the end, Van Rompuy went out into the snow with European Commission president Barroso to tell the media what had been agreed. The description of a French daily speaks volumes:

> At his [Van Rompuy's] side Barroso, normally very much at ease with the media, is forced to remain silent and smiles. With the flaws of debutants, Van Rompuy reads his text first in English, then in French. But he remains so distant from the microphones that he has to start it all over from scratch. He closes in just a bit, stammers in English, keeps on and decides it is useless to repeat in French. Fair enough: markets speak only English.[21]

In the final text, the EU leaders canceled the references in the earlier draft to the markets' speculative behavior and to generic commitments and substituted a sentence referring to the principles of sound national policies and shared responsibility inscribed in the treaties since the Maastricht text: "All euro area members must conduct sound national policies in line with the agreed rules. They have a shared responsibility for the economic and financial stability in the area."[22] The reference to the treaty was essential for Merkel in consideration of any eventual legal questions. On its face, the phrasing was neutral, but in reality the two principles of sound policies and shared responsibility were put on equal footing, something that was not evident to all the leaders around the table.

As a consequence, the responsibility of the Greek government was articulated more sharply than in the first draft and Athens was called upon to implement measures "in a rigorous and determined manner to effectively reduce the budgetary deficit by 4 percent in 2010."[23] Fixing the numerical goal so clearly was unusual for a council declaration. The roles of the various institutions in the monitoring of Greece commitments were much more clearly defined than in the earlier draft. The task of following up, with a tight control, was explicitly mandated to the ECOFIN, while the IMF was mentioned but basically only as a provider of expertise, as probably Sarkozy wanted. The leaders assigned a more important role to the ECB than to the IMF, that of monitoring the implementation of Greece's promised policies. This was a crucial decision in the context of the divergences that had opened between the austerity-only line of the ECB and the more fiscally supportive approach of the IMF.

The council's text ended with a fundamental sentence: "Euro area member states will take determined and coordinated action, if needed, to safeguard financial stability in the euro area as a whole."[24] Since that day, determined and coordinated action was indeed taken only when it was subordinate to the financial stability of the whole of the euro area, rather than the needs of one country or another. The "stability of the euro"—so relevant for the interests of the German public and for the correct interpretation of the treaty by the German Constitutional Court, not that of Greece—became the focus of the crisis.

The European Council declaration, couched in the foggy language of international diplomacy, was actually a fundamental step forward. Before February 11, 2010, the debate within the EU was still prey to an emotional contrast between those who thought that solidarity was mandatory within a community-of-destiny (as Konrad Adenauer and Helmut Kohl used to call Europe) and those who thought that Greece did not deserve solidarity because of its having fudged its bookkeeping and/or that helping such a country would mean the end of the monetary union because of the moral hazard that inevitably would draw many other countries into a debt spiral. The February 11 statement redefined the ground rules of the debate without even mentioning the question of solidarity. It said officially, and for the first time unequivocally, that euro area member states were expected to step in to rescue a fellow member. It based the reasons for the intervention on the principle of defending the stability of the common currency grounded in the EU treaty.

*Merkel between the Constitution and the Citizens:*
*Not for Greece, but for the Euro*

The result of the European Council meeting represented a crucial strategic coup for Merkel. As usual, the German government had very clearly in mind that its room to maneuver was defined by legal considerations. The German law approving the Treaty of Maastricht carried out the transfer of responsibility for monetary policy to the EU in the context of monetary union but based it on precise rules. The relevant 1998 ruling by the German Constitutional Court interpreted stability of the euro as Germany's precondition to the agreement. "The basis and justification" of the transfer of powers was the concept of monetary union as a "stability-oriented community," which the federal constitutional court defined as follows: "The scale of the monetary union is the stability of the euro. The goal of stability is secured in the procedures regulated by the Treaty." The court explicitly mentioned in this context Article 124 of the Treaty on the Functioning of the European Union (TFEU), which prohibited public authorities from violating the autonomy of the monetary institutions, and Article 125, which ruled out the responsibility of any member state in the financial obligations of another member state. In the context of a bailout, any form of financial assistance would seem to be excluded, since the no-bailout clause is a substantial part of the stability concept. Violation of this clause, according to the federal court, would imply the eventuality that Germany must abandon the euro if the monetary union does not continuously develop in the agreed sense of a stability-oriented community. The precise formulation of the relevant paragraph in the 1998 ruling of the German court on the related Stability and Growth Pact was as follows: "This concept of the Monetary Union as a stability-oriented community is basis and justification of the German agreement to join it. . . . Should the Monetary Union with the entry into its third phase not be able to continuously further develop the existing stability in the sense of the agreed commitment to stabilization, then it would abandon the Treaty conception." In that case, the court announced, it would step in and take action; in other words, it would force Berlin to abandon the euro. And no government, no parliament, no referendum would be in a legal position to counter such a decision by the court.

The apparently shallow text engineered by Merkel, Van Rompuy, and Sarkozy for the European Council had the power to open a breach in a powerful German judicial offensive that could have threatened any attempt to aid an ailing country in the euro area. The statement countered the no-bailout clause with another constitutional prescription: the defense of the stability of the monetary union. The crucial point was that Merkel had to demonstrate that Germany was stepping in not so much to bail out Greece but to preserve the stability of the euro. In a sense, the stability of the German currency—or more appropriately now, the currency of the Germans—was the prime concern of the German Constitutional Court, as explicitly mentioned even in the text of the German Fundamental Law. In Article 88, that law stated: "The Federation shall establish a note-issuing and currency bank as the Federal Bank. Within the framework of the European Union, its responsibilities and powers may be transferred to the European Central Bank, which is independent and committed to the overriding goal of assuring price stability."

However, the fact that the European Council statement did not mention solidarity forced Chancellor Merkel to pay a price on the international stage. For the moment, it kept the resolve to aid Greece on a hypothetical level, rather than one grounded in political morality. The decision would later become a matter of contention and a primary cause of accusations against Berlin for its reticence and for the insensitive way Germany rebuffed the aid request by Greece. But for Merkel, mentioning solidarity reasons for aiding Greece would have meant an explicit admission of the unconstitutionality, from a German legal viewpoint, of the bailout. Anybody—as it actually happened—would have been able to present a complaint to the constitutional court alleging a patent violation of the no-bailout clause. Such a case would be brought to the court publicly, resulting in what would surely be a global disruption of financial markets. But for Merkel, an even worse consideration was another set of problems that posed politically catastrophic risks: in such a critical environment, the German population might side, by an overwhelming majority, with a protest against the euro and German participation in Europe.

According to all the polls at the time, a vast majority of Germans denounced the violation of the EU treaty resulting from a Greek bailout. On average, two of three Germans were against any transfer of money to Athens. Once legitimated by the constitutional court, this relatively silent majority might find a new political expression and fall prey to some new political movement outside the postwar parliamentary tradition. Merkel's conservative governing party would have been forced on the defensive, exposed to the accusation of betraying the Germans. The same would happen with the two main opposition parties, which were more in favor of helping Greece than was the government. A fringe protest party with a national conservative platform might find favorable ground. Germany had been the only European country not to fall prey to populism in the past twenty years. Different from France, Italy, Austria, the Netherlands, Belgium, Poland, the Czech Republic, and even Switzerland, Germany had shown an impressive solidity in respecting a democratic consensus, even during a major scandal that had involved the CDU and former chancellor Helmut Kohl at the beginning of 2000.

How fast such a test might happen had been demonstrated by the shocking events in Bavaria in September 2008, when the CSU lost its majority for the first time in fifty-four years. Even more startling had been the case of Ronald Schrill in Hamburg, a "zero-tolerance-of-foreign-criminals" populist who had founded a party and collected a stunning 19.4 percent in his first appearance in local elections. Extreme right and anti-democracy parties like the National Democratic Party or the German People's Union had managed to overcome the electoral thresholds and were represented in the regional parliaments in Sachsen and Mecklenburg-Vorpommern. On the opposite side, an extreme left party had made its way into the Bundestag. According to Forsa, one of the largest German poll organizations, the potential for an extreme right-wing populist party in Germany should be limited to 10–15 percent of the total electorate. Emnid, another poll organization, forecast a 20 percent limit for such a party. Even so, the public's agreement with right-wing slogans can reach a stunning 60 percent.[25]

The peculiarity of the German federal system is such that populist parties can post impressive results in local elections but then struggle to extend them to the federal level. Faced with such challenges, the establishment manages to react, sometimes absorbing the slogans of the populists by appealing to the population with a sort of "centrist populism." That had been the strategy of Konrad Adenauer after World War II when he succeeded in removing from the political agenda the prosecution of former Nazi party members, thus cutting the ground under the feet of a new Nazi-nostalgic formation. With obvious differences, Merkel was following a similar line by taking a hardline stance against Greece.

Just one day before the February 11 EU Council, a poll by the Emnid Institute revealed that 71 percent of the German respondents were against a Greek bailout by the European Union. Only 25 percent said that it was right to ask German taxpayers to step in. This was especially true in consideration of the popular characterization of Greece. For all the efforts that the new government in Athens was making and for the suffering and sacrifices that Greeks were undergoing, the image fixed in everybody's mind outside Greece was that of a country that fudged its accounts to the detriment of other countries and that had lived irresponsibly beyond its means. This image made it difficult, if not impossible, to create solidarity with Greece in the rest of Europe.

## Only as the Last Resort

The situation posed a dramatic challenge for Angela Merkel. It should not come as a surprise that during a meeting of ECOFIN, German finance minister Schäuble called the decisions on the euro Chefsache—an issue that could be decided only by prime ministers and other heads of government. The connection between national democratic responsibility was too tight and delicate not to be dealt with directly at the highest level of governments. This very fact was to shape the rest of the diplomatic developments. Merkel would take over personally and require that discussions be conducted at her level.

The ultimate paradox was that, in one sense, Merkel became stronger the more she made the euro weaker. To avoid any rebuke by the constitutional court, Merkel had to bring the debt crisis to the brink. That was the reason for the famous Latin expression she repeatedly used at that stage of the crisis: ultima ratio—only as a last resort.

The ultima ratio was also a camouflage enabling her eventually to make a difficult political choice on the basis that there was "no alternative." In this way, a politician can cut the ground from under the opposition's feet. Helmut Kohl had brilliantly done it when he rushed the German unification in 1989–90. Gerhard Schroeder did the same when he pushed through his reform agenda more than a decade later. Merkel's coalition had also used the "no alternative" explanation to bail out banks in 2008 over public opposition. Through the ultima ratio doctrine, the Greek bailout became the bailout of the euro, simply because there were no alternatives.

This mechanism enhanced Merkel's leadership in Europe. Her resolve to intervene would develop only when the stability of the euro area was in question, so the crisis had to get worse.

# 12

## Sell Your Islands

### *Papandreou's Bold Move and the Frankfurt Consensus*

Hoping to break the gridlock between Greece and Germany, Prime Minister George Papandreou visited Angela Merkel in Berlin on March 5, 2010. Even before he arrived, however, the chancellor announced what would not be discussed: "I expressly want to say [that the meeting] isn't about aid commitments, but about good relations between Germany and Greece." For Papandreou, that was like the crack of the whip. "We have fulfilled to the utmost all that we must from our side; now it's Europe's turn," Papandreou told his fellow ministers just before taking off for Berlin. The Greek government had just announced a new raft of fiscal measures to help achieve the ambitious deficit reduction targeted for 2010, equivalent to 4 percent of GDP.[1] It was the third belt-tightening since the beginning of the year. In total, this made a sizable fiscal effort of around 6.5 percent of GDP—something very similar to the overall fiscal tightening that had taken place in Ireland. Once he arrived in Berlin, Papandreou added a subtle threat: if Europe was not up to the historic moment, Greece might have to turn for help to the IMF in Washington.

With that threat, Papandreou succeeded in gathering sound bites of solidarity from Berlin, although the actual policy line remained unchanged: Athens would have to help itself.

The European Central Bank also gave Athens an endorsement but no relief: The promised measures were "convincing," the bank said in a statement. The bank added that it appreciated the Greek government's recognition of the need to "rapidly adopt and implement decisive structural reforms." It then emphasized that the "reform program will bring the economy back on a sustainable medium-term growth path with increasing employment."[2] The endorsement reinforced the idea that the current euro area economic policies were still correct: the core of everything remained the fiscal adjustment plan. Swiftly implemented with strong structural reforms, it would guarantee the necessary adjustment in 2010, while helping Greece regain competitiveness and lay the basis for sustainable growth and debt dynamics. During the monthly press conference on March 4, ECB vice president Lucas Papademos, a Greek (and future successor to Papandreou), explained how a credible fiscal consolidation would lower borrowing costs and bolster credibility, confidence, and competitiveness, thus subscribing unconditionally to the theory of "expansionary fiscal contractions" that had been orthodoxy at the ECB—a sort of "Frankfurt Consensus" in tune with the German cultural heritage of the bank.

The ECB's unmitigated praise for Greece's draconian fiscal plan was in contrast to the IMF's stance during the crisis. The IMF had emphasized the fact that its new generation of adjustment programs, mostly implemented in the euro zone's backyard of Central and Eastern Europe, was much lighter on fiscal adjustment and conditionality, reflecting the lessons of past mistakes (notably, the IMF's controversial heavy-handed treatment of Asia in the late 1990s). The euro zone, meanwhile, seemed instead to have rediscovered the wisdom of the "old" IMF.[3] In fact, ECB president Trichet released a strong statement against the IMF, observing that it would be inappropriate to have the Fund step in with a loan facility because the conditionality attached to such a loan should be imposed strictly within the euro zone and in the framework of the EU's Stability and Growth Pact. The official reason was that Trichet feared that the IMF might insist on influencing the monetary conditions in any Greek aid package, thus impinging on the ECB's autonomy. That was a particularly sensitive issue since the IMF's chief economist, Olivier Blanchard, had just published with others a paper wondering if it was not advisable in the current situation for a central bank to adopt an inflation target higher than the ECB's target of 2 percent.[4] Blanchard proposed a 4 percent target, although his original proposal was even higher, around 5 percent, overlooking the fears of undermining credibility, pushing up long-term interest rates, or disrupting inflation expectations.[5]

Faced with daily strong popular protests on the streets of Athens against the austerity program, the Greek government sent again its ultimatum to the European partners: if financial assistance was not forthcoming, Athens would bring the IMF horse through the Trojan walls. Finance Minister Papaconstantinou briskly pointed out that the EU was unwilling to put its money where its mouth was, which is what the IMF would instead do.[6] Papandreou skillfully played his hand and announced that after meeting with Merkel in Berlin and then Sarkozy in Paris, he would fly to Washington to meet with President Obama and—though never officially confirmed—with IMF managing director Strauss-Kahn.

## The Elusive European Monetary Fund

By evoking the IMF, Papandreou was playing not only a strong diplomatic card, but a substantial one. The euro area countries had to reckon with the absence of their own mechanism to address financial crises that could threaten, via contagion, the whole European market. The problem was well understood since the first moves toward a common currency. The agreements of 1978 that produced the European Monetary System as a comprehensive fixed exchange rate regime provided for a European Monetary Fund within two years. Then German chancellor Helmut Schmidt, who along with French president Valéry Giscard d'Estaing was the driving force behind European monetary integration, thought an EMF should have an analogous role to that of the International Monetary Fund in the Bretton Woods regime.[7] In particular, countries that were hit by a sudden or unanticipated crisis could draw on the resources of such a fund that, like the IMF, could impose formal policy conditions in exchange for aid. Actually, finance and economics ministers meeting as ECOFIN had revived the issue occasionally during 2009 and the early months of 2010.

German finance minister Wolfgang Schäuble picked up suggestions formulated by two German economists—Daniel Gros, head of the Brussels think tank Center for European Policy Studies, and Thomas Mayer, chief economist at Deutsche Bank—who had been working on a proposal for a European Monetary Fund since the beginning of 2009. On March 8, Schäuble disclosed an exit strategy from the Greek crisis: a new financial facility, with strong political conditionality that was necessarily accompanied by more European integration at the political level. "For the first time, we in the euro zone are engaged in full surveillance over the fiscal and economic policy of one of the member countries,"[8] he wrote. But the proposal was muted by the coolness that Chancellor Merkel let show by commenting that a full-scale negotiation among the EU's twenty-seven member states would be needed to set up a European Monetary Fund. "Without treaty change we cannot found such a fund," Merkel said, raising the spectre of an uncertain and extremely long ratification process, an assumption sure to frighten French leaders, who in 2005 had failed to convince their own voters to support a proposed EU constitution. Schäuble's ministry retreated, saying that the project was actually only an Ideenpapier (idea, or concept, paper).

That Merkel had to walk a fine line was demonstrated by the commentaries in the German press. Jürgen Stark, an economist sitting on the executive board of the European Central Bank, wrote in the German newspaper *Handelsblatt* that an EMF would breach the treaty rules of the euro zone and undermine public support for the euro and the EU; "instead of a European monetary fund, budget rules must be strengthened and implemented with the help of a stringent supervisory mechanism." Stark's logic—appealing to the German Ordoliberal school, rejecting the interference of public powers in the management of the economy once the rules have been fixed—had to be carefully considered since it resonated in the German public. "A European monetary fund would be the start of a European financial compensation mechanism which could be very expensive," he wrote. Moreover, countries in fiscal disorder would not change their behavior, he added, expressing fears that even "public acceptance of the euro and of the European Union would be undermined."[9]

The *Frankfurter Allgemeine Zeitung,* considered close to the Bundesbank, dubbed the monetary fund a "Debt Fund." The EMF "would be the beginning of the end of national tax sovereignty. What would the Federal Constitutional Court say about that? . . . To express it in numbers: Until in the EU the voice of one Luxembourger counts as much as that of ten Germans, Brussels should not decide on the use of German tax money. Chancellor Angela Merkel thinks the Euro-debt fund is a good idea. Why? She'll get little applause from voters."[10]

The risk of a revolt by the German public was the worst eventuality for Europe. Schäuble seemed to understand what was going on and considered the real risk that some in Germany might demand distance from Europe. He wrote a remarkable piece in the *Financial Times:* "If we wish the euro to be strong and stable on a lasting basis—our condition for bringing the DM [deutsche mark] and its high credibility into the euro fold—we have to be prepared to integrate further in the euro zone. Co-ordination between euromembers must be more far-reaching; they must take an active part in each other's policymaking." He said this taking the integrationist line. But he also acknowledged: "I understand that a great deal of political resistance will have to be surmounted. Nevertheless, I am convinced that from Germany's perspective, European integration, monetary union, and the euro are the only choice."[11]

The way he reiterated his proposal for an EMF is revealing of the ambivalent agenda of German politicians: on the one hand he proposed that "euro zone members could also be granted emergency liquidity aid from a 'European monetary fund' to reduce the risk of defaults." But he added: "Emergency liquidity aid may never be taken for granted. It must, on principle, still be possible for a state to go bankrupt. Facing an unpleasant reality could be the better option in certain conditions."[12]

Unfortunately this was a strange form of stick and carrot policy. For the first time ever, the markets had heard from Berlin that Athens risked being ousted from the euro. Schäuble had not explicitly referred his comments to the Greek situation, but he obviously took a false step and underestimated the markets' negative reaction.

## Expelling Countries from the Euro Area

Germany ended up in the line of fire for its delaying strategy. Greece was again under market pressure little more than one week after its third painful austerity program, but it was not Greece alone that complained about the obstacles coming from Berlin. There was a widespread sense in Europe that Germany did not understand its own responsibility. As a "surplus country," which regularly exports more than it imports—also thanks to a wage policy that constantly underbids productivity gains—Germany was considered a source of instability both at the global level and, even more, within the euro area. Martin Wolf, an influential economics columnist for the *Financial Times*, coined the phrase "Chermany," a blend of China and Germany, the two countries that ran the world's most persistent current account surpluses and wanted their respective trading partners to deflate.

Since 2009 the countries belonging to the Group of Twenty (G-20) had engaged in macroeconomic coordination through the "Framework for Strong, Sustainable and Balanced Growth." This framework differentiated the responsibilities of countries running external surpluses, to "strengthen domestic sources of growth," from those running deficits, which needed to raise their domestic savings rates and reduce fiscal deficits.[13] Although the United States and European countries tended in the past to have a significant conflict over macroeconomic policy about once a decade, changes wrought by the euro had altered actors' bargaining positions fundamentally.[14] U.S. current account deficits and German current account surpluses lay at or near the heart of most of the imbalances in the global economic system at least since the early 1970s. U.S. administrations pressed the German government for more expansionary fiscal and monetary policies at several stages: after the breakdown of the Bretton Woods regime in the early 1970s; after the second oil shock with the controversy over the "locomotive theory" that was resolved at the Bonn summit of 1978; when balance of payments diverged markedly in the mid-1980s and gave way to the Plaza and Louvre accords; and finally since the adjustment dispute at the end of 2008. Almost as regularly—and with the further episode of the Exchange Rate Mechanism crisis in the mid-1990s—the deutsche mark appreciated substantially, benefiting the United States and European partners.

German chancellor Helmut Schmidt had responded to his experience in the late 1970s by engaging French president Giscard d'Estaing in launching the European Monetary System. The two leaders actually began negotiations over monetary integration as the dollar fell to its record lows against the deutsche mark in 1978. The European Council decided to create the new system in December 1978, and it became operational in March 1979. Schmidt thought that a currency agreement would be an instrument to strengthen European economic and political integration but also would be "an incentive for the Americans to under-stand that they must not let the dollar go down the drain." Schmidt explained his view very clearly in a piece for *Die Zeit* in 1990: "The reckless conduct of the United States with respect to monetary policy and the dependence of the monetary policy of the European countries on the dollar, on dollar interest rates, and dollar speculation has had painful effects. . . . We knew that the national European economies individually were not in a position to arm themselves suf-ficiently against the turbulences of the world. For that reason we wanted union and common success."[15] The result was that Germany was finally shielded from American political pressures. Indeed, when asked to reflate in order to rebalance its current account surplus, Berlin regularly cited the fact that the balance for the euro zone as a whole was in equilibrium and that internal euro imbalances were mainly caused by other countries' inefficiencies. The normal adjustment of global disequilibria through the exchange rate had been defused. For the first time in its recent history, Germany was reaping the benefits of its industrial organization, thanks to a relatively weaker—but still very stable—currency. Fred Bergsten, the American economist who headed the Peterson Institute for International Eco-nomics, defined the German situation as "a Nirvana."

Schäuble took a hard stance on this subject in a speech to the Bundestag: "I want to repudiate, very clearly, calmly, and coolly, the criticism—whether within the framework of the G-20 or from within Europe—that those who are reason-ably successful in competition are to blame for the problems of others."[16] In fact, data analysis was not unequivocal in this regard. More than productivity, the main factors in Germany's exporting success seemed to have been wage compres-sion and a great ability to organize outsourcing, that is, a form of international industrial cooperation where Germany could play an upper hand due to the size and specialization of its industrial corporations; this was hardly a factor that any other euro zone country could imitate.

As happened many times in the past, national competitiveness assumed the position of a positive, shared national culture, but this time, in Germany, it was with little remorse. German reunification had removed from the myth of eco-nomic primacy the national interest in income redistribution in favor of the dis-advantaged. The stress, all through the 1990s, of absorbing the new Laender in the east had saturated whatever disposition Germans had for redistributing limited resources. The new German economic doctrine—centered on painful reforms, a rudimentary concept of stability in terms of monetary restraint, and skepticism about the virtue of state expenditures—became a sort of civil religion. A daily prayer was sung from the minarets of some of the press against the arche-type of un-German vices: Greece. And there is never a shortage of candidate aya-tollahs when orthodoxy gains popularity. The four professors who took the Ber-lin government to the federal constitutional court in 1998 over Germany's entry into the euro used this latest opportunity to take to the stage: "There is no short-age of proposals to help the Greeks, including assistance from other euro zone governments—a move that would contravene the 'no bailout' rule enshrined in the treaty setting up monetary union," they wrote in a March 10 op-ed column for the *Financial Times*. "There is, sadly, only one way to escape this vicious circle. The Greeks will have to leave the euro, recreate the drachma. . . . We would like to state clearly that, should euro zone governments provide assistance to Greece in a manner that contravenes the no bailout rule, we would have no hesitation in lodging a new lawsuit at the Constitutional Court to enjoin Germany to depart from monetary union."[17]

On March 17 Merkel shocked all Europe by spelling out, in strong words, the option of excluding a country from the euro zone. During a debate at the Bundestag, she said that Finance Minister Schäuble had presented a proposal to expel from the currency union countries "that on the long term repeatedly fail to respect the conditions. Otherwise we will not be able to work together." In order to do that Merkel wanted to be able to change the European treaty. In response, the markets pushed down the euro by 1.1 percent, to $1.3587. Papandreou called the next day for urgent decisions from the euro-partners on aid to his country, because in just a few weeks Greece needed to float €5 billion in bonds. Papandreou seemed to win some support from ECB president Trichet, who, in an appearance before the European Parliament on March 22, indicated for the first time that the bank might continue providing liquidity against Greek bonds, even if the country was downgraded further by ratings agencies. Trichet also strongly rejected Merkel's suggestion that countries unwilling or unable to make reforms could be expelled from the euro zone. "The euro area is not à la carte. We enter the euro area to share a common destiny," he said, adding that exiting the euro zone was legally "impossible."[18]

## Help with Strong Conditionality

With events moving quickly, Merkel asked her two closest advisers, Uwe Corse-pius and Jens Weidmann, to speed the preparatory work with their counterparts in Paris for the EU summit of March 24–25. Markets all over the world consid-ered that meeting to be a moment of truth for the euro crisis. But Merkel had a different agenda, having decided to maintain the hard line against bailing out Greece for domestic reasons because her coalition's poll numbers had fallen to an all-time low. She decided to lead the European summit negotiations personally without letting anybody interfere. She informed Sarkozy through a constant line among her advisers Corsepius and Weidmann and their French counterparts, Jean-David Levitte, the president's diplomatic adviser, and Xavier Musca, the deputy secretary general at the Elysée. On the afternoon just before the council meeting was to begin, Merkel and Sarkozy worked for two hours on a draft text, not allowing even Herman Van Rompuy, the EU Council president, to join them. When they were done, Merkel and Sarkozy presented a statement to Papandreou, Trichet, and Van Rompuy shortly before the opening council session at 3 p.m. on March 25. Van Rompuy made only marginal amendments, though one had major political relevance: he replaced the words "economic government" with "economic governance" to ensure acceptance by Prime Minister Gordon Brown, who reflected Britain's wariness of mandates from Brussels. At the opening of the council the other heads of state and government were informed of the Franco-German text. The atmosphere immediately became tense. Spanish prime minister José Luis Zapatero, who held the six-month presidency of the EU, protested the lack of consultation. The same complaint came from Dutch prime minister Jan Peter Balkenende, who had been explicitly mandated by the Dutch Parliament not to enter into any binding commitments to help Greece.

The final statement represented the German position, though with some French amendments. Far from delivering a final counterattack to the crisis, it marked a shift back to negotiating rigidity. Here is the core:

> Euro area member states reaffirm their willingness to take determined and coordinated action, if needed, to safeguard financial stability in the euro area as a whole, as decided the 11th of February. As part of a package involving substantial International Monetary Fund financing and a majority of European financing, Euro area member states, are ready to contribute to coordinated bilateral loans. This mechanism, complementing IMF financing, has to be considered ultima ratio, meaning in particular that market financing is insufficient. Any disbursement on the bilateral loans would be decided by the euro area member states by unanimity subject to strong conditionality and based on an assessment by the European Commission and the European Central Bank. We expect Euro-Member states to participate on the basis of their respective ECB capital.[19]

The phrase "determined and coordinated action" would involve a series of bilateral loans that each euro member state would offer to Greece. No common pool of resources would be made available, but rather a web of fifteen national loans to the sixteenth country, Greece. This was nothing more than a "mechanism" complementing the IMF financing, even though Paris managed to insert the obvious remark that the majority of the funds were to arrive from the euro area members. The role of the IMF itself was completely different from the one envisaged in the statement of the February 11 European Council meeting. At that point, the council had described the IMF's role in marginal terms, as a simple provider of expertise ancillary to the ECB and the European Commission. Now, the EU leaders described a new euro area mechanism that was complementary to IMF financing. This represented a surprising U-turn even considering the fact that the Fund was not expected to give Greece more than €10 billion (based on the Greek share of IMF capital and applying the same multiplier that the IMF had used to assist the Baltic countries), while Athens's required funding for 2010 was in the range of €50 billion.

Berlin used many official reasons to explain this move, starting with the fact that involvement by the IMF would lend credibility to the operation, plus its money was immediately available. But the real reason was that leaving the leadership to the IMF made it possible to cut the lifeline if things became unsustainable. Allowing Greece to default would not have been possible if the decision had to be made by the EU Council, which required unanimity for all of its actions. The IMF role remained a bone of contention between Merkel and her finance minister, Schäuble, who still opposed the involvement of the Washington-based authority. Bringing in the IMF also was a serious setback for the European Commission, whose members believed they had been able to develop capacities in policy design on a level comparable with those of the IMF. Olli Rehn, the new economic and monetary affairs commissioner, reacted by saying that he would "prefer" aid for debt-laden Greece to be "under the clear lead of the EU," and not the IMF. Strong positions against the involvement of the IMF also came from the ECB.

The really non-negotiable part of the council statement was that the euro area mechanism of bilateral loans "has to be considered ultima ratio, meaning in particular that market financing is insufficient." The Latin expression favored by Merkel had finally found its way into official language of the EU. The European Commission and the European Central Bank would have to assess the financial straits of the requesting country. No automatic funding was allowed. And if Germany did not like the assessment of the two European institutions, it could block any disbursement of aid because a unanimous decision was required. Furthermore, the loans would come with strong conditionality attached and at a cost that would rule out any interpretation of the loans being an easy bailout. Finally, the EU leaders endorsed Merkel's preoccupation with the need to ensure fiscal sustainability through a reinforced Stability and Growth Pact. The idea of a European Monetary Fund was put aside because establishing such a fund would have required a formal change in the EU treaty, a laborious step fraught with difficulties. Instead, the mechanism of bilateral loans had superseded the need for an EMF, and there was no guarantee that the mechanism would evolve into a new permanent facility to deal with any future problems.[20]

## Sell the Parthenon, Too

Merkel's rigidity was greeted in Germany by the media far beyond what was reasonable; she was called the Euro-Retterin, the savior of the euro and of its stability. A consensus had been building around the image of Germany forced to defend itself from disorderly neighbors. The narrative behind this consensus represented a new German normality. Berlin felt it could openly defend its national interests just like any other nation and no longer had to pay a price for its past misdeeds, as it did in the rhetoric of Europas Zahlmeister, the official paymaster for Europe. This narrative was very appealing to citizens who could ground their skepticism, or lack of solidarity, behind the idea that they were exactly like all the other Europeans, and in any event better than the Greeks.

The mass-circulation newspaper *Bild Zeitung* played a very important role in orienting the public discourse in Germany, with its extreme language disparaging Greeks. The so-called boulevard-newspaper had 800 journalists, a circulation of 3 million, an estimated 12 million daily readers, and 27 local editions. Starting in February 2010, *Bild* mounted an unprecedented campaign against Greece. A first round of headlines on the front page asked, for example, "Is Greece making the German banks bankrupt?" This was followed by a formidable escalation of rhetoric: "Greeks quarrel and strike, instead of saving," "So the Greeks burn our nice Euro," "No Money to Greece," "You get nothing from us," "Why should we pay Greeks luxury pensions?" topped with the demand, "Sell your islands, you rotten Greeks, and the Acropolis too." This last story was accompanied by a financial estimate of the value of the Parthenon. A reporter was sent to Athens to be pictured distributing drachmas to the population. The title was "*Bild* gives rotten Greeks back their drachma." The pressure on the government was unequivocal: "Frau Merkel, stand by your Nein." As the mainstream weekly magazine *Der Spiegel* observed, *Bild* "has taken the role of opinion leading. In fact, time and again, it takes over the role of a right-wing populist party, otherwise not evident in German politics."[21]

Even beyond the excesses of the populist media, the mirage of a new German normality as the main force in Europe was too catchy to resist. A profound change in Germans' self-awareness came from the realization that Berlin could impose its will even beyond its economic weight. Non-euro countries within the EU were relieved not to be asked to participate in the rescue operations; they simply endorsed Germany's position. The Mediterranean countries and Ireland also were intimidated by the prospect of eventually depending on aid similar to Greece's. In short, practically all of the EU silently followed the hardening of Merkel's stance, which resulted from two factors—that she had received advice that Greece was insolvent and the consequences for the German banking system were very uncertain and that she faced political ramifications. As a consequence, she determined that Athens had to go through a draconian austerity program imposed by the IMF, similar to the experience of Latvia and Hungary. And Merkel's governing coalition was at a historical low in the polls and risked losing its majority in the Bundesrat (upper chamber) as a result of elections in North Rhine-Westphalia in May.

# 13

## Contagion

### Markets against Political Hesitations

At the beginning of April 2010, the Greek situation seemed to be getting worse by the day, and the markets questioned whether the European partners were committed firmly to giving Athens a chance to avoid default. The interest rate premium Athens was asked to pay over benchmark German bonds rose by more than 4 percentage points, its highest level since Greece joined the euro in 2001. The interest rate was above the threshold of 7 percent, considered an alarm bell for unsustainable borrowing costs. By the end of May, the Greek government faced a total financing requirement of around €29 billion. There was only a minimal chance that Athens could successfully ask the markets for that much money.[1]

Things took a clear turn for the worse when Greek citizens started withdrawing their money from the banks. A run on the banks is the origin of most disorderly defaults. When that happens, banks face a shortage of liquidity and in turn request funds from the national central bank. In the case of the euro area, the transfer of liquidity from the European Central Bank is only partly automatic and in case of an emergency must be authorized by a qualified majority of the central bankers. If the ECB rejects such a request, the national central bank might then be forced to issue electronic money that is different from the common currency, in effect breaking the country free from the euro. In April 2010 the four largest Greek credit institutions had to seek government support to help counter a liquidity squeeze resulting from the significant flight of deposits in the first two months of the year. Finance Minister George Papaconstantinou announced that the banks "have asked for access to the remaining funds of the support plan"—a €28 billion government package that was put together during the 2008 global credit crunch.[2] The banks' request, which came as spreads on ten-year Greek bonds remained at record levels, heightened concerns about the growing impact of the country's debt crisis on the financial sector. Local savers transferred about €10 billion of deposits—equal to about 4.5 percent of the total in the banking system—out of Greece between January and February, according to the central bank. Many savers had chosen to move funds to their banks' subsidiaries in Cyprus or Luxembourg. Others had transferred funds to local subsidiaries of foreign banks. That was a disastrous combination, pushing the Greek economy to the brink, aggravating the fiscal situation, and infuriating public opinion in foreign countries that were called on to help the Greeks who were running for the exits.

The prevalent analyses in the markets were drawing the conclusion that the Greek situation was unsustainable. Credit-default swaps on Greek debt surged to an all-time high, as did the spread between ten-year bonds for Greece and Germany. Red lights started to flash in the financial markets over the differences among euro zone governments on the details of any rescue. The source of growing disillusion was once again linked to doubts about the political commitment of the euro partners. Differences had emerged over how much Athens should pay for the cost of the financial support. Most euro zone nations were prepared to offer loans at 4 to 4.5 percent, the rate paid by the euro zone's other big debtors, Ireland and Portugal. But Merkel wanted to keep loans to Greece at a nonconcessional level to prevent a legal challenge in her own country. She insisted that Athens should pay 6 to 6.5 percent, the market rate it was currently paying on its ten-year bonds.

The situation was so desperate that on April 8 Prime Minister Papandreou called Prime Minister José Luis Zapatero of Spain, who then chaired the EU, asking him to mediate and to call for an urgent meeting of the Eurogroup. The two leaders got the green light from French president Nicolas Sarkozy and ECB president Jean-Claude Trichet, but European Council president Herman Van Rompuy opposed the request, anticipating that the Berlin government would object because there was no concrete plan ready for an aid package. The technical bodies in charge of the preparatory work for the European Council—first of all the Economic Financial Committee (EFC)—were still working on the complex legal aspects of mobilizing funds for Greece in anticipation of an informal meeting of the Economic and Financial Affairs Council (ECOFIN) to be held in Madrid. Merkel wanted to see the details of the technical preparatory work before committing to any funding. She wanted a precisely spelled-out sequence of steps. First of all, an agreement was needed on the total amount of the aid for Athens and how it had to be shared between the EU and the IMF. The second step was a formal request by Greece for assistance. The third was the mission to Athens of the newly established troika (a joint staff in charge of designing the strategy for Greece and formed by economists of the European Commission, the ECB, and the IMF) in order to complete the assessment of the Greek situation and set the conditions attached to the loan. Finally, a unanimous vote was needed by the heads of state and government of the Eurogroup.

## Eurogroup's Swift Assistance to Greece Takes Shape

Eventually, after the most turbulent week on Greek financial markets since the onset of the crisis and a two-notch downgrade of Athens's rating by the credit agency Fitch, an urgent extraordinary video conference of the euro zone finance ministers (in their capacity as the Eurogroup) was set for Saturday, April 11. The ministers were in direct contact with their principals. They agreed on the financial terms to be attached to a joint euro zone/IMF support package for Greece that would be made available, were it to be activated, as follows:

> Euro area Members States are ready to provide financing via bilateral loans centrally pooled by the European Commission as part of a package including International Monetary Fund financing. The Commission, in liaison with the ECB, will start working on Monday April 12th, with the IMF and the Greek authorities on a joint program (including amounts and conditionality, building on the recommendations adopted by the ECOFIN Council in February). In parallel, Euro area Members States will engage the necessary steps, at national level, in order to be able to deliver a swift assistance to Greece. Euro area Member States will decide the activation of the support when needed and disbursements will be decided by participating Member States.[3]

Several new elements emerged in this text, starting with the idea that the aid in the first year was part of a three-year program. The relationship between aid from the EU and the IMF was fixed in financial terms, as a two-to-one ratio for the first year (€30 billion from the euro member states and €15 billion from the IMF), with a decreasing IMF contribution expected for the following years. The European Commission would pool the national contributions and unofficially was expected to take over the lead in managing the loan program starting in the second year. Additional support for the second and third years was to be decided upon agreement of the program being worked out jointly by the Commission, the ECB, the IMF, and the Greek authorities. The total package for the first year amounted to almost 20 percent of the Greek annual GDP, larger than had been generally expected. The €30 billion just from the euro zone would entirely cover Greece's remaining financing needs for 2010 and into early 2011. The figures for 2011–12 were not mentioned in the statement released by the Eurogroup but were estimated to range between €50–€75 billion just from euro member states.

The text stated that "states loans will be granted on nonconcessional interest rates." The cost of the bilateral loans was one of the major points of disagreement within the Eurogroup. As noted earlier, the Germans wanted the interest rate to be clearly "nonconcessional" to show to the Constitutional Court that the loans did not provide a subsidy to Greece and were only dealing with the inability of markets to finance a euro zone member country. The rate was set at 300 basis points above euro swap rates for loans with less than a three-year maturity (400 basis points for longer-term loans), with an extra one-time charge of 50 basis points to cover operational costs. The implied interest rate of around 5 percent on a three-year loan—specifically mentioned in the Eurgroup text—was actually significantly lower, by more than 200 basis points, than market rates.[4] This was a compromise that left everybody unsatisfied. Analysts considered a 350 basis points spread over swap rates (especially in an environment where interest rates were likely to rise in the future) as still too high a cost of funding for Greece relative to what the country could afford to stabilize its debt-to-GDP ratio, given the poor outlook on nominal GDP growth. The credit line seemed especially unattractive in the longer term, above a five-year maturity. This confirmed the council's description of the package as "nonconcessional" and as maintaining incentives for the Greek government to increase its fiscal efforts to achieve more favorable borrowing conditions in the markets.

The technical details of the deal revealed a number of issues that had been difficult to settle since the beginning of the year, both among states and inside the EU-ECB-IMF troika. Immediately after receiving the mandate from the April 11 Eurogroup, the troika partners could not even agree where they had to meet. The European Commission, which had improved its capacity in policy design, had asked the IMF to hold the meetings in Brussels for the set-up of the conditionality of the Greek loan, but the IMF refused. They agreed instead to meet in Athens where, by sheer coincidence, the flight schedules had been disrupted by the eruption of a volcano in Iceland.

Agreement on the amount of money and on the timeframe had been difficult to reach. John Lipsky, the managing director representing the IMF, had stated plainly that what was needed was the classic IMF multiyear package—three years—for a total amount of €70–€100 billion. Germany wanted a one-year commitment, which was more palatable for its domestic politics, and a total loan of €40 billion. At the last minute, the president of the Bundesbank, Axel Weber, made another unsuccessful attempt to shut the door on the involvement of the IMF. Weber's objection was related to the independence of the ECB: the ECB probably would need to raise rates in the next two years, which would modify the terms of the Greek package and offer an opportunity for the IMF to meddle in the ECB policy. That was one of the reasons why the Greek financing deal used as a reference the "Euribor plus premium." The Euribor is a market rate and, although influenced by the ECB rate policy, does not reflect it mechanically. One further major aspect of the April 11 decision was that there was no indication that loans would be released automatically. As a German finance ministry spokesman confirmed, a parliamentary approval was "obviously" required, for example, in the case of a bilateral loan by Germany to Greece. In other words, the game of chicken between politics and markets was going to continue.

## The World Fears of Contagion

Initially the bond markets welcomed the loan package by substantially cutting interest rates for Greece across the maturity range.[5] But in a matter of days, markets started to take a more skeptical view of the agreement. The risk of a default had not been prevented, and the real test was expected to come in two weeks when the Greek government had to decide how to meet its €10 billion funding requirement to replace bonds that matured by the end of May.

Athens again found there was a risk of running out of time and on April 15 took an important step toward requesting a bailout from its euro zone partners and the International Monetary Fund by formally seeking "consultations" over the loan package to stave off a default. In a letter to the European Commission, Greek finance minister Papaconstantinou said Athens wanted to discuss "a multi-year economic policy program with the Commission, the European Central Bank and the International Monetary Fund." This prompted a reaction of "rage" among Greeks surveyed in a poll. Nine of 10 people surveyed said they expected the IMF to insist on more belt tightening. Labor unions threatened new strikes, but very impressively the Greek government managed to ride out the storm of public protest, which for the most part proved reasonably peaceful. A preliminary meeting in Athens with the IMF, ECB, and EU delegation was scheduled for April 19, with the talks supposed to take two to three weeks to complete. On April 23, Prime Minister Papandreou decided to call formally for the activation of the agreed-upon loan package. The request came one day after the yield on the country's benchmark two-year note topped 11 percent, nearing that of Pakistan, and Moody's Investors Service lowered Greece's creditworthiness by one notch to A3 and said it was considering a further cut to junk status.[6]

The risk of contagion was on everyone's mind when the IMF and World Bank spring meetings in Washington commenced on April 23. An IMF report on Global Financial Stability had just been released with a repeated alarm on the consequences of sovereign debt instability: "Financial sector linkages can transmit one country's sovereign credit concerns to other economies."[7] According to one participant in a restricted meeting with the finance ministers of the Group of Seven (G-7), Tim Geithner, the U.S. Treasury secretary, "was the most alarmed of all of us, due to the level of the U.S. debt." Olli Rehn, the

EU's monetary affairs commissioner, months later recalled that "very serious concerns were expressed about the danger of global contagion. There was very straight talk."[8] Talking with American officials was extremely helpful in focusing global attention on the need for action, especially considering the level of alarm of the Europeans.

As could be expected, Geithner was primarily worried about the effect on the American economy of a crisis in the euro area. "We were at a cusp in the economic cycle," a U.S. official explained. A new wave of instability coming from Europe could disrupt the very difficult recovery that was trying to take hold in the American economy. The jobless rate was unusually high and persistent, reflecting directly the declining approval of the president. Nevertheless, households were trying to gear up their consumption and needed credit from the banking system to keep going. Only a continuation of the very risky "return to abnormality" of a leveraged economy would encourage private investments and eventually produce sustainable growth. A new credit crisis would disrupt this fragile—although, to European eyes, reckless—way to sustain growth. A high-ranking representative of the administration denied that the White House or the U.S. Treasury could really pressure their European counterparts. "First of all, neither the President nor the Treasury secretary are psychologically and culturally inclined to lecture the others. Secondly and more importantly, we were all well aware that the crisis was originated here. It would have been embarrassing to pretend we had a better solution to the problems we had provoked. . . . Our best contribution to the solution for the euro crisis was to highlight timely and strongly on the usefulness to involve the IMF from the start," the official said.

## German Banks Would Fail with Greece

While the Washington meetings were ongoing, on April 24 German finance minister Wolfgang Schäuble went public in a television interview announcing officially that Germany would participate in the Greek loan program through the state bank KFW, backed by federal guarantees. The goal was to support the "extraordinarily ambitious" plan to which Athens had committed, he said. Schäuble recalled the agreement reached by the European Council on March 25 and defended its legal basis: Germany was not taking the responsibility for other countries' debts, as expressly forbidden by Article 125 of the Maastricht Treaty, but was making a voluntary loan to combat the excessive speculation against a member of the euro area and was, therefore, defending the stability of the euro with a credible plan. "We can help, but we don't have to," he said. In an important explanation issued much later, the German government observed: "A strict interpretation of Art. 125 could speak for a denial of support measures even in case of a threatening danger . . . but each mechanical application of Art. 125 would substantially endanger the economy in the euro zone and beyond.

The norm is not apt to be applied in the case of a present and severe danger for the financial stability of the euro-system." According to the government, the main failure of the treaty was in not considering the possibility of a threat to the whole euro area. This was the main line of interpretation that Merkel was going to hold all through the crisis: the threat was not about Greece but over "the euro area as a whole."[9]

Two days later Merkel gave a televised statement from the Chancellery where, visibly cautious and sticking to simply phrased concepts, she confirmed that Germany was participating in the three-year plan suggested by the IMF. "Nobody can say that we have not stressed the need for sustainability and severity, but I am convinced that Germany must do what is needed," she said. Merkel stressed the longer term commitment—repeatedly quoting Dominique Strauss-Kahn, the managing director of the IMF, on the successful past experience in Hungary and Latvia—to avoid being forced into new emergencies year-by-year. "We are now convinced that we need a prompt reaction for the stability of the euro as a whole . . . for Greece and for the German interest in a stable euro."

The conservative press in Germany reacted furiously, but the head of Deutsche Bank, Josef Ackermann, countered that without the European support, Greece would default and so would some German banks and other southern European countries. One day later, Standard & Poor's downgraded the Greek bonds to junk status; as a consequence the Dax, the main German equity index, lost 3 percent in a matter of hours.

The issue of banks was crucial to the debate in Germany, where most of the parliamentary groups still wanted to force the banks to pay for having been active parties in creating financial instability. Merkel too—but not her liberal ally the FDP—had been seriously considering a move in that direction. The opposition parties had been pressing strongly for a tax on the credit institutions that had exposed the country to the Greek risk. However, Schäuble was more cautious than Merkel. He knew that an involvement of the private sector directly connected to the sovereign bonds could be risky. The finance minister had tried to reach an agreement at the EU level on a common tax and tabled a different proposal that had been floated also by Merkel: a tax on financial transactions. Again, no agreement had been possible even within the EU, let alone with Washington, in that regard.

## Contagion Reaches the Core of Europe

Merkel's political discomfort in helping Greece was expressed in a board meeting of the Christian Democratic Union party. The chancellor admitted that it was "very difficult to justify help for Greece" but said it was necessary to prevent an even worse outcome. In order to rein in protest within her own government, Merkel organized a meeting in Berlin of the heads of the parliamentary groups from the Bundestag (the lower house of parliament) with IMF managing director Strauss-Kahn and European Central Bank president Trichet. Merkel needed all parties to agree to a fast-track procedure to pass a law in one week and be ready to help Greece. Trichet helped the parliamentarians understand the urgency of their commitment: "Every day we waste, things get worse." Finally, in an interview with the conservative newspaper *Bild,* even Bundesbank president Axel Weber sang the right tune: "Greek default would have an incalculable impact on markets and other countries." Contagion was accelerating, with interest rate spreads for short-term Portuguese and Irish government bonds reaching the same levels as Greece's just one month earlier. EU president Van Rompuy promptly announced a summit of the heads of the euro area countries "at the latest" on May 10—the day after Merkel's coalition faced crucial elections in North Rhine-Westphalia.

The sell-off came on April 28, a day after S&P cut Greek debt to junk and pulled Portugal's debt down two notches. Greek debt markets had all but frozen amid fears the country might default if it could not repay bondholders by the end of May. In a matter of hours, the euro area discovered the real scope of systemic instability. Contagion started to spread to Ireland, Portugal, and Spain. This expansion of the debt crisis beyond Greece also focused attention of the markets on the German and French banks, which had high exposure to the debt of several weak countries. French banks had nearly €60 billion in Greek exposure, followed by Germany at €35 billion. The prospect of contagion sweeping through European sovereign debt markets intensified as Spain's sovereign rating also was downgraded by Standard & Poor's, triggering a sell-off of Italian government bonds as well. Italy was the elephant in the room because no pool of resources would ever be sufficient to avoid a default of the country with the third-highest public debt in the world (€1.8 trillion). Investors were looking past Greece's well-known woes and pondering the possibility of a much larger European government debt crisis. Greek rating downgrades had heightened financial market contagion first to the weakest members of the euro zone, then to risk across all asset classes. S&P took Spain's long-term sovereign rating from AA+ down to AA with a negative outlook. Even France felt it was under attack. French budget minister Francois Baroin tried to ease public worry that French credit might encounter the risk of being downgraded. "There is no risk to see the bill (French debt) degraded," he said. "We are still a signature refuge" for investors.

## Merkel's Ethics

When the Greek crisis was perceived primarily as a short-term liquidity problem, because of the concentration of its refinancing needs in April and May, the contagion remained limited. However, as the markets began to see that forced fiscal tightening (and high borrowing rates) would cause—and be impaired by—lower growth in Greece, they began to shift their attention to the country's real problems of solvency and long-term sustainability. Analysts, investors, and others began discussing possible scenarios for Greek insolvency and subsequent default on its debts, raising what had been the taboo topic of a possible sovereign restructuring of an advanced economy. Once the taboo was broken, and Greece defaulted, all the other weakened countries became potential candidates for the same status. This would have several impacts, starting with higher sovereign risk premiums, which would put even more pressure on heavily indebted countries such as Italy and Belgium. To refinance their outstanding liabilities, these countries would need to access the bond markets more frequently and for relatively more money than other, less debt-ridden countries. Moreover, if Greece defaulted, other countries would be scrutinized in relation to their similarity to Greece, that is, whether they also had both high fiscal deficits and current account deficits. This meant that Ireland, and to some extent Portugal, Spain, and even Italy, would be next in the line of fire.

Seen from this perspective, letting Greece default might have been fatal for the euro and even for Germany itself. Once these potential consequences were taken into account, it became clear that the insistent use of moral categories in public discourse and in political judgments, particularly in Germany, was naïve and misplaced. Punishing Greece and the banks might seem correct, and even self-satisfying, from an ethical point of view, but it would be suicidal, which is hardly an ethical attitude. The logic of markets is, of course, neutral to the ethical dimension that was—often with populist distortions—leading German public opinion. Even so, elements of morality are indeed intrinsic in financial behavior, starting with the idea of moral hazard. So a moral element in the political debate was significant for the markets, as well. It was difficult, however, for the democratic procedures of political systems to work at the speed demanded by the markets, where computers often operate in terms of split seconds. At an even more profound level, democracy was attempting to reconcile the respect for the principles of our societies—honesty in the first place, plus credibility and trust—with the need for defending the stability of society itself.

This is an archetypical German dilemma, one that sociologist Max Weber characterized as between the ethic of ultimate ends (*Gesinnungsethik*) and the ethic of responsibilities (*Verantwortungsethik*). The shift in Europe from a purely national community, based on each country's own recognizable constitutional values, toward an interdependent—but not yet supranational—political environment represents a form of disenchantment (*Entzauberung*), where a community is deprived of the powerful forces of identity and left mainly to the rational discernment of human beings in what Weber called the "collision" of values. Once they do, they lose the orientation of responsibility and become purely cynical. Thus, the German chancellor faced a fundamental political dilemma in dealing with the Greek crisis. In the eyes of Angela Merkel, the only strategy that would work was to demand that Greece impose severe domestic policies as a condition for the bailout, thereby reconciling a moral commitment with the desired consequences.

But there was a problem with this simple equation. It might be satisfactory for Merkel's scientific mind, but such an algebraic prescription completely neglected an important factor: future uncertainty. Against all available evidence, Merkel's logic required an assumption that the future was already written as a pure consequence of the present. Or, as Hegel once noted, she seemed to assume that what was rational was also real.

## The Agreement on May 2

Merkel's equation took shape. The agreement that the EU-ECB-IMF troika finalized on May 2 with the Greek government was both severe in the austerity demanded of Athens and huge in its size.[10] The final amount was set at €110 billion over three years; €80 billion was to be provided by euro area member states and €30 billion by the IMF. The agreement consisted of a twenty-six-page text with precise technical details. As previously agreed, the aid was to come in the form of pooled bilateral loans channeled through a bank account opened by the European Commission at the ECB. The €80 billion loan from the European states had a maximum term of five years, and Greece had the option of not repaying it during the first three years. Greece was to pay a 3 percent premium over Euribor rates for the first three years; after that, the premium increased to 4 percent, and by 2 percentage points in case of arrears (missed repayments). If any single country could not extend credit to Greece, for instance, for political reasons, the initial loan could be financed by just some of the euro zone countries.

The rest of the text contained several hints of the German special position. Germany was the only country that would participate not as a state party to the loan but through the state-owned bank KFW—even though it was clearly stated that Germany acknowledged and guaranteed all the obligations of its agent bank. The last point in the text—"If the European court, or a constitutional court in a euro zone country, rules that the loan to Greece violates European Union or national law, the loan agreement for the country, or the euro zone as a whole, would be void"—raising the possibility of a judicial opposition to the deal, obviously was a very German position that gave the German people and its judges a formidable power. This point was taken up by *Bild:* "If the German Federal Constitutional Court decides against the billion-euro assistance, our contract with the Greeks will be void. We won't have to pay anymore!"

In return for the financial package, Greece agreed to new huge austerity measures amounting to €24 billion over three years. The aim was to reduce the budget deficit by 13.6 percent of GDP to below the Stability and Growth Pact's

3 percent threshold by 2014 and to stabilize public debt at around 140 percent of GDP. As Van Rompuy announced, "A major program has just been concluded. The agreement is both ambitious and credible, given the efforts it foresees in budgetary terms and in terms of competitiveness."[11] The measures to which the Greek government committed included an increase in the value-added tax from 21 percent to 23 percent; significant cuts in bonuses, pensions, and subsidies to the public sector; changes in the complex provisions regarding retirement, including an end to early retirement agreements; an increase in the official retirement age to sixty-seven and a loosening of the restrictions surrounding the laying off of workers. Even before the agreement was reached, George Papandreou justified the government's decision to accept harsh aid terms in appropriately dramatic language: "The economic measures are necessary for our protection and the country's survival. This is our patriotic duty, which we will carry out regardless of the cost."[12]

# 14

## Dr. Faust Saves the Euro

### Beginning with a Small German Village

The fears and the fury of the markets could not be contained by the painstaking and long negotiations over the Greek loan. European leaders needed urgently to grapple with a host of broader issues, first of all, setting up a sizable financial fund, especially for a number of countries looking less and less stable. The Greek agreement had simply come too late. Contagion was vigorously proceeding and the euro area was never so close to collapsing as at the beginning of May 2010. To counter the disruption in the markets, two more high-level meetings were scheduled, the first at the level of the heads of state and governments (the Euro-summit) and the second at the level of the finance ministers (the Eurogroup) to approve the bailout package. During those incredibly hectic and dramatic days, a number of coups-de-theatre happened entirely behind the scenes.

The untold story of the negotiations reveals a reality of European politics that turns upside-down the conventional understanding that later took hold, one in which Germany was betrayed, pushed into a corner, or even simply outvoted by its euro zone partners and forced to accept ECB involvement in the Greek bailout, thereby violating the bank's mandate. That version, which formed the standard narrative of the euro crisis and helped shape all the future events in the crisis, was simply not true.

Germany was, in fact, betrayed, but not by the crucial decision on the role of the central bank. The real betrayal came instead at the end of May when, as we will see, France broke a secret and informal commitment on the future defense of the debt-ridden countries by using a subterfuge that would also influence the rest of the crisis. But the complex story of May 2010 needs to be told from its very beginning and by highlighting the roles of two of the most secretive and influential actors: the European Central Bank, the only financial powerhouse truly capable of saving the euro, and its most powerful governor, Axel Weber, the president of Germany's central bank, the Bundesbank.

In the months before May 2010, Weber had been feeling the terrible pressure of the crisis on his shoulders. Since he had become president of the Bundesbank in 2004, the valiant monetary economist had tried to keep under control the personality cult that seemed to come with his new job. He did not rise through the ranks of the respected institution and had been a surprising choice as an outsider to lead it. But since taking charge of the bureaucratic monster of roughly 10,000 employees, he had behaved high-handedly—often refusing to discuss, let alone negotiate, his decisions with his colleagues. Weber had been the helpful partner of ECB president Jean-Claude Trichet in convincing Angela Merkel in 2008 to bail out Hypo Real Estate at the very last minute, defusing what could have been a devastating crisis for Europe. He had seen in that case the mediocrity of bankers and the ignorance of politicians. Ever since, Weber had seemed to believe, with some legitimacy, that he had become essential to his country in mastering the crisis.

The Bundesbank building is a dull glass and concrete complex on the outskirts of Frankfurt. It is so ugly that one of Weber's predecessors, Karl Otto Poehl, ascribed to it only one clear advantage: "It is the only place in Frankfurt from where you do not see it." Entering the building is a somewhat cultural experience. Visitors notice the glass cases showing 1 billion deutsche mark banknotes of the German hyperinflation between the two world wars. Then the visitor enters an elevator and is left in pitch darkness. It may be many seconds before the operator turns a little key and the energy-saving system allows the lights to go on. Every cent is valued here. And values and moral high ground are often too easily associated with the bank's tasks of protecting German monetary stability.

Before settling into his Bundesbank office on the coveted twelfth floor, Weber had followed a very German academic career. He was born in Glan-Muenchweiler, in Kusel county, with just 5,000 inhabitants. He had studied economics at the University of Konstanz and later taught at the University of Siegen, hardly primary addresses in the world of monetary studies. But at age thirty-seven the talented scholar had reached a professorship at Bonn, then Frankfurt and Cologne, and he became a regular presence at academic monetary conferences across Europe. Later, he was named to the Sachverstaendigenrat, the independent body advising the government on economic policy. "It is impressive," the wife of his former teacher at Kostanz told him one day, "how lucky you have been to obtain your reward." Weber responded, "It has nothing to do with luck, only with knowledge."

## On the Brink of the Abyss

During the eighteenth century, the cannons used by the French and Austrian armies were engraved with the words *ultima ratio regum,* the last resort of the kings. A similar inscription might have been engraved on the dossiers concerning financial assistance to Greece. The decision about the date of the all-important summit of the heads of state and governments of the euro zone was changed under the buildup of market pressures. In his letter, sent during an official visit to Tokyo, European Council president Herman Van Rompuy had indicated that the meeting would take place on May 10 "at the latest." The reason for the vague indication was obviously the regional election in North Rhine-Westphalia on May 9. Merkel had been accused, both inside and outside Germany, of dragging her feet on difficult decisions about Europe just to avoid being punished by an irritated German electorate. According to the polls, North Rhine-Westphalian citizens were among those showing the greatest disapproval of transferring money to Greece. The western Land is also the most populous in the country. The May 9 election was considered pivotal because if the opposition won, Merkel's new government—in power for just six months—would lose its majority in the Bundestrat (the upper chamber of parliament) and therefore its ability to adopt major laws easily.

Following the EU-ECB-IMF agreement producing the Greek loan deal on May 2, Van Rompuy tried to convince Merkel to drop her political maneuvering because Europe was rapidly running out of time. If the leaders waited to meet on May 10, the day after the local elections in Germany, to approve or adjust the troika's plan, they would be discussing and negotiating in the very extreme and volatile climate of open markets still uncertain about the outcome. That was not a risk that Europe could run. Moreover, even after the summit meeting, markets would remain in a climate of uncertainty for several more days. The heads of state and governments could not be expected to finalize the enormous amount of technical details implied by the agreement in such a short time. So, the May 10 meeting would have to be followed by another one, this time among the finance ministers of the Eurogroup. And even that technical meeting could require more than one day. Waiting as long as ten days before a final resolution could be announced was outright suicidal. The alarm about the situation was extremely clear during the continuous contacts among the G-7 finance ministers, who were discussing the implications for the international bond markets of the Greek debt debacle. U.S. Treasury secretary Timothy Geithner, who was less inclined than his predecessors to interfere with other countries, expressed his worries about the impact of European inaction on a U.S. economy that was on a cusp between recession and recovery. Australia's prime minister, Kevin Rudd, was scathingly critical of the EU package for Greece agreed the weekend before by fifteen euro zone countries and the IMF: "Markets have judged those arrangements to be inadequate," he said.[1]

"This is a global issue," Japan's deputy finance minister, Rintaro Tamaki, said. "All the financial markets are now in turmoil. . . . The impact of the Greek crisis has gone beyond the euro area."[2] Waiting for the vote in North Rhine-Westphalia could not be the only priority.

There was something of destiny in that date game: on May 8 European leaders were to attend the celebration in Moscow commemorating the end of World War II in Europe sixty-five years earlier—and Merkel, in consideration of the special role of her country, was the only European leader who felt she could not miss it. May 9, "Europe Day," marked the sixtieth anniversary of the Schuman Declaration, the proposal by the French foreign minister, Robert Schuman, to create a supranational organization of states in war-ravaged Europe. Finally, Van Rompuy had to ask the chancellor whether she would mind if the summit meeting was held on May 7 instead of May 10. This would leave the whole weekend for the finance ministers to implement whatever the heads of state and government decided before the financial markets reopened on Monday morning. In Berlin the debate on aid for Greece was extremely heated, but both houses of parliament were bound to approve the highly unpopular bailout (the opposition Social Democratic Party ultimately opted to abstain). In a desperate attempt to put a favorable spin on the situation, Merkel changed her communications strategy and rounded furiously on the markets, rather than on Greece. "Politics has to reassert primacy over the financial markets," she said describing speculators as "our opponents" and the banks as "perfidious." Merkel added, "Like all my colleagues, I want to win this fight." Adopting this new strategy implied reacting as fast as possible, and preempting if possible, any attacks from the markets. Consequently, Merkel agreed with the new date.

Due to the delays caused by Berlin's "ultima ratio" policy and by the connected sense of precarious political support, financial investors were all but dropping the bonds of the euro zone peripheral countries. Days after the troika group had agreed on the bailout package, yields on Greek two-year bonds were still above 10 percent, and the euro weakened further. Although everybody was now expecting a resolution at the May 7 meeting, the situation in the financial markets was rapidly getting out of hand. The spiraling of interest rates on sovereign bonds that started in Greece spread to Portugal, then to Spain, Ireland, and Italy. From London, Paris, and Frankfurt financial associations and representatives of bond dealers hammered ECB officials with calls to make them aware of the turmoil and to demand a solution. "There were no buyers at that point. We felt that if the ECB would announce that they would operate as a buyer, the markets would know there was a floor to the prices."[3]

The ECB normally intervenes only in the secondary market for bonds—the market for securities after their issuance—while it is impeded by its statute from buying bonds directly from states when they are issued. Moreover, the bank can buy on the secondary market for reasons related to the regular management of its huge portfolio, or for limited monetary policy goals, but not for the purpose of promoting financial stability, as in this case. Central bank officials were receptive to the comments they received but without revealing whether they had any plans for a so-called nuclear option: countering the market attacks by buying the sovereign bonds of the weaker euro area countries.

## The ECB: The Reluctant White Knight

The situation was indeed similar to that in September 2008 when Lehman Brothers failed: banks were increasingly reluctant to lend to each other because of worries that other institutions could fail to pay back their loans. At that time the ECB provided for a huge amount of liquidity to overcome the impasse in Europe (the Federal Reserve did the same in the United States). Similarly, the ECB in 2009 engaged in its "Grand Bargain" of making loans to banks so they could purchase bonds from governments in trouble—a procedure that kept the ECB one step removed from buying such bonds itself (see chapter 7).

Now, nearly two years later, a decision by the ECB to buy government debt directly would have shored up the euro zone bond markets by reassuring investors they could always sell to the central bank. But such a decision could have been fatal for the central bank. In several countries, most prominently in the United Kingdom and the United States, deficits had been financed by the central bank creating new money. If the ECB followed the same practice, it would have to rip up the euro zone rulebook and its first commandment: the independence of the central bank from political pressures. Printing money to buy sovereign bonds would mean that the distinction between monetary and fiscal policy would melt away, together with the autonomy of the central bank from the political powers, its supranational public legitimacy, and its coveted anti-inflationary credentials.

The ECB knew that strong speculative attacks could have been countered only by a central bank threatening to mobilize its theoretically infinite amount of financial resources. Within the bank there was no consensus at all for a so-called quantitative easing of that kind, especially one used for fiscal reasons. The only option considered was eventually to buy sovereign bonds without changing the quantity of money—that is, "sterilizing" the money used to buy bonds by avoiding an increase in the monetary base as a result of the bond purchases. However, even for this less extreme option there was no unanimity within the bank's governing council and executive board. The two German board members,

ECB chief economist Jürgen Stark and Bundesbank president Weber, had stated their opposition very clearly at every opportunity. In theory, sterilizing money would avoid the fiscal policies of governments directly influencing ECB monetary policy, but it would have changed the role and the status of the bank, making it responsive to the policy priorities of euro zone member governments.

This was a crucial issue at the core of the central bank's identity. Independence from political powers—the cherished heritage of the Bundesbank—had been transmitted to the new institution, which, not coincidentally, also was based in Frankfurt. ECB president Trichet was well aware of that. He traced his own admiration for the Bundesbank back to a specific episode in 1956: "One of the most impressive [events] has been the open conflict with Chancellor Konrad Adenauer, who wanted the Bundesbank [it was actually its forerunner, the Bank deutscher Länder] to decrease interest rates. But the Bank refused. It proved to be really independent." Trichet saw a direct line binding the ECB to the German institution: "At the beginning of 2004 shortly after I became President of the ECB, three heads of member states asked publicly to lower rates: The Bundeskanzler of Germany, Gerhard Schröder, the President of the French Republic, Jacques Chirac, and the Prime Minister of Italy, Silvio Berlusconi. The ECB demonstrated its independence. We did not comply."[4] Still, the situation of the euro was so critical that all options were analyzed in all aspects—and this was done in the greatest secrecy.

The reason for the secrecy at the ECB was that if governments knew that the central bank might ultimately step in and defend the euro, they would probably avoid any fiscal efforts on their own. In other words, the concern in Frankfurt was the classic one of moral hazard: allowing sinners to escape penalties for their sins. Moreover, regardless of whether the bank intervened directly, governments would have to agree on a European stabilization mechanism of some kind: an institutionalized, firm commitment to mobilize huge funds to help countries hit by unjustified financial difficulties. This would be the final stage of a debate about a European Monetary Fund that had been going on for three decades. The new institution could show to the markets that the euro area countries were in fact committed to preserving the stability of the monetary union. With such an institution in place, an eventual commitment of the ECB to buy bonds would not be bottomless and with time was likely to be superseded by the stabilization mechanism itself. Fiscal policy problems would be solved with fiscal policy instruments, leaving the credibility of monetary policy untarnished.

For the ECB the possibility of an ultimate intervention in the bond market was particularly embarrassing because it had always ruled out any bond purchase in the past. Doing it now would smack of a U-turn affecting its future credibility. The justification for such a dramatic policy change—for the ECB and for Berlin—was that the current exceptional circumstances required an intervention for the sake of overall stability. There was a clear risk of financial disorder and grave economic consequences, so any past commitment had to be calibrated on the current set of risks.[5] Still, it was important for the ECB to be particularly vocal in ruling out any form of quantitative easing and, instead, calling for peripheral countries to reduce wages and their public deficits. Behind the scenes, it was important to obtain strong commitments from Spain, which was about to announce spending cuts (including a 5 percent cut in public sector wages), that would bring the deficit to 6 percent of GDP, and Portugal, which promised to hike taxes in order to bring its deficit to 4.6 percent of GDP. The positive answers by the two Iberian countries demonstrated that, as a central banker put it, instead of moral hazard, what was at work was moral suasion.

## The Faustian Moment

Even though some governments, such as Spain and Portugal, were promising reforms, the ECB was wary that governments in general were slow and hesitant in their responses to the crisis. It had repeatedly called for more decisive fiscal action and for setting up a stability mechanism to convince the markets that governments were serious about dealing with their fiscal problems. So, when the bank's board held its monthly meeting in Lisbon on May 6, in the midst of the crisis, Trichet denied vehemently that the option of buying bonds had been on the table. A journalist asked him directly about the option of purchasing government bonds during a press conference, and Trichet replied, "We did not discuss this option."

He should have added, "not yet." In fact, something completely unexpected happened after the board meeting and the press conference. The top officials of the European Central Bank were sitting down to dinner with their spouses in the Emperor's Room of the Palacio da Bacalhoa, a fifteenth-century estate and winery south of the Portuguese capital. Suddenly, all the Blackberries of the central bankers started to vibrate simultaneously. News alerts flashed on the screens. On Wall Street, the Dow Jones Industrial Average was plummeting in what became known as the "flash crash." A U.S. government report later said, "May 6 started as an unusually turbulent day for the markets," and the U.S. stock markets opened low on worries about the debt crisis in the euro area.[6] At 2:42 p.m. New York time (8:42 p.m. in Lisbon), with the Dow Jones down more than 300 points for the day, the equity markets began to fall rapidly, dropping more than 600 points in five minutes for an almost 1,000 point loss by 2:47 p.m.[7] It was the largest intraday loss in the history of Wall Street.

The news deeply upset everybody around the table in Portugal. For all their rational discipline, a group dynamic began to breed sentiments of increasing discomfort. Unaware of the technical reasons behind the event on the New York Stock Exchange, the European central bankers feared that they had somehow provoked the dramatic market disruption, as a result of the council's tepid statements and what markets might have perceived as their reluctance to commit to strong measures defending Greek bonds. President Trichet immediately convened, in the palacio's cellar, a conclave of the ECB's governing council to debate the situation. After a first broad assessment of the situation by Trichet, a profound sense of alarm prevailed during the forty-five minutes of discussion about the market tensions and preoccupation with the euro area.

All of a sudden, the unspeakable option was raised by the most unexpected source—the president of the Bundesbank, Axel Weber. "The ECB must buy government bonds!"

Many of those present could not believe their ears. The hawkish leader of the conservative German institution had launched the most compromising challenge for a central banker, to bend the rigor of monetary policy to the rescue of profligate governments. Central bankers were thought not to be unanimous in their views about such a contentious matter as buying the bonds of governments that seemed unable to access the markets. But one thing had seemed certain until that very moment: Weber would never support the idea. In the informal talks of the previous days the German board members—Weber and ECB chief economist Stark—had equated the step to "printing money," anathema for the Bundesbank, a step that could stoke inflation. Now, in response to a market crash across the Atlantic, suddenly the most orthodox defender of a purist monetary policy, a man rigorously indifferent to the claims of politics, bent his creed to the need of governments. It was truly a Faustian moment. Science traded for survival. Shockingly, Weber exposed his conversion and was the first to throw the issue on the table: "We must buy government bonds, this is a monetary policy decision!"

Jürgen Stark was opposed, but took a cautious position. Other board members were also opposed, but were now upset, completely taken aback by the unforeseen situation. In fact, after Weber's conversion, the die was cast. Around the table, it was easy to form a clear majority in favor of buying bonds of the ailing countries.

The ECB bond purchasing plan, later called the Securities Market Program (SMP), was intended as "one of the transitory non-standard measures of monetary policy," as one of the participants to the dinner meeting explained later. "We deemed it necessary in view of the abnormal situation in markets, to help restore a normal transmission of monetary policy." But that is likely to be an ex-post rationalization. That evening Europe seemed to be on the brink of a financial collapse, for the second time since the dark days of September 2008. Weber had lived through the first post–Lehman Brothers crisis—at Hypo Real Estate's bedside—and had seen how close Europe had been to the disaster. Now, he seemed to react instinctively as a firefighter and ran for the water pump. Although the decision was actually made that night in the Lisbon cellar, the group decided to keep their resolution under wraps and to postpone a formal decision until they had seen the euro zone governments adopt tough measures of their own. Consequently they did not release any statement after their meeting.[8]

## Close to the Global Meltdown

Once more, the market pulse was out of tune with the bipolar nature of the responses by the policy authorities. Despite the €110 billion lifeline to Greece agreed by the troika on May 2, and the repeated commitments by European institutions and leaders to save the euro, markets kept on savaging the peripheral countries. A major hit came on May 6—the same day of the ECB meeting in Lisbon—when Moody's highlighted a risk of contagion from the Greek debt crisis, which it warned could spread to five other EU states: Spain, Portugal, Ireland, Italy, and the United Kingdom. This warning also came on the very day that Britain was holding its eventful general elections that ended the long rule of the Labor Party and produced a new coalition government led by the Conservative Party's David Cameron, a government that was widely expected to be more skeptical about ties to Europe. The British government had also recently published data on its fiscal situation that showed a long-term explosion of public debt reaching levels not far from that of Greece (relative to the overall economy) and the highest per capita deficit of any advanced economy in the world. The involvement of Britain in the contagion chain was particularly dangerous because in recent months public finance economists had been inclined to put it on the same footing as the United States. A transmission of contagion from Greece to the United States, via the United Kingdom, was suddenly a concrete possibility. It was no surprise, then, that U.S. president Barack Obama intervened, repeatedly calling Angela Merkel and urging the German government to stabilize the European crisis.

Overall, the cacophony of statements by European policymakers was deafening—except on the subject of contagion, where the strategy of denial seemed to defy logic. Trichet had tried to defuse the rationale for contagion: "Greece and Portugal are not in the same boat," he told journalists in Lisbon. "This is very clear when you look at the facts and figures . . . Portugal is not Greece."[9] But the European political arena was out of control. On May 4 Antonis Samaras, leader of the Greek opposition party, Nea Dimokratia, announced that his party would vote against the EU/IMF loan package, denting severely any hope of a bipartisan consensus for reforms in Greece. In Germany, in view of the upcoming vote in North Rhine-Westphalia, Merkel released hawkish remarks to German public television inadvertently envisaging the possibility of a default in Greece. The same thing happened to Finance Minister Wolfgang Schäuble, who told reporters, "We need . . . the possibility of a restructuring procedure in the event of looming insolvency that could help prevent systemic contagion risks."[10] The prospect of losing money on investments in peripheral bonds, so clearly expressed by senior German leaders, contributed to a fall of the euro to 1.30 against the dollar, its lowest level of the year.[11] The yield on two-year Greek bonds soared to an astounding 14.5 percent. Acceptance of austerity in Greece seemed definitely to waver when, on May 5, three people died in a bank fire in Athens as the Greek capital descended into chaos amid protests over government austerity measures. Greek president Karolos Papoulias said the country was "on the brink of the abyss."[12]

At the same time, Robert Fico, prime minister of the euro zone's newest member, Slovakia, announced that his government did not want to vote on financial aid for Greece before Slovakia's June 12 national election.[13] The Slovenian prime minister, Borut Pahor, endorsed Merkel's suggestion of excluding countries violating the fiscal deficit rules from the euro zone. Moody's May 6 report listing a number of countries as targets of "potential contagion" aroused strong reactions from the French and German governments, both of which announced retaliations against the credit agencies.[14] Jean-Claude Juncker, chairman of the Eurogroup finance ministers, said he suspected an "organized worldwide attack against the euro." That wording may seem Machiavellian, but exactly the same language came from the White House. Finally, as previously mentioned, on May 6 Wall Street collapsed as a consequence of technical flaws. In Asia, the Shanghai stock market fell to an eight-month low, down a choppy 6.8 percent from the previous day, and the euro fell to 1.27 against the dollar. Clearly, markets were panicking.

Against that backdrop, the political reaction seemed far less sharp than would have been desirable. Just a few hours before the Eurosummit, Sarkozy and Merkel issued a joint letter that seemed to present a common front, or at least a façade of one. The two leaders called for a number of initiatives to stabilize the financial markets and tighten control of euro zone countries' finances. The letter was remarkable because it did not mention Merkel's idea of ousting undisciplined countries from the euro zone, or other forms of severe penalties (like cutting the transfer of EU funds to the delinquent country). The letter served both as an endorsement of the Greek package and as an orientation for further steps. An EU consensus had been building along three lines of action: strengthening fiscal surveillance by highlighting the need for more ambitious reductions of long-term debt (not only of annual deficits); setting up a framework for interdependent economic surveillance, extending it from purely fiscal matters to competitiveness-related policies and "strengthening the effectiveness of EU recommendations on economic policy"; and establishing a permanent resolution mechanism that could also include warning systems.[15]

A few hours before the May 7 meeting in Brussels, European Commission president José Manuel Barroso announced that the European Commission was ready to mobilize financial resources—€60 billion—to set up a lifeline for countries in need under Maastricht Treaty Article 122.2, which contemplates aid in the case of a country hit by externally caused, exceptional circumstances.[16] According to rumors in Brussels, such a proposal had long been anticipated, but market participants had expected the euro partners would offer funds of around €100–€120 billion. Barroso's announcement was nowhere near that scale. The commitment had to be extraordinary and Thomas Wieser, the president of the Economic and Financial Committee (EFC) working on the deal, sounded the alarm in a letter to Eurogroup chairman Juncker. In a revealing paragraph, Wieser called on the euro area member states to "express their willingness to take all necessary measures to protect the integrity and stability of the euro." Just how difficult it was to get such a commitment from the governments was revealed by another diplomatic incident that happened on the evening of May 6 when Herman Van Rompuy circulated a draft of the statement summarizing the next day's summit meeting. In the draft, the heads of state and government were called to "demonstrate our commitment today and tomorrow to ensure the stability and the integrity of the euro area and to use the full range of means available to the euro zone and its members to this end." But the next morning, on May 7, a few hours before the beginning of the meeting, Uwe Corsepius, the German chancellor's EU adviser, expressed reservations to Van Rompuy about the reference to "the full range of means available." Van Rompuy had to call the chancellor herself, who agreed immediately that it would be sensible not to delete the phrase.

Also in advance of the leaders' meeting, finance ministers and central bank governors of the G-7 held a conference call to address growing concerns that a failure to effectively contain the Greek financial crisis could cause it to spread quickly to other European countries and beyond, further roiling world markets. Officials in Washington said the one-hour call was hastily scheduled after the steep market drop on May 6. Dominique Strauss-Kahn, the managing director of the International Monetary Fund, took part in the call, and Treasury secretary Geithner and Federal Reserve chairman Ben Bernanke represented the United States. Market instability was actually spreading well beyond Europe: jittery investors forced Brazil to scale back bond sales as interest rates soared and caused some Asian currencies to weaken. Ten companies around the world that had planned to issue stock delayed their offerings, the most in a single week since October 2008.[17] Overall, United States banks had $3.6 trillion in exposure to European banks, according to the Bank for International Settlements. That included more than a trillion dollars in loans to France and Germany, and nearly $200 billion to Spain. American money market investors were nervous about hundreds of billions of dollars in short-term loans to big European banks and other financial institutions. "Greece may just be an early warning signal," a prominent Wall Street strategist told the *New York Times*. "The U.S. is a long way from being where Greece is, but the developed world has been living beyond its means and is now being called to account."[18] There is a limit to the effectiveness of U.S. pressure on European decisions. A source very close to the president said that the White House and the Treasury were clearly inhibited in their criticisms, since the United States had been the original source of financial instability for the whole world. Nevertheless, U.S. Treasury officials confirmed to a Greek government source that they feared a direct contagion to the United States because of Greece's ballooning public debt. In the early hours of Friday, May 7, Barack Obama called Merkel and Sarkozy to urge them to ensure that the EU was "taking resolute steps to build confidence in markets." It was the third time in four weeks that Obama called Merkel to urge her resolve. "We agreed on the importance of a strong policy response by the affected countries and a strong financial response from the international community," the president said afterward. "I made clear that the United States supports these efforts and will continue to cooperate with European authorities and the [International Monetary Fund] during this critical period." Obama also admitted that "I am very concerned about what's happening in Europe."[19] A new call was made by the president at 10 a.m. on Sunday, May 9, after the Eurosummit. According to a German source, Obama used dramatic tones: if Europe was not going to act decisively, nobody could guarantee what would happen to the euro. The White House had spotted signals that a massive attack on the common currency was in the pipeline for the next Monday.

### Dinner on May 7: The ECB as the Main Course

As euro zone leaders prepared for their May 7 meeting, they saw three critical issues at stake: the volume of money that euro area governments could mobilize; the mechanism they were going to use to pool the funds; and, most important, the role of the ECB in the rescue package. In fact, the whole meeting—the most crucial up to that point in the history of the crisis—must be viewed through the lens of the ECB question.

According to sources, Merkel was not prepared to commit to an exorbitant amount of money. She clearly considered the €60 billion mentioned in Barroso's statement as insufficient, but the right amount, in her view, was far from clear. What she surely wanted was a liquidity ceiling for the stability mechanism, which others thought was meant to offer a limitless guarantee. At the same time, she wanted to defend the autonomy of the central bank while also getting it to participate actively in the rescue. Sarkozy, by contrast, favored putting on the table the highest possible stake and urging—even commanding—the ECB to buy sovereign bonds. Beyond these divergent tones, however, the positions were actually very close. The real bone of contention was the role of the ECB. Any other possible solution that the European Council would come up with would require time. A short-term policy response was therefore necessary, and that could come only from Frankfurt. Both Trichet and Merkel themselves had already concluded that the bank's purchase of bonds was indispensable, but they could not allow the ECB to appear as having obeyed a request, much less a demand, from the governments.

The French president was extremely active after his arrival in Brussels. He had gathered a solid consensus among the prime ministers of the Mediterranean countries and with Barroso. But he also held well-advertised bilateral meetings with Trichet, Van Rompuy, and Merkel. The chancellor had canceled a campaign event in North Rhine-Westphalia in order to fly early to Brussels. The press reported that Sarkozy entered the meeting with Merkel, followed by a scrum of French journalists and cameramen, and announced theatrically: "This is the moment of truth." The French activism already had alerted Merkel and Trichet, both of whom were clearly fearing a public attack on the ECB autonomy. They could count on the support of the prime ministers of Luxembourg (Jean-Claude Juncker), the Netherlands (Jan-Peter Balkenende), and Finland (Matti Vanhanen). The crucial preliminary meeting was between Merkel, Sarkozy, and Trichet, around a table with a few cookies, some glasses of water, and two telephones. Sarkozy tried to pin down a solution within the day, urging his two interlocutors to commit in a hurry. Merkel, as usual, wanted to stick to the formal rules of European meetings, appealing to the EU procedures and delegating the details to the finance ministers. By doing this, she spared the ECB from facing pressure from the heads of governments for a swift decision.

The preliminary discussions went on for two hours beyond the official starting time of 7 p.m. that Van Rompuy had fixed for the formal dinner. To Merkel's relief, news came from Karlsruhe that the German Constitutional Court had just rejected the motion of four professors who had wanted to block Germany's participation in the Greek aid package.

### *"Live Up to Your Responsibility!"*

The working dinner finally got to the heart of the matter with George Papandreou's lengthy opening statement on the dramatic situation in Greece. It was then Trichet's turn. The ECB president launched into an explanation of the broader situation facing Europe. He did it in a quiet voice and with the help of charts illustrating the risk of contagion, including one graph showing an impressive parallel with the 2008 Lehman Brothers failure. Trichet explained the mechanics of contagion, warning that if governments refused to act, Portugal would be the next victim, as demonstrated by a second graph showing Portuguese government bond yields tracking exactly the same path as Greek bonds.

Turning to what governments had to do, Trichet stressed that the first priority was fiscal consolidation. The challenge facing some governments was undoubtedly large, but it was not hopeless. He showed another graph on Belgium's fiscal trajectory, which demonstrated that cutting public debt could be done. The euro area governments also had a collective responsibility, however, to show that they were serious about the reform of the Stability and Growth Pact and other aspects of the area's economic governance. Trichet finished with a passionate defense of the role the ECB had played throughout the crisis. "We have done what we had to do. It is you, the member states, who have failed in your duty." The ECB had kept inflation under control, even though in some member states wages had risen by 100 percent or more since the introduction of the euro a decade earlier, and public expenditures were out of control almost everywhere. It was at that stage that he launched his anthem around the table: "Live up to your responsibility!"

Sarkozy expressed clearly the strategy of collective action that he envisioned based on two centers of power: the European Commission and the ECB. Analyst Peter Ludlow describes Sarkozy's words as follows. Concerning the role of the ECB, Sarkozy promised "he would not talk in these terms outside the room, but speaking frankly, behind closed doors, he urged the ECB to follow the example of the Federal Reserve and the Bank of England, both of which had bought bonds." In subsequent statements, prime ministers Silvio Berlusconi of Italy, José Luis Zapatero of Spain, and Jose Socrates of Portugal endorsed Sarkozy's line. Trichet's reaction to Sarkozy was more than angry. Unusual for him, the central banker raised his voice in stating that the ECB was not taking orders from anybody and warning that if the heads of state and government tried to apply pressure, the ECB Council would react negatively "with disastrous consequences."[20]

It was at that moment that Angela Merkel spoke up and sided explicitly with Trichet. She agreed that the crisis was systemic. Greece had set a courageous example of what had to be done by every member state, including Germany. The ECB also had been exemplary, and whatever else the heads of state and government did, it was crucially important that they should respect its independence. As for her own role, which she knew had been criticized, she was proud of the way in which she had been able to bring the German public opinion so far. Looking to the future, she, like Trichet, stressed the importance of fiscal consolidation and of the reinforcement of the Stability and Growth Pact. The most interesting parts of her statement, however, dealt with a possible stabilization mechanism and the role of the ECB. As far as the stabilization mechanism was concerned, she agreed that it was needed. Unlike Sarkozy, however, she made no mention of the European Commission in this connection. She did not want to resort to solutions that could be seen as conflicting with the European treaty. She dreaded the accusation of violating the words of the treaty and thereby being exposed to a constitutional claim in Germany, and she referred specifically to potential troubles with the Karlsruhe Court. For that reason, she wanted governments to act in a voluntary, if coordinated, capacity; in other words, an intergovernmental mechanism requiring Bundestag approval was preferable to any measure based on the treaty.[21]

On the ECB, Merkel made three points that she repeated several times during the evening. First, it was crucially important to respect the central bank's autonomy. Second, this meant that "hectoring" of the bank had to stop. And third, all parties—the heads of state and government and the president of the ECB—had to "trust each other."

As the evening wore on, the hardliners gradually established their ascendancy.[22] When Merkel and Sarkozy seemed unable to reach agreement, Van Rompuy brokered a late-night compromise: the leaders would announce the creation of a stabilization fund, or of a "robust crisis mechanism," which finance ministers would flesh out and finalize during the weekend. A full announcement would be made on Sunday night in order to impress the markets before Monday opening. For all the arm twisting behind it, the Eurogroup final statement resulted in the first comprehensive response to the crisis since it started in 2008.[23]

The first point of the final statement concerned implementation of the support package for Greece:

In February and in March, we committed to take determined and coordinated action to safeguard financial stability in the euro area as a whole. Following the request by the Greek government on April 23 and the agreement reached by the Eurogroup on May 2, we will provide Greece with €80 billion in a joint package with the IMF of €110 billion. Greece will receive a first disbursement in the coming days, before May 19.

The leaders added that their decision reflected "the principles of responsibility and solidarity . . . which are at the core of the monetary union."

The second point dealt with the response to the current crisis through the full range of means available to ensure the stability of the euro area. They were specified as follows:

—First, consolidation of public finances is a priority for all of us and we will take all measures needed to meet our fiscal targets this year and in the years ahead.

—Second, we fully support the ECB in its action to ensure the stability of the euro area.

—Third, taking into account the exceptional circumstances, the Commission will propose a European stabilization mechanism to preserve financial stability in Europe.

The stabilization mechanism ultimately was named the European Financial Stability Facility (EFSF), to be substituted starting in 2013 with a permanent European Stability Mechanism (ESM). In addition to these agencies, the

European Commission itself was to launch a European Financial Stabilization Mechanism (EFSM) as the agency to lend the €60 billion to troubled countries.

The leaders also said they had decided to "strengthen the governance of the euro area" and were prepared to:

—broaden and strengthen economic surveillance and policy coordination in the euro area, including by paying close attention to debt levels and competitiveness developments;

—reinforce the rules and procedures for surveillance of euro area Member States, including through a strengthening of the Stability and Growth Pact and more effective sanctions;

—create a robust framework for crisis management, respecting the principle of Member States' own budgetary responsibility.

The final element of the communiqué that the leaders had to discuss went practically unnoticed at the time, in part because it disguised an issue that would determine more than anything else the future of the crisis. Actually the wording seemed innocuous. Under the heading of "regulation of the financial markets and the fight against speculation," the leaders said they "agreed that the current market turmoil highlights the need to make rapid progress on financial markets regulation and supervision."

The background to this statement is as follows. During the May 7 meeting, as part of the general discussion on financial regulation, Chancellor Merkel described vividly the need to have some form of involvement by banks in shoring up Greek sovereign securities. The issue was bound to become of paramount importance in the future months, but was seriously underestimated by the whole European Council. The chancellor had already mentioned the issue in her face-to-face meeting with Sarkozy. She needed to highlight banks' responsibilities in causing the crisis and to "punish the bankers" in order to appease German public opinion and to tame the anti-bankers rhetoric in the Bundestag. To her eyes, that was the only way to get the German Parliament to approve the Greek bailout. What she had in mind was at least a public commitment by banks in each euro zone country not to sell any Greek sovereign bonds in their portfolios for three years, that is, until May 2013. The details had to be approved by the finance ministers meeting on Sunday, and she relied on Wolfgang Schäuble to get it passed. Merkel's colleagues did not pay much attention to this request, and many apparently thought it was a cheap way to buy Berlin's involvement in the deal.

By the end of the meeting, a full range of instruments had been agreed among member states and all the institutions. These evidently involved a trade-off between the request by the southern countries to the ECB to take part in the rescue and the strong commitment to consolidate their fiscal positions by the end of June. The European Financial Stabilization Mechanism (EFSM), launched by the European Commission, was to be put into action that weekend, although important differences remained between Angela Merkel and her group and Sarkozy and his camp about both the size and the legal basis of this new mechanism. Merkel apparently acknowledged that part of the job could be done under Article 122.2 of the European treaty, referring to financial assistance under exceptional circumstances. But the amount of money that could be made available by this means was limited. A prospect of further integration was opened by the mandate assigned to a task force headed by Van Rompuy. This group would present proposals both on fiscal and on economic coordination, the latter topic emerging from the darkness where it had been kept for a decade. The ECB was just briefly mentioned, and there were no hints of pressures on its autonomous decisions. However, what was still missing in the communiqué was a discussion of an adequate amount of money to support the ailing countries through the new European stabilization mechanism. Without such an announcement, the following Monday would have seen the end of the euro.

## The Last-Minute Agreement at the ECOFIN

The euro area governments had in mind much more. The idea was of a three-pronged intervention: €110 billion was confirmed for Greece and a date for transfer of the money had been fixed—that money represented a real transfer from the other euro zone countries to help Athens cover its financial needs for the next three years; another €60 billion was to be made available by the European Commission (that is, by the twenty-seven countries, not just those in the euro zone) through the European Financial Stabilization Mechanism (EFSM), which would issue bonds and make funds available to countries in need; and, finally, a much larger amount of funds was to be offered in some as yet unspecified form by the euro zone countries.

Preparations began early the following Saturday (May 8) for the extraordinary ECOFIN meeting and went on more or less continuously until the finance ministers assembled on Sunday at 1:00 p.m. It was the responsibility of the European Commission to produce the proposals on which the finance ministers were to work. The first sign was not encouraging: the British government, although directly interested in the contagion mechanism, was ready to spell out that, based on an agreement of the Labor government with the main opposition party, London would not take part in a special plan to save the euro.

On Saturday at 6 p.m., Sarkozy called Merkel from the Elysée Palace, where he had summoned a restricted government cabinet, and agreed on the size of the fund. This time Merkel, who was already on her way to Moscow for the World War II celebrations, surprised her counterpart by confirming the unexpectedly high amount of €500 billion for the whole stabilization fund. The decision to add €440 billion to the €60 billion already announced by the European

Commission was, in fact, less contentious than might be imagined. The rationale was to cover the possible financial requirements of Ireland, Portugal, and Spain for the following three years through the new mechanism—later named the European Financial Stability Facility (EFSF). The EFSF framework agreement stated that each state was to guarantee an amount proportional to 120 percent of its ECB capital share. Excluding Greece, Ireland, Portugal, and Spain, 120 percent of the ECB capital shares of the other euro countries would be exactly €441 billion. The entire bailout guarantees, included in all programs, would then amount to €860 billion: €110 billion for Greece from the EU and the IMF; €440 billion for the EFSF; €60 billion for the commission's fund (EFSM); and €250 billion from the IMF. This total was slightly less than the aggregate government debts of Greece, Spain, Portugal, and Ireland (€1.064 trillion by the end of 2009). The French president could finally call the American president in Washington and reassure him.

But Merkel had attached a number of strings to the financial package that she wanted to be approved by the finance ministers, including those to prevent fiscal profligacy by countries in the future and to assure the German Constitutional Court that the bailout did not violate the European treaty. Among the conditions, Merkel mentioned the involvement of the IMF, the need for a unanimous vote in favor of a rescue, and the temporary nature of the stability mechanism. These conditions did not represent Sarkozy's vision, or the vision of the European Commission, which on Sunday, May 9, at 2.45 p.m., signed off on a draft pact that envisaged an opposite strategy: that a majority vote would suffice to make the money available, that the mechanism would not expire, and that the commission itself would raise the funds for the whole package except for the IMF's money issuing EU-bonds.[24]

Wolfgang Schäuble had therefore to overturn the Brussels position in the course of the negotiations and also to advance a new proposal of great importance for Berlin: the commitment of the banks to hold in their portfolios the bonds of the countries under assistance, the embryo of the involvement of the private sector in the crisis. On his way to the negotiations, however, Schäuble fell ill from an allergic reaction to a medication and was rushed to the hospital. "Wolfgang's absence came as a shock," recalled Christine Lagarde, his French counterpart.[25] At 3:45 p.m., Schäuble's undersecretary, Jörg Asmussen, announced that the minister would not be able to participate. His replacement was Thomas de Maizière, Germany's interior minister, Merkel's former right arm at the Chancellery, who had built a technical competence on financial matters only during the crisis but had the complete trust of the chancellor and was considered a tough negotiator. He was summoned from a walk with his wife in the woods outside Dresden and flown on a government plane to Brussels, where he arrived at 8:30 p.m., visited briefly with Schäuble at the hospital to receive instructions, and immediately rushed to the summit, thus leaving only a few hours to reach the deal before markets opened the next morning.

The design of the new mechanism endowed with €440 billion was problematic.[26] ECOFIN's plan foresaw a euro zone rescue fund, operating under EU authority and selling bonds backed by government guarantees. The proposal was completely unacceptable to Berlin. Germany did not want the fund under EU auspices because that would have opened the issue of compliance with the treaty and directly exposed any agreement to a claim by the constitutional court. Berlin insisted that any country requiring financial assistance should receive it, as Greece had done, in the form of bilateral loans from other governments. However, bilateral loans presented a problem for the other ailing countries. Such loans would be counted as liabilities, thus increasing the public debt, and so were a very problematic instrument for highly indebted countries, such as Italy, or for countries smaller than Greece, given the relative higher impact on their fiscal accounts. Some donor countries also resisted using bilateral loans for political reasons, because it would have implied asking their national parliaments to vote again, just days after the approval of the €110 billion Greek aid package. Spain and Finland had limited flexibility in negotiating because of their constitutions.

Berlin wanted to avoid having common guarantees offered jointly by EU countries because they could become a precedent for a common public debt, a step that might one day be used for issuing euro-government-bonds. De Maizière was in touch with the Chancellery, where Merkel had gathered a small group of ministers. When the impasse seemed impossible to overcome, the ECB president, although maintaining secrecy over the decision of the ECB on the purchase of bonds, let the governments know that if no commitment for the fund was agreed to, the bank would not be involved in any way. It was an ultimatum. But not even that fatal prospect could force de Maizière to change his position. Merkel was hammered with telephone calls from other leaders, among them President Obama.

In the meantime, the exit polls in North Rhine-Westphalia revealed that Merkel's CDU was heading for a major defeat and might lose its majority in the Bundesrat. Around midnight, de Maizière proposed that all the other countries proceed with a common fund, while Germany would stick with lending the money through a bilateral loan. The Dutch finance minister said that, in that case, he would ask for the same treatment.[27] The prospect of a fund made up only of weak donor countries was unacceptable, as monetary affairs commissioner Rehn explained. The agreement was once more on the brink. De Maizière again called Merkel. The message he received was clear: "Stay firm. We still have two hours to negotiate."

Commissioner Rehn later said that the compromise enabling a breakthrough came from Maarten Verwey, director of foreign relations at the Dutch finance ministry. Verwey proposed a "special purpose vehicle"—the EFSF—with the right to raise funds, backed by the €440 billion in government guarantees. More precisely, the facility was to be guaranteed by the euro area member countries, proportionate to their capital contribution at the ECB. Backed by these guarantees, the facility was to raise funds in the markets to provide loans to the euro area member countries requiring financial assistance. That would have spared countries like Italy, which would have struggled to raise additional funds to aid another country.

In their final statement, the ECOFIN ministers gave this description of the financial stability facility, using Verwey's terminology: "Euro area Member States stand ready to complement such resources through a Special Purpose Vehicle that is guaranteed on a pro rata basis by participating Member States in a coordinated manner and that will expire after three years, respecting their national constitutional requirements, up to a volume of €440 billion. The IMF will participate in financing arrangements and is expected to provide at least half as much as the EU contribution through its usual facilities in line with the recent European programs."[28]

Finally, the French and the Italian ministers endorsed the Dutch proposal and pushed Berlin to seal the deal a few minutes before the opening of markets in Tokyo. As soon as the agreement on the €500 billion was found, Sarkozy called Trichet in Basel, where he was attending the regular monthly meeting of the world's main central bankers. Dominique Strauss-Kahn was also at the Basel meeting and in constant touch with French finance minister Christine Lagarde, in Brussels, and with his headquarters in Washington to prepare his substantial part of the financial package.

### Weber's Second Conversion

Also on Sunday, May 9, 2010, ECB president Trichet convened (for the second time that week) a meeting of his board to put the seal on the Securities Purchase Mechanism that would have allowed the bank to intervene in the government securities market. In Frankfurt and in Basel, the ECB was at the hub of a consultative process, which involved at least two telephone conferences of the whole ECB Governing Council during the course of the weekend. The informal decision on purchasing sovereign bonds had already been taken at the ad hoc meeting in Lisbon. But another coup-de-theatre occurred on the way back from Portugal. Only a few hours after surprising his colleagues in Lisbon by launching and endorsing the idea of buying bonds, Bundesbank president Axel Weber had changed his mind again. He sent an e-mail to his colleagues, when they had just returned home from Lisbon, saying he denied his support to the purchase of government bonds. After Weber's shocking second volte-face, the ECB council, in a teleconference meeting, split by a much deeper extent than it ever officially admitted. This time, it was not two council members in the minority opposing the idea, as in Lisbon, but five.

Early on Monday morning, before the opening of the European markets, the ECB announced its decision to buy sovereign bonds.[29] Weber, however, went public, announcing he was against the bank's decision. He feared that the role he had played in Lisbon would be leaked and that he would be singled out as the person responsible for the decision of buying bonds. According to a colleague of his, Weber was especially afraid that his associate Jürgen Stark would denounce his "betrayal" of the Bundesbank orthodoxy, something that Stark never did. In an interview with the financial newspaper *Börsen Zeitung*, conducted on Monday and published on Tuesday, Weber said loudly that he regarded the decision of the ECB board as "critical" and warned that the purchase of sovereign bonds would "entail considerable stability policy risks."[30] His ECB colleagues were furious and completely upset by his behavior. Weber lost that day any chance to become the next ECB president.

The ECB official announcement followed the ECOFIN communiqué in the early morning of Monday, May 10. The bank listed a set of extraordinary measures, including purchases of sovereign securities in the context of interventions in the euro zone public and private debt markets. "In view of the current exceptional circumstances prevailing in the market, the Governing Council decided to conduct interventions in the euro area public and private debt securities markets (Securities Markets Programme) to ensure depth and liquidity in those market segments which are dysfunctional."[31] There are limits to the money supply that a central bank can mobilize and to the risks of losses that it can bear on its balance sheet. But at the end of the game, markets cannot fight central banks that have almost unlimited resources. Also on Monday morning, the euro zone central banks announced—loudly and in a clearly coordinated fashion—that they had initiated purchases of sovereign securities from Ireland, Portugal, and Greece. As could be expected, these announcements produced extreme reactions in the market. The euro, which had closed the previous Friday at 1.277 against the dollar, shot up to above 1.30. German ten-year benchmark yields were up by 18 basis points. The Eurostoxx 50 index went up by about 7 percent, and the banking sector rebounded by about 11 percent.

## The Secret Side of the Agreement

In a crisis atmosphere, and acting out of fear of the consequences of inaction, the European authorities were giving shape to a greater policy coordination and to better economic governance. On May 11 Barroso received from former EU commissioner Mario Monti the report on the Single Market, aimed at abating the barriers that still hampered the full integration of the EU economies. On Wednesday, May 12, the European Commission published an extensive set of

proposals that included several innovative elements; the first step was a reinforcement of compliance with the Stability and Growth Pact and deeper fiscal
policy coordination. A "European semester" would be called every year to coordinate the fiscal initiative and the reform programs of each national government
in a European framework. All combined, the policy actions represented a great
step forward in euro zone economic policy coordination. An arrangement for
issuing bonds in a coordinated way sounded very much like an embryonic eurobond. A surveillance mechanism that delved into the quality of each country's
fiscal policies—as well as economic policy at large— was to be spelled out in the
coming months.

Still, the political dimension of the package proved elusive to the markets.
This was especially true in the financial capitals of London and New York, where
the complexity of European policy commitment appeared abstruse and where
the deal was scrutinized in its most critical aspects. And, indeed, it was easy to
find the weak spots: too many caveats, too much arm twisting, and all accomplished too late. Shortly after the ECOFIN meeting, even former Federal Reserve
chairman Paul Volcker said that he was concerned the euro area might break up.

The question of whether Greece would—or should—default remained somehow unanswered. The severe adjustment was aggravated by the onerous interest rates placed on the financial assistance. Projecting the cost of financing was
not reassuring, given the possibility that Greece might have to support a public
debt that would climb to 150 percent of GDP in 2015. At first, the figures
in the European aid plan were impressive, but the level of political commitment did not correspond to the nominal size of the package. Nearly two years
after September 2008, exactly the same mistakes were made: the common rescue
action—just as in the case of the banking fund, another second-best solution—
was a sum of separate financings. As in the case of bank rescues, the sustainability of state fiscal budgets would remain unclear, creating a number of zombie-
like states suspended between life and death.

The debate at the Bundestag about the agreement was profound and articulated—much more so than in any other euro zone country. Government and
opposition parties in Germany discussed the matter, defusing any populism. It
was an impressive demonstration of German democratic debate. But a deep mistrust seemed to take over when the country had to deal with its euro zone partners. For example, the German law implementing the EFSF put a detailed interpretation on the procedure to be followed for providing loans to Greece; this
interpretation was more strict than the vague language EU leaders had agreed
to in their meetings approving the aid mechanism. The German law stated that
help could only be provided as an emergency measure to preserve a country's
solvency. Under the German law, a clear sequence had to be followed after a
country applied for help. First, all euro states (excluding the endangered country

or countries), the ECB, and the IMF had to unanimously agree on the looming insolvency. Then, the European Commission and the IMF, in cooperation with the ECB, had to negotiate a consolidation plan with the country requesting help. And, finally, this plan would have to be unanimously accepted by all euro countries, including those in danger. Given that the EFSF was formed by an international agreement formally outside the EU, Germany's interpretation was binding for the German government and could not be overruled. In other words, Germany reaffirmed its right to veto any bailout.

While the public debate was focused on Greece, an even more fundamental process was under way almost entirely hidden from the public. On the day after the ECOFIN meeting each of the euro area finance ministers summoned the largest banks of their countries to urge them to keep the stressed sovereign bonds in their portfolios. The success of the bailout depended on minimizing opportunistic sales of sovereign bonds and, therefore, stabilizing the sovereign markets of the periphery and making it possible for the ECB to intervene on the bonds market with the minimum amount of purchases.

Chancellor Merkel had raised the issue in the meeting of the leaders on May 7 and in the bilateral meetings with her colleagues. She had stumbled on an annoying legal hurdle on what she had defined as the "private sector involvement in the bailout package." The problem was that any commitment by the largest euro area banks not to sell Greek bonds had to be informal and voluntary—at least officially—or it would infringe the core principles of the EU treaties. In fact, this issue was not openly mentioned in any of the official statements but was agreed to very clearly among the governments of the euro area and, first of all, by Greece's largest creditors in Germany, France, and the Netherlands. Each of the sixteen finance ministers agreed to ask their banks to make the commitment to hold the bonds in their portfolios.

In the case of Germany, a recovered Wolfgang Schäuble convened a meeting at the finance ministry in Berlin on May 11 of the country's largest banks. Some banks, among them the Sparkassen (public savings banks), declined the request to hold onto the bonds. They maintained that the request should be addressed to those banks that had invested recklessly in risky assets and in Greece specifically, first of all the Landesbanken. Other banks accepted only reluctantly, stressing the purely voluntary commitment "consistent with the specific capacity of each bank." Daimler, an industrial group with significant financial interests, was also invited but declined. Eventually, thirteen of the largest institutions accepted the government's request. As usual, the leader of the group was Josef Ackermann, the head of Deutsche Bank. The agreement stated that the banks would keep their bonds for exactly three years, until May 2013. Although they accepted it, the agreement did not go down well with the banks. Their relations with Schäuble were already difficult, since the finance minister had scorned the calls of the banks not to induce what they called financial repression in Germany: "If you want to dry out a swamp, you don't ask the frogs," he said.[32] A few days later Ackermann added more uncertainty in Europe by saying that Greece might never be able to repay its debt in full.[33]

Two weeks later, on May 29, the Bundesbank sent out an unusual alarm revealing that, according to its confidential data, the French banks had betrayed the commitment and started to massively unload their portfolios by selling Greek bonds directly to the European Central Bank. Since the start of its controversial European Securities Program—the bond-buying effort agreed to at the dinner meeting in Lisbon—the ECB had already bought about €25 billion in government debt of the euro area. A source at the Bundesbank leaked to the German media that the biggest sellers were French, adding a disturbing remark about the French nationality of the ECB president. The alarm reverberated across Frankfurt and up to Berlin, where Schäuble had to calm a rebellion by the German private banks. A confidence rift opened between politics and banks in those hours. The underlying mistrust would prove fateful for the rest of the crisis.

# 15

## From a New Complacency to the Irish Crisis

### *Merkel's Shoes in Kohl's Footprints*

"Ladies and gentlemen, let's not talk around it: The crisis over the future of the euro is not just any crisis. It is the greatest test that Europe has gone through since 1990, if not even in the fifty-three years since the adoption of the Rome Treaty. This test is an existential one. It must be passed. Failing it, the consequences would be incalculable for Europe and beyond. But succeeding, then Europe will be stronger than before," Angela Merkel declared.

Only three days after the last of the series of fast-paced EU meetings in early May 2010, and when markets had already started to undermine the first positive assessment of what had been accomplished, Merkel on May 13 gave a key speech in Aaachen, at the Karlspreis (Charlemagne Prize) ceremony honoring Polish premier Donald Tusk, a former dissident and protest leader under the communist regime.[1] The speech was almost overlooked by the international news media, although it initiated a completely different aspect of Berlin's European policy: its finally constructive long-term strategy. Merkel used the tone and the gist of her mentor Helmut Kohl's pro-European rhetoric. But the speech also made clear that, in Merkel's eyes, the solution of creating the European Financial Stability Facility (EFSF) was unsustainable unless, as the chancellor argued time and again in the months that followed, a new legal basis was established through a new treaty or an amendment to the current European legal framework.

Merkel was walking a fine line between the irritation of her public and the watchful control of the German Constitutional Court on the prerogatives of German national democratic institutions. A change in the European treaty would make the May 7 agreement and the broader violation of the no-bailout clause a temporary lapse from orthodoxy. As a result, the court would not need to address the question of treaty violations (even though it was just examining claims against the bailout of Greece), because the EU itself could correct the problem with a new piece of legislation. The best way to reconcile both the German public and the court to the continuing commitment to Europe, which was itself inscribed in the constitution, was to highlight the government's mission of preserving the stability of the euro in the longer term, even at the cost of raising short-term concerns of the financial markets. There was a clear timeline for this endeavour: as Berlin had requested, the EFSF was to last only for a limited period of three years. After that, a new crisis mechanism would be set up. Since the EFSF was initiated in May–June 2010, it would expire in May–June 2013, just a few months before the next German federal elections. As a result, there was no doubt that Merkel wanted to be sure that the new institution would be acceptable to the Germans.

In her speech in Aachen, Merkel put the questions facing Germany, and Europe, in completely new terms:

> Forget for a moment all the rescue packages, which we will discuss and pass during these weeks, forget for a moment all the sums of money that currently dominate the discussion—20, 40, 100, 400, 700 billion. Forget the stock market prices and the rating agencies. Forget for a moment the discussion about the triggers and causes of this crisis. Was it the Greeks, of whom it is said that it was always clear that they wouldn't play by the rules? Or was it the European institutions? According to some, only the naïve expect them to pay close attention where close attention is needed. Forget for a moment the differences in culture—here the southern countries, where, according to some, they have always seen these things in a more relaxed way; there the northern countries, which are said to tackle things in a more pedantic way; then the eastern countries, which are judged to make it impossible to know what they will do; and finally the countries that won't participate in everything that's planned for Europe anyway. Forget for a moment also the oft-repeated judgments regarding the—let's call it different characters of the political actors: on the one side the energetic, the brave, the quick; on the other side the hesitant, the irresolute, the one with the wait-and-see attitude, the one obsessed with stability, the one who decides late; and all possible variants in between.
>
> If we forget all that, what do we see? We see that officials of Europe and all member states, finance ministers, foreign ministers, heads of state and government worked day and night for months on end, burning the midnight oil in marathon sessions. Why did they do that? Of course, to rescue Greece. But why? . . . Because we feel that if the euro fails, not only

the currency fails. Much more than that fails. Europe fails; the idea of European unity fails.

The idea of European unity is the most captivating, most wonderful, most promising idea that Europe has ever seen. . . . And beyond economics, after the common currency we will venture to take further steps, for instance, steps toward a unified European military. In the end, it's about our values and principles: democracy, human rights, sustained economic growth, a stable currency, and social peace. The twenty-first century can become Europe's century.[2]

## Iron Discipline and the Stability Fund

Theoretically Merkel's high rhetoric was justified. The latest summits had shown that all euro area member countries could mobilize their citizens' resources in an act of solidarity toward four weaker countries: Greece, Ireland, Portugal, and Spain. Merkel in her Aachen speech added a historical framework consistent with the display of solidarity. By doing so, she countered the lack of the famous "narrative" that is often lamented by those studying the developments of the European Union. Saving the euro was the key test of implementing political integration, with subsequent ambitions including putting together a European army. But no narrative can be a substitute for facts. So in the weeks and months following mid-May 2010, European leaders had to prove step-by-step that their political determinations could be reflected in practical decisions: a new framework for economic governance; an effective implementation of the financial stabilization mechanisms; the enactment of structural reforms and of fiscal discipline by all countries; and, finally, the consolidation of the financial systems. The result was disappointing. Political divergences were reignited and the positions grew distant especially on the need for reinforced fiscal rigor, which was resisted by the majority of governments, but was crucial for the ECB, Germany, and the EU Commission asking for automatic sanctioning of countries that violated the fiscal rules. The apparently boring institutional debate showed the acrimonious juxtaposition of priorities that would accompany the rest of the crisis—especially when there were delays in setting up the new funds to aid the debt-plagued countries, delays that irritated the European Central Bank.

The final statement by the Eurosummit leaders on May 7 had outlined all the elements of the package, and in the third paragraph it specifically assigned a task force headed by Van Rompuy with a clearly profiled mandate: broadening and strengthening economic surveillance and policy coordination in the euro area, including by paying close attention to debt levels and competitiveness developments; a strengthening of the Stability and Growth Pact, including more effective sanctions against countries that violated it; and creating a robust framework for crisis management.[3] The structure of this so-called comprehensive solution for the euro crisis was founded on a bargain. Germany was available to lend help now, but in turn wanted a kind of a guarantee that any price that had to be paid now would not be asked time and again in the future. For Merkel, the essential clause of this bargain was strict fiscal rigor. From a long-term perspective, countries with relatively low debt levels would not require external help, so the design of the strategy rested on strong discipline in fiscal policy as its centrepiece.[4]

In June 2010 the proposals for a new economic governance became the core of the political debate among the capitals. Van Rompuy's task force was put to work immediately and met twice between May and early June. The task force had been asked to prepare a report before the end of 2010 indicating "the measures needed to reach the objective of an improved crisis resolution framework and better budgetary discipline, exploring all options to reinforce the legal framework." Merkel had especially requested language in the council's statement that the task force had to explore all legal options, thus leading the way to a possible amendment of the European treaty. This complication represented another element of uncertainty for financial observers, but it also testified to Berlin's long-term commitment to strengthening Europe.

The institutional debate was crucial in the mechanism of the crisis, because it opened a phase of disruptive noncooperation between the ECB on one side and the governments on the other. It was the consequence of the forced and controversial decision of the ECB to bail out Greece in the absence of the governments' full commitment. It is therefore crucial to understand the ECB position.

On June 10, just one month after the EU Council, the European Central Bank published its own set of proposals for a fiscal policy framework for the euro area under the title "Reinforcing the economic governance in the euro area." The ECB proposed a system with much stronger automaticity in rules and procedures than in the past, showing its mistrust in governments' discipline. Fiscal surveillance was to be given a real upgrade through the very ambitious proposal of creating an independent EU fiscal agency under the competence of the European Commission. This proposal was aimed at de-politicizing the whole structure of fiscal control by taking away from governments their much-abused inclination to offer excuses for their failure to exercise restraint. But crucially, the ECB, in addition to asking for stricter and automatic fiscal surveillance, called for a prompt activation of the European Financial Stability Facility (EFSF), the new institution funded by the governments to absorb the role of purchasing bonds and bailing out the debt-ridden countries—a task that the ECB, torn and bitterly divided by Weber's criticism, did not want to carry out.

The first answer to the ECB came from the EU Commission endorsing the line of strict rigor on fiscal policy. In its framework, issued on June 30, the commission insisted that national fiscal frameworks be strengthened and the Stability and

Growth Pact focus on the issue of long-term debt dynamics as well as annual fiscal deficits.[5] The commission also wanted to "set out effective enforcement mechanisms to ensure that member states will act in compliance with the EU framework they have agreed. Where developments in member state economies pose a risk to the overall development of the Union, a series of preventive and corrective measures are proposed, including a range of sanctions that could be applied where breaches occur." Finally, the commission envisaged mechanisms aimed at addressing imbalances through stronger macroeconomic surveillance proposed to "establish a European semester for policy co-ordination and explain the process and timing that will provide a European input to national policy decisions, leading to more effective ex-ante policy co-ordination. This also applies to the structural reforms and the growth enhancing elements of the Europe 2020 strategy."[6]

If implemented fully, this proposal would represent quite an improvement in the fiscal solidity of the euro area. The two supranational European institutions, the ECB and the EU Commission, clearly asked national politics to take a step back and relinquish its often abused discretionary fiscal powers.

On June 17 the heads of government met at the European Council in Brussels, pretending to be in a completely different atmosphere from one month earlier and showing a sense of normality after the storm. EU Council head Herman Van Rompuy opened the first session, when journalists were still in the room, by saying "There is no crisis today, so we can begin." He wanted to steer the meeting away from the fiscal emergency and back to the long-term policies of the Europe 2020 strategy, the ten-year program launched by the commission on March 3, 2010, aimed at reviving the European economy through "smart, sustainable, inclusive growth" after the, at best, mixed results of the previous Lisbon Strategy. Merkel and French president Sarkozy had a completely different sense of the situation, however. The German chancellor intervened at the beginning to urgently gear the discussion toward a more profound reflection, as she put it, on "where we are in Europe, where Europe is in the world and how we can progress." Her goal was to give a sense of direction to the efforts in sorting out the crisis. Between the long-term strategy and the short-term problems, she worried about the problem of economic governance.

Van Rompuy presented the preliminary work of his task force on the new governance, and some of the points he expressed were in line with some of the commission's earlier proposals: more attention to differences in competitiveness; the establishment of a crisis resolution mechanism; the inauguration of the "European semester" in the first six months of the year when national governments would have to submit their budgets to the European Council and to the commission for examination even before national parliaments would be asked for approval; a greater attention to public debt levels; and a strengthening of the system of statistical information either at the national or European levels.

However, Merkel was disappointed with the plan for imposing sanctions against countries that violated fiscal rules because it contemplated the possibility that the heads of governments could retain the ultimate control of the sanctioning procedures. For the chancellor, as well as for the ECB, the accent on discipline was not explicit enough because sanctioning had proved impossible in the past when it was left in the hands of the governments.

One month after the Greek bailout plan, the political fronts in Europe were again diverging and hardening. Merkel had just received approval from her coalition in Berlin to move forward with her toughest plan yet on German fiscal consolidation. The German fiscal package was impressive at first sight. It amounted to a cumulative cut in deficits of €80 billion to be accomplished by 2016, when a new German constitutional rule imposed a deficit limit of 0.35 percent of GDP. The impact of the cut would not be felt in the critical first budget year; instead, the biggest chunk of the fiscal restraint would fall in 2013—the year of the next planned federal elections, a paradoxical choice in all other countries of the world, but not in Germany, where Merkel knew the preference of her electors for fiscal rigor.

The quest for the sanctions' automaticity responded to another of Merkel's fundamental worries: the risk of losing control of the euro area dynamics in favor of Paris. Three French nationals had been given central roles in the management of the latest events: President Sarkozy himself, through his influence within the European Council and Eurogroup; Dominique Strauss-Kahn, the IMF managing director; and Jean-Claude Trichet, the ECB president. Moreover, Sarkozy had created a strong compatibility of interests with the leaders of two other large countries, Italy's Silvio Berlusconi and Spain's José Luis Zapatero. Adding to the French camp the other peripheral countries facing fiscal trouble—Greece, Portugal, and Ireland—would put Germany in a less than central position. This was an especially disquieting prospect for Merkel since the key pillars of German influence in Europe—the Stability and Growth Pact, the no-bailout clause, and the absolute autonomy of the central bank—had proven fragile and were subject to complete revision. To regain control of the situation, Berlin and Paris negotiators developed a paper, presented by the finance ministers of the two countries on July 21, one month after the June European Council. The Paris-Berlin paper emphasized that a large part of the exercise had to do with sanctions for violations of deficit rules, including sanctions that had a political component. As an example, the paper suggested that "suspension of voting rights for member states that materially and/or repeatedly fail to comply with joint commitments should be established. This mechanism would have to be included in any revision of the Treaty that may in future be agreed to." Berlin was trying to limit the maneuvering room of those governments, including the French, who wanted some more fiscal flexibility. At stake, ultimately, was the future economic governance of the euro area after the traumatic experience with Greece.

In fact, the gist of the debate was definitely political. As ECB board member Lorenzo Bini Smaghi put it:

> There are two avenues. The first is to recognize the limited powers of the Eurogroup and move to a rules-based system, with automatic procedures and sanctions. That was the approach followed by the ECB in its published proposal for reform of the SGP [Stability and Growth Pact], and partly also the approach of the European Commission. The Heads of State and Government of the European Union followed a second avenue, as they wanted to retain the ability to decide on budgetary matters, in particular concerning the imposition of sanctions on countries not respecting the rules. They did not want to deprive themselves of their powers in favor of the European Commission, nor to bind themselves with a rules-based approach. This position might be understandable from a political point of view. But it doesn't resolve the problem that I raised previously, concerning potential sinners forgiving the current ones. No change has been made to the system of governance aimed at reducing the perverse incentives. Why should the Eurogroup be expected to behave in the future any differently than in the past?[7]

In May the ECB had paid a high price in terms of political autonomy and of financial aid, but that price seemed not to be repaid with adequate compliance on the part of the European governments.

## The Other Side: Banks' Problems and the No-Stress Tests

Against that backdrop, the European Central Bank—caught in a conflict among EU governments over the need for more fiscal discipline—carried out its task of supporting the bond markets reluctantly. In fact, markets remained skeptical about the solidity of the euro area, and pressure remained very high, especially on two countries: Spain and Ireland.

Revealingly, the responsibilities of governments still seemed completely absent in the financial sector domain. The lack of transparency concerning the solidity of banks in Ireland, France, and Germany amplified the problems connected with the risk of national defaults. Markets still perceived risks related to debt restructuring, and uncertainty was stoked by the fact that investors were kept in the dark concerning the European banking situation. Interest rate spreads started to climb again from the levels reached in mid-April, as if May—with its crisis escalation and historic meetings—had never occurred.

Spain, at loggerheads with Berlin, made a wise decision and took the lead by aiming exactly at the German weak spot. Apparently acting on advice from the president of Spain's national central bank, Zapatero quite unexpectedly announced in mid-June that he would initiate a strict stress test of Spanish banks and make the result public. Berlin was completely taken aback. At first Merkel balked, asking Van Rompuy not to list the issue of Spain's bank tests on the agenda of the EU Council on June 17 and surely not to go public with the results. But evidently once Madrid had upped the ante, all others had to follow, or they would be exposed to market reaction. In their statement summarizing the June 17 meeting, the leaders said, "The European Council agrees that the results of ongoing stress tests by banking supervisors will be disclosed at the latest in the second half of July."[8]

Market worries about the banks were very easy to detect. Over the previous few months, European banks had seen sharp rises in their funding costs and a significant sell-off of their equity. Uncertainty about the capital positions of these banks relative to the risk in their portfolios had been the driver of this negative market reaction. The correlation between bank credit default swaps (CDS) and sovereign CDS showed how connected the two sides of the crisis—financial and sovereign—had been.

The launch of the stress tests in June and July was the much-awaited effort to clarify the European situation. It was believed that analogous tests in the United States a year earlier had led to improvement in American public sentiment. The Committee of European Banking Supervisors (CEBS) and the national banking authorities coordinated the tests, in cooperation with the ECB and with the national authorities. In line with its mandate, the CEBS regularly monitors and tests the vulnerabilities of the banking sector, but this was the first time the results of these analyses were to be released to the public on such a wide scale. The tests would cover ninety-one banks in twenty countries, which collectively accounted for 65 percent of total assets in the EU banking system. The tests also were designed to cover at least 50 percent of each national banking sector, and to incorporate a significant share of public banks (most notably the German Landesbanken and Spanish Cajas) for which financial clarity normally is minimal.

The tests were meant to measure the resilience of the capital held by the banks in response to a series of potential shocks—a sudden decrease in the GDP, or a fall in sovereign security prices affecting the trading portfolios of the banks (although not the hold-to-maturity portfolios). However, market analysts were less than convinced by the lack of details provided by the European authorities, and some suggested that the test was suspiciously non-transparent. Even the IMF recommended full disclosure of results to guarantee the tests' credibility, observing that "some uncertainty regarding the stringency of the tests is likely to remain." An IMF staff report finalized on July 1 said, "To reduce aggregate uncertainty and induce a greater willingness to tackle troubled banks, [IMF] staff called for a more detailed disclosure of inputs and outcomes, possibly at the institution level." But it reported resistance from euro zone authorities to the idea of more transparency. "Supervisors felt that disclosure of individual bank results could prove too market-sensitive and some national authorities noted legal impediments to publication," the IMF said.[9] In other words, national authorities were influencing the nature of the test. So, while Spanish regulatory bodies opted for a wider and more rigorous test, others, first of all their German counterparts, went particularly soft on their domestic system. Eighty-five European banks provided breakdowns of their government-debt holdings when they published the stress test results. All of the six that did not were German banks, including Deutsche Bank, the country's biggest bank. A German financial newspaper broke the story that Bundesbank president Axel Weber supported German banks in their opposition to complete and uncontrolled publication of stress tests against pressure of the EU and even the German government.[10]

When the results were released on July 23, the tests found that only seven banks needed to raise capital. Only Germany's Hypo Real Estate, Agricultural Bank of Greece SA, and five Spanish savings banks lacked adequate reserves to maintain a Tier 1 capital ratio of at least 6 percent in the event of a recession and sovereign-debt crisis. The total amount of capital required by the seven banks was only €3.5 billion, about a tenth of the lowest estimate by analysts, leaving doubts about whether regulators were tough enough.[11] Barclays Capital, for example, said at that time that European banks would require as much as €85 billion. An article published in September by the *Wall Street Journal* revealed the extent of the manipulation of test results by some banks and banking regulators, quoting explicitly the evidently well-informed Barclays Bank.[12]

A paper from two economists at the Organization for Economic Cooperation and Development (OECD) highlighted the flaws in the tests, which had looked only at the government bonds that the banks were holding in so-called trading books, containing short-term investments that must be valued at market prices.[13] The stress tests ignored bonds held in financial institutions' much larger banking books. The OECD economists reasoned that "over the two years considered [by the tests] default is virtually impossible in the presence of . . . the €750 billion fund to bail out troubled governments, which is certainly large enough to meet funding needs of the main countries of concern over that period."[14] Moreover, it is assumed that bonds in the banking book will be held to maturity, so banks do not have to recognize losses unless the issuer defaults—an outcome that the regulators explicitly ruled out over the stress tests' two-year horizon. According to the OECD paper, the banking books contained more than €1.6 trillion in EU government bonds, compared to only €336 billion on the trading books. Using the stress tests' own worst-case scenario, the authors estimated that banks' total losses would be €165 billion, compared to the stress tests' estimate of only €26 billion. Lenders held about 90 percent of their Greek government bonds in their banking books and 10 percent in their trading books, according to a survey by Morgan Stanley. The example in Germany of Hypo Real Estate (yes, again the Munich bank) showed that virtually all of the exposures were in the banking book—around 98 percent according to the OECD, and therefore were excluded from the stress test.

Needless to say, the stress test backfired and uncertainty remained in the market. In a matter of days, the costs of insuring many bank and government bonds against default in countries such as Portugal, Ireland, Greece, and Italy jumped above their pre-stress-test levels.

## Ireland: A Rude Awakening

One of the most surprising outcomes of the stress tests was that the Dublin-based Anglo Irish Bank had somehow passed the examination. Reality, however, was not long in coming. At the end of August, the Irish bond spreads started to widen significantly, driven by fears over the cost of bailing out the banking system and the nationalized Anglo Irish Bank in particular. Ireland had won a lot of praise for tightening fiscal policy relatively early and aggressively in 2009, but its government, as others, was trying to hide a banking situation that was notoriously problematic. Between 1999 and 2007 total assets and loans and advances to customers had increased by a factor of twelve. By the end of 2007 Anglo Irish posted total assets of €96.7 billion and loans and advances to customers of €65.9 billion. Debt securities in issue increased from €100 million to €23.6 billion. Anglo Irish's rapid expansion was based largely on increases in lending to property developers. By September 2007 more than 80 percent of all loans made by Anglo Irish Bank related to loans for construction and property, excluding residential mortgages (equivalent to 12.5 times the bank's capital base). According to an EU report prepared for May 2010, "This property lending was of a common-or-garden kind: not exotic or complex or hard to assess through esoteric statistical models. And it constituted a sword of Damocles hanging over the banking system."[15]

In early 2009 Finance Minister Brian Lenihan estimated the total cost of recapitalizing Anglo Irish at €4.5 billion. A first estimate of the total cost of bailing out the bank had been advanced at the start of 2010 by the Irish government, which had deemed it "infuriating but manageable." Nobody had been particularly surprised about the bank's poor standing for the first half of 2010, but little information was actually available. Private analysts were no longer scrutinizing the bank since it was publicly owned. By March 2010 Dublin indicated that the total cost of re-capitalizing Anglo Irish was likely to be around €25 billion (or 16 percent of Irish GDP, in addition to the current public deficit of 11.5 percent), but the rating agencies were estimating the total cost would be much higher. Standard & Poor's put the estimate around €35 billion: above

23 percent of Irish GDP. A rough-and-ready estimate of another €10 billion was to be taken into account for capital injections needed by other Irish banks. All in all, Ireland was faced with a minimum jump of 40 percent in its debt-to-GDP ratio. Through September, the government pledged €33.5 billion in capital support to domestic banks, in the form of "promissory notes," but when Lenihan declared at the end of the month that a further €12.8 billion in capital injections would be needed, uncertainty about the final cost for supporting the banking system became palpable. Obviously, doubts also were growing about the manageability for the government itself. The spread between Irish and German ten-year government bonds had increased by 130 basis points in one month, reaching more than 360 basis points at the start of September. The yield on Irish ten-year government bonds had climbed to 6 percent, dangerously close to the 7 percent threshold that was considered a conventional alarm bell for potentially defaulting countries. The main reason was that Anglo Irish had around €7 billion in government-backed, medium-term debt that was maturing in September in the context of heavy refinancing needs across Europe.

Ireland's success since the 1990s in catching up with European standards of living had been taken as a model for other countries. From 80 percent of the euro area average in 1993, GDP per capita (in purchasing power parity terms) rose to 134 percent of the euro area average by 2007. This rate of income growth was unsustainable, however, and so it is probable that Ireland's strong budget performance in the past had masked a great deal of hidden vulnerability. Every year between 1990 and 2007, Ireland managed to keep its deficit within the maximum 3 percent of GDP level specified by the Maastricht Treaty. In ten of the eleven years leading up to 2007, Ireland posted a budget surplus. But once the downturn hit, the extent to which the government was reliant on "boom-related" taxes quickly emerged. Between 2000 and 2008, the public sector wage bill rose 145 percent, compared with increases of 92 percent, 82 percent, and 24 percent in Greece, Spain, and Portugal, respectively—although at 11 percent of GDP, the total bill in Ireland was the lowest of the EMU peripheral economies.[16] While in 2007 the headline (nominal) budget balance stood at 0.1 percent of GDP, Ireland's structural budget balance (after eliminating vagaries of business cycles) in 2010 stood at a negative 7.7 percent of GDP, according to an IMF estimate.[17]

The apparent—but, in reality, misleading—solidity of its fiscal position had given legitimacy to Dublin's policy of lowering the corporate tax rate, once 10 percent (and later 12.5 percent), to a fraction of the European average, thus drawing huge foreign direct investments, which of course were diverted from other countries. The blind eye lent to the unsustainable situation in Ireland probably reflected the country's impressive economic results over an extended period, but without taking into consideration the web of interests offered by such a low taxation base in the European Union. Probably no research published by investment banks—not even those that had a furiously critical attitude toward the EU peripheral countries (by then Portugal, Ireland, Greece, and Spain) and in general toward the monetary union—ever criticized Dublin and instead defended Ireland's performance, even up to the point when the EU had to intervene with aid. Some investment bankers admitted that they had ceded to pressures by the Dublin government, fearing it would retaliate against them if the analysts released unfavorable comments on the Irish economy. But international institutions also were generally more generous toward Ireland than Portugal or other periphery countries. No analysts spent a minute in highlighting how much of the Irish boom depended on subtracting from the welfare of other countries instead of increasing it. Once the crisis struck, the domestic debate in Ireland also was devoted largely to blaming the EU itself—rather than the country's own policies—for the predicament.

The artificiality of the "Celtic boom" was actually evident even in hard data. Between 1993 and 2000, average annual GDP growth approached 10 percent, but as *The Economist* remarked: "Over the last decade the boom turned bubbly, as low interest rates and reckless lending, abetted by dozy regulation, pushed up land values and caused Ireland to turn into a nation of property developers. In County Leitrim, in the Irish Midlands, housing construction outstripped demand (based on population growth) by 401 percent between 2006 and 2009, according to one estimate."[18] Few minded. The Irish became, by one measure, the second-richest people in the European Union. "The boom is getting boomier," said Bertie Ahern, Ireland's taoiseach (prime minister), in 2006.[19] The government began exporting the "Celtic Tiger" model, telling other small countries that they, too, could enjoy double-digit growth rates if they followed Ireland's lead. Accusing the global crisis of having triggered the eventual decline is misleading, however, because property prices in Ireland started declining in 2006–07, before the rest of world markets, thus leaving the local banks exposed.

Two weeks after the Lehman Brothers failure in September 2008, Dublin took the fateful decision to guarantee liabilities worth €400 billion at six financial institutions without even informing its European partners. This action created the first connection between a real estate–banking crisis and the sovereign debt crisis that exploded in the following months across Europe. There are few analogies between Greece and Ireland, but one has a psychological character: the sense of being the center of the world even if relatively isolated. In both countries, pride in sudden economic success made it difficult for both the Greeks and the Irish to see just how tenuous that success really was. Another analogy is described again by *The Economist*: "The radical transformation of Ireland into a globalized economy left some old attitudes untouched. Voters continued to tolerate levels of misbehaviour and, in some cases, outright corruption in their politicians that in other countries would have ended careers."[20]

The boom made things fuzzier in both the public and in the private economies. The concentration of risks in lending was a feature that made the banking system particularly vulnerable. Cycles in credit to commercial real estate are
prone to particularly wide swings; and during the upswing in Ireland, there is
wide agreement that property development was well ahead of trends that fundamentals could justify.[21] Tax-induced capital inflows had increased domestic
wages beyond productivity gains, thus making part of the economy uncompeti-
tive. Investments flew ever more to the real estate sector, inflating the bubble,
while production started to stumble concurrently with the crisis. Partly as a
consequence of the crisis and partly to cut costs, Dell, Ireland's largest exporter,
moved its manufacturing facilities to Poland in 2009.[22]

During the crisis nobody in Europe had the least interest in stressing the
peculiar potential of the Irish crisis. Much more than Greece, Ireland had a
mainly financial problem that could easily and swiftly transfer to the rest of
Europe. Assets in the Irish banking system amounted to €1.7 trillion (that is,
a stunning 1,060 percent of Irish GDP). Of this huge amount, 70 percent was
held by foreign banks with branches in Ireland or banks that were registered in
Ireland but conducted the bulk of their business abroad. The Irish economy
represents only 2 percent of the euro zone GDP, but evidently the banking system is more than 10 times greater, and the ripple effects of a failure would be
hard to measure.

In the summer of 2010, the fifty-one-year-old Irish finance minister Lenihan
was waging a personal battle as well. Stricken with pancreatic cancer, he was
undergoing rounds of chemotherapy and seemed increasingly despondent, Irish
journalists reported. He grew disillusioned and doubted that anything he did
to improve Ireland's finances would satisfy bond markets. While Lenihan cast
about for ways to reduce Ireland's budget, the crisis worsened. In September
Irish banks' borrowings from the ECB increased by €23 billion. The *Wall Street
Journal* gave a vivid description of the situation:

> Frantic, Irish banks turned to a little-used emergency lending program run
> by national central banks, which are effectively appendages of the ECB.
> Ireland's central bank doled out €7 billion to Irish banks this way, accept-
> ing low-quality collateral. For example, Anglo Irish Bank offered a gov-
> ernment IOU as collateral, thus converting a promise into instant cash.
> "Financial gymnastics," one Irish banker called it. On September 30, Mr.
> Lenihan announced that Ireland would funnel billions more in taxpayer
> cash into the banks. He promised a new deficit-cutting plan. When Mr.
> Lenihan got on a conference call with hundreds of investors to sell the
> plan the next day, he was drowned out by a deluge of derision. Callers
> heckled him and shouted, "Short Ireland!"[23]

News of instability started to circulate, more deposits were withdrawn from the Irish banks, which had to turn more and more often to the ECB for their funding needs. By mid-October 2010, Dublin was considered unofficially as the next candidate for European aid. At the end of the month the European Central Bank had €130 billion of outstanding loans for the funding needs of Ireland's banks. The central bank's financial exposure was mainly against Irish public debt. The level was growing by the month, following the intervention to support the banking system. Of an estimated €85 billion of public debt, 85 percent was held abroad, with the largest part held in the United Kingdom, Germany, and France. But the Irish banks' debt securities, totaling €80 billion, also were mostly held overseas. Even if the official government deficit was already financed and its needs covered until the following year, the potential disruption throughout Europe of a collapse of the banking system was too big to be tackled by the Irish government alone. For the EU as a whole, the problem of Ireland posed another moment for self-interrogation: How was it possible that the stress tests had been so crassly fudged, and how could a country formerly held up as a model of fiscal propriety suddenly turn into a most critical case?

# 16

## *A Sophisticated Way to Commit Suicide*

### *A Walk on the Beach*

October 18, 2010, was the much-awaited deadline for accomplishing the resetting of the economic governance of the EU. It turned out to be a fateful day, one of the worst for the whole crisis. That something was going wrong became evident during the morning. When EU finance ministers arrived in Luxemburg for a meeting of the Economic and Financial Affairs Council (ECOFIN) on that Monday, Germany's Wolfgang Schäuble and France's Christine Lagarde were not among them.

Ireland was on the brink, but was still resisting the pressures from Brussels, from the European heads of governments, and from European Central Bank president Jean-Claude Trichet, to ask swiftly for aid by the European Financial Stability Facility (EFSF), the fund instituted for bailouts in May 2010. In fact, the other EU countries did not allow the Irish government to impose losses on senior bondholders of the country's banks, including the deeply troubled Anglo Irish Bank, because of repercussions that might develop for the fragile continental European banks. By the end of September, the ECB had lent Irish banks €83 billion—roughly one-half of Ireland's annual economic output. In August and September, spooked depositors and investors pulled their money, and the banks grew even more desperate for cash. Considering the financial interconnections, a disorderly default in Ireland would have been more catastrophic than one in Greece, resulting in EU banks losing an appalling amount of money. Germany and the United Kingdom, in particular, would be directly affected. For Ireland, however, the burden of fiscal adjustment would be much greater if bondholders—including the banks in the rest of Europe—were not forced to share in any losses. Protecting those bondholders, while Irish citizens had to accept austerity, opened an understandable reaction in the Irish political debate against the European partners.

The worsening situation in Ireland also posed political problems for Chancellor Angela Merkel in Germany. Beyond the potentially immeasurable financial consequences of a new, widespread financial contagion, the situation was becoming too delicate politically for Merkel to remain passive. Either an Irish default or a bailout would pose a whole set of unpleasant problems for Merkel in terms of German public opinion. Bankers had become the target of popular discontent in Germany as well as elsewhere in Europe. Politicians in her government's coalition parties had raised the idea of punishing banks as a core program of their rather wobbly alliance. Paradoxically, the German banks responsible for faulty investments in Greece or Ireland were often state-owned or controlled by politicians. But the rhetoric was heated and had become a landslide. As often was the case, Merkel's priority was to search for the lowest cost and reasonable safety in the longer term for her voters: particularly in the absence of automatic sanctions on fiscal indiscipline in the other countries, German involvement in future bailouts had to be as limited as possible, and the costs had to be shifted onto the banks.

Looking toward the ECOFIN meeting in Luxembourg, the chancellor did not think that the finance ministers would come out with a strong decision meeting her goals: spelling out clearly the word "default" for ailing countries and calling on bankers to help foot the bill. This issue, soon to be known as "private sector involvement," became the most important political objective that Chancellor Merkel wanted to bring home to appease German public opinion. She had already laid the foundations of a role for the banks in May, when she obtained an informal agreement by EU leaders to demand that banks hold their Greek bonds in their portfolios until May 2013. Now, it was time for Merkel to take a decisive further step of making it clear that banks would have to bear the brunt of any future burden for the faulty investments they had made. She wanted the European Council to approve a formal rule according to which private creditors—and not just governments—would help pay for a default by a European country after 2013. For the first time ever, the eventuality of private involvement in a sovereign default was to be explicitly pinned down ex-ante in all future sovereign securities in the euro area issued after 2013. It was a promise of future losses: hardly a way to encourage investors.

Although Schäuble and Lagarde, the two most important ministers, were not present, the ECOFIN meeting in Luxembourg on October 18 proceeded as usual. European Council president Herman Van Rompuy was to present the outcome of the last meeting of his task force. The conclusions, which he made public following the meeting, envisaged a system composed of widely discussed pillars: greater macroeconomic surveillance based on an early warning system that "will detect the risk of real estate bubbles or of unsustainable patterns on the balance of payments, or strong divergences in competitiveness. . . . We recommend this surveillance mechanism, as a macro-economic pendant of the budget-focused Pact. Ultimately this may result in sanctions for countries in the euro zone only." The second recommendation concerned the Stability and Growth Pact, where a greater emphasis would be placed on debt, in addition to deficits, and a wider range of sanctions with a significant degree of automaticity. Policy coordination would be enhanced through the "European Semester" (formal reviews by the EU of budget plans by the individual governments). Finally, a robust framework for crisis management was proposed, but without many details. Van Rompuy's task force also recommended setting up independent fiscal councils, a greater degree of coordination by the governments, and the improvement of legal frameworks, even at national level.[1]

A high-level decision on these recommendations was evidently necessary, and it was hardly imaginable to have it without the personal endorsement of the two most influential finance ministers. Moreover, Van Rompuy's work was limited by the attempt of the task force to remain within the domain of the existing EU treaty.[2] As he had communicated to Merkel four days earlier, establishing new rules for the Stability and Growth Pact and for the European Stability Mechanism (ESM), a permanent agency that would take the place of the EFSF in 2013, would indeed require changes to the treaty. However, French opposition made that difficult.

Franco-German bilateral negotiations on economic governance questions had been under way at the highest levels since September. Merkel and Sarkozy met at the Asia-Europe summit in Brussels on October 4–5 to search for a common position. Germany needed support for the proposed involvement of private creditors in future debt restructuring and more particularly for the treaty change required in order to hallow the new fiscal framework and make it credible for the German electors.[3] Eventually, France, worried by its ballooning deficit, obtained a softening in the new agreement's procedure that any sanctions recommended by the EU Commission under the new Stability and Growth Pact could be blocked only by the vote of a qualified majority (the so-called reverse majority). Germany, however, won a round on its much bigger priority: financial investors (notably, the banks) would be called on to foot the bill for any future debt restructuring in the euro zone; in other words, they would be forced to suffer losses when countries such as Greece received EU aid to restructure their debts. This "private sector involvement" clause would prove to be the game-changer in the future of the crisis because of its effect of destabilizing investors, but none of the high-level officials in Berlin or Paris seemed to understand the consequences of what they were doing.

The deal was done when Germany backed down on how many "steps" states would get before automatic penalties would kick in and France agreed on a so-called soft change in the EU treaty. Before presenting the agreement publicly, Schäuble and Lagarde needed approval from their bosses (Merkel and Sarkozy), and they also wanted to avoid subjecting their compromise to haggling with the other countries, so the two finance ministers decided not to show up for the ECOFIN meeting in Luxembourg. Moreover, Merkel and Sarkozy had planned to meet in Deauville, France, on the day of the ECOFIN meeting for a trilateral session with Russian president Dmitry Medvedev, so they decided to finalize the agreement there.

When Merkel arrived at the Hotel Royal in Deauville, Sarkozy embraced the German chancellor and led her into a small salon with views of the English Channel. According to a journalist present at the scene, the French president ordered an aide to fetch Merkel's coat, before the two leaders set out for a private walk on the boardwalk, because there was a chill in the autumn air. But Sarkozy was expected to help with more than the coat. Germany could not accept an extension beyond 2013 of the €500 billion safety net that had been created after Greece's bailout. Some euro zone countries wanted to repeal the expiration date of the fund, saying ending it would prejudice the credibility of any bailout. But Merkel sought exactly the opposite: she wanted to change the EU treaty and introduce a completely different category of crisis management, calling for investors holding bonds in insolvent euro zone nations to shoulder losses on them, starting precisely in 2013, the year of the next German federal elections. Merkel proposed to the French president a cheap compromise. Germany would drop its demand for strict automatic sanctions, a procedure that had been feared by Sarkozy because he faced popular protests against France's own cost-cutting measures in pension reform and the recently submitted national budget. In exchange, the chancellor wanted Sarkozy to support the idea that in the future, if a euro zone country needed a bailout, bondholders would accept a reduction in what they were owed, an automatic "haircut," as it was known in financial circles. That would induce discipline in all countries, she thought. Such a step would also calm her voters in 2013 because they would finally see the bankers bearing the brunt of the cost of their misdeeds.

Unfortunately, by pressuring Sarkozy to agree to this demand, Merkel was explicitly stating that a western European nation might actually default on its debts. That had not happened since Germany had emerged from World War II.

### "You Are Going to Destroy the Euro"

Unaware of the agreement between Merkel and Sarkozy in Deauville, the finance ministers and other ECOFIN officials began their meeting the same day in Luxembourg believing they were close to accord on a procedure for imposing quasi-automatic sanctions against fiscally irresponsible countries. Such a procedure would reassure financial markets about the credibility of the EU's fiscal framework. Entering the meeting room, EU monetary affairs commissioner Olli Rehn said finance ministers faced a "litmus test" that would show "whether states are genuinely for reinforced economic governance or not," adding that "now is the moment of truth."[4] Accounts of the meeting reported ECB president Jean-Claude Trichet talking of "the beginning of a new era." The tightening of margins for political interpretation of fiscal restraint would reinforce the credibility of the euro, and the positive effects on the interest rate spreads could be potentially decisive in changing the course of the crisis for the better. However, the central bank still had concerns, including that the reform of fiscal rules risked setting overly generous goals for deficits and debt. "To ensure strict enforcement of the provision, it is important that the room for interference is limited to the absolute minimum," Trichet told the ministers. As to the enforcement of sanctions, the ECB also had serious concerns regarding the provisions according to which, following a request by the relevant member state, or on grounds of "exceptional economic circumstances," the sanctions could be lifted. The assessment had to be more independent, by reinforcing the European Commission's internal procedures and setting up an independent body of "wise persons" at the EU level, the ECB president argued.

However, soon after the start of the meeting, Jörg Asmussen, the state secretary in the German finance ministry, who was sitting in for Schäuble, announced that the German government would support the French position on the Stability and Growth Pact of not asking for a strong automaticity of sanctions. This surprised the finance ministers of the countries that had taken hardline positions on fiscal rectitude, notably the Netherlands, Sweden, and Finland. But Van Rompuy, who knew what was happening in Deauville, seized on the opportunity offered from Asmussen to press for a closure of the discussion on a compromise that was close to the newly flexible Franco-German position. All in all, the softening of the sanctions was not dramatic. In the text that Van Rompuy delivered on October 21, the voting procedure for imposing sanctions was clearly stated: "It is proposed to introduce a reverse majority rule for the adoption of enforcement measures. This means in practice that Commission recommendations would be adopted unless a qualified majority of Member States in the Council votes against within a given deadline."[5]

The new accent on the public debt was stated at the beginning: "The Task Force recommends to operationalize the debt criterion in the Treaty by defining an appropriate quantitative reference, and to apply it effectively—due account taken of all relevant factors—notably as a trigger in the excessive deficit procedure."[6]

The sanctions of "both financial and reputational/political nature" were instead only very broadly described. But the enforcement procedure provided for a very accelerated mechanism:

In case of significant deviation from the adjustment path, the Commission shall issue an early warning. The Council will, within one month, adopt a Recommendation for policy measures setting a deadline for addressing the deviation. . . . If the Member State concerned fails to take appropriate action within five months, the Council will immediately adopt a Recommendation stating so, on the basis of a Commission Recommendation based on article 121.4 of the Treaty. At the same time, an interest-bearing deposit will be imposed on the euro area Member State (by reversed majority rule). The whole process will be no longer than six months. The time period of five months shall be reduced to three if the Commission in its Recommendation to the Council considers that the situation is particularly serious and warrants urgent action.[7]

Jean-Claude Trichet was rabid about the disregard the governments had shown for the ECB requests for credible automatic mechanisms needed to lend credibility to fiscal discipline. He was even more unhappy about the delay in setting up the European Stability Mechanism, which was just vaguely mentioned in the text: "The Task Force considers that in the medium term there is a need to establish a credible crisis resolution framework for the euro area capable of addressing financial distress and avoiding contagion. It will need to resolutely address the moral hazard that is implicit in any ex-ante crisis scheme."[8] Evidently, the governments wanted to leave the task of remedying the risks of default on the shoulders of the ECB for as long as possible. The text concluded with the observation that "setting-up of a crisis resolution framework requires further work. As it may imply a need for Treaty changes, depending on its specific features, it is an issue for the European Council."[9]

After Van Rompuy had finished presenting his report at 4 p.m., taking into consideration all the objections, but not releasing a final text—which appeared only three days later—news started to flow from Deauville where the French, apparently without properly negotiating it with the German delegation, released a formal communiqué about the "walk on the beach" between Merkel and Sarkozy. The first press reports arrived in Luxembourg about 5 p.m., followed later by the French communiqué, as the finance ministers were still engaging in their meetings.

The Franco-German text announced that Berlin had accepted that a "qualified majority," that is the vote of a higher number of governments, was needed to sanction a country (rather than to suspend sanctions). The text added that "these sanctions should be more automatic [than in the past], while respecting the role of the different institutions and the institutional balance. In enforcing the preventive arm of the [Stability and Growth] Pact, the Council should be empowered to decide, acting by QMV (qualified majority voting)." Moreover, the text added: "France and Germany consider that an amendment of the Treaties is needed and that the President of the European Council should be asked to present, in close contact with the Members of the European Council, concrete options allowing the establishment of a robust crisis resolution framework before its meeting in March 2011."[10] In Luxembourg, Italian finance minister Giulio Tremonti put it well: "Habemus Novum Pactum. It is a compromise," he said, "that allows for some flexibility," which was precisely what the European Central Bank did not want.[11]

Just after 5 p.m., Germany's Asmussen "printed out an email outlining the proposal and passed it around to finance ministers."[12] This message contained the even more surprising news that the French and German leaders had also cut a deal behind everyone's back, one that meant that private creditors would have to worry about losing their money. According to two participants, Trichet turned to the French delegation shouting: "You're going to destroy the euro,"

## Haircuts for Everybody Starting in 2013

For some reason, the introduction of a "promise of losses" was overlooked at the time by the press and the markets. Most of the communication in Deauville and Luxembourg was focused on the rhetoric concerning sanctions and on the rivalry among countries. The attention was centered more on the Stability and Growth Pact—where Germany seemed to have given in—than on the more elusive crisis mechanism and its powerful implications. For ten days most observers simply did not understand what was going on. The involvement of private creditors was approved officially in the final statement of the European Council meeting on October 28. Release of the statement finally exposed the plan publicly, to the horror of world investors—but evidently not of the finance ministers or the euro zone leaders: "The European Council welcomes the intention of the Commission to undertake, in close consultation with the President of the European Council, preparatory work on the general features of a future new mechanism, i.a. the role of the private sector."[13]

During the discussion, the only loudly discordant voice was that of Jean-Claude Trichet. He is reported to have said that he did not doubt the need for a crisis mechanism but he was greatly concerned about the consequences: "We must be clear about how the markets work. If the crisis mechanism involves the private sector, it will be much more vulnerable. If the new mechanism provides ex ante for private sector contributions, the conditions on which the contributions will be demanded will be crucially important. We will also need to have the IMF on board. Lastly, I would strongly advise against 'haircuts.'"[14]

Van Rompuy's text for the European Council statement absorbed Angela Merkel's requirements. It said that the European Commission and the president of the European Council will work on "the general features" of a crisis resolution mechanism, including "the role of the private sector, the role of the IMF and the very strong conditionality under which such programs should operate." The statement also said the European Council's meeting in December would, on the basis of this work, take "the final decision both on the outline of a crisis mechanism and on a limited treaty amendment, so that any change can be ratified at the latest by mid-2013."[15]

Trichet again tried persistently to make the leaders aware of the risks that this would provoke in the markets. Analyst Peter Ludlow provided an interesting description of how Trichet was silenced: After a firm but polite reply from the German chancellor, in which she explained why she thought that the private sector must be involved in the new arrangement, Sarkozy exploded in terms that had relatively little to do with the matter under consideration and much more to do with Trichet's status as an appointed official and Sarkozy's as a head of state. "You are trying to convince the world that it was you who saved the euro. It wasn't. It was us, the heads of state and government, who took the vital decisions."[16]

Speaking to other central bankers after the summit, Trichet called the outcome "abhorrent" and worse. He was right to state his objections so forcefully. The decision that starting in 2013 all members of the euro zone would be obliged to introduce "collective action clauses" when they issued new government bonds—and thus opening the possibility that private bondholders would be asked to share in any restructuring of the debt—had the gravest consequences. The collective action clause was a mechanism that had been invented by the IMF to help emerging market countries. By adopting such a requirement themselves, the euro area countries implicitly were "downgraded" to the financial status of emerging markets. Instead of creating certainty in the solidity of the euro, the European Council enhanced tensions and made investors more—not less—worried about investing in the weaker countries. But the real extent of the damage could not be understood without taking into account the secret and informal agreements reached by the EU finance ministers with their national banks. Back in May, just after the decisive meetings of May 7–9, governments had obtained from the largest banking institutions in their countries a commitment not to sell the Greek bonds in their portfolios until May 2013. Now those bonds, locked in the banks, were directly exposed to the risk of default starting in 2013 and now their prices would need to take into account their new riskiness for investors.

Trichet explained rather clearly his opposition to the "haircut" for investors during his monthly press conference in Frankfurt on November 4:

> Comparing with what we are reflecting on in Europe, the IMF does not make necessarily the ex-ante working assumption that the relationship with markets, investor and savers is interrupted. Let us look back over the

past 20 or 30 years and estimate the proportion of cases in which this kind of intervention by the IMF occurred alongside the interruption of the normal functioning of the financing of the economy through haircuts and generalised restructuring. Depending on the period under consideration, the proportion might be the following: in more than 75 percent of cases there was no such interruption of the normal relationship and only in less than 25 percent of cases there was. Of course it can never be excluded, but this assumption is not made as compulsory ex ante. I would say the assumption made is the contrary.[17]

The disruptive potential of what the leaders had decided has to be put in the context of the euro area fragility. At the beginning of November 2010, a shortfall of credibility undercut the Irish government's efforts to design a fiscal plan based on the assumption that GDP growth was not particularly affected by the debt crisis.[18] Irish interest rates climbed toward 6.7 percent on November 11, when ten-year bonds rose to an explosive 9 percent. News of the finally revised (for the twentieth time) Greek fiscal deficit for 2009 exposed that it had reached an appalling 15.4 percent of GDP (implying that the 2010 deficit would end above 9 percent rather than under 8 percent). As could be expected, this news deepened skepticism among investors about the sustainability of the euro area.

Meeting in Seoul for a G-20 summit, finance ministers of Germany, France, Italy, Spain, and the United Kingdom tried to limit the damage by emphasizing that the EU was still considering its options and that no decisions about the new mechanisms had yet been taken: "Whatever the debate within the euro area about the future permanent crisis resolution mechanism and the potential private sector involvement in that mechanism, we are clear that this does not apply to any outstanding debt and any programmes under current instruments. Any new mechanism would only come into effect after mid-2013 with no impact whatsoever on the current arrangements."[19]

According to the Wall Street Journal, Schäuble spent much of the ten-hour flight to Seoul encouraging Merkel to change her tune. Germany, he argued, had to help others in order to help itself. "We must not always talk about what we don't want," the sixty-eight-year-old veteran politician told Merkel and her advisers. "We must say why the euro is in Germany's interest."[20] Apparently on that occasion Schäuble sold Merkel on a plan that would come to be known as another "grand bargain": Germany would increase its financial commitments to Europe's rescue funds, but only if all members of the euro zone agreed on a common economic strategy and more fiscal rigor. However, a different version of Merkel's change of strategy is common among informed sources. Merkel had resumed intensively her contacts with Trichet, who actually convinced her to change her strategy, abandon the automatic imposition of haircuts, and adopt as a market-tested system the one used by the International Monetary Fund in its bailouts. The IMF applies haircuts only when the rescue proves really impossible otherwise. The IMF makes a series of assessments over a period of time, and only if success is precluded, is a restructuring of the debt implemented. The medium-term strategy of an IMF-like bailout could be accompanied by the "grand bargain," in other words, trading resources for conditionality.

Eventually, Merkel acknowledged that her diktat had upset the markets, but she continued to insist that it was unfair for taxpayers to be saddled alone with the cost of sovereign rescues. In Seoul, she stated clearly a crucial dilemma that is both effect and cause of the whole crisis: "Let me put it simply: in this regard there may be a contradiction between the interests of the financial world and the interests of the political world. We cannot keep constantly explaining to our voters and our citizens why the taxpayer should bear the cost of certain risks and not those people who have earned a lot of money from taking those risks."[21]

It was a very crucial point, one that should be taken into account along the whole story of the European crisis. Democracy—not only politicians—and markets had been at loggerheads. They have different timings, different priorities, and different ways of reacting. Both democracy and markets are essential for countries—Germany included—that need to borrow to survive. They borrow from their citizens, even from the sometimes ugly institutions of banks, insurance companies, hedge funds, or even pension funds. But the power of the markets was infinitely larger than in the past and dictated the timing and the content of policy decisions in a totally unprecedented manner. At that juncture politics had probably only one option: to learn to use the power of the markets instead of fighting it.

### Ireland Has to Be Rescued

A final assessment of the reasons for the worsening of market conditions was released in December 2010 by the Bank for International Settlements:

> The surge in sovereign credit spreads began on 18 October, when the French and German governments agreed to take steps that would make it possible to impose haircuts on bonds should a government not be able to service its debt. Spreads widened further after a European Council statement on 28 October made it clear that other EU governments had agreed to the proposal. In the following two weeks, Irish spreads went up by more than 200 basis points and the CDS spread curve inverted, indicating that market participants now saw a more immediate risk of a negative credit event. To forestall further spread increases, the finance ministers of several European countries on 12 November reiterated that burden-sharing would apply only to bonds issued after 2013. This announcement

brought merely a temporary calm. Focus quickly turned to the Irish banking system, which had grown more reliant on the central bank as repo market loans using Irish government bonds as collateral had become prohibitively expensive.[22]

In fact, markets grew nervous from day to day, and even the spreads between the yields on French and German ten-year bonds widened when analyses circulated observing that France might not be immune from the contagion. Indeed, France was paying higher interest on its sovereign bonds than Malaysia or Chile, and there were rumors that credit rating agencies were contemplating a change in France's AAA status. Officials at the finance ministry in Paris admitted they were severely intimidated by the risk of losing the valued status of a risk-free, almost-German debtor. That influenced directly the stance of Paris in following Berlin's policies. French finance minister Lagarde rushed to support Merkel, defending the "principle" of bondholders assuming bailout costs. "All stakeholders must participate in the gains and losses of any particular situation," she said.

Irish finance minister Brian Lenihan attributed the pressure on his country to "unintended" remarks from German officials about new rescue measures that would compel private lenders to shoulder some costs in future bailouts. The British and the Irish press sponsored the view that Ireland was a victim of Europe.[23] Hostility toward Germany was palpable in Brussels, and even German parliamentarians admitted their country's image had been damaged. Greek prime minister George Papandreou warned repeatedly that Germany's insistence on investors sharing the pain in any future mechanism for a euro zone bailout was damaging some economies. "This could break backs. This could force economies towards bankruptcy," he said on a visit to Paris.[24] Europe seemed once again divided and the euro once more on the brink.

After several days when Dublin tried to resist resorting to external aid, and the interest rate spreads on bonds had fallen slightly to below 6 percent, on November 18 signs of a bank run made the situation unsustainable. A story by the *Financial Times* reported that analysts saw growing evidence that Irish bank deposits were dwindling, after Irish Life & Permanent said corporate customers had withdrawn €600 million—more than 11 percent of total deposits—over a matter of weeks in August and September.[25] Bank of Ireland reported a similar trend, and Allied Irish Banks was expected to have been hit by a similar exodus. Compounding the outflow of customer money, LCH.Clearnet, one of Europe's biggest clearing houses, doubled the down-payment it required banks to place with it as an indemnity against default when trading Irish sovereign debt.

On November 21, European finance ministers agreed that providing assistance to Ireland was warranted to safeguard financial stability in the EU and the euro area. In their statement, they confirmed that the joint EU-IMF financial assistance package would be financed from the European Stabilization Mechanism (ESM) when it came into play in 2013, and in the meantime by the European Financial Stability Facility (EFSF). In addition, this aid could possibly be supplemented by bilateral loans to be negotiated by non-euro EU member states. The United Kingdom and Sweden had already indicated their readiness to consider such loans. A €85 billion rescue package for Ireland was formalized one week later. "The Irish began by saying they didn't want the IMF, but that only lasted two weeks, where it lasted four months with Greece," Dominique Strauss-Kahn said about the resistance to an IMF involvement in Europe.[26]

As the Bank for International Settlements observed, "Investors reacted positively to the announced support package, but the respite was short-lived due to a number of new developments. First, disagreements within the Irish coalition government resulted in an Irish election being called for early 2011. Second, on November 24, Standard & Poor's downgraded Irish government debt from AA– to A with a negative outlook, prompting further increases in Irish credit spreads. With no obvious new information as the trigger, investor attention turned first to Portugal and Spain and later to Belgium and Italy. Government bond and CDS spreads in those countries reached new highs."[27]

What spooked the markets was that the Irish banking system was still exposed to default risk, even if Irish sovereign risk had been guaranteed by the EU funds. The banks' previously unexplored obscurity hid bad surprises that were partially disclosed by analyses of the BIS. According to the data, Ireland's banks were among those most exposed to some of the other weaker euro zone nations, in spite of the Irish industry's tiny network of foreign operations. Combined, Irish banks were the fifth-largest lender in the world to Italy, with total outstanding credit of more than €30 billion. Among the leading lenders to Portugal, Greece, and Spain, Irish banks collectively ranked fifth, fifth and seventh, respectively, even though Ireland's economy is only the fifteenth biggest in the European Union.[28] The interconnectedness of Ireland's banking system to other peripheral economies was exacerbated by some foreign banks' use of Dublin's financial center as a low-tax conduit for business. The data highlighted that the interrelationship among the troubled nations of Europe was more deep-seated than many people had realized, suggesting that the risk of contagion was still very high.

### Merkel versus Ackermann and the End of the Euro

Tensions among the European banks' top managers were extreme, and especially in Germany the proposal for investor haircuts was dreaded as a lethal threat, given the heaps of government bonds in the portfolios of banks and insurance companies. In two private meetings, Deutsche Bank's Josef Ackermann tried to convince Merkel that her initiative was damaging the stability of the euro area. The new collective action clauses made it easier for government issuers to revise the terms of bond contracts once they could find agreement with a majority of bondholders, thus forcing a minority to take the losses. The bankers concluded there was a near-certainty of incurring high losses.

In mid-November Ackermann, who was also chairman of the Institute of International Finance, a powerful global lobby for the banking industry, had tried to convince Van Rompuy and Barroso to stop the initiative. He was made aware that the stumbling block was much closer to home: at the Chancellery in Berlin. On November 27, during a closed conference in southern Germany, Ackermann tried again to convince Merkel to back down from her haircut proposal.[29] It was too late. The next day, the European Council confirmed the collective action clause. In the following days, German banks broke out of the commitment, made in May, to hold onto the bonds of the peripheral countries in their portfolios. The Deutsche Bank moved quickly and extended its sales to Spanish and Italian bonds, with fateful consequences.

On that very same November 28, the Eurogroup was asked, at the end of a series of informal meetings, to approve as rapidly as possible the European Stability Mechanism (ESM) that would replace the EFSF in 2013; the goal was to give some clarity to the markets. Under the pressure triggered by the haircut dispute, Paris and Berlin had taken up new bilateral meetings to prepare for a smooth conclusion of the negotiations on the "Grand Bargain." But they finally involved the offices of both Van Rompuy and Barroso, represented by Antonio Cabral and Marco Buti, the director general of ECOFIN, who was the commission's leading representative to the euro working group. The final discussions took place among ministers and EU officials on Sunday, November 28, then a video conference involving Van Rompuy, Merkel, Sarkozy, Juncker, Trichet, and Barroso was held to get approval of the final text. The document itself was released as a collective statement by the Eurogroup later the same day. Negotiated against the background of the sharp dispute about the obligations of private creditors—a dispute between Trichet on the one hand and Merkel and Schäuble on the other—the Eurogroup statement carefully and repeatedly highlighted the similarities between the new ESM and the IMF. Like the IMF, but unlike the temporary EFSF, the new institution, once it took effect in 2013, was to be a treaty-based international organization with capital paid in by participating countries. The rules covering case-by-case participation of private sector creditors were to be "fully consistent with IMF policies." The procedures to be followed for approving loans were similar to those of the IMF, and the IMF itself was to be involved in them. The ESM was new therefore, but at the same time it would have the reassuringly familiar characteristics of the IMF.[30]

The statement explained that the rules for the new ESM "will be adapted to provide for a case by case participation of private sector creditors, fully consistent with IMF policies. In all cases, in order to protect taxpayers' money, and to send a clear signal to private creditors that their claims are subordinated to those of the official sector, an ESM loan will enjoy preferred creditor status, junior only to the IMF loan."[31] The involvement of private creditors in eventual losses was aggravated by the fact that the ESM loans would be reimbursed before the privately held bonds (the ESM loans were not "pari passu," as the legal status is defined in such cases, but enjoyed a privileged status). Moreover, an aid program would require a unanimous vote within the Eurogroup; in other words, just one country could block a proposed loan. In order not to spook investors, a further specification helped to put this decision in a more reassuring legal framework:

> In the unexpected event that a country would appear to be insolvent, the Member State has to negotiate a comprehensive restructuring plan with its private sector creditors, in line with IMF practices with a view to restoring debt sustainability. If debt sustainability can be reached through these measures, the ESM may provide liquidity assistance. In order to facilitate this process, standardized and identical collective action clauses (CACs) will be included, in such a way as to preserve market liquidity, in the terms and conditions of all new euro area government bonds starting in June 2013."[32]

Despite the reassuring language, the effect on the markets was catastrophic. On November 29, interest rate spreads widened rapidly and abruptly across the euro zone, reversing the stabilization that had started with the leaders' crisis responses in May. In the markets, it was called the "Merkel Crash, indicating that investors knew who to blame for their potential losses on failing bonds. Irish ten-year spreads moved toward 5 percent and Greek spreads toward 9 percent, but a particularly dangerous alarm rang with a spike in yields on Spanish bonds. The euro, which had traded above 1.42 versus the dollar in early November, ended the month flirting with the 1.30 level after weeks of heavy selling. The decision of the EU heads of government to create a "permanent crisis mechanism to safeguard the financial stability of the euro area as a whole"—one that involved the private sector—raised the probability of a sovereign debt rescheduling or restructuring starting in 2013. However, it also immediately impacted existing debt. The eventuality of a default after 2013 opened the possibility that even in the run-up to 2013, financing the debt in countries like Greece or Ireland would become much more dangerous and expensive, impacting the bonds that some banks had kept in their books only because of the pressure of their governments. The crisis suddenly, and yet again, changed course for the worse.[33]

## The Mortal Danger

The official reaction of the ECB president was diplomatic. Trichet tried to reassure markets by saying current bond holders were secure, in line with precedents set by the International Monetary Fund in dealing with other sovereign defaults. "In stating very explicitly that Europe will be 'fully consistent with IMF policy' and 'IMF practices' as regards private sector involvement, the position made public by governments last Sunday is a useful clarification," Trichet told the European Parliament on November 30.[34] During his testimony, Trichet added a very crucial remark. He started cautiously: "I wouldn't comment" on the bond-purchase program put in place by the ECB, which had been a stronghold of defense for all the euro countries attacked by the markets. But he immediately admitted that "the program was ongoing" and that the governing council of the bank would make decisions on its future path. De facto, he was hinting that the ECB would soon be back in the market for government bonds.

Trichet's words came just in time. Its Securities Market Program (SMP) was indeed at work, and after Trichet spoke to the parliament, the ECB placed large orders for tranches of €100 million in Irish and Portuguese debt. Investors reacted euphorically. On December 2, the ECB announced that it also would continue to provide exceptional liquidity support to the banks of the euro area via three-month financing at fixed rates with full allotment until April 2011.[35] Together with the ECB bond purchases at larger-than-usual trade sizes on that same day, the new measure made yields fall by around 50 and 25 basis points on ten-year Irish and Portuguese bonds, respectively, in just a few hours. On that same day, Tommaso Padoa-Schioppa, the architect of the euro and former ECB board member, wrote a private letter to Greek prime minister George Papandreou that revealed the real situation, which would become visible to the others only in 2011:

> The crisis has hit Greece, then Ireland and is now menacing Portugal, Spain, Italy, Belgium, perhaps France. But the lack of confidence is not about individual countries. It is about the euro-zone: the issue is whether the euro-zone is willing and capable to act as a true union and as an effective policy maker. This lack of confidence persists in spite of the very important decisions taken since May and constitutes a mortal danger. A collapse of the euro would disintegrate the single market, destroy relationships by countries based on the Rule of Law and undermine the prosperity of all participants, the strong and the weak alike.[36]

A few days after sending his letter, this visionary man died suddenly, as if overwhelmed by the European tragedy.

## The Crucial Deadline of March 2011

After the huge dislocations created by the haircuts issue and the subsequent bail-out by the ECB, the European Council on December 16 was the crucial event for the design of a sensible package, including treaty amendments that would be needed to establish the new crisis mechanism. The final statement at the meeting on December 16 gives the sense of the difficult negotiation: "The member states whose currency is the euro may establish a stability mechanism to be activated if indispensable to safeguard the stability of the euro area as a whole and. . . . The granting of any required financial assistance under the mechanism will be made subject to strict conditionality."[37]

During the discussion, British prime minister David Cameron reiterated his request that no money from the European Union as a whole should be employed to bail out the euro. As a consequence he requested that article 122.2 of the treaty—which had been activated in May for the European Union's €60 billion facility—would not be used again. That was very hard to swallow for the European Commission, and for the European Parliament, because such a limitation would make impossible any future bailout packages. A ban on using article 122.2 also would have a broader consequence: if the entire European Union of twenty-seven nations was to play no role in the destiny and sustainability of the euro area, the development of solidarity policies in the euro zone would follow a purely intergovernmental path. It would be entirely dependent on negotiations among states with no supranational mediation.

The profile of the political answer to the crisis was becoming clearer. The Eurogroup was the new perimeter of stronger coordination, and its modus operandi would be intergovernmental and therefore inevitably influenced by the country that—as the chancellor herself said, in an admission that none of her predecessors would ever have dared use—is the economically strongest country. Once Germany was satisfied, the agreement on the crisis mechanism had been found. It was necessary, and ultimately possible, for the political leaders to deliver a decisive signal of their commitment to act. This was done in the morning of the second day of the European Council with a statement that was intended to put an end to the crisis: "The Heads of State or Government of the euro area and the EU institutions have made it clear . . . that they stand ready to do whatever is required to ensure the stability of the euro area as a whole. The euro is and will remain a central part of European integration."[38]

Could they do or say anything more clearly? In one sense, this statement echoed the grand words of Helmut Kohl, in January 2002: "The introduction of the euro is not only an important decision for the EU; it is an important turning point in European history. . . . The single European currency has made European integration irreversible."[39] As president of the European Commission,

Romano Prodi went one step further: "Some day there will be a crisis and new (economic policy) instruments will be created." Or, were the words of the European Council statement simply worn out by months and years of dithering action and empty rhetoric? Never before had the European leaders used the phrase "whatever is required"—a phrase that was especially meaningful in connection with calling the euro a "central part" of the European project. In other words, if the euro fails, Europe fails. No one could think of such an eventuality. Even so, these were nothing more than words.

# 17

## A Fateful Fight between the ECB and the Heads of Governments

### Trichet's Alarm

European Central Bank president Jean-Claude Trichet was very alarmed when he understood that the heads of governments intended to delay the launching of the weaponry necessary to defend the euro—particularly the "stabilization" funds that were to relieve the Central Bank from the burden of purchasing sovereign bonds. For months, he had been asking for a "quantum leap" in economic governance and had warned that defaults would be made more likely as a result of suggestions that private bondholders might be forced to accept losses. Indeed, the markets had received that idea very badly, increasing Trichet's concerns that the crisis was threatening the very existence of the euro.

An improvement of the planned European Financial Stability Facility (EFSF) was "necessary both in quantity and in quality," Trichet said in Frankfurt on January 13 when the ECB's governing council met for the first time in 2011. "Everything is urgent in the present circumstances, and we are asking authorities in general—public authorities, European authorities and governments—to be up to their responsibilities."[1] The ECB had again bailed out the euro in December 2010, but wanted to be relieved by the governments of the task of purchasing bonds. Euro zone leaders had agreed the previous May to establish the EFSF, but in the following months the crisis had widened and it was necessary to endow the fund with a larger amount of money so that it could be credible. Even so, governments seemed reluctant to commit swiftly to lend it more money. An unusual rift was opening between Berlin and the ECB, with profound consequences. Trichet was supported by José Manuel Barroso in asking for a swift implementation of the stability funds, but the reactions in Berlin against the head of the

European Commission were blunt: the requests were "incomprehensible" or "non-constructive," members of the German government replied. The German media's new mantra was "kein Blankoscheck": we want to be sure that the money requested by any future fund—the EFSF or the future ESM—is not limitless.

National governments had a solid motivation not to rush to pour money into the EFSF, which was that the funds used to purchase bonds would have to be accounted as national debts while loan guarantees would not. That, of course, would impact directly the governments' budget balances, thereby increasing the debt-to-GDP ratio levels in all countries and hampering national policy programs. The governments preferred to wait until the ESM was established in 2013 because that new stability mechanism, unlike the EFSF, would have an own juridical personality. The ESM would be an international organization, just like the International Monetary Fund, and therefore its debts would be its own and would not reflect on the national accounts.

Beyond the delay in the activation of the EFSF, the second reason Trichet was angry was, again, the possibility of "private sector involvement" (PSI), or mandatory haircuts for private bondholders. He was convinced that its application might destroy the euro. Forcing bondholders to accept losses had occasionally been used in resolving past sovereign debt crises because it could help sovereign borrowers to regain fiscal sustainability more rapidly. It was also considered as a measure to ensure burden-sharing between the public and private sectors, in other words, punishing the banks. However, Trichet feared that within a monetary union, the application of PSI to the bonds of one member country might put at risk the financial stability of the currency area as a whole. Given the strong interdependency of financial actors, banks in all countries would be affected even if losses were forced only on bonds for one single country. According to Trichet, doing this was likely to trigger a need for large-scale bank recapitalization at a time of financial stress and in the absence of a well-endowed EFSF that could help banks, as well as countries.

Trichet also was surprised that the leaders could neglect the risk of "confidence effects": if the application of PSI in one member country led to a sudden increase in risk aversion among financial market participants, the market access of other countries might also be hampered. This might occur even if the economic fundamentals of the other countries remain unchanged. As a result, solvent countries could easily be drawn into a lethal crisis. The weakness of the banks and the risk of sovereign debt were likely to be mutually reinforcing, creating a vicious feedback loop.

According to the ECB president, the risks of PSI underlined the importance of strong governance in the euro area to ensure sound fiscal positions in all member countries at all times. The risks also highlighted the need to have an effective crisis resolution mechanism at the European level—the European Financial

Stability Facility and, from mid-2013, the European Stability Mechanism—to ensure that financial assistance could be provided effectively and under strict conditionality should a euro area country experience future problems in obtaining refinancing in the markets. It was evident that Trichet thought that the crisis could become deadly soon and that he needed to put pressure on the governments to set up timely defenses.

## Markets Shared the Same Fears

In fact, the reactions of the markets to the decisions of the December European Council meeting were not encouraging.[2] As soon as January began, the markets started hitting not only Ireland, whose repayment capacity had just been criticized by the IMF, but also Belgium, where domestic political instability was becoming chronic, and Spain and Portugal. Once more, Moody's stepped in to announce a possible downgrade for Lisbon, as well. Rumors about Portugal asking for aid from the EFSF started to circulate.

What upset the markets was the word "default," which was frequently evoked by the EU leaders and implicitly attached to the PSI clause. Each time, the d-word set off a reassessment of risk in portfolios of the financial intermediaries, and investors reflexively shifted funds from marginally riskier countries to sounder ones. Within the euro area, the cross-country reshuffling of funds was much stronger than anywhere else, because of the absence of the currency risk among countries sharing the euro and because the banking systems of creditor countries (countries regularly posting surpluses in their balance of payments), notably Germany, had risks hidden in their balance sheets that had accumulated for a decade. Those banks were eager to get rid as fast as possible of any further risks, especially after they had learned of the possibility they might be forced to suffer losses through PSI. Moreover, depositors transferred their money from the banking systems in countries that were perceived as more fragile—at the beginning of 2011, Spain or Portugal—to Germany or other AAA-rated countries. The drain of liquidity from weaker countries to stronger ones—a "sudden stop" in the language of the crises—could be immediately felt in Iberian banks. And then, since monetary conditions were regulated by the ECB for the euro area as a whole, no specific expansion of the money supply could be engineered for the two Iberian countries.

In the specific framework of a monetary union, such as the euro zone, that lacked both a common fiscal policy and common guarantees behind the national debts, a breach of trust set off by a faulty political statement about the lack of solidarity can trigger a liquidity crisis that, if large enough, would push interest rates higher. The resulting tightening of monetary conditions can slow down one or more economies in the union and even degenerate into an insolvency. This is a specific technical fault-line beneath the ground of a monetary union. Countries outside such a union can always resort to policies such as monetary expansion, debt reduction through inflation, or currency devaluation—as the United Kingdom did—and avoid the immediate risk of a default. However, countries "trapped" into a monetary agreement have access to none of those instruments. Moreover, if the monetary agreement is not backed by fiscal unity, a snowball effect can come into play: fears of a solvency problem in one country can trigger emergency budgetary cutbacks that might force the country into a recession. Eventually, political management of the recession—under the pressure of markets and of other partners in the monetary union—can make life extremely difficult for the government and set off social protests once social expenditures are curtailed or automatic stabilizers (such as unemployment benefits) come to a halt. In the fragile setting of a monetary union, the snowball can originate from a relatively minor liquidity problem, even one caused somewhere else, for instance a contagion from another country or a general sentiment of risk aversion around the world.[3] As a consequence of these factors, the offhanded mentioning by European leaders of default as a possible option fed into a sentiment of distrust and self-fulfilling destructive dynamics.

## To Default or Not to Default

The question also needs to be asked: was the commitment of ruling out any default really credible? Markets seemed unconvinced, as demonstrated by the frequent spikes in interest rate spreads for the most fragile countries. None of the heads of governments wanted to spell out clearly why default made no sense, and it can be argued that they had done the opposite by threatening investor losses (through the "PSI" clause) on some government securities. The lack of political cohesion made it reasonable to think that at some point in time, for debtors or even for creditors, the cost-benefit of a debt restructuring would be unbalanced. Debtors might imagine that a clear reduction in their debt would be more acceptable to their population than years of painful domestic deflation. A rapid reduction in the debt burden avoids implementing an overly restrictive fiscal policy, which may further hamper growth and lead to social tensions. It spares taxpayers from having to pay for mistakes made also by investors, especially foreign ones. At a certain point in time, even creditors might find that a default by some smaller country, after ring-fencing (protecting) the others, could be costly but probably less than going on for years helping more and more countries.

The main rationale supporting the logic of default is indeed that fiscal adjustments required by a country such as Greece or Ireland might be just too heavy just to stabilize the debt-to-GDP ratio at a safer level, if not at an acceptable 60 percent of GDP, at least below 90 percent. However, as an analysis of the IMF fiscal staff observed in September 2010, "fiscal adjustment on the requisite scale is historically not unprecedented. During the past three decades, there were fourteen episodes in advanced economies and twenty-six in emerging economies when individual countries adjusted their structural primary balance by more than 7 percentage points of GDP."[4] The feasibility of the adjustments was proven by the fact that in most cases, even in the peripheral European countries, the primary surpluses required for stabilizing the debt would be close to or even lower than their average primary surpluses in the 1990–2007 period. In Greece and Ireland, the data showed that the surplus required had been reached only in rare cases, but it had been done.[5]

Default, or any kind of debt restructuring, is not an economically attractive option for advanced economies. Even for Greece, it would not meaningfully reduce the still-necessary painful fiscal adjustment. Actually, a default would make it very difficult to access funding from international markets. As a result, the government of the defaulting country would be forced to return to a primary surplus more abruptly and potentially in a more disorderly manner than otherwise. This would be difficult to accept for citizens who would suffer a loss of private wealth and who in some cases would have reason to believe that their problems were made unsustainable by the global financial shockwaves.

The core idea that a default would not be politically convenient for any government lies in the stigma and in the fact that a default has not occurred for decades in an advanced economy. As ECB executive board member Lorenzo Bini Smaghi highlighted in December 2010:

> An oft-made assumption is that governments can renegotiate with their creditors the terms and conditions of their debt instruments without this having major repercussions on the rest of the economic and financial system. This assumption is largely based on the experience of developing countries with underdeveloped financial systems and mainly foreign creditors. What is generally not well understood is that, in advanced economies, public debt is the cornerstone of the financial system and an important component of the savings held by citizens. As recent events have shown, the simple fear of a default or of a restructuring of public debt would endanger the soundness of the financial system, triggering capital flight. Without public support, the liabilities of the banking system would ultimately have to be restructured as well, as was done for example in Argentina with the corralito (freezing of bank accounts). This would lead to a further loss of confidence and make a run on the financial system more likely. Administrative control measures would have to be taken and restrictions imposed. All these actions would have a direct effect on the financial wealth of the country's households and businesses, producing a collapse of aggregate demand. Taxpayers, instead of having a smaller burden of public debt to bear, would end up with an even heavier one. Many commentators fail to realise that the main impact of a country's default

is not on foreign creditors, but on its own citizens, especially the most vulnerable ones. They would suffer the consequences most in terms of the value of their financial and real assets. The economic and social impact of such an event is difficult to predict. The democratic foundations of a country could be seriously threatened. Attentive observers will not fail to notice that sovereign defaults tend to occur in countries where democracy has rather shallow roots."[6]

Between 2000 and 2010 default occurred in countries such as Ivory Coast, Pakistan, Nigeria, Ukraine, Argentina, Venezuela, and Zimbabwe. Based on all available data collected by the IMF, there also were thirty-six instances during that same period in which a country's interest rate spreads rose above 1,000 basis points. Of those instances, seven eventually resulted in default; in the remaining twenty-nine cases, however, the spreads stayed high for a few months and eventually fell back well below 1,000 basis points, with no defaults.

It was the availability of alternative funding sources and the political aid provided by non-national institutions—by supervised implementation of fiscal and structural reforms, for instance—that were crucial in avoiding a default in four out of five past sovereign debt crises even in countries that did not have the benefit of the strong institutional framework supporting Greece and Ireland by the European common institutions. The prospect of more countries needing that help made it all the more urgent for the EFSF to be made working.

Unfortunately, the lack of clarity on the future value of the Greek debt, inherent in the Deauville decision to force private investors to suffer losses after 2013, created an ambiguous situation where default was neither denied nor practiced. Rather than preventing contagion from spreading to the rest of the euro area—as policymakers had intended—the denial of default as a possibility maintained a heightened degree of risk aversion and market turbulence across the whole European financial system. The Deauville disaster—Chancellor Merkel's insistence on punishing private investors—and the lack of a strong EFSF were enhancing instability. Finally, the ambiguity on Greece, whose need for debt restructuring had been firmly denied since 2009, reduced the credibility of the same denial for other countries, making life for all the euro sovereigns extremely precarious.

## Whatever the Euro Is, the Money Is National

The debate on saving Greece and the other countries had a direct impact on the taxpayers of the wealthier countries. With its limited budget, the European Commission had little control over where hundreds of billions of euros would be spent by national governments. At that time, the EU's common finances were already under intense pressure from the net contributors to the EU budget (that is, Germany and other countries that contributed more money to the EU than they received in direct financial benefits). A simple calculation gives an idea of the relevance of national fiscal decisions as opposed to those taken at European level: the public expenditures deliberated yearly by the German Bundestag are equivalent to 11–12 percent of the euro area GDP, while the entire annual EU budget is barely over 1 percent.[7]

Inevitably, the euro area crisis fell prey to a national debate in the creditor countries entirely centered on the presumed failures of the European partners. In Germany, in particular, a simplified moral argument dominated the public discourse: the blame for the flaws of monetary union was laid entirely on countries like Greece, Spain, Ireland, and Portugal, which had been "living beyond their means" in the first ten years of the euro. Debt levels were the consequence of irresponsible management by both public and private consumers, described by Germans as Defizitsuender, or "fiscal sinners" whose countries had become insolvent through their own mistakes. It was not only unethical to bail them out, it would be a mistake because financial assistance would provide them with the wrong incentives to persevere. It is not by chance that this motivation is called "moral hazard." The moral motivation became the false-science that Leo Tolstoy thought of as typical of German culture: "The German's self-assurance . . . imagines that he knows the truth—science—which he himself has invented but which is for him the absolute truth."[8] In this interpretation of the crisis, aid should come only after self-redemption and, in the absence of a political authority that could force the sinners to repent, financial markets had to be given the maneuvering room to impart the discipline. Hence, the threat of PSI losses for the banks and the need to leave the EFSF uncertain until a strict framework for economic governance would enforce fiscal discipline.

Through the political agreement in December 2010, the EU had activated a number of conspicuous innovations in its system of economic governance. At the beginning of January, Barroso launched the Annual Growth Survey, which was intended to "advance the EU's comprehensive response to the crisis." The policy recommendations in the report focused on fiscal consolidation, labor market reforms, and growth-enhancing measures, "to keep pace with our main competitors and prepare the EU to move towards its Europe 2020 objectives."[9] In the same period, the EU inaugurated the so-called European Semester, a review of national budget plans that was expected to harmonize the legislative cycle of national fiscal policies and to activate a system of reciprocal surveillance through the European Council's machinery. Moreover. the six-bill legislative package on economic governance, designed to lend substance to economic policy coordination, had been presented by the European Commission the previous September and was progressing through the Council-Parliament approval procedures. A European Banking Authority was also due to be launched at the beginning of 2011. Finally, an important agreement had been reached on a treaty amendment establishing the permanent European Stability Mechanism (the ESM) starting in 2013. Work on the details had been switched from the European Council to an ad hoc task force of senior officials chaired by Maarten Verwey of the Dutch finance ministry.

In Merkel's view, however, all those instruments came a distant second to the priority of ensuring that the other countries were adhering to German discipline and had come to understand that they should not count on continued bailouts in the future. The idea, which the chancellor conveyed to Barroso during a dinner in Berlin at the end of January, called for closer cooperation among the member states of the euro zone but under a new architecture. This would entail more closely harmonizing the national financial, economic, and social policies. Merkel hoped that this would prevent the economies of the euro countries from diverging as much as they had over the past few years.

Merkel's strategy was based on three elements: a "pact for competitiveness" including, not incidentally, the same components already tested in Germany (wage moderation, reduction of pension benefits, and constitutional constraints on public debt) and to be applied to all countries of the euro area; a new president of the European Central Bank who would reassure the German electorate about the future stability of the currency; and, once these elements were in place, a German willingness to extend, within strictly defined limits, fiscal solidarity among the countries of the euro area. This last element was the bone of contention for the negotiations of the Spring European Council on March 24–25. Before that date, Merkel wanted to get the rest of the package in safe hands.

The first element—the pact for competitiveness—was intended to export the successful experience of Germany during the previous fifteen years of implementation of structural reforms. The good performance of the euro area in terms of growth and employment in the years before the crisis was largely ascribed to the surprising recovery of the German economy after years of low growth. It took a decade of sacrifices, salary compression, raising the retirement age, industrial restructuring, and so on, before the country in 2004–05 could again be the engine of European growth.

## Weber or Draghi

At least as delicate was the second element of Merkel's package: the choice of the future head of the ECB, to replace Trichet once his term expired in late 2011. Merkel thought that the president of the German Bundesbank, Axel Weber, would be the undisputed guarantor of the continuation of the stability culture at the ECB, or a "sop for the German public opinion" as the conservative newspaper *Bild Zeitung* wrote.[10] However, the possible choice of a deficit hawk like Weber was not well-received in many other capitals, especially in Paris.[11] Weber's strong public criticism addressed to Jean-Claude Trichet on the purchases of sovereign debt by the bank did not argue in his favor. According to the French press, Nicolas Sarkozy was hostile: "The euro area needs someone who can change his mind when the situation requires it, therefore someone with great mental agility."[12] The French president was personally interested in choosing a man in whom he had confidence for the role at the bank. Sarkozy's frequent conflicts with Trichet during the previous twenty months had been blunt.

To understand the complexity of the choice, one has to consider the peculiarity of the ECB, which is different from all other central banks given its multinational nature.[13] The ECB determines the monetary policy in a system of seventeen countries, each of which retains substantial control of the rest of the economic policy instruments. Decisions are taken according to a simple majority of the governing council, which is composed of six members of the ECB executive board and seventeen national governors. The ECB president, in such a context, is supposed to help coalesce the consensus of the council, or at least contribute to forging the consensus and then reflect it before the public. He has no power to determinate decisions on his own initiative, as often happens in most other central banks.

This is all the more true given the "strategy" of the ECB, that is, the method that the bank has adopted in taking its monetary policy decisions. The bank president is transparent in following always the same scheme when he is called upon to explain the bank's strategy and its monetary decisions. Both during his monthly press conferences and his quarterly appearances at the European Parliament, his analysis starts always from an "economic analysis," basically the real economy and price indicators, followed by a "monetary analysis" of detailed evidence about the money and credit developments, then an assessment of fiscal policy, and finally his synthesis of all these considerations. "It is a constant analytical and expository scheme, which after being criticized in its first years is now generally accepted," observed ECB economist Ignazio Angeloni.[14] The strategy has not only lent consistency and discipline to the internal discussion at the ECB and to the resulting decisions of the governing council, it has also made them more objective by limiting the influence of individual viewpoints. That was why an experienced broker of consensus was better suited to the job than a polarizing figure like Weber, who after May 2010 found himself isolated from the rest of the European central bankers. Against that backdrop, an alternative candidate came to the fore: the Italian central banker Mario Draghi, a highly respected public official who at the time also was president of the Group of Twenty's Financial Stability Board.

## Another Paris-Berlin Disaster

The European Council meeting on February 4 was considered the right moment to get an agreement on the pact for competitiveness. But only a few days before the meeting, German magazine *Der Spiegel* revealed the existence and substance of the proposed pact for competitiveness.[15] In the proposal, Merkel called for an immediate program "that will be implemented on the national level within twelve months." This would entail the member countries adapting "the retirement age to demographic trends" and introducing financial policy rules modelled after Germany's so-called debt brake (an amendment to Germany's constitution that requires the government to virtually eliminate the structural deficit by 2016). Furthermore, within one year the countries would have to mutually recognize each other's educational and professional qualifications, as well as introduce a standardized means of assessing corporate taxes to avoid so-called tax dumping (that is, when countries try to attract companies by having an artificially low tax rate). The pact was designed to complement the so-called "European semester," but there was also a need for states to agree to coordinated tax, wage, and social policies.

The disclosure of the plan— before Merkel had a chance to discuss it privately with her fellow leaders—was a major setback for the chancellor. The way the pact was presented smelled strongly of the "Germanization" of Europe.

With backing from Sarkozy, Merkel had planned to describe the merits of the plan over lunch when the euro zone leaders convened on February 4, then details were to be thrashed out at a specially convened summit in March, together with an already-scheduled EU summit later that month. "We need to increase competitiveness and the yardstick should be the member state that is leading the way," Merkel told journalists immediately prior to the lunch. Sarkozy hailed the initiative as a major step forward. "France and Germany are working hand in glove to defend the euro," he told the joint briefing.[16] However, the idea that two of the seventeen leaders could meet and decide that the others should raise the retirement age in their countries was so naïve that it is difficult to understand how Berlin and Paris believed they could succeed.

In fact, it was a perfect disaster. Merkel tried to defend the position paper, unofficially circulated among the euro area leaders after the lunch in a form that was not even translated from the German. But the Berlin-Paris plans hit a hurdle immediately, with Belgian prime minister Yves Leterme blasting them as being overly constrictive. "There must be more economic cooperation, but member states must be left the room to carry out their own policies," Leterme said. "Each member state has its own accents, its own traditions. We will not allow our social model to be undone." During unusually heated discussions, Spain, Luxembourg, and Portugal objected to the wage-indexation proposal, while Austria, in particular, criticized the plan to increase retirement ages.[17] "We welcome the move toward greater economic governance as step in the right direction. However, the method being proposed will not provide the required result as it is purely intergovernmental," said the leader of the European Parliament's Liberal group, Guy Verhofstadt. "The only effective way of ensuring the discipline and objectiveness that is required, is through the Community method and with the empowerment of the Commission to act and set real sanctions." Some of the ten EU leaders whose countries are not in the euro zone, including Poland and the United Kingdom, said some of the suggestions could undermine the single European market. The Polish prime minister, Donald Tusk, spoke of "humiliating methods" used by Paris and Berlin. "There were 18, 19 countries who spoke up to make known their regret on the way it was presented and also on the content," said Leterme. "It was truly a surreal summit."[18]

The negotiations failed so evidently that all of Merkel's package started to look wobbly. In addition, the flare-up over the competitiveness proposal helped keep from public view another issue, that of the nomination of Trichet's successor. A majority of Merkel's colleagues, including Sarkozy, strongly objected to Weber. Shortly after the summit, Sarkozy secretly met in Paris with Mario Draghi. This was followed by incredible news from Frankfurt: Axel Weber announced he would not accept a second term at the Bundesbank. The news was unexpected in Berlin, even by Merkel, who reportedly was furious. It became very clear that she had no Plan B for the post. Still, she badly wanted a person at the head of the ECB upon whom she could rely, especially given the new role of the bank in financial supervision, which meant that the next president would preside over the German banking overhaul. Balance sheets hiding the sancta sanctorum of German political compromises would be unravelled and unearthed, and the state-owned Landesbanken would be reduced to three. It was essential for the pillars of the German social model—and of its political wardens—that the ECB tread cautiously on the national financial graveyard. Merkel summoned Weber immediately to the Chancellery. "I do not want to be a ball in the game of politics," Weber said in an icy atmosphere. "I want to remain independent." For months, the head of the Bundesbank had actually been isolated by his European colleagues, and he knew that he had no chance.[19] The way was free for Mario Draghi.

## A Threat from the ECB

Trichet's reaction to the Merkel-Sarkozy strategy was one of scorn and disappointment. Asked what the new pact for competitiveness implied he answered:

> We do not yet know what exactly this pact comprises. If its aim is to improve the functioning of the economic union through greater coordination and integration, we will support it. Ironically, however, we are already talking about this new pact, while the countries of the euro area are, at the same time, still discussing the reform of their Stability and Growth Pact and the other elements of economic governance. . . . And these reforms are, in our view, not ambitious enough. The proposals made by the European

Commission went in the right direction, but were already not ambitious enough in our view. And the Member States—including Germany, France and other countries—have watered them down further. Our message is clear: we have to go as far as possible in reinforcing European economic governance, at all levels. We won't give up on that.[20]

The ECB was worried primarily that the delays in institutional matters were in turn delaying the commitment of the leaders to take up the role of purchasing the government bonds of Greece and Ireland that were burdening the balance sheet of the Central Bank. The position of the bank was widely discussed within the board at every meeting. Trichet was relentlessly putting pressure on Merkel and Sarkozy about the need to create an adequate financial stability facility before the market jitters could get worse. During the ECOFIN meetings in February, Trichet started threatening the finance ministers that the bank would stop buying government bonds if they did not carry out their promises.

Trichet's suspicions were well-founded. Resolving remaining questions about the EFSF and the preparation of the ESM were the critical issues. Although the political agreement to establish a treaty-based crisis mechanism had already been achieved at the European Council of October 28, and the Eurogroup finance ministers adopted a description of the "general features" of the new European Stability Mechanism one month later, important questions remained to be sorted out. These matters had been assigned to the special task force chaired by Dutch finance minister Verwey. As far as the EFSF was concerned, three issues needed to be resolved urgently at the euro area summit of March 11: the effective (as distinct from the nominal) lending capacity of the facility; whether or not the EFSF should be authorized to purchase bonds (and not only lending money); and the terms of the Greek and Irish loans. A clear indication on those issues would be helpful in appeasing the markets. At the beginning of March, there was general agreement that the EFSF's effective lending capacity should be raised and brought into line with its nominal capacity of €440 billion.[21] But Berlin was not in favor of engaging the EFSF in the secondary market of government securities.

A crucial issue was the revision of the term of the loans granted to Greece and Ireland. The past loans were by far too onerous and were killing the bailout, making a recovery even more difficult. The market had also interpreted the high rates imposed on the loans as a sign of riskiness of the recipient countries. In fact, the high rates were a consequence of the German demand that the loans not be concessional, to avoid a domestic legal complaint about an alleged violation of the no-bailout clause in the European treaty. The debate about the level of the rates was even more political in Ireland, which had just been through an election campaign in which the fierceness of the terms imposed on the country and

accepted by the government was one of the main election issues polarizing sentiments against the foreign diktat coming from Brussels and Berlin. It was widely
expected that the incoming prime minister, Enda Kenny, would ask for a term
revision. The same would be necessary for Greece to convince the markets of the
sustainability of the existing aid package. Prime Minister George Papandreou
had expressly requested that a cut of 200 basis points in the rates be applied to
the loans. The Germans had acknowledged the necessity of a term revision, but
resistance was still strong within the Dutch government. The negotiations were
hampered by the political nature of the conditionality of aid. As a matter of
fact, Ireland was confronted with a request from France and Germany to engage
in serious discussions about its corporate tax, hitherto held at such low levels
to be considered a source of distortional fiscal dumping in the EU. The tax
issue, raised particularly by Paris, went to the core of national sovereignty and
was a sign of the political capital that creditor countries were capable of using
to extract political concessions from the debtor countries.[22] The demand was
different, but also straightforward, in the case of Greece. If the Greek government was prepared, in addition to carrying out the structural reforms, to fully
and speedily complete the €50 billion privatization and real estate development
program that it had already announced, its creditors would be ready to increase
the maturity of the loans under the program agreed in the previous year from
three years to seven-and-one-half years, thereby bringing the EU loans into line
with those of the IMF.

## Trichet and the Leaders Clash

In the preparation for the March 11 euro area summit, the debate on the EFSF
reverberated inevitably on the design of the successor, the ESM. Strict conditionality was the crucial aspect of the new institution, which had been shaped on the
footprint of the IMF. As noted earlier, the ESM, unlike the EFSF, would have
had the juridical personality of an international organization. Its debts would not
be reflected on the national debts of member nations, and it would constitute an
institutional filter between the debt problems and the common solution mechanism. It had been very clear that the rules covering case-by-case participation
of private sector creditors, although intended to be "fully consistent with IMF
policies," were still to be tested in the context of a monetary union. Other issues
to be clarified on the ESM concerned the rules for approving loans, decision
rules, and the possibility for the ESM to offer precautionary and flexible credit
lines, once more in a manner similar to that done by the IMF.[23] Finally, the most
important issue concerned ESM purchases of government bonds on the primary
or on the secondary markets. Germany again had significant reservations about
bond purchases of any kind, although its hostility was particularly strong in the
case of secondary market operations. This was another source of conflict with

the ECB, which wanted to hand off the bond-buying task to another entity so it could regain some margin of distance between its monetary policy operations and the improper fiscal role that it had been playing. Again during the ECOFIN meetings, Trichet criticized the strategy of the governments and threatened to drop the bank's purchases of government bonds. The harshness of the discussions at the ECOFIN was described by a participant as "unprecedented."[24]

The March 11 summit found an agreement to increase the European Financial Stability Facility's effective lending capacity from around €250 billion to its headline figure of €440 billion. Together with money provided by the IMF and the European Commission (the €60 billion EFSM program), this meant that some €750 billion would be available to address any liquidity problems faced by a euro zone country (€67.5 billion of this had already been earmarked for the Irish financial support program). Merkel conceded that the ESM would be able to purchase government securities on the primary markets, and many thought that it could be considered a success for the summit. The effective lending capacity of the ESM was expanded to €500 billion, slightly above that of the EFSF, and it was given the possibility to buy substantial amounts of debt in the primary markets directly from crisis-stricken euro zone governments. This ability could become a potentially very important "safety valve" if, for instance, Greece in 2012 or later still did not have access to private funding. At that point, Greece seemed to have an avenue to get additional funding from the EFSF/ESM—in return for explicit political concessions—which would prevent it from having to default on private bondholders.

Merkel did succeed in blocking permission for the ESM to buy bonds in the secondary markets, which the European Central Bank's Securities Markets Program had been doing. This was a bitter defeat for Trichet, who did not want to engage in such quasi-fiscal purchases in the name of maintaining financial market stability. EU political leaders said no, however, clearly intending to limit the potential scope of their own purchases of euro area government-financed bonds. The main reason was that buying government bonds in the primary market does not require much technical capacity, while handling a portfolio on the secondary market would require a great deal of sophisticated analysis by well-qualified personnel. Markets have to be monitored minute-by-minute, different strategies must be implemented to optimize the purchases, and an uncertain amount of financial resources would have to be pre-funded to make the bond purchases possible. In practice, one would need to set up a European Debt Agency, a step that Berlin would see as too close to a common treasury minister for the euro area and as a harbinger for the issuance of a eurobond. It was easy for Berlin to point out that the ECB already had both the professional capacity and the financial resources to manage the activity on the secondary market, even if the bank did not want to engage in that activity.

As soon as Trichet was allowed to speak at the summit meeting, it became immediately clear how unsatisfied the ECB president was. Trichet used the highest tones of his rhetoric and spoke of an apocalyptical scenario facing the euro if the governments failed to accept fully their responsibility to set up a proper common financial fund with the due operational flexibility and if they did not adopt stricter rules and automatic sanctions for financial discipline. Unfortunately, the ECB president's cries fell on deaf ears.[25]

## The Systemic Response—A Comprehensive Solution

For all the alarms sent by Trichet and by the markets, the strategy of the leaders, foremost among them Merkel and Sarkozy, focused almost entirely on the reform of economic governance and on the guarantee of future fiscal discipline and economic convergence. The leaders met again at the spring European Council meeting at the end of March. The aim was to get hold, once and for all, of the whole array of problems that had emerged in the architecture of the euro area during the past three years: fiscal discipline, economic coordination, crisis interventions, divergent competitiveness, and banking weaknesses. As the European Commission pointed out, "these systemic responses constitute the EU's comprehensive approach to tackling the crisis."[26]

The pillars of the systemic response were

—a framework for strengthening the surveillance of the economies (the so-called "governance package");

—a calendar of commitments by national and European institutions, which would have allowed for the surveillance and coordination (the "European Semester");

—the definition of the permanent crisis resolution tool (the European Stability Mechanism);

—a pact for monitoring the competitiveness of the economies (called Euro-Plus Pact); and

—a reinforced system for solving the banking problems (the European System of Financial Supervisors).

The new strengthened surveillance framework was comprised of six legislative proposals that had been adopted by the European Commission on September 29, 2010. They aimed to overhaul the EU economic policy framework by reinforcing the Stability and Growth Pact, strengthening national budgetary frameworks, preventing and correcting harmful macroeconomic imbalances, and establishing an effective enforcement arm for euro area countries. The reformed Stability and Growth Pact would place more emphasis on debt, so that countries whose debt was more than 60 percent of GDP would be obliged to reduce their debt every year by 1/20th of the excess above the 60 percent threshold. The changes also aimed to take revenue windfalls into greater account when assessing the fiscal situation of a country by introducing a reference value for expenditure growth that should not exceed "a reference medium-term rate of GDP growth." Finally, the new pact would be stricter in enforcing national programs, imposing sanctions earlier in the process, and "ensuring a higher degree of automaticity."

The second element of the comprehensive solution, the "European Semester," drew together all the elements of EU economic surveillance, including policies to ensure fiscal discipline, to promote macroeconomic stability, and to foster growth. The processes under the Stability and Growth Pact and the Europe 2020 growth strategy would thereby be aligned in timing, while remaining legally separated.[27] The aim of the European Semester was to provide ex ante policy guidance for the national policymakers to help strengthen policy synergies and avoid policy inconsistencies. A third element was the European System of Financial Supervisors, established in November 2010 to monitor macro-financial risks and strengthen financial oversight in the EU in response to the lack of consistent and rigorous financial oversight in the EU prior to the crisis.[28] The central task of the European Systemic Risk Board (ESRB) was to monitor and assess macro-financial systemic risk to mitigate the exposure of the system to systemic failure and to enhance the financial system's resilience to shocks—in other words, to contribute to preventing financial crises.

Finally, the European Council agreed to adopt the "Euro Plus Pact" (EPP) with the goal "to strengthen the economic pillar of EMU [the Economic and Monetary Union], achieve a new quality of economic policy coordination in the euro area, and to improve competitiveness and facilitate convergence."[29] The Pact, which was the successor of Merkel's Pact for Competitiveness, addressed some of the more structural underlying problems of the euro zone. The added value of the EPP was that it expanded the coordination beyond the regular fiscal surveillance and focused on areas that previously fell under national competence but that were integral to competitiveness and the avoidance of harmful imbalances. In the words of the EU Council, the pact "will further strengthen the economic pillar of EMU and achieve a new quality of economic policy coordination with the objective of improving competitiveness and thereby leading to a higher degree of convergence reinforcing our social market economy." Each year governments will have to come up with a list of concrete measures that will be implemented in the following twelve months. The implementation of these measures were to be monitored politically by the heads of state of government.[30]

The most critical decision of the leaders—and for the ECB—concerned the need for a permanent crisis resolution mechanism, which was addressed by the European Council in establishing the European Stability Mechanism (ESM). As described by the European Commission in its quarterly euro area report, "Financial assistance will be provided by mutual agreement, if and when euro area Member States are experiencing or are threatened by severe financing problems, in order to safeguard the financial stability of the euro area as a whole."[31] The ESM was to take over the role of the European Financial Stability Facility (EFSF) and the commission's European Financial Stabilisation Mechanism (EFSM) after their expiration in June 2013. The agreement explicitly adopted a provision for private sector involvement (PSI, the bondholder haircuts): "The ESM will mobilize funding and provide financial assistance under strict conditionality, whereby the beneficiary Member State will be required to put in place an appropriate form of Private Sector Involvement (PSI), according to the specific circumstances and in a manner fully consistent with IMF practices."[32] Support from the ESM would be conditional on the adoption of an appropriate macroeconomic adjustment program by the recipient country and based on a rigorous analysis of public debt sustainability, conducted by the European Commission together with the IMF and in liaison with the European Central Bank.

During the EU Council meeting, the difficult political situation in many countries was apparent, leading to approval of stricter rules to be applied in bailout cases. The main issue was, once again, the involvement of private creditors in case of a default. Politicians wanted to state clearly to their citizens that taxpayers were not the only ones to bear the financial brunt of bailing out other countries and that bankers, or investors, or "speculators" also could be forced to pay.

## The ECB Punishment of the "Administrative Egoisms"

The rationale of the latest "Grand Bargain"—German willingness to step up its aid to ailing states in exchange for increased control over other euro zone members' economic policies—was not so different from the arrangements of the past. The economic governance of the euro area remained stuck in the hybrid structure combining a single currency safeguarded by an independent central bank on one side and a decentralized economic system, in which fiscal policy remained the responsibility of the member states, on the other. Discipline and harmonization still rested on a rules-based regime oriented at reducing political discretion in the management of common problems. De facto problems involving collective actions were denied, and much confidence was put on a system, which had already failed in the past, of mutual surveillance, rules, and self-discipline. National sovereignty was still the cornerstone of the new architecture, even though all kinds of relevant new problems had suggested that the degree of interdependence requested a vision of the euro area as a systemically integrated economic and policy area.

Many of the solutions of this Grand Bargain had to be tested. The lines of action of the Euro Plus Pact, for instance, were similar to those of the 2000 Lisbon strategy, which aimed in vain to make the EU "the most competitive and dynamic knowledge-based economy in the world" by 2010. Although the new monitoring system of the pact seemed arguably stricter than the simple peer review of the past, it remained uncertain how much traction the new method would gain in the end. No sanction was foreseen in case a country failed to reach its own commitments. Because the fiscal framework was much more focussed on fiscal restraint than on coordination, the surplus countries were exempted from any effort of rebalancing. The execution of the stress tests of banks remained influenced by the reluctance of some countries to cut deep into the bones of their domestic banking systems. Eventually, it was very clear that the new system was more rigorous on fiscal policies, but it was to be tested how successful it would be in developing a capacity to stimulate structural reforms and productivity gains. Finally, and most irritatingly for Jean-Claude Trichet, most of the burden of intervening in the markets remained on the shoulders of the ECB. This was even more disturbing to him because the leaders had kept, and even reinforced, the rule of a private sector involvement, which he was certain would further destabilize the euro area.

The disappointment of the ECB appeared clearly in a speech that Trichet gave on March 18 before a caucus at the European Parliament. He used the speech to launch a systematic criticism of the agreements the leaders would discuss one week later at their summit in Brussels:

> We are at a point where it is time for decisions, and the matter before us is complex. Parliament has received about 2000 amendments on the six legal texts. Therefore, specificity in recommendations is essential.
>
> First, all surveillance procedures have to be faster and more automatic, including the new macroeconomic surveillance framework. We . . . cannot wait months or even a year until policies are corrected. In the meantime, spillovers would hurt other Member States. . . .
>
> Second, the enforcement tools also need to be more effective. For example, the new macroeconomic surveillance framework needs to provide clear incentives by envisaging financial sanctions already after the first instance of non-compliance. . . .
>
> Third, the policy requirements should be more ambitious to match the current reality of the euro area. . . .[33]

Let me borrow the words of Willy Brandt, speaking as the first Head of Government of a member state of the European Communities to address the plenary of the European Parliamentary Assembly, back in 1973. "This is where the political will should, at long last, carry the day over the many national administrative egoisms, which may be justified individually, but all in all can no longer be tolerated. Having gone so much astray in the past years, we must now achieve a better harmonization of our economic policies. New decisions are needed which place more precise obligation on us, and bind Member States more closely.[34]

Trichet and his fellow European central bankers were bitterly disappointed with the outcome of the EU councils. The private sector involvement had been maintained, and even reinforced, and more importantly the ESFS had been shifted further down the path and prevented from acting on the secondary market. The national political leaders had again left it to the ECB to counter the markets, using its own resources, without the guarantee of an adequate political initiative against the crisis.

Confronted with potential disruptive risks accumulated in its balance sheet, the Council of the ECB decided—but never announced its decision—to suspend immediately the purchases of Greek, Irish, or Portuguese sovereign bonds, taking the safety net of the ECB from beneath the feet of the European political leaders. A participant says that the decision was taken after a formal vote of the council in March. It was an incredibly strong reaction by the central bankers against the idleness of the "Heads." Trichet had repeatedly floated the threat of taking this step in all the meetings with the leaders and the finance ministers, to no avail. His colleagues decided that the time was ripe for following the words with facts. Come what may.

# 18

## The Crisis Reaches Italy and Spain

### Earthquake in the Making

The decision by the European Central Bank to stop buying the bonds of Greece, Portugal, and Ireland was a major episode of the tug-of-war between the ECB and the national governments. Both sides underestimated the unintended consequences that their conflict—centered on the institutional setting of the stability funds and on future economic governance—would have on the private economy. It was a fatal mistake.

Carried away by the dominant rhetoric that described the crisis as the consequence only of fiscal profligacy, European governments seemed unable to understand that the mechanism for transmitting contagion of the sovereign debt crisis was actually buried within the balance sheets of their banks. The banking problems, however, might as well have been on the dark side of the moon—hidden from sight but perfectly complementary to the more obvious sovereign debt crisis. As weaker countries were struggling to pay their debts, the value of banks' assets was declining. As a result, banks felt forced to reduce risk by selling other assets, most likely government bonds. After the European Central Bank decided in March—without making any announcement—to stop buying government bonds issued by Greece, Portugal, and Ireland, certainty about the price of those assets eventually vanished. Investors began counting the days when the ECB was not showing up on the market. Around the sixth or seventh week, they understood that the ECB had changed its policy. One after the other, the banks started selling other assets in their portfolios with a risk profile similar to that of the bonds of the three weakest countries, which now were seen as unsellable.

Banks therefore unloaded Spanish and Italian bonds, making contagion reach very close to the core of Europe.

The reshuffling of bank portfolios had accelerated since November 2010, when the European Council first reaffirmed the principle of private sector involvement (PSI) in future sovereign restructuring. Before then, German banks had remained committed to the government's request of not selling those bonds while the bailout was still under way. But soon after PSI became official, German banks started selling bonds of the periphery countries, especially those of Greece. In fact, they had been extremely irritated by knowing they were almost the only ones to adhere to a commitment that was intended to be common across the EU, as described in chapter 14. According to data from the Bank for International Settlements, between April 2010 and December 2010, German holdings of Greek sovereign bonds had only marginally declined from $23.1 billion to $22.7 billion. In the same period French banks had sold almost half of their Greek portfolios (from $27 billion to $15 billion). Spanish, Italian, and British banks had behaved well, selling only low amounts of Greek government bonds, but the rest of the euro zone banks—first of all the Dutch—had cut massively their holdings from €22.9 to only €7.7 billion.

A classic "stab-in-the-back syndrome" developed one more time in Germany. The disturbing element was that the worst perpetrators were France and the Netherlands, possibly Germany's closest allies. The discovery, coupled with Chancellor Merkel's stubborn insistence on PSI, caused a sudden change of strategy among the financial actors in Frankfurt.[1] Between the end of 2010 and February 2011, the Bundesbank detected that German banks sold 40 percent of their Greek bonds. In the first three months of the year the German insurance industry cut its holdings by more than half. Deutsche Bank, often the first mover in German finance, sold 70 percent of its holdings in the periphery countries between December 2010 and June 2011.

Deutsche Bank started unloading a shocking 88 percent of its Italian government bonds.[2] The sell-off by German institutions happened almost one year after the more vicious dumping of bonds by major French banks, but the dynamics behind the decisions of the banks of the two countries were widely similar. The peculiar situation of the banking system in the two largest countries of the euro area was well documented in a remarkable graph published by the IMF, according to which French and German banks stood out in 2007, along with Belgian and UK banks, as the lowest capitalized and most reliant on wholesale funding to keep their capital-assets ratios low.[3] But what was most shocking was that while all other banking systems had lowered their leverage and improved their stability in recent years, German and French banks had not significantly reduced their leverage. French banks especially appeared to have a lower level of equity than three years earlier. Moreover, German banks' profitability was about half of the average in the OECD group of advanced countries, and their capacity to return to a good profitability was questionable.

The banking situation was difficult to assess even for market operators who started musing over a number of hidden risks.[4] The interaction between sovereign and bank debts was very simply expressed in April 2011 by the International Monetary Fund:

> At the heart of the global financial crisis was an abrupt rediscovery of credit risk. Focused initially on problems in the U.S. subprime mortgage sector, the reassessment of credit risk broadened over time, affecting households, nonfinancial corporations, banks, and sovereigns across much of the industrialized world. The turbulence in some euro area financial markets over the past six months suggests that the process is still ongoing. Nearly four years after the start of the global financial crisis, confidence in the stability of the banking system as a whole has yet to be fully restored. Markets remain concerned that some banks are too highly leveraged and have insufficient capital, given the uncertainty about the quality of their assets.[5]

Since the end of 2010, banks had been trying to raise both the quantity and quality of capital, but European banks had generally been lagging U.S. banks and had also remained highly dependent on wholesale funding (loans from central banks and other banks aside from core deposits). The dependency on short-term wholesale funding requirements could bring further vulnerabilities, given the need for constant roll-over of the funds in a context of volatile prices. The IMF noted also that some of the larger European banks funded a significant part of their short-term positions in foreign currency, much of which came from U.S. money market funds. But this funding was subject to further risks as it could be subject to quick withdrawal by money managers, as had been seen in the past. "The result," the IMF said, "is that global banks face a wall of maturing debt, with $3.6 trillion due to mature over the next two years. Bank debt rollover requirements are most acute for Irish and German banks, from 40 percent to one-half of all debt outstanding is due over the next two years."[6]

European banks were facing pressures not only on the funding, but also on the asset side of their balance sheets, reflecting concerns about exposure to troubled sovereigns and to property markets in Ireland, Spain, the United Kingdom, and the United States. After four years, the original sources of financial instability were still working under the surface. The policy decision-making of the previous six months—especially the PSI debate—had been aggravating the situation, as the IMF acknowledged:

> In Europe, the entire liability structure at banks is being repriced given investor concerns about potential future private sector burden sharing.

The repricing follows the initial communication of the future European permanent crisis resolution framework, the debate on the Irish private sector bail-in, and the Amagerbanken insolvency in Denmark.[7] As losses on senior debt become a credible threat to market participants, demand for bank debt from some current investors will decline, potentially reducing the overall funding pool available to banks.[8]

As a consequence, credit growth, although steadily recovering, remained sluggish and well below pre-crisis levels. The reduced volumes of credit were hampering growth and this was aggravating the debt problems. Furthermore, although some of the major sources of concern about banking were located in the core EU countries, as a consequence of the link between banking and sovereign problems, wholesale funding pressures reflected in sharp rises in bank debt yields in the peripheral countries.

Finally, and most importantly, the banking and the sovereign debt problems were mutually reinforcing as a consequence of the uncertainty about the value of bank exposures to troubled sovereigns. In Europe, the majority of sovereign debt is held in banking books (as opposed to trading books) and so is accounted for at book value. But investors feared legitimately that the market value of some of those bonds might be considerably lower than the accounting value. "Bank holdings of government bonds issued by countries facing fiscal pressures are large in relation to capital in several banking systems, so the market value of these assets is an important factor in assessing the overall health of these banking systems," the IMF noted.[9]

In fact, European banks were still holding a lot of critical assets of different nature on their banking and trading books. First of all, the exposures to sovereign assets were not evenly distributed—with the banks in some countries more heavily exposed to the countries at the focus of the sovereign debt crisis than others. Nor was the distribution of exposure spread evenly among individual banks within a country. As we have seen, for a whole array of contingent or historical political reasons, European governments resist being transparent about their banks. Financial protectionism applies not only to "national systems" but to single institutions. Still under this veil of ignorance, the obscurity of bank balance sheets accentuated a sense of fragility in market assessments about the crisis. Eventually it was likely that individual banks would see latent losses on their trading books realized. Trading books were considered irrelevant to the first two stress tests because the tests were based on the assumption that no country would have to restructure its debt before the expiration of the EFSF in 2013. But markets remained uncertain about the longer term, especially after the German request to involve private creditors in the haircut. So even after their respective "bailouts," Ireland and Greece had seen the price of their sovereign bonds discount a 30 percent haircut. Those countries were joined by Portugal on April 7 when a formal request for financial assistance was made. It was enough to increase the worries about the risks hidden in the trading books of all the European banks.

The interconnection of financial problems was better known in 2011 than it had been in 2008. It was still true that banks tended to be heavily exposed to the sovereign debts of their own countries. According to OECD calculations dated August 2010, the exposure of Greek banks to Greek sovereign debt represented 226 percent of their Tier 1 capital. In Italy, Hungary, Spain, Portugal, and Ireland these numbers were 157 percent, 133 percent, 113 percent, 69 percent, and 26 percent, respectively.[10] But large cross-border exposures to Greece were still present for systemically important banks in Germany, France, Belgium (and Cyprus and Portugal).[11] Large exposures to Portugal were present in Germany and Belgium; to Spain in Germany and Belgium; to Italy in Germany, France, the Netherlands, Belgium, Luxembourg, Austria, and Portugal; and to Ireland in Germany and Cyprus. Many banks, especially in France, had been trying to wiggle out of that situation by unloading their bonds onto the ECB, which had found itself at the end of 2010 holding 15 percent of the total Greek public debt. Since May 2010 a strong flow of repatriation of funds had been detected in the euro zone, paradoxically aggravating the situation of the weaker debtors. The third set of stress tests, to be done in June–July 2011, would publish more detailed data and might give a clearer idea of the process of recapitalization that authorities had to undertake and eventually also allow an orderly resolution for those banks that may prove to be insolvent. But in the general obscurity, diffidence was growing.

As sales of euro area bonds by French and especially German banks became massive, they did not go unnoticed on the market. The Wall Street financial powerhouses, whose links to the major French and German banks are tighter than publicly acknowledged, were ready to jump the gun as well and started cutting credit lines not only to the periphery but also to the other European heavily indebted countries. Finally, in the spring of 2011, the American money market funds, which normally hold around $350 billion in European assets, scaled down their credits to the periphery. European equivalents did the same and in the second quarter of 2011 sold 10 percent of the $512 billion invested in the issuances of the euro area by shifting the money to precautionary deposits or cash. In the following weeks, some German banks, first of all NordLB (one of the most beleaguered), started to mark down the value of the Greek bonds in their portfolios, effectively discounting for a default. Rapidly the general assessment in the financial industry was that Greece would never be able to repay fully its debt.

## Doubts and Desperation in Athens

Now that the ECB was no longer buying sovereign bonds on the market, financial investors were nervously pondering the chance of defaults in the euro area.

Inevitably, and for the euro leaders unexpectedly, Greece returned to the center of the financial analyses as a litmus-test of a debt restructuring.

Since the end of 2010, and especially between February and March 2011, the ECB and the IMF had been alerted that the Greek reform plans were wobbling. In its third "Program Review," released on March 14 (but based on discussions that ended on February 11), the IMF added a note of severe caution, highlighting that there were "substantial risks" that Greece would not be able to re-access markets before the economy got back onto a growth path and debt dynamics had changed course. The sustainability of the debt depended on two factors: the recovery taking hold toward the medium term with a potential that the IMF estimated around 2.5 percent of GDP in real terms; and the fiscal deficit declining markedly. Unfortunately, neither element was developing in the right way. Early in 2011, the IMF noted that "tensions have been evident through the 2010 budget implementation cycle."[12] As for growth, "near-term risks remain skewed to the downside," the IMF noted. "Market sentiment remains fragile, and much fiscal, financial sector, and structural adjustment lies ahead. In this environment, contagion is a risk, and sovereign spreads could increase sharply if market doubts about the response to the crisis in the Euro area intensify."[13] The extent of risks related to the scenario were evident once the implications on the Greek banking system were taken into account. Under a banking shock, and without even considering the so-called "second round impacts" (for example, via higher interest rates), debts would jump to over 200 percent of GDP.

"It is clear that the program design was flawed and had to be subsequently corrected," observed Greek finance minister George Papaconstantinou. "The interest rate was set too high and the repayment period too short. And capacity problems hampering implementation were not addressed vigorously enough."[14] Actually, the fiscal projections contained in the Greek reform program were far too optimistic. Moreover, the sustainability of such a high stock of debt and of a primary surplus of about 6 percent of GDP was the subject of intense debate. The need to lower the absolute level of the debt became even more of an open issue. According to a document provided by a representative of the EU-ECB-IMF troika, "in the event of an extension of the maturity of the loans provided by the EU and by the IMF, amortizations during 2013–15 would drop by a third from €163 billion to €110 billion, which in turn would raise the probability of earlier market access on better terms." De facto, a renegotiation of the loans to Greece had to be undertaken immediately.

The failure of the Greek intervention by the EU-ECB-IMF program was dramatic for the credibility of the euro area. The original mistake was to have overlooked the unique nature of Greece, which had the most inward-looking economy of the euro area. Almost 90 percent of the profits of the Greek manufacturing industry derive from business inside the country (as opposed to a

European average of below 50 percent). As a consequence, austerity alone—cutting domestic wages and prices—undermined the expected profitability of Greek businesses. Firms stopped investing or downsized their activity, thus triggering unemployment and causing an even deeper recession. Evidence that the plans were off track became dominant and public in April.

During the winter of 2010–11, banks and law firms had repeatedly advised Athens to study a restructuring of the debt to skip the pain of a decade of austerity.[15] The packages were prima facie appealing to the government, which was about to face three dire years of painful adjustment of the economy, starting particularly in the second half of 2011.[16] Prime Minister Papandreou was cautious, but some of his ministers were loudly refuting the troika policies, insisting that the debt could be cut through higher economic growth rather than through austerity. The government was shocked by the attitude of the troika. The first labor market reform was written in Washington and Frankfurt, then taken to the Athens branch of a major international law firm and written to comply with the Greek legislation. Finally, it was delivered to the Greek government so that the Parliament could not change a word of the text. In more general terms, a default was appealing for the whole Greek political system, which could then resist changes undermining its grip on power and wealth, for instance through privatization of state-owned enterprises or cuts in public employment. Finally, public opinion was being misled by the nationalistic rhetoric of politicians who insisted that foreigners were imposing blood and tears on the Greeks.

European governments were tempted to enact some form of "soft restructuring"—for example, a simple extension of debt maturities, thus postponing repayment of the outstanding debt and lowering its overall cost. However, even if, in a hypothetical case, a soft restructuring would not be classified as a default, it would have strong negative sides. Any form of revision of a debt would increase risk premiums on debt securities across Europe. In the case of the periphery, it could disrupt the bond markets. As a second-grade consequence, markets likely would extend contagion to the other indebted countries. Revising the terms of sovereign debts was also likely to hit the stocks of banks in the core countries. Indicators of systemic risk—cross correlation of credit default swaps and yield spreads in the euro area—showed that they were reacting with a higher degree of sensitivity than even in September 2008. All in all, changing the terms of debt was likely to set off a chain reaction across Europe that could slip out of control. Ultimately, the huge costs would fall onto the shoulders of the taxpayers of all the countries, not only of Greeks, causing stunning justice and democratic problems. Once more, these "political" aspects of issues linked to the "restructuring" of debt were raised foremost by the European Central Bank, which was particularly vocal in crying foul whenever the "R" word was mentioned. Trichet, ECB governing council member Lorenzo Bini Smaghi, and ECB chief economist Jürgen Stark pressed hard to stop the train from entering what they saw as a black tunnel. Still, the ultimate decision might be influenced by Greek citizens, who rebelled against austerity in a national-partisan hyperventilated political environment.

## Akropolis Now

In an internal paper written in April, the IMF delegation to Athens acknowledged the situation: "Greece is at a critical choice between continuing with the bold reform program, or in the face of the difficult headwinds, to allow the pace of reform to slow."[17] According to the plans of the Greek government, wages and pensions were to be cut eventually by 20 percent. The government obviously dreaded the moment when the sacrifices were going to bite the flesh of households. Notwithstanding its responsibilities, the opposition party was not helpful. As the IMF noted "wavering political support for the program and domestic infighting has increased uncertainty." The heated partisan dialectic was troubling and made it more difficult for leaders to present to their citizens a lucid analysis of their real situation and of their responsibilities. As a consequence, the government's action was less convincing than nominal figures purported to show. "The structural fiscal reforms have been slow to show yields . . . the deficit could get stuck at 10 percent of GDP going forward," the IMF noted. Privileges were still maintained, as the German press relentlessly highlighted: officials working with Papandreou were still receiving sixteen monthly paychecks per year; a day of leave for train drivers had twenty-eight hours instead of twenty-four; bonuses were granted to public employees just for their punctuality, or even for washing hands, or for working at low temperatures (between 0 and 8 degrees Centigrade). Priests received from the state a reward for each service they celebrated; bus drivers started their working day when they left their homes; in some public firms, employees got eighteen monthly pay checks each year and luxury holidays. At Hellenic Petroleum, for instance, the average pay was 50 percent higher than in the equivalent job in Germany. Retiring members of Parliament got a golden handshake of about €250,000, while those who had served since 1993 got a doubled pension. The public economy, which employed one-fourth of all Greek workers, was rotten, with no state firm reported to make profits. Owners of some 200,000 private houses were still escaping real estate taxes. In some cases, Greece did not even have a land register. Even at the sacred monastery of Mount Athos, illegal land trades had been denounced. Since the crisis had broken, Greeks had transferred abroad at least €30 billion, probably as a cautionary measure. But for all these characterizations, the real drama in Greece was the steep increase in unemployment and the sudden discovery of poverty by multiple layers of the society.[18]

In May 2011, exactly one year after Greece had been bailed out, the situation looked critical again. During that year, as finance minister George Papaconstantinou explained relentlessly:

[P]ublic sector nominal wages had been cut by 15 percent, pensions by 10 percent, public sector employee rolls by 10 percent, operational and military spending was slashed, the value added tax raised by 4 percentage points, and excise taxes increased 30 percent. Fiscal consolidation was accompanied by long overdue structural reforms. A comprehensive pension reform raised the retirement age and linked pension benefits to lifetime contributions. Labor market reform reduced severance payments and cut overtime remuneration. The statistical authority was granted full independence, while fiscal management was strengthened. Tax reform shortened judicial procedures for tax cases, and included a determined—but as yet incomplete—effort to combat tax evasion. Local administration reform reduced the number of municipalities from 1,034 to 325. The start-up of businesses was simplified; a 'fast track' process for large investments was legislated; the road haulage sector was liberalised; cabotage was abolished; closed professions were opened.[19]

Prime Minister Papandreou had introduced a great many reforms, but the "implementation of the broader real economy structural reforms has slowed down in 2011," according to the IMF, hampered by an inefficient public administration.[20] According to international observers, the Greek reform program had been purposely scaled down by the government, as it waited for a decision on restructuring the debt.

## People against Power

In Athens, the large Syntagma Square each day saw an increasing crowd gathering in front of the Greek Parliament—the seat of the country's democracy and, indirectly, a symbolic cradle of democracy in human history. At the end of May, dozens of thousands of citizens protested against the government's austerity policy and the whole political system. In one of the relatively few tense moments of the demonstrations, members of parliament were dubbed as "thieves" and objects were hurled at them. Greek citizens were asking for new transparency in national democracy, they wanted parties to admit their responsibility in creating the problems, and polls showed that a strong majority was in favor of extensive sales of state-owned businesses and properties to save the country. Papandreou was weakened. Even members of Parliament of his PASOK party were digging in their heels against sacrifices. The opposition, led by the Nea Dimokratia party, was completely uncooperative and voted against the austerity measures. For all the efforts of the European partners and of the president of the republic, Karolos Papoulias, there seemed to be no way of achieving the much-needed bipartisan agreement on the future course of the country.

Many protesters attacked the troika, the IMF, and particularly Berlin for blackmailing Greece and imposing hard conditions on the population. Some also called for Greece to exit the euro area and return to its former currency, the drachma. Social conditions were worsening. Unemployment had jumped to 16 percent and the economy was performing worse than expected. Five thousand people were reported as having lost their homes and were living on the streets of Athens. Two hundred thousand families were expected to be forced to sell their homes because they were unable to pay their mortgages. The number of suicides had doubled between 2009 and 2010, according to charity organizations.

An escalation of social protests might lead to a refusal by the Greek Parliament to comply with the plans of the troika, which would immediately put a stop to the financing and lead to a disorderly default—the worst possible end to this troubled story. However, the protests in Greece were not isolated. A sense of decline on the continent was making citizens insecure all across Europe. On April 17, a general election in Finland, normally ignored by international political analysts, sent shivers down the European backbone. Citizens' protest took the shape of unprecedented support for a nationalist and populist party, the "True Finns," which had conducted its campaign on one single issue: no money to Greece. The True Finns did not manage to get into the government but came close to a stunning 20 percent of votes, showing the potential for popular rebellion and anti-European sentiments.[21] Anders Borg, the Swedish finance minister and exponent of a young, pragmatic generation among the Northern European politicians, explained the Scandinavian reaction in simple terms:

> At the beginning of the nineties, my mother, who was working for the state in Sweden, lost her job three times. We know what it means to suffer a financial crisis and to change. Finland underwent a dramatic crisis between 1991 and 1994. Unemployment increased by a factor of ten, but the Finns paid back every single marka of their debts. It is not easy to explain to our citizens that Greeks are different and that they can get away for free.

At the same time, debt-ridden Portugal was drowning in a political crisis, which made aid negotiations with the European partners more and more difficult. Even France saw an upsurge of anti-European sentiment stoked by a nationalist fringe party, Front National, led by Marine Le Pen just one year before the next presidential elections. Around Europe, polls reflected the disappointment of the electorates with all their governments.

In Spain, a citizens' movement had been growing daily, with meetings in Plaza Major in Madrid and in other major cities. Los Indignados became a symbol of juvenile protest against the political class and the privileged. The peacefulness of the protest should have not been mistaken: youth were the real losers in the crisis and were paying the highest cost of the austerity measures. Most young workers in Spain had been hired in temporary jobs and were the first to be fired once the crisis bit. The scandal of financial greed was still burning, but not on the skin of bankers. Nobody could deny that the los Indignados had justification for their indignation. In fact, their protests took hold in other countries as a new form of contagion.

## German Hysteria

A form of popular protest also was taking hold in Germany. Stuttgart, the capital of Baden-Württemberg, was the scene of a grassroots movement (Leben in Stuttgart, Living in Stuttgart) against a controversial urban construction plan ("Stuttgart 21"), which became a synonym for the crisis of political parties. Tens of thousands of citizens had camped for weeks in the center of the city to protest a major new railway project and the razing of old buildings and trees. The protest movement had crystallized a civic sentiment that cut across the political spectrum and at the end of March landed a historical defeat for the conservative Christian Democratic Union, which lost control of the regional government for the first time since 1953.[22] For Merkel it was a new and intimidating sign of popular rebellion against mainstream national politics. Merkel was in a very defensive mood, greatly accentuated by a faux pas involving a March 17 vote on UN Security Council resolution 1973 on the use of military force against Libya; in opposing the resolution, Germany had appeared isolated from its traditional allies by siding instead with China, Russia, India, and Brazil. The immediate consequences were strong critical statements around Europe about Germany's fitness to lead Europe and about the relevance of Europe as a foreign policy actor. The chancellor's image suffered at home as well. The continuation of the euro crisis, which meant that Germans were still making disbursements to other countries, added to the discontent. Part of the government was musing about the possibility of a once-and-for-all surgical cut on the debtor's flesh—cutting off further aid and thus forcing Greece into default. The priority for northern European politicians was to avoid the sense that southern Europe was going to be a bottomless pit forever. Citizens in Germany, especially, would rebel if they saw a repetition, for decades, of the yearly income transfers that they had experienced after reunification in the early 1990s. Some in the former West Germany had dubbed Eastern Germany the "German Mezzogiorno," explicitly referring to the historical backwardness of southern Italy that burdened the rest of that country.

On one hand, the German attitude was surprising. For all the talk of the past months, no tax money had been transferred from Germany to any of the periphery countries—at least not yet. The financial support had been granted only as loans and based on strong political conditionality. Indeed, Greece, Ireland, and Portugal had already implemented substantial policy corrections to reduce their future funding needs. The loans also came with a rate of interest that equalled or exceeded the funding cost of the lenders, potentially providing for a profit. Nevertheless, Germany was assuming a risk that the loans could not be paid in full. On the other hand, Germans were connecting the current European developments to their domestic experience with their country's fiscal union, where conditionality does not exist or has little traction and money flows from the same three states to the rest, just like in the United States, where transfers always seem to flow from a few wealthy states to the less-fortunate ones.

The need for a second loan to Greece became evident by the day, thus aggravating the German irritation. The Greek outlook seemed so precarious that Berlin was tempted to cut the rope and let Greece default one way or the other. Different plans started to circulate around the European capitals. Many of the German government's advisors—for example, the Ifo Institute's Hans-Werner Sinn and Deutsche Bank's Thomas Mayer—were unequivocal in calling for a debt restructuring in Greece. Merkel's former economic adviser Jens Weidmann, now Axel Weber's successor as Bundesbank president, in his first speech in his new capacity said, "the Bundesbank in itself does not speak against a debt restructuring."[23] Almost 200 German economists, few of them known in international levels, signed a manifesto along the lines of Ordoliberalismus (the Austro-German liberal school of thought according to which the state has primarily to establish a strong legal framework; a stable monetary, fiscal, and social condition; and market-friendly antitrust regulation, without interfering directly in private activities) opposing state support for Greece and warning about future calamities if the EFSF were to be made permanent.[24] Dissenting voices became almost inaudible. Belgian Paul de Grauwe, one of the most original European economists who had pointed out the institutional fragility of the euro zone, had an easy time criticizing the simplistic analysis behind the statement of those who opposed aid for Greece; he pointed out that they did not distinguish between a solvency crisis in Greece and liquidity crises in Spain, Ireland, Portugal, Italy, and Belgium:

> This opposition is based on an incomplete diagnosis of the sovereign debt problem in the euro zone. For the 189 German economists the story is simple: some countries (Greece, Ireland, Portugal, Spain) have misbehaved. Their governments have irresponsibly spent too much, producing unsustainable debt levels. They are now insolvent through their own mistakes. There is no point in providing financial assistance because this does not make them solvent. It only gives them incentives to persevere in irresponsible behaviour (moral hazard).[25]

As so typical among German academics, even the sophisticated intellectual Zeitgeist coincided with the "vox populi." According to Hans-Werner Sinn, an influential and outspoken figure, an internal devaluation of 20–30 percent—that is, cutting prices and wages by at least one-fifth—as requested of Greece had a historical precedent in Germany in the early 1930s with the emergency decrees ("Notverordnungen") of Weimar Republic chancellor Heinrich Bruening. His government cut wages and welfare while raising taxes, in order to repay Germany's war reparations. The deflationary policies caused social unrest that was exploited by political actors to bring democracy to an end. "In practice the consequence is civil war," Sinn concluded. But now, the beacon of rigidity was inside the Bundesbank, the German central bank. Since Weber's false myth on the betrayal of the purity of central banking through the purchase of government bonds—although not excluded by the ECB statute[26]—the Bundesbank had mobilized its influence to undermine the bailout of the ailing countries by the ECB. Coupled with the populist accents adopted by mass communication, the mix became almost irresistible for Chancellor Merkel, who had to maintain an artful balance. "In Germany sometimes hysteria prevails," commented Klaus Regling, the experienced German head of the EFSF.[27] Regling thought that the manic fear by Germans of a new "Transferunion" made no sense. The Bundesbank had a different reason to fear an extension of the purchasing program of the ECB: since the beginning of the crisis the German bank's balance sheet had been loaded with claims by the other euro area central banks. The amount of the claims had skyrocketed from €18 billion to €338 billion. The potential losses were immense. Paradoxically, observed Regling, by "only letting Greece get out of the euro area, as some economists are calling for, financial transfers would become almost surely unavoidable."

More than hysteria, what was going on in Germany was the same self-protecting, knee-jerk reaction that had characterized the German unification twenty years earlier. German unification took place in the 1990s with the aim of safeguarding the social and political equilibrium of western Germany. Chancellor Helmut Kohl imposed an unrealistic exchange rate between the two Germanys in a bid to avert "demographic contagion" or migration to the west of the eastern German population. High-wage contracts were applied to the new regions in order to prevent the creation of low-wage enclaves in the east capable of exercising competitive pressure on western businesses and employment. The two primary elements of cost—the exchange rate and labor—caused an immediate decline in economic activity and exceptionally high unemployment rates in the new Laender. The burden was so heavy that it weighed on the entire country, increasing unemployment and stagnation also in western Germany. Finally, the Bundesbank reacted to the German reunification with a mistaken monetary tightening that closed the loop exporting high interest rates to all of Europe, plunging it into a crisis and causing the breakup of the European monetary system, a disquieting precedent.

## Was Not Defaulting More Destabilizing than Defaulting?

At several stages during the spring of 2011, Athens forced new negotiations with the European authorities, looking for an improvement in the terms of the EU loan. Papandreou came close to threatening to step out of the agreements Greece had signed with the troika. However, when the Greek government discussed the default option with representatives of the ECB and the European Commission, it was confronted with the dire consequences such a step would cause at home and all around Europe. In the worst-case scenario, Greek banks holding €55 billion in Greek sovereign bonds would go bankrupt immediately and the country's payment system could break down. In such a case, capital controls might become necessary—exactly as happened in Argentina in 2001–02, often evoked as a virtuous example of debt restructuring—to avoid a definitive capital flight that was already taking place any time the word restructuring was even mentioned. Contagion would spread around other countries.

But how was it possible for Greece to live with a public debt that was going to reach a level equivalent to 160 percent of GDP? Evangelos Venizelos, who was nominated as the new finance minister, gave his sense of the endeavor:

> Just picture this: From €100 billion of income officially declared annually by Greek taxpayers, only €30 billion is taxed by an average rate of 30 percent, which generates around €9 billion. Thus, the average taxation for all the declared taxpayers' income (€100 billion) is only 9 percent! If the officially declared annual income is increased by 30 percent—totalling €130 billion—and if all of it is taxed at a 15 percent average, this would generate €19.5 billion. Relieving Greece's fiscal problems at a great extent![28]

Furthermore, the IMF calculated that Greece had state assets, eligible for privatization. worth an equivalent of up to 60 percent of its GDP. Maybe only a third of that was a realistic target. Privatizations, therefore, could help bring the Greek debt level down to 120–130 percent of GDP in five or six years, once the public debt had already started declining. However, selling assets equivalent even to 20 percent of Greek GDP was a daunting program in a damaged financial and economic environment. Furthermore, the prospect of selling the entire Greek OTE telephone company to the German Telekom, along with selling the lottery company and many other activities to foreigners, was also problematic because it seemed clearly dictated by external interests (although it would have been risky for outsiders to purchase assets of such a beleaguered economy). This potential conflict of interest was the reason why the intervention of the IMF was badly needed as a more neutral referee. Unfortunately, at the same time these matters were being discussed, the pro-European head of the IMF, Dominique Strauss-Kahn, was imprisoned in New York in a sex scandal. The IMF itself was divided internally on the attitude the fund should have toward Greece. While the head of the European division, Antonio Borges, and the two highest figures of the Fund, Strauss-Kahn and his deputy John Lipsky, were in favor of helping Greece to avoid a default, other IMF representatives—some of them very influential in the negotiations—were pushing for a default as soon as possible. Although the overall commitment of the IMF was not in question, for a while the sudden disgrace of Strauss-Kahn seemed to tip the balance and move the IMF toward a less cooperative stance.

In that period, a harsh confrontation developed inside the troika. In the July 2011 IMF staff report on euro area policies, a clear sign of dissent between the ECB and the Commission, on one hand, and the IMF staff, on the other, became unusually evident, as was clear in this IMF staff report: "Both the Commission and the ECB considered that a sovereign default or a credit event would likely trigger contagion to the core euro area economies with severe economic consequences. [IMF] Staff however also saw serious risks of contagion, even under a strategy which tries to avoid default or credit events."[29] The report observed that "cross-country financial exposure and the risk of contagion remain high. In the absence of mitigating policies, a sovereign default or disorderly bank failures could send shockwaves through Europe's financial sector and liquidity could well dry up again, with potentially strong and negative global spillovers, underscoring the need for actions to mitigate contagion." Evidently, the dispute about whether to default or not to default was not resolved, since the conclusion of the troika was that the priority was not to avoid a default at any cost but only to avoid a disorderly one.[30] The IMF observed that the dogmatic assumption that no default was allowed even for an insolvent country was flawed. It was not only unsustainable because eventually Greece needed to restructure its debt, but it was destabilizing other countries. Whenever authorities said that Spain had a liquidity problem but was solvent, investors could not but think that those were the same words used to describe Greece. And the Greek debt was going to be restructured.

## A Default in Disguise

On May 4 during an informal and restricted meeting of EU finance ministers in Luxembourg, German finance minister Wolfgang Schäuble went public by asking to discuss the issue of a Greek default and even advanced a German plan.[31] At mid-May the ECB announced that in case of restructuring of the Greek debt—even through the "soft" version of compulsory extension of the maturities of Greek bonds—it would not continue accepting Greek securities as collateral for loans to the Greek banks. If that happened, the Greek banking system would not be able to finance itself and the whole payment system would come to a standstill.[32] Someone in Frankfurt dubbed this strategy "showing the nuclear bombs to the enemy." A crucial role was played by Merkel's former aide, Jens Weidmann, in his new role as president of the Bundesbank. In a secret missive sent to Merkel early in June, Weidmann made simple calculations on the direct costs for Germany of a Greek default, reckoning that, in the best of cases, they would amount to €40 billion. A second loan to Greece, considering voluntary involvement of the banks, would cost only €12 billion (roughly one-third of the €40 billion paid in by the euro area countries).[33] In a worse but likely scenario, a Greek default would spread contagion all over Europe and cut the whole periphery out of market financing. In that case, the direct costs for Berlin were in the range of €70 billion, but the total amount of money needed to limit the damage across Europe would drain all of the EFSF and put in danger even the solidity of the central banks.[34]

In the meantime, the EU had created a task force on the "private sector." It was led by the same Dutch finance ministry official who had gained plaudits in May 2010 for configuring the formalities of the EFSF. The Dutch government was on the same wavelength as Berlin. Finally, Merkel had to step in. On June 8, returning from a Washington visit, when President Obama had publicly called on her not to let Greece fall because it would disrupt the world economy, she recorded one of her weekly web-messages trying to put a patch on the situation: "We must not undertake anything that could put the global recovery in jeopardy . . . we cannot afford an unruly default by any country in the euro zone." On June 10, the German Bundestag approved participation in a second loan package for Greece that euro zone leaders expected to forge at a forthcoming EU summit on July 21 and that was considered vital for the funding of Athens debt. Since part of the total amount (then estimated at €80–€90 billion, but which eventually surged to €130 billion) had to come from the banks, the Bundestag approval came only on the condition that private sector involvement was approved by the EU Council.

The strategy of the European authorities was to buy time for Greece while waiting for anticipated good news in the coming months—at the latest in September—from Ireland and Portugal. Ireland was especially seen as being on the right track because it was respecting the plans set out with the troika in exchange for the €85 billion loan in late 2010 and was on the way to recovery. Dublin's GDP expanded in the first quarter of 2011 by 1.3 percent over the preceding quarter, driven by strong exports. In June, Ireland's trade surplus came in at a record €4 billion. Portugal also was observed with confidence, although its economy was not going to grow visibly in the foreseeable future. The terms and conditions of the financial assistance package for Lisbon had just been agreed by the Eurogroup and by the ECOFIN on May 17. The financial package would cover Portugal's financing needs of up to €78 billion. EU officials believed at the time that once these two countries were getting sounder, showing that austerity and rigorous monetary policy were not hampering the recovery, Greece would appear as the single problematic case for the euro area. Greece was a difficult case indeed, but still a relatively small one.

On June 20 the Eurogroup met to discuss the PSI and reached an agreement on the principle of letting private investors foot part of the bill but not on the technical means of doing it. Four days later, the European Council decided to eliminate the option of a hard default and instead stick to the original plan for the Greek fiscal targets and an extension of the lifeline—one that would also involve the voluntary rescheduling,[35] with technical details to be approved in July.[36] The decision was intended to provide a long-term commitment of the euro area for Greece and to exude a new sense of common destiny. Unfortunately, what struck the markets was a much more prosaic pronouncement in the text: "The euro area Heads of State or Government . . . endorse the approach decided by the Eurogroup on 20 June as regards the pursuit of voluntary private sector involvement in the form of informal and voluntary roll-overs of existing Greek debt at maturity for a substantial reduction of the required year-by-year funding within the programme while avoiding a selective default."

For the first time, the principle of private sector involvement was specifically prescribed, at the highest levels of government, in the sovereign debt crisis of the euro area. Furthermore, the ECB had clearly demonstrated—by abstaining from purchases of sovereign bonds on the market—that it did not intend to be the agent of financial solidarity for much longer. But the leaders gave no clear indication about the promptness of the EFSF (except to call for its "rapid entry into force") or exactly when the ESM would take over that role from the bank.[37]

Finally, the Greek Parliament did its work and approved by a thin majority (155 to 138) the new severe austerity package prepared by Papandreou. Finance Minister Venizelos had announced the creation of a privatization fund to sell off €50 billion in state assets.[38] In that context the role of private sector involvement in support programs raised the possibility of rapid contagion and of a downward spiral. On July 5, Moody's cut Portugal's credit rating to junk status, citing concerns that the country would likely need a second bailout.[39] But Moody's main worry was caused by the new mechanism just established by the euro partners; the agency said the EU approach to financial assistance "implies a rising risk that private sector participation could become a precondition for additional rounds of official lending to Portugal in the future as well."[40] PSI appeared to have become a matter of Realpolitik in the creditor countries, not as a solution to the debt crisis.[41] The political nature of the decision, imposed by the German government, convinced rating agencies and the markets that Ireland and Portugal would follow Greece. In a matter of days, credit default swap spreads for those countries reached quadruple-digit levels. The bonds of Greece, Ireland, and Portugal became de facto non-marketable. Investors, worried by the increased risk implicit in their trading and portfolio books, started to look for the next risky bonds to unload.

## An Italian Midsummer Nightmare

Since he first stepped onto Italy's political stage in 1993, Silvio Berlusconi had been a challenge for his European partners. In their eyes, he represented a departure from the contemporary "European ideology" of government by law and not by men, or worse, by one man.[42] Once in a governing position he could rule by the laws by changing them to his own advantage, albeit following democratic procedures. Formally there was no way to dispute the outcome of the elections that brought him to power, although everybody understood the electoral process was influenced by Berlusconi's conflict of interests as a media tycoon. Germany's Helmut Kohl, in the 1990s, turned a blind eye to Berlusconi's exceptionality and let him into the European Popular Party family. But Berlusconi came across to the Italians as the symbol of both politics and of anti-politics, both power and anarchy. In this state of grace, although mercilessly surrounded by judicial inquiries, Berlusconi had built a personal system of power whereby the government was primarily meant to keep him in power instead of serving the interests of the country.

In May 2011 Berlusconi's governing coalition was bitterly defeated in a number of local polls across the country. Opposition parties took control of major cities and of a majority of regions. The results demonstrated that prime minister Berlusconi, whose image had been tarnished by a string of sexual scandals, for all his innate popular charisma, had lost touch with the Italian public opinion. Although Berlusconi could stay in power, the ineffectiveness of his government was heightened by the defeat. For investors the political development was reason for concern because of the dismal growth prospects of the country and of the second-thoughts that might prevail about the politically costly fiscal rigor previously promised by Finance Minister Giulio Tremonti. A laxer fiscal attitude and still-lower growth would result in greater public debt.[43] In the weeks after the electoral defeat, government politicians voiced the idea of postponing the target of a balanced budget from 2014 to 2016. It was the coup-de-grace to an already precarious economic situation.

The reason for the vulnerability of Italy was its dismal economic growth. Italy's GDP had declined by 7.5 percent from its peak (the first quarter 2008) to its trough (second quarter 2009). In 2010, the economy rebounded by a modest 1.3 percent. In the first quarter 2011 the economy again stalled (+0.1 percent) comparing very unfavorably with the relatively ebullient German performance (around 1.5 percent). How could the Italian economy keep pace with core Europe? Wasn't it only a matter of time, at best years, before Berlin and Rome had to acknowledge that they had not been made to live under the same currency? Actually most of the Italian reality was literally obscure, and not only in the notorious murky reality in the southern regions where organized crime still had a role in the society. The second manufacturing powerhouse in the European Union was the cradle of 30–40 percent of the EU's small and medium-size enterprises, a molecular system reflecting the individualism-entrepreneurship of its citizens and generally flying below the radar of international analysts. This was a hidden strength of the economy, coupled with the archetypal financial solidity of the Italian families. But the fragmentation of the Italian economy also mirrored the lack of unity in the country and the lack of trust in national politics, which had often found no better way to hold together than being governed from abroad, most recently by the European rules. Now, with Berlusconi silently isolated by his European colleagues as someone morally unfit to rule a country, the link with Europe was looking weaker than ever.

The reason why Italy was the make-it-or-break-it case for the euro is purely algebraic. Between the second half of 2011 and the end of 2014, Italy needed to roll over €679 billion of debt redemptions. According to its National Stability Program, it would also need to issue €135 billion of new bonds to cover the planned budget deficits. As a whole, the government financing need was €813 billion. If Italy needed assistance, even the financial resources provided by its European partners would prove insufficient. Assuming that the IMF provided half of the commitment made by the EU, the total lending capacity of the European Stability Mechanism would reach €750 billion, enough to finance a three-year program for Greece, Portugal, Ireland, and even Spain. But once Italy suffered from the contagion, Germany and France would have to issue guarantees, including those already issued, for an equivalent of around 23–25 percent of their GDP on top of the current unprecedented levels of their own debts. France would see its implicit debt-to-GDP ratio rocket to an Italian level and would immediately lose its AAA rating. As a consequence, Germany would bear almost alone the whole burden of assistance of the euro area—a burden higher than that of the German reunification but concentrated in one-third of the time—and would be overwhelmed by it. In simple terms, Italy was too big to be saved.

In 2010 foreign investors held more than 50 percent of the €1.8 trillion Italian public debt. According to market analysts, all of a sudden at the beginning of July 2011, the share of foreign bondholders plunged below 45 percent. An estimated amount of €100 billion was sold at the end of June and in the first weeks of July before and after the European Council statement confirming the private sector involvement. The share of Italian and Spanish assets in the portfolios of money market funds plunged, respectively, from 0.5 percent and 0.2 percent of the total to zero. The Italian government aggravated the situation and presented at the end of June a fiscal "correction" (that is, budget cutback) that was nominally huge (€47 billion) and would bring the balance close to equilibrium in 2014. Unfortunately the fiscal correction was seen by the markets as "backloaded." More than 80 percent of the correction was due in 2013–14, after the next elections and therefore highly uncertain.[44] Berlusconi's weakness assumed a tragic note when he inserted into the fiscal package an ad-hoc article intended to benefit him personally.[45] In the meantime, prosecutors also had sought the arrest of one of Tremonti's closest advisers, who was suspected of accepting bribes. Berlusconi's ad hoc article was finally expunged under the outrage of the Italian public opinion, but the credibility of the two most prominent figures of the government plunged to a miserable level.

Between July 7 and 8 a chaotic spiral started to develop on the markets. Default fears had gripped Portugal as a consequence of the downgrading by Moody's, and the credit default swap spreads on Lisbon's debt had reached a historic level. Surprisingly, notwithstanding the incipient storm, the ECB raised its refinance rate to 1.5 percent, in what appears either another confused assessment of the European economic situation by ECB chief economist Jürgen Stark or a hostile message from the ECB to the national governments. The Dutch finance minister called for Greece to default. Interest rates on Italy's government five-year bonds jumped up over 5.2 percent, the highest in three years, seemingly moving along the same path that Greece, Ireland, and Portugal had gone one year earlier. Spain moved in parallel. The main source of instability was probably contagion from Greece.[46]

Financial investments in the euro area were shortened just on fears of self-fulfilling doubts about the sustainability of the euro area or in view of heightened volatility. At 6 percent the service of Italy's debt was still bearable, although it would add, in the medium term, a further €20 billion in costs over the debt service of one year earlier; any step higher would create expectations of a default. As the past experience in Ireland and Portugal showed, once a country loses the confidence of the markets, it was extremely difficult to regain it. Scaling up the riskiness of Italian securities meant an automatic reweighting in global portfolios and a likely massive sell-off. All of a sudden the presumed strengths of the Italian fiscal position turned out to be reasons for weakness: the size of its bond market was not a reason for liquidity anymore but the ballpark for global risk reduction. The significant share of domestic investors in the Italian debt also backfired because once the sovereign debt started looking wobbly, the largest Italian banks also seemed less safe than before. Italian banks' borrowing from the ECB via open market operations almost doubled from €41 billion at the end of June to €80.5 billion at the end of July. The potential impact of disruption in Italy was far beyond any means not only in Europe. Italy and Spain are the third and fourth biggest countries in the euro zone, respectively, accounting for more than 28 percent of the area's gross domestic product. Adding the 6 percent total represented by Greece, Ireland, and Portugal reveals concerns about the creditworthiness of more than one-third of the euro zone. The risks to the European and to the global banking systems, with their intricate patterns of multibillion-euro, cross-national loans and investments, were immense. In the United States, banks are more exposed to Italy than to any other euro zone country, to the tune of $269 billion.[47] If Greece for twenty months had threatened to destabilize an entire continent, a default in Italy had the capacity to change the face of global capitalism. The euro itself could not survive. Once the crowning achievement of the post-1945 European political and economic integration was gone, the rest of the European project would lose sense and direction. Europe's influence in the world would disappear. Since the first signs of a sovereign debt crisis, the nightmare haunting the continent's policymakers had been the prospect of the crisis reaching Italy. Apparently, in the second half of 2011, the nightmare was becoming reality.

### Summer Is Hot, Let's Meet in the Fall

The weekend of July 9–10 saw preparations for the end of the world. Chancellor Merkel had phoned Berlusconi to urge him to act swiftly. "Italy must send an important signal by agreeing on a budget that meets the need for frugality and consolidation," she said to the Italian premier.[48] Senior officials in Berlin, Paris, and Brussels discussed convening an emergency summit, One of the diplomats preparing the meetings said that "the Berlusconi-problem" was "at the top of the agenda" for Sarkozy and Merkel. But Merkel's negotiators officially wanted to wait at least until Monday, July 11, when a Eurogroup meeting was already planned before taking any decision. The chancellor's goal—notwithstanding the incredible danger building on the markets—was to postpone any initiative until September, probably hoping that the political situation in Italy would become clearer with markets' pressure forcing the exit of Berlusconi, a scenario that was discussed also in Italy. On July 11, fears hit stock markets not just in Italy, where the major index fell nearly 4 percent, but across much of Europe. The selling continued amid fears that several European banks had not passed the latest round of stress tests—the results of which were going to be published on Friday, July 15. Of the ninety-one European banks that had undergone the stress tests, about 15 were expected to fail. The United States was affected, too, with the Standard & Poor's 500 stock index down about 1.8 percent on European debt fears and worries about a partisan showdown in Washington over raising the United States debt limit.

The meeting of the Eurogroup on Monday evening was judged catastrophic by many participants. The final statement made the right sounds but no detailed program was spelled:

> Ministers reaffirmed their absolute commitment to safeguard financial stability in the euro area. To this end, Ministers stand ready to adopt further measures that will improve the euro area's systemic capacity to resist

contagion risk, including enhancing the flexibility and the scope of the EFSF, lengthening the maturities of the loans and lowering the interest rates, including through a collateral arrangement where appropriate. Proposals to this effect will be presented to Ministers shortly.[49]

The debate on the deadline for the proposals was a shocking test of the lack of understanding of the extent of the crisis. Germany's Schäuble at first asked to postpone action to "the Autumn." After an outburst of criticism he tried to settle for "the coming weeks." Only at the very end of their meeting did the Eurogroup ministers converge on a vague and still-harmful "shortly."

The disappointment among many EU officials was so deep that many thought the whole euro area was in danger. Some of them confessed confidentially their doubts about Germany's real will to defend the euro. Many euro zone leaders tried to convince Merkel that an emergency summit was unavoidable. Former chancellor Helmut Kohl was quoted as saying "this girl (Merkel) is destroying my Europe," a comment he later denied.[50] As usual the chancellor, who had planned a journey to Africa, did not want to be forced into a decision under the pressure of emotion and extreme financial emergency. However, French president Nicolas Sarkozy forced her hand proposing a summit for Thursday, July 14, and European Council president Herman Van Rompuy finally settled for July 21. The invitation to the special summit was sent out on July 15, but a number of meetings had already started at the technical level. The goal was to compose a reassuring message to the markets, but in order to do that, it was necessary to produce another comprehensive package. What was needed was a consistent orientation toward the final and stable arrangement within the euro area, first of all a credible crisis mechanism.

One of the main negotiators offered this explanation of the challenge facing the leaders four days before the summit. "The crisis is of systemic nature and after four years the markets are finally going to hit the jugular of the euro attacking Italy. If they succeed, the crisis will not be financial or economic, it will develop into a political and institutional breakdown."[51] The agenda of the summit had to be built on two goals: solving the Greek problem once and for all, and setting up a systemic response to the crisis. The uncertainty of the solution of the Greek problem was reverberating onto the rest of the euro area. The shadow of a disorderly default was still hanging. It was therefore necessary to decide about PSI (private sector involvement). Although it seemed clear that Berlin would not backtrack on that, it was still unclear whether the technical form of PSI was consistent with the resolution of the Greek problem. The main option was to extend the maturity of the EFSF loans to Greece and to cut the rates to a level just slightly above financing costs. The price of the loans would then be similar to those granted in past years to the EU non-euro countries

(Latvia, Romania, and Hungary) or to non-EU countries in the context of a program known as "macro financial assistance." Depending on the amount of PSI, it was possible to envisage the right form of selective default (a default affecting only the private creditors involved in the PSI program), which could bring down the level of the Greek public debt.

### "Complete Lack of Trust"

Once more the European Council needed to overcome the resistance of the European Central Bank to any form of selective default. Negotiations started at the highest level with Trichet. The head of the ECB was offered a number of guarantees to ensure that the ESM, when it began in 2013, would have strong shoulders and would be able to take over the role that the ECB was surreptitiously and unhappily doing to support the critical countries. One of the participants to the negotiation spoke of "complete lack of trust" on the part of the ECB president toward the governments. The ECB felt it had been "stabbed in the back" after its agreement in May 2010 to intervene on the bond markets and asked to cancel the PSI. Privately, a central banker described the situation as "a very strong institutional conflict between the ECB and the ECOFIN [the finance ministers]." The anger in Frankfurt was not due only to the €75 billion spent to purchase government bonds of the three countries under assistance, but because the potential losses were much higher once the amount of collaterals (against banking refinancing) was taken into account. Greek banks alone had turned in to the ECB domestic paper for the equivalent of €100 billion. Any kind of selective default could imply very substantial losses for the ECB and for the national central banks. In theory, such losses could be covered by the member states with taxpayer money, but the political implications would be huge. Central banks would be seen as an extension of political power and by citizens as a source of taxes. Their sacred autonomy and independence would become a fiction.

Trichet explained to Merkel that the ECB would support—essentially by backing the banking systems with a huge lending facility—the financial assistance to the countries if the governments agreed on a common guarantee on the debts or alternatively on higher capital for the EFSF. In order to lend credibility to the financial assistance, it was necessary to recapitalize the EFSF at least at the level of the ESM. But the problem was relevant because the EFSF had no juridical personality and, therefore, the level of its debts reflected directly into higher debts of the national governments. By contrast, the ESM was to be an international organization, autonomous from national governments, and so its balance sheet would not formally affect the national accounts of euro area member states. Eventually, an institutional filter might be indispensable before 2013 to make it credible that the euro area might step in and help countries larger than Greece, Ireland, and Portugal.

Trichet had lost confidence even in Merkel and decided to send letters to her and Sarkozy pinning down their future commitments and fixing exactly the scheme by which the ECB in 2013, at the latest, would be free of its current unorthodox tasks. He said that it was necessary to grant to both the EFSF and the ESM an "operational flexibility" enabling them to buy and sell government bonds on the secondary market (as well as on the primary market), absorbing the ECB's function of market stabilizer. What had happened in April after the ECB stopped buying the bonds demonstrated that the bank could not be both the rescuer of last resort and the policy enforcer. The two roles are contradictory, especially so for a central bank that has no democratic legitimacy. In his letters, Trichet highlighted the risk of contagion ingrained in the application of PSI and asked Berlin and Paris to state very clearly that the selective default would be a unique case for Greece only.

The negotiations started in the afternoon of July 15 in Rome with a meeting chaired by Vittorio Grilli, the new head of the Eurogroup working group (EWG) (the high-level committee that prepares the Eurogroup meetings), who opened the discussion about PSI between the European authorities and the representatives of major banks.[52] Bankers were acting mainly through the Institute for International Finance, the powerful global lobby chaired by Deutsche Bank's head Josef Ackermann. On the evening of Monday, July 18, the working group met again in Brussels to sum up the outcome, which at that moment seemed a fairly good deal for the banks.[53] Two meetings followed in Brussels on Tuesday, July 19. The first was joined by the highest officials of the European Council, of the European Commission, of the ECB, and by Nikolaus Meyer-Landrut, the new European adviser to Merkel, and Xavier Musca, secretary general for the French presidency. The issue, reduced to the bone, was finding a compromise between the German request for a sizable PSI and the French insistence on a more powerful and flexible EFSF.

Behind the scenes, France and Germany were once again taking control of the European negotiations. In Berlin the development was justified by the fact that Germany represented the group of the creditor and fiscally rigorous countries, while France was heading the group of the weaker countries. The first meeting failed very clearly. Meyer-Landrut thought that EWG's Grilli had given in too easily to the bankers, that the designed PSI was too soft on the private sector because it implied only a 10 percent haircut, that is a loss for private bondholders of 10 cents for each euro. France suggested substituting the PSI solution with a general tax on financial transactions as a direct compensation for the state interventions on behalf of Greece. The latter was a cheap trick to spread the PSI from the banks directly involved in the Greek credits—most of them French—to all the others. Meyer-Landrut made it clear that in such circumstances Berlin was strongly opposed to increasing the flexibility of the EFSF. The meeting ended with the sense that Berlin was willing to wreck the summit of July 21. A second, more restricted, meeting that morning was needed between Musca and Meyer-Landrut to design a possible compromise on a more substantial PSI, which would have doubled the burden on the banks to 21 percent (21 cents lost on each euro). What remained unresolved was the new endowment of powers to the EFSF. To solve this problem and fix a comprehensive package, a direct negotiation was needed between Merkel and Sarkozy, and the French president offered to fly over to Berlin on the evening on July 20.

## "Governments Finally Did It"

The meeting began at the Chancellery around 5:30 p.m. and went on for almost seven hours. During the day, the chancellor had received a call from President Obama, who had highlighted how important it was for the whole world that Europe could find an agreement. The meeting opened in the small Kabinettsaal on the sixth floor and later moved to the dining room on the eighth floor. The bone of contention was the role of the EFSF, with Merkel resisting the idea of giving it too much power and endowing it with too much money. The official explanation for her position was that providing more capital would be an invitation for speculators to drive up Italian bond costs then wait for an intervention by the euro partners. After one hour, it became clear that no solution could be found without having the ECB around the table. Jean-Claude Trichet was in a meeting with his colleagues in Frankfurt preparing for the European Council when he was contacted by the Chancellery and asked to come to Berlin. He got on the latest flight to Tegel Airport and reached the Chancellery at 10:25 pm.[54] The story of the Franco-German meeting is generally told as a compromise between the two countries, but in fact it was a deal of the two countries with the ECB. The main point was giving to Trichet the necessary guarantees about the future developments of the euro area to buy his consent for defending Italy and Spain until the stability mechanism (the EFSF) began work. Trichet reiterated a number of requests: The euro zone leaders had to say as clearly as possible that private sector involvement for Greece was a unique case; that the governments were to provide credit enhancement to underpin the quality of collateral; and that they would also provide adequate resources to recapitalize Greek banks if losses connected with PSI would weaken their balance sheets. Finally, in the context of the agreements on the set-up of a crisis mechanism, Trichet wanted to be sure that the ECB would have a central role in determining when and how the EFSF would make its purchases of government bonds in the secondary market.

According to one account, "After a great deal of hard bargaining, the job was done and a phone call was put through to Van Rompuy in Brussels. It was in some respects a moment of low comedy after several hours of high drama. As there was apparently no fixed line within easy reach, the Chancellor, the French president and the president of the ECB shared a portable phone, which they passed to each other depending on who was speaking. They got their message across, but in a fairly chaotic manner."[55] A clearer message was sent through an e-mail to the EU authorities and to the other leaders at 4:00 a.m., summarizing the agreement.

The leaders met in Brussels at 1 p.m. the next day, July 21. In the rooms close to the one of the meeting there were the representatives from the banking lobby (the Institute for International Finance) and other EU officials. The first set of measures regarded Greece. The support for Papandreou was substantial, as noted in the final statement: "We agree to support a new program for Greece and, together with the IMF and the voluntary contribution of the private sector, to fully cover the financing gap. The total official financing will amount to an estimated €109 billion. This program will be designed, notably through lower interest rates and extended maturities, to decisively improve the debt sustainability and refinancing profile of Greece."[56]

The PSI was by far the most important novelty, although the four options presented in the text left some uncertainty about the real scope of it. The financial sector had indicated its willingness to support Greece on a voluntary basis through a menu of options that would strengthen overall sustainability. The net contribution of the private sector over the years 2011–14 was estimated at €37 billion.[57]

Further requests by the ECB were clearly stated in the following lines and in the paragraph dedicated to PSI: "Credit enhancement will be provided to underpin the quality of collateral so as to allow its continued use for access to Eurosystem liquidity operations by Greek banks. We will provide adequate resources to recapitalize Greek banks if needed. . . . As far as our general approach to private sector involvement in the euro area is concerned, we would like to make it clear that Greece requires an exceptional and unique solution."

The other issue of the negotiations was the character of the crisis mechanisms or "stabilization tools" intended to contain the risk of contagion and of systemic risk. The chief novelty was the decision to approve a precautionary program involving the establishment of a facility that resembled the special credit line of the IMF and was to be used also for "non-program countries," that is, Italy and Spain. The biggest concession by Merkel was to allow the EFSF to intervene in the secondary markets, an option she had fought fiercely in the previous EU Councils. Trichet obtained agreement that the ECB had a primary role in activating the interventions.[58]

The strict connection between fiscal support and political conditionalities emerged in the paragraphs dedicated to Portugal and Ireland. Dublin in particular agreed to mentioning the discussion on tax cooperation while receiving much better terms for the financial assistance from the EFSF: "We note Ireland's willingness to participate constructively in the discussions on the Common Consolidated Corporate Tax Base draft directive (CCCTB) and in the structured discussions on tax policy issues in the framework of the Euro+ Pact framework."[59]

In the final point of the text, the leaders announced the direction for the institutional development of the euro area: the eventual "economic government" would be an offspring of the process of intergovernmental coordination chaired by Van Rompuy. The statement said, "We invite the President of the European Council, in close consultation with the President of the Commission and the President of the Eurogroup, to make concrete proposals by October on how to improve working methods and enhance crisis management in the euro area."[60]

Given the preliminary conditions, the outcome of the special summit seemed, at first glance, to be impressive. The support measures were at the top end of market expectations. The announcement of a second Greek rescue package of €109 billion reduced instantaneously the two-year bond yields of Greece and the other program countries by hundreds of basis points. Trichet described the outcome of the summit to his G-20 colleagues in Basel as a good agreement. He probably needed to justify the fact that the ECB had abstained from purchasing securities in the past four months just to put pressure on the governments. And he could say that risky strategy had now led to good results.

In fact, anyone who knew that the core of the negotiations was about the governments relieving the ECB from its bond purchasing program would realize that the outcome was disappointing. The unwillingness of the leaders to increase the size of the EFSF should have been clear. On the other hand, unless the ECB signalled that it was willing to resume using its Securities Markets Program for bond purchases, the market was going to question quickly the adequacy of the EFSF. Furthermore, the date from which the EFSF would be able to use the new framework to support the Italian and Spanish sovereign bond markets remained unclear. Unfortunately, the awareness that the EFSF had no financial capacity to resist the markets in case of an attack against Italy became evident just a few hours after the summit. In the following two weeks, the stocks of euro zone banks fell on average by 20 percent, and the Italian spread over German bonds rose from 283 basis points to 416. The idea of a Greek default "by stealth"—a loss in the value of the credit without the legal guaranty of a formal default—increased the riskiness of the euro area. This would especially be true for those investors who hedge their bonds through the credit default swaps. The soft restructuring was designed exactly to avoid triggering such swaps. Suddenly, investors in the euro area felt they had one less tool to protect themselves. The situation was aggravated by one more unilateral decision by the Irish government to force a restructuring, on very punishing terms, on the bondholders of the Bank of Ireland. This action again raised the specter of defaults in the banks of the euro area, as explicitly mentioned by Moody's when it warned of the possible downgrade of the subordinated bonds of eighty-seven banks in the euro area. The interaction between banks and the debts of states now appeared more dangerous than ever, and the spreads between the German ten-year bonds and the Spanish and Italian bonds started widening implacably. At the beginning of August 2011, Madrid and Rome were exactly on the same path as Athens had been in early 2010, then Dublin in autumn 2010, and Lisbon a few months earlier. Trichet, confident that the EFSF was finally coming, saw the need for the ECB to build a bridge until the EFSF was operative. So the ECB decided it could start purchasing Italian and Spanish bonds.

# 19

## Berlusconi's Moral Hazard and the German Waterboarding Strategy

### *Mr. Prime Minister, You Got Mail*

Maybe for the first time in his life as a politician, Silvio Berlusconi had lost his touch with the public. Scandals had marred his charisma and poor results had tarnished his image as a successful entrepreneur on loan to the world of politics. Fearful of being judged, condemned, and finally jailed at age 75 for personal improprieties, he was determined to hold onto his power as long as possible. Since the beginning of the financial crisis, national governments in Europe had suffered a string of losses at every election. In France and Germany, the opposition had taken the lead in the polls. In Finland and the Netherlands among others, minority parties were holding the public debate to ransom. But financial markets had put a special pressure on governments in the most debt-stressed countries and forced several leaders to resign. Changes of government had already occurred in Portugal and Ireland. The Greek crisis had also coincided with a change of government in October 2009. Spanish prime minister José Luis Zapatero announced at the end of July 2011 that early elections would be held on November 20, four months ahead of the scheduled date, to promote stability and have a new government in power by year-end, one that would have broader political support. Against this backdrop, nothing seemed to be happening in Italy.

Under attack at home Berlusconi was also increasingly isolated abroad. Nicolas Sarkozy and Angela Merkel avoided any non-institutional meeting with him in public and reduced their regular bilateral meetings with Italy. His credibility around the world was diminished because everybody knew he was accused of dubious private and public behavior. Unfortunately, the results of his years in power also were disappointing. Italy's economy was at a standstill. During his two previous governments, public expenditures in nominal terms had been double and even triple the average of the previous two decades, but it had not helped economic growth, demonstrating the limits of government policy. The tax rate had escalated and economic growth had halted. The foreign press saw him as "the man who screwed an entire country," as *The Economist* wrote on its front page.[1] He probably thought the remark was not entirely offensive.

Between the end of July and the beginning of August 2011, the spread of Italian ten-year bonds over the equivalent German Bund rose to unprecedented levels. Italy was on a slippery slope: the self-perpetuating dynamics gathered pace through July, with bondholders selling in anticipation of future losses in their portfolios, thereby raising volatility and perceived risk, which led to further selling. Interbank markets in the euro area came close to a heart attack. Nobody was lending money to anybody. The financial conditions were on the same track as in September 2008, with Italy now in the role of Lehman Brothers. Berlusconi and his finance minister Giulio Tremonti announced that the Italian government would improve the fiscal correction that had been presented and already changed in the first half of July, but shockingly they pushed the deadline for action to September. The Italian Parliament was closed for its customary summer lull, probably the longest in the western democracies. The "caste," as Italians snub their political class, seemed to be dancing on the deck of the Titanic.

The reason behind Italy's political gridlock is crucial to understanding the developments. In the face of the crisis, Berlusconi would opt for assistance from the European Central Bank, through its Securities Market Program, while Tremonti preferred to use the card of asking assistance from the IMF. The two policymakers also had a different view of the crisis; Berlusconi described it as temporary market hysteria, while Tremonti had been speaking for months confidentially of a forthcoming Armageddon that would change the face of the world. But the really decisive and Machiavellian reason for their differences was that the ECB purchase of Italian bonds would happen behind the political scene, allowing Berlusconi to stay in power, while the visible arrival of an IMF program—the first to an advanced economy in decades—would have huge political consequences and open the way to a "grand coalition" government that Tremonti could head. Berlusconi understood Tremonti's visions and, not incidentally, relations between the prime minister and the Treasury minister in his government were so bad that they did not communicate with each other.

On August 4, yields on Italian and Spanish government bonds spiked to 6.2 percent, approaching the 7 percent level considered the threshold of unsustainability. The global situation was deteriorating. In the United States, congressional negotiations on the debt ceiling came close to putting the country on the brink of default; on August 5, Standard and Poor's announced the downgrade of its long-term credit rating for the U.S. federal government debt, changing it from

AAA to AA+ with a negative outlook. Concerns about a serious deterioration in the outlook for global economic growth, and especially in the United States, triggered a flight to quality, causing severe tensions in several market segments.

The European Central Bank was expected to step in to save the euro by renewing its policy of full allotment liquidity (fulfilling all loan requests from banks) to keep the European banking systems afloat. Rumors spread that the bank would start buying Italian and Spanish bonds, officially to restore functionality in the money markets of the euro area. The purchase of Italy's securities was obviously the make-or-break decision and not an easy one. By purchasing government bonds in large amounts the ECB would de facto assume a fiscal policy role; that is, instead of worrying only about inflation, the bank would be pressuring governments to be accountable to the taxpayers. Once the bank started to purchase such bonds, it would find itself in a trap: how could it decide to let a country go bust by denying further purchases? The bank had no democratic legitimacy to take such a fateful decision. Still, in the incomplete institutional framework of the euro area, the ECB seemed the only possible lender of last resort. There were actually two other possibilities to provide the euro area with an ultimate backstop: the issuing of eurobonds and the expansion of the European Financial Stability Facility (EFSF), which was to buy bonds from debt-ridden countries. Yet these steps faced political resistance and even if approved would still need time to be activated. Confronted with a full-blown crisis, the ECB decided to spell out precisely the economic policies that countries would have to respect in return for receiving loans from the bank. Since the bank's role of dictating economic policy actions was not acknowledged officially by the Maastricht Treaty that created the bank, or by the bank itself, the ECB had to follow a strictly confidential procedure.

On August 5, ECB president Jean-Claude Trichet and his successor, Bank of Italy's governor Mario Draghi, sent a letter to Berlusconi, in the name of the European system of central banks, spelling out the initiatives that the ECB insisted be undertaken by the Italian government.[2] Since the stated justification for the bank's purchases of Italian bonds was a technical one (restoring the functioning of the monetary market), formally the letter did not set the requests as conditio-sine-qua-non for aid. But the meaning of the letter was unequivocal and the tone was very harsh. The letter was a diktat: it asked extreme urgency in policy action and even suggested the parliamentary procedure to shorten the time and asked the government to prepare a fast track decree. Although it was not specified in the text, Trichet and Draghi clearly wanted Berlusconi to resort to a confidence vote to get a swift parliamentary approval.

Similar missives had been sent in the past to Greece, Ireland, and Portugal when the ECB started purchasing their government securities. At the same time as the letter to Berlusconi, Trichet and the governor of the Spanish central bank sent a similar letter to Prime Minister Zapatero in Madrid. The only letter whose existence became public was the Italian one, because Berlusconi thought he could use it as an excuse for unpleasant and politically costly fiscal initiatives.[3] He wanted to use the ECB as a shield, leveraging on the trust that the Italians have for guidance from abroad, rule out an IMF intervention, and eventually lay the blame for tax increases on Trichet.[4] Tremonti described the letter as one of two missives received in August by the government: "The first was from terrorists, the second from the ECB. The second was the worst."

The letter was an impressive testimony to the loss of sovereignty suffered by a country that was not even under an official and publicly acknowledged financial assistance program. Officially, Italy had only a liquidity problem derived from the exogenous and imported instability. In reality, its policy priorities were now being designed and dictated by unelected officials who had to consider as a first goal the stability of the euro area. In fact, in all respects, the tone of the letter was unusual and harsh. The ECB called for pressing action by the Italian government to restore the confidence of investors. It did so by stressing the commitments made by European leaders at the July 21 summit, as if to question Italy's compliance. The lack of action was denounced at the start of the letter, which said the bank's Governing Council believed that Italy needed to urgently underpin the standing of its sovereign signature and its commitment to fiscal sustainability and structural reforms. In simple words, the ECB questioned the political credibility of Berlusconi and Tremonti and clearly stated that their economic policy was not sufficient.

Draghi and Trichet called for significant measures to enhance potential growth, observing that "more needs to be done . . . to increase competition particularly in services, to improve the quality of public services and to design regulatory and fiscal systems better suited to support firms' competitiveness and efficiency of the labour market." Full liberalization of public services, reform of collective wage bargaining, and new rules for the hiring and dismissal of employees were openly called for.

"Additional corrective fiscal measures are needed," Trichet and Draghi wrote. "We consider essential for the Italian authorities to frontload the measures adopted in the July 2011 package by at least one year. The aim should be to achieve a better-than-planned fiscal deficit in 2011, a net borrowing of 1.0 percent in 2012 and a balanced budget in 2013, mainly via expenditure cuts." Among the other measures the central bankers requested were interventions on the pension system and reducing the cost of public employees if necessary by reducing wages. "We regard as crucial that all actions be taken as soon as possible," they said.

Significantly, the central bankers did not limit their prescription to indicating broad economic parameters. They entered into the crevices of specific legislation and its implementation. The salient point was the recommendation that Berlusconi act by issuing decrees with the force of law, followed by parliamentary ratification by the end of September 2011. The decree is a measure that article 77 of the Italian Constitution allows "in cases of extraordinary need and urgency," originally tailored to meet possible military emergencies. The procedure is often abused by governments wanting to circumvent parliamentary debates, but it was shocking to read that a supranational technical body strongly urged a government to resort to a method overriding the long parliamentary debates in the name of an emergency dictated by financial markets.

In the face of obstinate denial of reality by the national political class, the ECB assumed a political role for which it was unwilling to take full responsibility and which it had no legal power to assume. The bank's role also was one that undermined national democracy. The push for circumvention of traditional democratic debate was evident in other passages of the letter where the "large-scale privatization" of local public services was requested despite a recent referendum opposing such privatizations. Although not belonging to a political party, the monetary authorities nevertheless had become political in the fullest sense. They were reflecting a dimension of politics where interdependence and financial emergency (contagion is also a form of interdependence) took priority over the traditional considerations of justice and liberty that normally orient national parliamentary debates. To some extent, even the classic left-right internal balance of politics was diminished by the necessity to commit over the long term to economic prescriptions set out as a condition for the bank's support, notably the request for a constitutional reform tightening fiscal rules.

The bank's interference with national fiscal sovereignty also was shown by the recommendations both on the timing and size of the fiscal corrections, and even more interestingly, on the quality of the measures. Bringing forward the planned balanced budget to 2013 was a political necessity for the euro area and would please Germany and the ECB, but it was a mistake in economic terms. In addition, the letter asked that primary current expenditures be further reduced by more than 5 percent in real terms in the period 2012–13. It also urged the government to implement the fiscal correction by cutting expenditures rather than by increasing taxes. Draghi was worried about sacrificing capital expenditures more than already envisaged by Tremonti's fiscal plans and recommended that the government act instead on pensions—especially on those regimes allowing workers to retire at an early age and allowing women working in the private sector to retire earlier than men. This recommendation was a slap on the face for Tremonti's political backers in the Northern League. The novelty of the letter was especially striking when compared to the recommendations issued just a few weeks earlier by the European Council on the advice of the European Commission.[5] The Brussels bodies had more political legitimacy than the ECB in such an exercise, but they were more restrained in making only limited and general policy suggestions.[6]

The bank's letter was not a platform for a political government, and Draghi was not its first mover. It was inspired foremost by the urgent need for fiscal action to guarantee the bonds purchased by the ECB. Of course, it represented a politically non-neutral template. In a country with a yawning gap in income distribution, for instance, growth could be dependent also on principles of equity. But that was a second-order consideration for the ECB. The letter was intended as an insurance policy for the ECB to buy Italian bonds. In this sense the ECB letter revealed the poor state of Italian politics but also the limited ability of an unelected, non-democratic body to carry out national policies.

Berlusconi and Tremonti blamed "Europe" for forcing a belt-tightening policy on Italy. At the same time, as if to show that they were still in charge of defending their people, they tried to hide the compelling character of the ECB conditions for help. Just before receiving the letter Berlusconi spoke to the Senate, playing down the fiscal dangers, in one hazardous attempt to deny reality. But the day after his speech, while markets reacted furiously to the inertia in Rome, the Italian media revealed that failure to comply with the ECB conditions would leave the Italian sovereign debt in a precarious position. What Tremonti especially wanted to hide was that without the back-up of the purchases by the ECB (soon to be headed by Draghi, whom he perceived as an arch-rival) Italy would default in a matter of days. In fact, politicians panicked under the urgency to revise the fiscal balances and under the hourly pressure of the markets.

Berlusconi's rhetoric had been torn apart. Tremonti had been downgraded from the savior of the indebted country to the ballast preventing necessary reforms. Tremonti's usual line of defense based on denial—the crisis comes from abroad, other countries are more exposed, our deficit is low—broke into pieces. Ant-like panic and further denial inspired four subsequent and contradictory versions of the same fiscal package required to appease the markets and keep the ECB at bay. The degree of confusion seemed to grow day-by-day, together with an array of proposals advanced and then retired in a matter of hours, even as Italy's interest rate spreads, compared to German bonds, went higher and higher.

*A Drama Inside the ECB*

To understand the difficulty of the ECB position, it is necessary to step one day back. While Italy and markets were panicking, on August 4 after the monthly meeting of the bank's board, Trichet announced in the usual press conference the monetary policy decisions of the ECB. The board had left interest rates unchanged but expanded its non-standard measures by introducing a new six-month full-allotment refinancing operation (in other words, expanding its lending to commercial banks). But the crucial issue was the reopening of the Securities Market

Program (the purchase of government debt). Under the pressure of reporters' questions, Trichet made a cryptic comment: "You will see what we do." In fact at the same time the ECB was intervening on the market, although buying only Portuguese and Irish bonds rather than the stressed Italian or Spanish paper. During an unusually tense news conference, Trichet said the decision on the reactivation of the SMP was not unanimous, but taken with an "overwhelming majority."[7] A few minutes later, the head of the German Bundesbank, Jens Weidmann, said he had opposed the decision to resume the bond purchase program.

The board meeting at the ECB was described as divisive and bitter as ever. A participant remembers a number of statements reflecting the lines of national interests, which was highly unusual for the ECB: "some governors seemed to act as official[s] of their governments." Weidmann and ECB board member Jürgen Stark opposed the reopening of the bond purchase program, as did ECB members from the Netherlands and Luxembourg. Harsh tones were used to describe Italy and Spain, with board members agreeing that those countries had not done enough to put their houses in order. But the German central bankers did not want to contemplate the possibility of even starting to buy Italian bonds because of the size of the Italian debt market. The sterilization of such a market intervention would be difficult and automatically this would create enough money to build up inflationary potential, violating the mission of the ECB to prevent any increase in future price levels. Although inflation was a very remote possibility, the sacred inflation-fighting principle that the ECB had inherited from the Bundesbank would break into pieces.[8]

The reaction of the Germanic component of the ECB—Weidmann and chief economist Jürgen Stark—has to be understood in context. For many observers it was provoked by the interests of a country being called upon to pay for others, but the interests of Stark and Weidmann must be explained in cultural terms, as well. First of all, they had reasons not to trust Berlusconi as a symbol of foreigners' unreliability. Secondly, as the mistake in forcing an interest rates increase in July had demonstrated, they were prey of fundamentalism. Both seemed to be defending their principles by acting in the spirit of Michael Kohlhaas, the fictional hero of Heinrich von Kleist's nineteenth-century novella who set fire to the walls of Leipzig to secure justice. Stark and Weidmann, like Kohlhaas, were not looking for a revolution or a new set of rules. They were not revolutionary spirits, but rebels who wanted to restore the laws and the order that they loved and that inspired their identity without the need for an ideological alternative. In this non-Machiavellian mindset, order proves always fragile and its absence is frightening. If the ethos is a substitute for psychic solidity, the Bundesbanker can substitute the complexity of reality only with his own craving for the absolute. But the absolute purity, in the ambiguity of the historical events, drives inevitably to tragedy, not least for its actors. In a destiny resounding the tragic end in Kohlhaas's life (and even in von Kleist's), Stark announced to his colleagues his decision to resign from the ECB. Ironically, and revealingly, none of his colleagues believed his threat.

The reason why Weidmann was not taken too seriously by the others was that Weidmann had made his career out of mediating between politics and the Bundesbank and was not credible now as a purist. As for Stark, his mistakes in suggesting the interest rate policy of the ECB had corroded his standing inside and outside the bank. Furthermore, he had been the undersecretary in the German finance ministry who had strongly tried to hide Germany's violation of the Stability Pact in the early 2000s and fought against the imposition of sanctions by the European Commission.

On August 7, the ECB approved and released its statement on the bond purchases for Italy and Spain:

> The Governing Council of the European Central Bank (ECB) welcomes the announcements made by the governments of Italy and Spain concerning new measures and reforms in the areas of fiscal and structural policies. The Governing Council considers a decisive and swift implementation by both governments as essential in order to substantially enhance the competitiveness and flexibility of their economies, and to rapidly reduce public deficits.[9]

The ECB board also welcomed the joint French-German statement on renewed commitment to the EFSF changes agreed at the European Council meeting on July 21, especially the facility's new ability to intervene on the secondary market—even though nothing had been said from Paris or Berlin about the central bank's request for increasing the size of the EFSF.

> It equally considers fundamental that governments stand ready to activate the European Financial Stability Facility (EFSF) in the secondary market, on the basis of an ECB analysis recognising the existence of exceptional financial market circumstances and risks to financial stability, once the EFSF is operational. . . . It is on the basis of the above assessments that the ECB will actively implement its Securities Markets Program. This program has been designed to help restoring a better transmission of our monetary policy decisions—taking account of dysfunctional market segments—and therefore to ensure price stability in the euro area.[10]

The Italian government started immediately to prepare a second fiscal package to follow the one approved earlier in July. It would take forty days to complete. The two combined packages produced savings in the budget of around €60 billion between 2012 and 2014 on top of cuts approved in 2010. The total amount of planned savings represented 5 percent of GDP. A balanced budget was also anticipated in 2013. Unfortunately, a disconcerting back-and-forth in the negotiations of the package, carried out in the unique cacophony of Italian politics, highlighted the disconnections between the poor adequacy of political personnel and the gravity of the situation. Nevertheless, on August 8, the ECB started buying Italian and Spanish sovereign bonds. The scale of purchases, at €22 billion in the week ending 12 August, represented the bank's largest intervention to date, albeit small relative to the outstanding stocks of sovereign bonds. Even so, market participants interpreted the intervention as an important signal that the Eurosystem, which many regarded as the most credible buyer at that juncture, would bridge the gap until the EFSF was authorized to purchase debt on the secondary market. Over the following days, Italian and Spanish ten-year benchmark yields declined by over 100 basis points to settle below 5 percent. The ECB thus had initiated a stop-and-go style of intervention aimed both at punishing market exaggerations and political hesitation.

It had never happened that a sovereign country, without even asking for financial assistance, was dictated a policy agenda and not given a chance to discuss it. Only the ineptitude of the Italian ruling class could accept and even publicize the letter of the ECB. But a further humiliation was to come yet. On August 7, the same day of the ECB announcement of the Italian and Spanish bond purchases, Merkel and Sarkozy issued a joint statement which seemed to put sub judice the Italian government. "France and Germany welcome the recent measures announced by Italy and Spain with regard to faster fiscal consolidation and improved competitiveness. Especially the Italian authorities' goal to achieve a balanced budget a year earlier than previously envisaged is of fundamental importance. They stress that complete and speedy implementation of the announced measures is key to restore market confidence."[11]

## The Germanization of France

Just a few days after its start, the ECB's program of buying Italian bonds showed it was not at all the expected panacea. The internal tensions of the ECB had come across to the markets as a sign that the program was conditional and temporary. The ECB, divided by the German protests, avoided communicating any sense that the purchase was unlimited. Investors thought they had to grab the opportunity to unload their bonds until there was a buyer of last resort. The pressure of sales made Italian yields rise instead of climbing down.

The degree of uncertainty introduced by Italy's sudden entrance into the circle of heavily stressed countries proved, unfortunately, too severe to be absorbed. Sovereign strains spilled into those parts of the euro area banking system perceived to be heavily exposed to the peripheral countries, or to have a greater reliance on dollar or short-term funding, or to have an insufficient capital base. France was the first target of speculations. It was heavily involved in Italy's banking system and sovereign debt, and the capital cushions of its banks raised concerns. At the end of 2010, French banks carried $392.6 billion in Italian government and private debt, according to data from the Bank for International Settlements. Markets began putting pressure not just on banks in Italy and Spain, but then on those in Belgium and France, and later on banks across the entire continent, including those headquartered in the Nordic countries. Bank equity values plunged as asset managers reportedly lowered their overall allocations of bank equity as an asset class.[12] The sharp declines in bank equity prices prompted U.S. money funds to further reduce lending to European banks, leading to higher dollar funding costs for these banks and a widening of the dollar-euro basis spread. As a consequence, bank funding costs increased and cast new shadows on the economy. Again, the problem was particularly acute for France. Since 2002 trends in credit growth and nominal GDP showed that an increase in leverage was a striking feature of the French economy, especially when compared with the situation prior to introduction of the euro. French economic activity had become more reliant on the availability of credit than in other euro area economies. As a result, reduced credit availability was likely to have a negative impact on French GDP.

So it was the turn of France to come into the line of fire. The ten-year spread of French over German bonds rose from 35 basis points at the end of May to 89 basis points on August 8. These moves tested France's AAA rating following the U.S. credit rating downgrade, as investors fretted about France's structural deficit, low growth rate, and potential contingent liabilities to the EFSF in the event of a sovereign default by Italy or Spain. Markets started to wonder whether Paris could support Berlin without accumulating too much debt itself. President Sarkozy called an emergency meeting with key ministers to discuss the market situation and growing speculation that France's triple-A rating could be at risk. The statement released after the meeting confirmed France's policy commitment toward fiscal discipline. A cabinet meeting was scheduled for August 24 to decide on the new fiscal measures for the 2012 budget, a month earlier than the normal end-of-September schedule. Sarkozy also said the government wanted to include in the constitution a balanced-budget rule—similar to what Germany had recently done.

A shock arrived with the latest data on economic growth, especially in Germany and France. The economies of the two largest countries came to an abrupt halt in the second quarter of 2011, and growth forecasts had to be revised downward throughout the euro area. The deceleration in GDP growth was driven mainly by much tighter fiscal policy and financial conditions in response to the euro area debt crisis. Once France was considered to be in the same critical group as Italy and Spain, the crisis had a different dimension. These three countries together accounted for 50 percent of the GDP of the euro area, in contrast to only 6.2 percent for the aggregate of Greece, Portugal, and Ireland. All of these countries had announced substantial fiscal corrections, but the lack of fiscal coordination in the euro area left no possible counterweight through fiscal expansion by Germany or other countries. A deflationary trap was ready to grind.

As a symptom of fear, funds parked overnight by euro area banks at the ECB's deposit facility grew to €145 billion at the end of the second week of August, compared to an average amount of €25 billion in the previous three months. A fifteen-day ban on short-selling of financial stocks was introduced in France, Italy, Spain, and Belgium to prevent excessive market volatility. The ECB operated its bond purchases under the Securities Markets Program for €22 billion in the second week of August. As usual, the ECB did not provide details of the purchases with regard to the country and duration, but the settlement was the largest since the bank began buying government debt in May 2010. The overall amount of ECB holdings under the program was now €96 billion.[13]

Under such pressure, Sarkozy and Merkel announced, at a press conference in Paris on August 11, that they would meet on August 16, to discuss euro area economic governance. Expectations grew of a major common decision, and all eyes were focused on the possible introduction of eurobonds. However, German finance minister Wolfgang Schäuble clearly rejected that idea in the near term by saying, "I rule out eurobonds for as long as member states conduct their own financial policies and we need different rates of interest in order that there are possible incentives and sanctions to enforce fiscal solidity."[14]

In the eyes of market investors, when Chancellor Merkel joined President Sarkozy at the press conference and also ruled out the launch of eurobonds, the two leaders seemed to have just landed from Mars. Rather then announcing any measures to combat the financial instability in the euro area, they were asking for stricter fiscal discipline, stronger economic governance, and a new financial transactions tax. Instead of putting in more resources to support countries under attack, France and Germany were asking them to tighten their belts even more. Investors, who had seen Europe's response to the prolonged crisis as too little too late, repeatedly expected Berlin to jump ahead of the curve, but were once more frustrated. It appeared clear that the main short-term goal of the meeting was to support France, which had become a target of speculation, by promoting the idea that Paris was on the same political level of Berlin and the destinies of the two countries were intertwined.

The Paris meeting of the two leaders on August 16 provided a less exciting, but still significant, picture of the long-term design that Merkel had in mind. In a letter to European Council president Herman Van Rompuy, the two leaders carefully described a framework for a "new economic government of the euro area." They proposed to strengthen the governance of the euro area through regular meetings of the euro area heads of state and government:

These meetings . . . would in particular check the proper implementation of the Stability and Growth Pact by euro Member States, discuss the problems facing individual Member States of the euro area and take the requisite fundamental decisions on averting crisis. These summits will also assess the evolution of competitiveness in the euro area and define the main orientations of the economic policy in the euro area to promote sustainable growth, foster competitiveness and prevent the build up of imbalances.[15]

Merkel and Sarkozy asked Van Rompuy to take on the job of chairing the Eurosummit for a two-and-a-half-year term. They wanted to reinforce also the Eurogroup and improve the effectiveness and the analytical capacities of the EFSF and the follow-on European Stability Mechanism (ESM).

The new design for the euro area was rather simple: the fiscal positions of member countries must converge and the process will be monitored more closely than in the past by the leaders personally.[16] National ownership of fiscal discipline would be guaranteed by constitutional commitment in all countries, and surveillance will be extended to structural reforms. The rationale was that improving fundamentals would help to restore market confidence and allow countries to fund themselves at reasonable costs in the market.[17] As Merkel and Sarkozy were keen to spell out after their meeting, only at the end of this long and difficult process of structural convergence would the euro area consider the eventual introduction of common guarantees and specifically of eurobonds. The message, to its core, was a sort of "Germanization" of the other economies and of the euro area: fiscal austerity and structural reforms.

The success of these developments hung on a learning process by national legislators. Correspondingly, the management of the euro area would not respond to the supranational spirit of the European Union, but to intergovernmental negotiations. Providing a joint guarantee for national debts implies, for each of the participating countries, giving partners access to their own taxpayers. The traditional bedrock of democracies is the correspondence between taxation and representation, but the euro area was far from any system of democratic polity, and it was not imaginable that taxpayers in some countries—one country in particular—might be required to stand in for defaulting borrowers in all the rest of the euro area without understanding the policies of the other countries and even, in extremes cases, dictating the policies that debtors had to follow. In such an extreme configuration, a political hierarchy would be borne out of financial power, hardly a recipe for shared democratic values. In this financial hierarchy the degree of integration was to be dictated by the creditor countries that had political clout. Revealingly, on the same day of the meeting in Paris, Finland struck a deal with Greece compelling Athens to lend back cash collateral on the Finnish contribution to the Greek bailout package.[18]

A confirmation of Merkel's strategy came from the German Constitutional Court, which on September 7 published its ruling about the legitimacy of the Greek bailout. In a long and profound text, the Karlsruhe judges highlighted the centrality of national parliaments in the European policies. A core feature of the parliamentarian sphere of competence was the budget policy, which could not be alienated. The court set de facto limits to the maneuvering room of the German government.

> As representatives of the people, elected Members of Parliament must preserve, even in a system of intergovernmental governance, the control on fundamental budget-policy decisions . . . on this backdrop the German Parliament cannot transfer to other actors its responsibilities on the budget through indefinite budgetary empowerments. In particular, no financial mechanism can be emplaced, not even by law, which could incur substantial budget expenses through decisions taken with nontransparent procedures without a preliminary constitutive agreement.[19]

According to the court, no treaty-based mechanisms can be grounded on the extension of guarantees emanating from "the voluntary decisions of other states," especially in a case when the consequences are hardly measurable. For each decision (for example, a decision to support aid to another country), a preliminary vote of the parliament is required. The limit for assuming or guaranteeing the obligations of other countries must preserve the maneuvering room of the German budget policy. In the case of Greece, the losses could reach, according to the court, around €170 billion, a sum that would still not drain all the yearly financial resources of the German budget. Discriminating on the basis of the potential losses for the German budget, the court effectively cut off aid for larger countries like Spain, Italy, or France.

But the really crucial remark of the court regarded the "voluntary decisions of other states." In order to legitimate the intervention of the Berlin government in support of other states, the financial assistance could not be the result of a problem caused by the discretionary fiscal policy of the assisted country. In other words, in order to qualify for future assistance, euro area countries had to give up any margin of discretion in their fiscal policy to avoid that Germany's help would be caused by voluntary choices of other peoples, even if the decision of assisting the ailing country would be taken in the European institutions. Hence the need to impose on all the euro area countries automatic sanctions and the strictest fiscal rules. This was exactly what Merkel would pursue in the following weeks.

In the simplest terms, the ruling of the court allowed Germany to participate in the bailout of Greece but prevented the country from being part of any permanent mechanism—potentially putting in danger both the ESM and any eurobonds. Once more, action in the crisis was dictated by fears of the judges of

Karlsruhe. The constraints were so exaggerated that an enlightening judgment about the stance of the court came from Finance Minister Schäuble:

> We should not cling to the old regulatory-monopoly of the national State of the nineteenth century. This has been protracted ad absurdum. Obviously it is right, as the Court says, that the European integration one day has to reach a limit, and at that point one needs to consider a new Constitution. But at the present time the problem is to make Europe stronger and more efficient through the limited transfer of competences.[20]

## Policy of Uncertainty

In the European political vacuum, national strategies were noncooperative and even gravely dysfunctional. So Berlusconi's moral hazard was countered by another uncooperative political strategy on the part of Germany. What took shape in Berlin was a fully fledged strategy that had been developing behind the scenes ever since the first signs of the crisis. On the one hand, the Constitutional Court reduced the maneuvering room of the government and threatened to force the exit of Germany from the European monetary union unless all other states obeyed its diktat. On the other hand, in the absence of a political authority entitled to regulate the behavior of the less fiscally solid countries, the only solution—in particular according to the Bundesbank—was to not completely remove the risk of default and instead to rely on financial markets imposing appropriate fiscal behaviors. Moreover, to leverage on the markets, it was necessary that the crisis resolution mechanisms not be fully implemented. For example, the European Central Bank had helped countries against the risk of default, but not completely, and leaving interest rates at punitive levels was a strong spur to improving the public budgets. Despite the interventions of the ECB, for example, the Italian ten-year bonds had remained between 5 and 6 percent. The ECB representatives of Germany, the Netherlands, Luxembourg, and other countries practiced daily opposition to the limitless purchase of Spanish and Italian securities. The ultimate expression of this resistance was the resignation announced September 9 by Jürgen Stark, a German member of the board of the bank. Stark gave a resounding demonstration of the political constraints that limited the ECB in the purchase of euro area government bonds.

Much the same was happening with the European Financial Stability Facility (EFSF), which had made four loans in 2011, two to Portugal and two to Ireland, but was not yet strong enough to assume the role of purchasing government bonds in massive amounts, as the ECB was doing. Berlin resisted the necessary expansion of the EFSF and delayed parliamentary approval of decisions agreed with the euro zone partners on July 21. Even if approved, however, it was clear that the funds available to the EFSF were not sufficient to solve a liquidity crisis in a large country (such as Italy or France) and avoid it turning into a solvency crisis. Proposals had been put forward for increasing the capacity of the EFSF, for instance by allowing it to borrow at the ECB or to offer loans with a leverage in relation to its equity. But once again the proposals were vetoed by the creditor countries.

Finally, the eurobonds were kept as a possibility but only after all countries had brought their fiscal policies into line, at which point they were likely to be of limited value. The opposition to the eurobonds was exactly dictated by the German interest in maintaining differences in the levels of interest rates as an effective form of discipline. None of the instruments for the resolution of the crisis—the ECB, the EFSF, or the eurobonds—was in fact entirely credible or even fully available. What many dismissed as myopia or selfishness was instead a real strategy. Crisis resolution mechanisms were left incomplete in order to leave it to the markets to impose discipline where political coercion was not possible or when majority voting in Brussels failed to produce the prevalence of rigorous policies.

The strategy needed another pillar: the reiteration of the political commitment to the euro and to Europe. The existence of such an institutional horizon is essential for several reasons. It can dispel the doubts about the ultimate sustainability of the monetary union and vanquish pessimism during the troubled times ahead; it can provide incentives for countries faced with duress in the transition period; it can help investors to recover credibility and make visible the advantage of betting on the solidity of the euro area; it can make it tolerable for donor countries to consider their help as a transitory effort and not a waste of money; and finally it will give a new shape to the future of Europe. Since the summer of 2011 Merkel had to repeat every week her commitment to Europe and to the defense of the common currency: "If the euro fails, Europe fails," Merkel said as a mantra. The ultimate goal had to be preserved and gilded with promises of further integration, eurobonds, and common policies. That was a crucial element of the strategy: Once all countries had adopted balanced budgets and constitutional restraints to guarantee future fiscal prudence, then all the problems about a "Transferunion" would shrink dramatically. The total amount of debt in the euro zone would decline and so would interests rates. Finding fiscal room to deal with the problems of aging societies, or even for common investments, would become easier and possible.

On the other hand, and in the troubled short term, Berlin kept on leaving the rescue of affected countries constantly in doubt. Unfortunately, this "policy of uncertainty" only works in specific conditions: if it is short, if macroeconomic conditions are normal, and if markets are working very well. Starting with the second quarter of 2011, the long uncertainty about the euro area became ingrained into the real European economy. Even the economies of Germany and France were faltering. The German economy, where exports account for 50 percent of GDP, was affected by the slowdown of the euro area. But having placed all its cards on a strategy of self-proclaimed virtue—austerity, fiscal rigor, internal devaluation, automatic sanctions in a rule-based system of economic governance, and even constitutional commitments to balanced budgets for all the euro area— Germany could not now break ranks and reflate its economy, even if the goal was to benefit the whole euro area. In a global scenario plagued by pessimistic predictions for growth, uncertainty was coming to infect even Germany and, most surprisingly, the credit default swaps on its debt rose significantly.[21]

There were indeed several weak flanks in the strategy of uncertainty, and they all came to fruition in September 2011. Austerity policy was failing in the case of Greece, and at the aggregate euro area level it was even triggering a renewed recession. Secondly, the basic tenet of the policy of uncertainty was that markets work well, so they should be allowed to do their job and enforce discipline and stability. But evidence pointed to the contrary. Furthermore, could the ECB be left to act alone, or must governments take on the fiscal tasks? And finally, were the governments responding correctly, or were they running astray in the loose institutional framework of intergovernmental relations?

### An Elephant on the Bridge

The "policy of uncertainty" was particularly dangerous because Greece demonstrated that the European leaders were not dealing with hypothetical risks. The Greek problem remained an unsteady elephant on the unsteady bridge between austerity and the long term commitment to the euro. During the summer, Athens' central government budget data indicated that the deficit had resumed widening since the beginning of the year due to weakness in fiscal revenues as well as an increase in primary spending. As a result, in 2011 the primary deficit—which was the most important quantitative indicator in the EU/IMF aid program— clearly was growing, rather than shrinking. Between January and August the deficit increased by 20 percent in nominal terms. So, as of September, the year-end deficit was expected to come close to 9 percent of GDP, only slightly lower than in 2010, when the government had projected that the deficit would drop from €24.1 billion to €17.1 billion. GDP was expected to contract by 5 percent. Even the representatives from the EU-ECB-IMF troika were shocked by the lack of results achieved by the Greek fiscal officials. Between August and September they left Athens in a gesture that was interpreted as a sign of despair about the delays of the Greek government.

Many observers saw themselves proven right for having said that the decision in 2010 not to organize an orderly default for Greece—an alternative strongly opposed by the ECB—was a major mistake that had finally backfired. Rather than achieving the goal of preventing contagion from spreading to the rest of Europe, uncertainty about Greece produced a permanent heightened degree of risk aversion and market turbulence across the whole European financial system. The uncertainty about the inevitable haircuts on Greece then extended to the rest of the periphery. Even a low probability of a default was enough that other countries saw their bond rate spreads follow those of Greece. If the markets were contemplating a 20 percent haircut on Greece, then a 10 percent annual risk of default on Italian and Spanish bonds was such that the spreads climbed by 200 basis points. But if the haircut on Greece was 50–60 percent, the markets demanded an increased spread for Italy or Spain of 500–600 basis points.

For that reason, at their meeting on July 21, the leaders of the euro area had stressed extensively that the case of Greece was special and that the methods used to resolve its crisis would not be repeated elsewhere. This was crucial for the management of the crisis. But the markets never seemed to believe this statement that Greece was a one-time event. The consequence of the 2010 Deauville statement on private sector involvement was that every sovereign bond issued in the euro area carried an explicit clause of default that made private investors fear for their money and ask for an additional risk premium. Once the threat of investor losses became attached to the Greek case, it had become all too real for everyone else in the euro zone. In early September 2011, the credit default swaps on sovereign debt—which, by and large, measure the insurance cost against credit risk on sovereign bonds—of Italy and Spain were higher than those of Egypt, Lebanon, Vietnam, and Romania. Six euro area countries were regarded as among the twenty riskiest countries worldwide. Evidently, there was a problem between the functioning of the markets and the credibility of the political commitment of the leaders of the euro.[22]

## Markets Are Not Perfect

Blaming the markets is often a cheap trick, but in many circumstances markets do not work as perfectly as the prevalent economic theory often assumed before the crises of 2008 and even afterward. Unfortunately, investors are subject to crises of confidence and self-fulfilling dynamics—traits that can worsen the instability and push prices out of line with fundamentals. This seems to have been particularly true in the unique case of the European monetary union. The euro area is, in fact, the only area in the world where monetary and fiscal institutions are completely separate, in which the fiscal authorities cannot count on the monetary authority, not only to prevent a solvency problem but also a liquidity problem. On the one hand, such a separation is very healthy because it pushes the fiscal authorities to take the necessary measures to ensure solvency. The framework works well only to the extent that markets can properly distinguish long-term solvency problems from shorter-term liquidity problems. But when uncertainty becomes extreme, or contagion dynamics set in, market participants are no longer able to properly assess the risks.

Paradoxically, the more a monetary union is successful, that is, the more the financial systems are integrated and the economies become interdependent, the more single risks tend to turn systemic and are therefore difficult to assess. Contagion makes risk-aversion indiscriminate among the fundamentals of different countries. A prolonged liquidity problem in such circumstances can easily degenerate into a solvency risk through self-fulfilling speculative trends and through the balance sheets of banks.[23] In the special institutional framework of the euro area, a single monetary policy makes it difficult to spot and address liquidity problems within individual countries, although they can rapidly affect banks throughout the area. Once a liquidity problem results in visibly higher interest rates—and the cost of serving debt—it turns into a solvency problem for the affected country. In a monetary union, national monetary policy obviously is not available to widen the money supply and compensate for the liquidity shortage, so interest rates remain high and cause grievance for the national banks that have large holdings of sovereign bonds. The cost of credit increases, and credit availability goes down the drain. The economy stalls and the debt-to-GDP ratio automatically goes through the roof. Once a solvency problem sets in, restrictive national fiscal policies do not suffice to dispel a risk that has instantly turned systemic, thus putting in doubt the sustainability of the entire monetary union. In such a framework, even countries like Italy or Spain that are solvent—that is, able and willing to generate a primary surplus to stabilize and reduce the debt-to-GDP ratio—can lose the confidence of the markets and face severe difficulties in refinancing themselves, thereby shifting from what economists call a "good equilibrium" to a bad one.

Italy was a blatant example. For all the absurdity of the Italian political scene in 2011, Italy had been ruled for two decades by the external discipline of the process of monetary integration and by the consensus mirroring this discipline in the country's public opinion. Between 1996 and 2008, the accumulated primary surpluses posted by Italy had been equivalent to €500 billion, that is, more than the sum of the primary surpluses in Germany, France, and Spain together. Italy's primary surplus (the budget surplus net of the interest paid on the debt) in 2012 was expected to be at +2.0 percent of GDP: higher than in Germany (1.4 percent) and much higher than in France, where it remained in negative territory (–2.4 percent). In such circumstances, it was difficult to claim that Italy was not willing and able to carry out a sustainable fiscal policy. Italy's primary surplus was projected to reach 5.5 percent in 2014, in line with former surplus during the 1990s in the run-up to the euro.[24]

Nevertheless, in a matter of two months the yields on the ten-year fixed-rate bonds —the reference security for the Italian public debt—had doubled even without a radical change in the economic scenario. Economic growth was revised downwards for the Italian economy during August, but that had not affected the bottom line of the fiscal deficit because the Italian government, although clumsy, had introduced new fiscal corrections and even anticipated attaining a balanced budget within two years. The ECB estimated that contagion effects from the three countries then under EU assistance (Greece, Ireland, and Portugal) accounted for about 37 percent of the variability observed in the Italian credit default swap (CDS) spread. After July 2011, however, the observed deterioration in Italian and Spanish CDS markets, a senior ECB official said, "can be explained to a large extent by contagion effects from the three program countries."[25] The contagion was thereafter transmitted through the banking channels and through the technical use of the Italian fixed-rate government bond, as an alternative to the German Bund for investors in the euro area. A correlation also appeared between the CDS spreads of Greece, Portugal, Ireland, Spain, and Italy and those of the two largest French banks, Crédit Agricole and Société Generale, whose spreads doubled from early July up to mid-August.

Unfortunately, market dynamics can produce political inconsistencies because reacting in a timely fashion to counteract sudden gyrations of the markets is very demanding for policymaking. Confronted with market demands for immediate fiscal corrections, and with little time to react, a government almost has only one immediate option, that of raising taxes. Cutting expenditures can be a long and politically difficult process. But raising taxes has an impact on disposable income and on the level of domestic demand, thereby lowering the GDP. When Italy had to deliver a second version of its fiscal correction to contain the market pressure in September, its €60 billion budget improvement was highly skewed toward revenues: 73 percent of the package, giving Italy the second highest tax burden (after Belgium) in the euro area. The excess of fiscal pressure was likely to raise automatically the debt-to-GDP ratio. In fact, the estimated impact on the GDP of the fiscal package was −0.7 percent. Exactly the same depressive effects had occurred in the 1990s, when Italy's potential growth fell to minimal levels. So the interaction between short-term demands from markets and short-breathed policymaking can be self-defeating.

## ECB as Non-Elected Political Agent

After one accepts that the interaction between national politics and markets works far from perfectly; that markets, especially, may not be able to self-correct and restore conditions in line with the fundamentals; and that there is a constant feedback loop between the banking system and sovereign debt, then the option of interfering with the markets at the European level becomes a good policy.

In August the widespread sovereign risk had spilled over to the banking system. Banks that held substantial amounts of more risky and volatile sovereign debt faced strains in the markets. In fact, the equity market capitalization of EU banks had declined by more than 40 percent in one year. Instability spread from weaker euro area sovereigns to institutions in other countries where banks had high exposure in cross-border asset holdings or were lending to banks that held risky sovereigns. By August 2011 nearly half of the €6.5 trillion stock of government debt issued by euro area governments was showing signs of heightened credit risk. A coordinated policy response to increase the credibility of the euro as a whole was vital, and the ECB was still the only actor that could intervene.

In September the ECB was in serious embarrassment because its interventions on the sovereign debt markets had not been accompanied by the euro zone governments having made adequate progress in expanding the EFSF and making it operative on the government bonds market. The framework of the euro zone's economic governance was also considered too lax and too "political": its mechanism for imposing sanctions against laggard countries lacked automatic procedures, and it lacked the "independent fiscal agencies" at both the national and at European level that could impose controls and sanctions to the governments.[26]

More important, the slow response of the Italian government to the requests of the Trichet-Draghi letter in July confirmed that the ECB was merely venting steam from the situation and policymakers felt safer to slow down their reforming efforts at the national and European levels. This was a typical case of moral hazard. With its decision to support the Italian debt issue, the ECB found itself in the awkward position of not having other effective leverage on Italy apart from letting the Italian interest rate spread widen whenever the bank thought the government was not delivering. But even this market weapon could not be taken to the limit because almost 50 percent of the €1.9 trillion Italian debt was in the hands of non-Italian investors, thus producing another external factor with severe consequences on financial stability in the euro area as a whole. Inside the ECB, a rift opened between those who thought that the bank could actually become the real European Monetary Fund and those closer to the German vision, Jürgen Stark in the first place, who thought that any such development would risk contaminating the autonomy of the institution, a quality that was necessary in defending monetary stability.

Bundesbank president Jens Weidmann expressed the German line connecting the position of his bank, of the chancellor, and of the Constitutional Court:

> By supporting individual member states via the central bank balance sheet, monetary policy would redistribute financial burdens between the taxpayers of the different countries. If assistance for individual countries is considered essential for exceptional and overriding reasons, such as a threat to financial stability, it must generally be provided through fiscal policy, which is the responsibility of national governments and parliaments. The most recent ruling by Germany's Federal Constitutional Count was probably based on this reasoning.[27]

The ECB evidently could tolerate being a substitute for the governments for only a limited period of time. Behind the scenes, the unofficial deadline was the end of October. By then, the euro group was expected to operate through the EFSF. But the signals were not encouraging. The European Council on March 11 had already raised the resources to an effective amount of €440 billion, later to be taken to €500 billion once the ESM began to operate. On July 21 the leaders agreed to expand the EFSF's operational powers and approved its purchase of government bonds in the secondary market. However, the size and governance of the EFSF/ESM were inadequate to support the euro area now that contagion had spread.

A number of proposals had been discussed for how to increase the financial resources. Economists Daniel Gros and Thomas Meyer proposed to convert the ESFS into a bank, which could use its capital as a leverage and thus increase its resources by a factor of three.[28] Others, including U.S. Treasury secretary Timothy Geithner, suggested as a model the Federal Reserve Bank's Term Asset-Backed Securities Loan Facilities. Berlin instead adopted a proposal from Paul Achleitner, the financial director of Allianz (a major insurance company based in Munich), to use the available funds to insure the risk of the loans, granting a refund of 20 percent of the bonds in case of a restructuring; this would enhance the firepower of the EFSF by a factor of five. Other proposals dealt with other forms of leverage, but none of them provided a convincing solution.

## "The Spirits I Called"

Evidently, the EFSF could be endowed with more resources only if Germany agreed to do it. Apart from the obvious financial reasons for avoiding potential losses by German taxpayers, Chancellor Merkel had to reckon with the Bundesbank's opposition to using the EFSF/ESM as an all-powerful weapon against contagion or market misrepresentations. The Bundesbank's opposition especially denoted a determination to avoid moral hazard and to maintain a degree of uncertainty about the bailouts, thus allowing markets to spur the recipient countries to restore fiscal order in their budgets. "It is crucial to ensure that the specific design of the support mechanisms does not discard key basic principles—such as subsidiarity, independent national responsibility for fiscal policy and the no bail-out principle, and thus also the disciplining function of the capital markets—under the smokescreen of financial stability," the head of the Bundesbank said in mid-September.[29] Governments of other creditor countries agreed with that strategy. In September 2011, for instance, Greece was left hanging in uncertainty about whether it would receive enough money to avoid a default. The same uncertainty hung on whether the EFSF would be endowed with the level of resources it would need to defend larger countries. Uncertainty was still the name of the game, but it was coming close to a practice of waterboarding with the weaker countries.

As explained earlier, the strategy was two-pronged. On the one hand, Germany remained committed firmly to the "political project" of the euro and of the euro area. Chancellor Merkel ruled out the break-up of the currency by saying that it would open the way to the end of Europe. No one therefore should default openly—Greece had already started a default by stealth, as we have seen—and none would be forced or allowed to leave the euro area. On the other hand Berlin claimed that the markets, for all their imperfections, were to remain the driving force of fiscal discipline. No political institution had the power and the legitimacy by now to prevail on the sovereignty of national countries. Only markets offered enough leverage to impose policy choices. However, the Bundesbank was critical of key elements of the design of the crisis resolution mechanism, the EFSF and the ESM. In the view of the bank's leaders, the existing legal framework was based on countries bearing responsibility for their own finances. The looser credit conditions approved by the European Council on July 21 and the planned secondary market purchases by the EFSF would reduce the incentives for countries receiving assistance to take the necessary steps to return as rapidly as possible to sounder public finances. As Weidmann explained it: "A crisis management mechanism . . . should contain three key elements: attaching strict economic and fiscal policy conditions to assistance, ensuring appropriate interest rate premiums and a credible involvement of private investors in the event of a default." Weidmann also articulated an uncompromising version of the argument that markets should be used to enforce policy discipline:

> Regarding the disciplining of national fiscal policy through the capital markets, the rules for monetary union should be adjusted so that, when a euro-area country looks likely to experience difficulties, private creditors cannot rapidly shift their liability to the taxpayers of the countries providing assistance. The introduction of collective action clauses (CACs) alone, scheduled to start in 2013 within the framework of the ESM, is highly unlikely to be sufficient to achieve this objective. The approach of adding a trigger clause to the terms and conditions of bonds stipulating that maturities will be automatically extended for a fixed period of time (such as three years) in the event of the ESM granting assistance to the country in question, as proposed by the Bundesbank, should therefore be supported.[30]

Triggering market fears was a very dangerous game for a policymaker, including a central banker, to be playing. But using public statements to enhance the nervousness of the markets was almost suicidal. Simple statistical observations revealed that since 2010, financial markets were driven more than ever before by the public statements of German officials. This trend, as much as anything else, revealed the evolving prominence of Berlin in European politics, a prominence derived primarily from Germany's financial strength. Especially in the peripheral countries, the influence of domestic policymakers had been constantly declining since the introduction of the euro—a symptom of the interdependency of the economies. But after the crisis of sovereign debt took hold, the pronunciations of German policymakers on the interest rate spreads in the euro area had grown disproportionately. The paradox was that destabilizing statements had to be followed by stabilizing interventions from the ECB. Those interventions were a source of concern for German officials who, as a consequence, issued further destabilizing remarks in a feedback loop.

This destabilizing cycle of rhetoric could become unsustainable, and the Bundesbank position looked increasingly similar to that of Goethe's "Sorcerer's Apprentice": calling markets into life—Die Geister die ich rief—to take on the role that national politics was not able to address, but then markets rapidly slipped out of control, like the brooms carrying ever more water into the Sorcerer's laboratory. Once an attempt was made to stop the markets—with the threat of creditor losses (PSI)—they multiplied and carried ever more water until the Apprentice was overwhelmed and powerless. Merkel herself clearly recognized that she and other policymakers could not always control the relentless pressures of the markets. At the end of September she met in Berlin with Pope Benedict XVI. "We spoke about the financial markets and the fact that politicians should have the power to make policy for the people, and not be driven by the markets," Merkel said after the talks. "This is a very, very big task in today's time of globalization."[31]

### Rome: Free Ride the ECB

The interventions of the ECB let some steam off the euro area crisis but also bought time for the Italian government, some of which went partially wasted. Due to the loss of credibility of the government, the Italian fiscal response to the market pressures since July seemed to be little more than a string of delays. In July the first fiscal package was interpreted as an astute shift of the fiscal adjustment to a future legislature; then Berlusconi did not comply with the first requests of the ECB to correct the budget law. In four different chaotic steps during August and September, Rome tried to comply with the ECB's requests as outlined in the letter. In fact, the government did draw up a budget correction and got approval by the Parliament, but the quality of intervention did not correspond to what the ECB had requested. It took five increasingly confused weeks to convert into law on September 14 the decree (decreto legge) that Berlusconi had issued on August 7. The August package had followed a previous package approved in July (decree 98/2011 converted in law 111 on July 15). The two packages cut the net borrowing requirements of the government by a cumulative 3.5 percent of GDP (€59.8 billion) for the period 2011–14 on top of former measures.[32] Tremonti planned to bring the Italian deficit-to-GDP ratio to 3.9 percent in 2011, 1.6 percent in 2012, and –0.1 percent in 2013.

Asking for this much of a brutal fiscal adjustment was not justified from a macroeconomic point of view. However, the assessments by the ECB, the Banca d'Italia, and the European Commission were that the Italian government in August had used a higher-than-reasonable estimate of future growth, and by doing that, it would overestimate the fiscal revenues and therefore would not reach the balanced budget until 2014, at the earliest. Of the nominal €60 billion in proposed budget savings, at least €20 billion was doubtful. A reform of pensions was blocked by one party of the governing coalition (the Northern League). The only reform approved was a rise in the retirement age for women, but its effects would be postponed until after 2015. Behind the scenes, negotiations between the European institutions and the Italian government focused criticism on the incapacity of the government to re-launch the growth. No growth-enhancing reform had been implemented. The opening of "closed-shop" professions was ruled out by a coalition of defenders of the status quo in the Parliament. In order to reform the local governments, the Berlusconi government decided to initiate a revision of the constitution, a step likely to require one year to be completed. The center-right government did comply with the changes requested by the ECB to weaken collective bargaining rights, demonstrating once again that the ruling political majority—whether of the left or the right—tends to approve measures that punish the constituencies supporting the minority while protecting their own constituencies. But the measures on the labor market were not accompanied by the safety net called for by the ECB. Interestingly this asymmetric policy of "partisan protectionism," as far as policy changes are concerned, proved stronger than the classical ideological cleavage on taxation. Against the advice of the ECB, the center-right government approved a fiscal correction based primarily (about 73 percent of the whole) on more taxes. Even so, the fiscal correction had not followed the overall track set by the ECB. The government's goal for the budget deficit in 2012 was 1.6 percent, rather than the requested 1 percent (along with the enforcement of a safeguard clause that compensated automatically for the eventual fiscal slippages). However, even this goal was uncertain because it was based on too large and indiscriminate cuts on tax allowances. At the ECB headquarters, an alarm bell rang loudly.

In one of his last public speeches as governor of Banca d'Italia, before assuming his new post as president of the ECB, Mario Draghi criticized Italian policymakers:

> We must act quickly. Too much time has already been wasted. Rate increases of interest in the size of those that occurred in the last three months, if protracted, would result to thwart in no small part the

measures approved by the decrees converted into law in September, with a further possible negative effect on the cost of debt, in a spiral that could be unmanageable.[33]

There should have been serious macroeconomic reasons to consider the fiscal adjustment imposed on Italy as being already excessive. But the credibility problem of the government was stronger than any other consideration. So the ECB Council was summoned to consider sending a second letter to Berlusconi warning him against falling short of the requested measures. The idea of a quick fix of political flaws that had lasted for decades was unrealistic, but the Italian government was still in denial. The European Council was ineffective in forcing discipline onto one of its members. In such a context, the ECB as a nonelected body had reached the political limits of its ability to act. The letter was never sent.

# 20

## Solution or Dissolution:
## Political Union or the End of the Euro

### *The Looming Breakup of the Euro and a World Recession*

At the beginning of October 2011 a vicious circle seemed to be leading the euro area toward breaking up. The banks' fears had grown since the application of PSI (the so-called haircut of 21 cents for each euro the banks owned in Greek sovereign bonds). In September the EU-ECB-IMF troika alerted the euro zone authorities that, due to the worsening economic conditions and increasing Greek public debt, the "haircut" had to be much higher, around 50 to 60 percent of the debt in the hands of private investors.[1]

Once more, investors saw the Greek model as suggesting what could happen to the Italian and Spanish securities that burdened the banks' portfolios. As noted in chapter 19, simply applying a 10 percent annual probability of default to Italian and Spanish bonds, a 20 percent haircut implies an interest rate spread of 200 points, but a 50–60 percent haircut increases the spread to 500–600 points, levels that make public debts unsustainable. Once again, the euro area interbank market practically stopped functioning because every bank doubted the stability of its counterparts. The credit crunch that followed made it more difficult and costly for firms to fund their activities, especially in the weaker countries where interest rates jumped the highest. Fearing for their jobs and their futures, families also slashed their demands for loans to buy houses. In October the economy of the euro area was close to falling into a recession. Finally, the decline in growth further jeopardized the sustainability of public debts, leading to renewed calls for additional restrictive policies. The pattern resembled closely the debt-deflation spiral described by the American economist Irving Fisher after the Wall Street crisis of 1929.[2]

The consequences of this latest episode of the euro crisis were felt throughout the world. From September 2011, the weakening outlook for growth became the main driver of global asset prices. World stock prices closely tracked the value of the euro.[3] Greek and Portuguese bond yields rose further, reflecting those countries' difficulties in meeting fiscal targets with their economies mired in recession. Ratings downgrades and political uncertainty also pushed higher yields on Spanish and Italian debt. In October fears of default hit Italy.[4] With France exposed to Italy's risk, half of the euro area turned unstable, putting the whole world economy at risk.[5] The feedback loop expanded on a global scale. The ten largest prime money market funds cut back their European bank holdings by $79 billion between the end of May and the end of July, and by 97 percent vis-à-vis banks from Italy and Spain.[6] In July alone, banks in Italy had to double their borrowing from the European Central Bank to €80 billion, and they borrowed even more in August.[7] Several major French banks faced problems in funding over the short term, and finally the risk of major banking failures materialized when in September Dexia, the Franco-Belgian bank, announced it needed state intervention to face the risks hidden in its portfolios. The bank was hugely exposed to Greek and Italian risks for an amount more than double its capital. In the extreme case of a 50 percent haircut on the debts it held in those countries, the bank would see its capital canceled. The alarm was unmistakable. The ninety European banks subjected to stress tests by European authorities had an estimated exposure to the five countries of concern (Greece, Ireland, Italy, Portugal, and Spain) totaling almost €600 billion.[8] Dexia had been among the ten best-classified institutions in the stress test of July, showing that the danger hidden in the interaction between banks and debtor countries was still unresolved.[9]

Since July the markets had been assessing the value of banks on the basis of the risks of their sovereign debt exposures. The IMF had put enormous pressure on the European banks by estimating an oversized need for capital. Since August even the new IMF managing director—and former French finance minister— Christine Lagarde had put the European banks on trial, saying they "need urgent recapitalization."[10] To bring clarity to the issue, the European Banking Authority—one of the three new financial authorities recently introduced in the overhaul of European financial surveillance—decided that the only consistent policy response was to require the banks to adopt the accounting method that the markets liked: a valuation of the sovereign paper at current market value, rather than the usual historical value.[11] The banking authority estimated the "mark to market" accounting method would require banks in the euro area to increase their capital by a cumulative €115 billion to reflect their potential losses. Although the capital need was much lower than the one estimated by the IMF, the signal was badly received by the market.

Banks throughout the euro area started to sell the stressed public bonds, which they otherwise would have held on their books to maturity. However, banks in the ailing countries—holding larger quantities of their governments' bonds, suddenly priced lower than the others—especially needed to increase capital or reduce their assets, loans, and credit to keep the ratio between capital and assets at the desired level. By cutting credit, the banks again hampered overall growth, further worsening the sovereign risks. The sell-off of sovereign bonds of the peripheral countries by banks in the "core" countries was particularly intense because those banks were still sitting on heaps of toxic assets that they had kept on their books since 2007.[12] Unable to sell the toxic assets, the banks instead unloaded government bonds to limit their risks.[13]

## Washington Feels the Pain

Throughout the second half of 2011, Europe was at the epicenter of global criticism for destabilizing the whole world's economy. Fears of contagion from Europe were infecting the United States, where banks, struggling to cope with the new regulation on housing mortgages, led the S&P 500 into bear-market territory at the beginning of October. The parallel weaknesses in Europe and the United States finally hit the German economy, whose growth estimates for 2012 slumped from 2.4 percent to 0.8 percent.[14]

During the September 23–25 meetings of International Monetary Fund in Washington, European governments had to take stock of the fact that they were completely isolated.[15] World leaders demanded that Germany agree to approve larger funding of the European Financial Stability Facility (EFSF), and the follow-on European Stability Mechanism (ESM), to contain market panic, support the banking systems, and defend the solvent countries of the euro area. Apparently aiming also to divert domestic critics, the voices of U.S. officials grew louder in openly blaming Europe for the uncertain state of the U.S. economy. Washington started piling pressure on European leaders to hammer out a solution to the debt crisis before it slipped out of control. U.S. Treasury secretary Timothy Geithner said the threats of cascading default, bank runs, and catastrophic risk had to be taken off the table. "European governments should work alongside the European Central Bank to demonstrate an unequivocal commitment to ensure sovereigns with sound fiscal policies have affordable financing, and to ensure that European banks have recourse to adequate capital and funding," he said. "Decisions cannot wait until the crisis gets more severe."[16] On September 27, President Obama noted that Europe was scaring the world with its inaction.

Given its status as the largest shareholder, the United States could find in the IMF an important source of policy leverage. As overseer of the stability of the global financial and monetary system, the IMF has the duty to intervene in dangerous situations, such as the one in Europe. Furthermore, the IMF had jointly funded, with the EU, all the programs in the distressed euro area economies, committing more than $100 billion to Greece, Portugal, and Ireland. As a result, the fund had a fully legitimate role to play in future decisions. With the prospect of a sudden worsening of the euro crisis, the IMF also could rely on contingent credit lines through a financing instrument, the New Arrangements to Borrow (NAW), which provides a substantial backstop to its lending capacity. The total IMF firepower gave a stronger voice to the United States in European matters, but a similar pressure was produced by the voices of almost all the representatives of the so-called BRIC countries (Brazil, Russia, India, and China) and other emerging-market economies. During the IMF meetings, probably no single policymaker did not blame Europe for the delays in its response to the crisis. German and French ministers—who had arrived in Washington hoping to be praised for their capacity to maintain AAA credit ratings even after the United States had lost its vaunted status—felt humbled. Europeans had planned, in particular, to discuss in Washington a multipronged strategy whereby the United States would provide for a credible fiscal strategy at home, aimed at stabilizing the American economy in the medium to long term; Europeans would finally keep under control their crisis and promise to reinforce their economic governance; and eventually the Asians, primarily the Chinese, would use their $3 trillion in reserves as a stabilizer for global equilibrium, thus assuming responsibility for the disequilibria that they had contributed to during the previous ten years by accumulating excess savings and insisting on undervaluing their currencies to promote their exports.

At the Washington meetings, however, the situation replicated the dramatic period following the collapse of Lehman Brothers in the autumn of 2008. Once again, systemic instability threatened the whole world. But this time, the responsibility of Europe was singled out. With much of the world economy on the edge of the abyss, the European (and, in particular, German) "policy of uncertainty" and the insistence on losses for private investors in sovereign debt irritated the investors and could not be understood by non-Europeans. The uncertainty surrounding the European banks, in particular, had to be solved before it would scupper any attempt to revive the economy. Politically, there were all sorts of reasons to deplore that taxpayers would be called to prop up the banks, especially considering that the European banks had posted cumulatively roughly €50 billion in profits in 2010. European policymakers were asked explicitly to address the problem of recapitalizing the banks, in light of the outcome of the European Banking Authority stress tests showing that two dozen of the ninety largest banks in the euro area needed fresh capital. Despite the interest in this question, adding some more capital to the banks, though urgent, was far from the most fundamental thing that needed to be done. No matter how much capital any one bank could have, the potential losses to any bank portfolio because of the sovereign crisis were immensely higher. There was no solution for the banks without settling the much bigger sovereign debt crisis.

In fact, the banks' problem resembled closely the one in 2008. If each country was called on to offer guarantees for its banks, the risks for both the banks and the states would escalate. What was needed was some form of common guarantee—or "mutualization"—of the debts of both the banks and the states. All the problems had to be solved together. Parallel to the banks' recapitalization, it also was necessary to create a firewall around the EFSF and ESM to support Italy and Spain. Moreover, no firewall would be enough if the problem of Greek debt was not fixed and prevented from spreading its destabilizing effects on the rest of the euro area. The latest assessments of Greece's prospects, drawn by the EU-ECB-IMF "troika," made dire reading, especially in Berlin. Austerity had pushed Greece further into recession than expected; output was shrinking by 5.5 percent in 2011, and the economy would not be able to return to growth in 2012. Moreover, the looming stagnation in the euro area was making structural reforms even harder to implement in Greece. As a result, Athens's debt would probably peak at about 186 percent of GDP in 2013, instead of the 160 percent predicted just three months earlier, even with the 21 percent haircut on debt held by private creditors that was agreed on in July. As suspected, deeper restructuring of Greek debt was indeed inescapable. But the euro area had to give credible assurance that a default by Greece—and forcing bondholders to take losses effectively was a default—would be the first and last default.

## A Political Strategy to End the Crisis

Angela Merkel and Nicolas Sarkozy had to meet urgently one more time in Berlin on the evening of Sunday, October 9. "We need to deliver a response that is sustainable and comprehensive. We have decided to provide this response by the end of the month because Europe must solve its problems by the G-20 summit in Cannes."[17] They had multiple goals: coming up with a sustainable answer for ring-fencing Greece; increasing the leverage of the EFSF to avoid problems with Italy; and agreeing on how to recapitalize European banks and how to present a plan for accelerating economic coordination in the euro area. All this needed to be done before the scheduled European Council and Eurogroup meetings on October 23 and the G-20 summit in Cannes on November 3–4.

Behind the scenes, a strategy took place along the lines that Berlin had been defending for many months. The exit strategy had a strong political character and envisaged three steps. First, the lack of compliance by Italian prime minister Silvio Berlusconi with the demands made in August by the European Central Bank had shown a credibility gap in the countries that were under attack. Consequently, it was indispensable to convince the debtor countries—Italy in particular—to adopt important measures to mend their fiscal positions and enhance growth. Second, since any form of support would have a fiscal cost for Germany, the European Council needed to contain, in a credible and permanent way, the problem of moral hazard; this could be done by reinforcing significantly the surveillance of national political economies and getting all countries to adopt constitutional constraints that would force them to keep their budgets balanced. Finally, the euro area countries would create a convincing and permanent system of aid that would both contain the pressure of the markets and lead the euro area to embrace a system of fiscal union that stopped just short of a real political integration. Once the entire package of all three steps was completed, the ECB would feel reassured and could tackle the problem of financial stability by offering more intense support for the government bond markets. In particular, Merkel and Sarkozy hoped the ECB would restart the old formula of unlimited financing for euro area banks in the expectation that they might eventually purchase the bonds themselves—exactly along the lines of the first informal grand bargain enacted in May 2009. It was evidently a complex design that ultimately required nothing less than changes of governments in Italy and Greece and the definitive settlement of the fight between the ECB and the heads of government that had thwarted any previous attempt to solve the crisis.

## Role of the ECB and the Disagreements over the EFSF

The European Central Bank was the only source of potentially unlimited intervention in the markets of the euro zone and was inevitably the focus of attention for both the policymakers and the investors. It was evident to everybody that the European Financial Stability Facility (EFSF) had not been endowed with enough money to withstand a potential run on Italy and Spain. Ultimately, either the EFSF's loss absorption capacity had to be raised to €1–1.5 trillion, or the ECB had to stand ready to intervene on a similar scale to stop the Spanish and Italian sovereigns from defaulting.

Germany and the ECB itself had opposed any proposal to formalize the role of the bank as lender of last resort for governments. There were serious reasons of financial, juridical, and political nature. The financial reason was that the ECB would assume a huge amount of risk by accumulating securities on its balance sheet that could produce incalculable losses in case of default. The ECB might even be brought to its knees with regard to need of capital. That would put it at the mercy of governments and disrupt its reputation. It would also create a potentially enormous fiscal burden for the countries called upon to recapitalize the central bank. The political problem was also connected to fiscal redistribution, in this case taking shape through the purchase of different government securities with common resources. The cost to the taxpayers of the different countries could be massive due to the volume of purchases conducted by the ECB. The third problem, of legality, was potentially the most tricky. The direct purchase of securities might have been considered a violation of the European treaty. Any German citizen, in particular, could call on the German Constitutional Court to judge the violation and maybe declare that the lending operations—which ultimately could imply the creation of money—were conducted disregarding the bank's commitment to keep inflation under control and hence in violation of the absolute condition that the court itself had set for Germany to comply with the monetary union. Theoretically, such a step might lead to Germany exiting the euro.

Another political reason was that without a precise mandate by the euro zone leaders, the ECB could not at the same time be both the underwriter of last resort of sovereign debt and continue its self-assumed job as the "policy enforcer." Such a political function already was overburdening the bank, although some of its board members were in favor of assuming also the role of a European Monetary Fund, which would publicly admonish governments on what to do on fiscal and structural policies. Enforcing policies is inherently in contradiction to the role of providing an unlimited backstop for sovereign debt. In fact, the role of disciplining a government requires an ongoing threat of walking away from purchasing the stressed securities if the government involved does not fully implement the policies demanded by the ECB. This might require long periods of abstinence that can make the policy implementation much harder and the fiscal climate much more difficult. To preserve the autonomy of the ECB from politics, lending money against conditionality had to become the official role of the EFSF. In that case, the ECB would be free to pursue only the monetary goals—including supporting some government securities markets if they were hampering the functionality of the financial system—and would be more at ease slashing interest rates to reduce the risk of a recession.

The ECB's irritation at the governments' muddling through was clearly expressed in Mario Draghi's first speech as president of the central bank, on November 18:

> In the euro area there is an . . . essential element for financial stability and that must be rooted in a much more robust economic governance of the union going forward. In the first place now, it implies the urgent implementation of the European Council and Summit decisions. We are more than one and a half years after the summit that launched the EFSF as part of a financial support package amounting to 750 billion euros or one trillion dollars; we are four months after the summit that decided to make the full EFSF guarantee volume available; and we are four weeks after the summit that agreed on leveraging of the resources by a factor of up to four or five and that declared the EFSF would be fully operational and that all its tools will be used in an effective way to ensure financial stability in the euro area. Where is the implementation of these long-standing decisions?[18]

The two weeks that elapsed between the October 9 Merkel-Sarkozy meeting and the first round of summits on October 23 were dominated by the attempt to design a form of leveraging for the EFSF and its eventual successor, the ESM. In political terms, the discussion on the EFSF-ESM was linked to a further German request: a reform of the European treaty that put into writing all the fiscal constraints that euro area member states had to comply with before a permanent and richer fund could be set up. Virtually nobody outside Germany wanted to embark on a revision of the treaties so soon after the extremely tiresome process that had produced the Lisbon Treaty. For the German chancellor and her advisers, however, a decision to embark on treaty change was an indispensable element to tie the hands of the partners and to provide the German public opinion with a strict and coherent framework in response to the crisis. In the design of the Chancellery, a treaty reform would lead to what Merkel called a "Stability Union," and once fiscal discipline was accomplished and secured, one could then talk about eurobonds and deeper ECB involvement.

## A Comedy at the Opera

On October 19 all the important policymakers of the euro area had arrived at the Alte Oper, in the center of Frankfurt, for the ceremony and concert honoring Jean-Claude Trichet on his retirement from the ECB presidency. Unexpectedly, Sarkozy (whose wife, Carla Bruni, had just gone to hospital to give birth to a baby girl) flew to Frankfurt giving all the sense of the emergency and joined the other members of what became known as the "Groupe de Francfort," a small number of people who were taking the helm of the euro area. In addition to Merkel, Sarkozy, Trichet, and Draghi, the group included European Commission president José Manuel Barroso, European Council president Herman Van Rompuy, the IMF's new managing director Christine Lagarde, Eurogroup chairman Jean-Claude Juncker, and European commissioner for economic and financial affairs Olli Rehn. The group met in a room of the opera house while the concert was in progress. The real bone of contention between Merkel and Sarkozy was, once again, the role of the ECB. Sarkozy wanted to get a deal on the involvement of the ECB in a comprehensive solution, in order to raise a "wall of money" before contagion reached France. The main option was for the central bank to be assigned the task of direct lender to the EFSF, which itself would be transformed into a bank. In that case, the EFSF could use the limitless liquidity resources of the ECB, and the latter would be "in the front line intervening massively and playing the role of a federal central bank" as Sarkozy said to the members of the "Group."

The Frankfurt meeting was described by participants as "explosive." Merkel and Trichet firmly opposed Sarkozy's idea of letting the European Financial Stability Facility operate as a bank and borrow money from the ECB. Trichet, who had been fighting that issue since May 2010, was strongly opposed to what he saw as a surreptitious way of getting the ECB to finance the states. But eventually the real confrontation once again was between Merkel and Sarkozy. And, as usual, the German prevailed. Sarkozy tried again with another option: putting together the reserves of the central banks, especially those invested in the IMF's artificial currency known as special drawing rights, to grant capital to a special vehicle. There was a proposal for combining some of the central bank reserves in the form of special drawing rights— which represent the claims of states to the IMF—in a special fund that would be linked to the EFSF. The opposition to this idea came directly from the Bundesbank, which represents Germany in the IMF. In the following days the conservative *Bild Zeitung* newspaper soberly published the story of Germans deprived of their gold.[19]

Merkel was aware that there had to be a way to involve the ECB, but only if it did not violate the European treaties. That basically meant having the ECB act as a lender through the banks. Primarily, her strategy was to let the central bank decide by itself when and how to act. That would preserve the autonomy of the ECB and would relieve the German government of painful decisions that her voters would not like. Her coalition would suffer internal conflicts in case of open support for the ECB and might even break up. Therefore, Merkel resorted to the usual "policy of uncertainty," which left unspecified the terms of the support to the euro area. As French officials told it, the most obstinate resistance came from the head of the German Bundesbank, Jens Weidmann, captured by what another central banker defined as "the group of four to five high officials who embody the black soul of the Bundesbank." This was a remark that thinly concealed the same suspicion of a nostalgic nationalist sentiment lingering behind the walls of the German central bank that pushed former chancellor Helmut Schmidt to brand an ex-governor a Deutscher Nazionalist.[20]

Sarkozy tried another tack, urging his colleagues at least to mention in the forthcoming Eurosummit's final statement that the leaders were calling for the ongoing support of the ECB's use of its securities market program to prop up the government bonds of the weaker countries. But even that was too much of an interference in the ECB's autonomy for Trichet to accept. Although the confrontation between the two Frenchmen reportedly was harsh, a number of alternatives were studied. As a last resort, Sarkozy wanted to insert in the final communiqué of the Eurosummit that the leaders were "supporting" the ECB in the further purchase of bonds. That also was unacceptable for the central banker, who wanted nothing said about the ECB continuing its non-standard measures. They finally settled for a compromise. Mario Draghi, who was going to take over as president of the ECB on November 1, would mention in a speech in Italy during the summit that the ECB intended to continue the securities market program.[21] At that point the president of the EU Council would welcome from Brussels the statement of Draghi. It was a very discreet way to show cooperation between the political leaders and the central bankers.[22]

## Berlin as Center of the Euro Area

In the week preceding the leaders' summit, Merkel had to revise her plans on how to approach the meeting. As a consequence of a decision of the German Constitutional Court, she decided to look for a mandate from the plenary session of the Bundestag to negotiate the EFSF in Brussels. But to do that, the chancellor needed time. She could organize her troops and give her speech to the parliament only on Wednesday, October 26. She got agreement that the Eurosummit would meet twice—a preparatory session on October 23 and a full meeting on October 26, following her speech to parliament.

There were two ways to increase the firepower for combating the debt crisis. One was to receive help from outside the euro area, and the second was to find a way to endow the EFSF with more resources. Attempts to draw money from abroad had not fared well since the beginning. Part of the money had to come through the IMF. This was a plan much supported by Sarkozy and his former finance minister Lagarde. It had also gained the favor of Merkel because she knew the Bundestag did not want to commit additional funds to the rescue operations, and it was more expedient to channel resources through the IMF as a way to bypass national parliaments. But engaging the IMF meant convincing other countries to join with the fund in supporting Europe. Negotiations with the Chinese government had brought nothing because Beijing understandably observed the Europeans' reluctance to add money themselves. On October 20 a transatlantic conference call between Merkel, Sarkozy, Obama, and British prime minister David Cameron also brought no result. Obama's reaction to the idea that the euro area should supplement its efforts to reinforce the EFSF's funding by raising money from outside Europe was constrained by the fact that he had no chance of getting approval from the U.S. Congress for a disbursement in favor of the Europeans. For his part, Cameron lashed out so brutally against Germany and France for failing to solve the crisis that he probably marked a moment of no-return for Britain in Europe.[23]

The second way to increase resources—by bolstering the EFSF—also was not easy. From the outset the EFSF was conceived as a temporary facility set up to relieve the ECB of the burden of purchasing sovereign debt. Each country's share of the EFSF's capital guarantees was determined by its capital subscription with the ECB. The EFSF funded itself through the issuance of bonds backed by the guarantees corresponding to the share of each country in the fund's capital. The guarantees were "irrevocable and unconditional." They were also joint guarantees for an amount up to the maximum guaranteed by each country. This meant that each country would never be liable for more than the maximum amount it had pledged. If, for instance, one country was not able to repay a loan from the EFSF for €400 billion and the only other country able to honor its guarantee was Germany, then Berlin would only be liable for its maximum pledge, €211 billion. Because in September Merkel had committed to the Bundestag not to increase the maximum pledge, she had no leeway to approve any solution envisaging a loss higher than €211 billion. As a consequence, no increase in the EFSF endowment could be allowed. No use of the funds in the form of an indiscriminate leverage was possible (because potential losses would increase correspondingly to the leverage).

One possibility was to use the available amount of money as a guarantee offered to investors in euro area government securities against the risk of losing part of their money. It was a scheme that had been suggested in early 2011 by Paul Achleitner, the financial director of German insurance giant Allianz, and soon studied by the German finance ministry and tested with Deutsche Bank. In order to also cover the bond issuances of Italy and Spain, the insured volume had to reach roughly €1.2 trillion. While the amount of guarantees of the EFSF stood at around €780 billion, the actual lending capacity of the EFSF was only about €440 billion, corresponding to the amount of guarantees given by only AAA-rated countries. After deducting the loans already committed to Greece, Ireland, and Portugal, the remaining money was now around €250–€300 billion. To reach €1.2 trillion, the maximum "leverage" should use a factor of four or five (€250 billion, for instance, is 20 percent of €1.25 trillion); or equivalently the insured losses had to be no more than 20 percent of the total investments. It was no surprise that, having previously obtained the desired guarantees that the total burden on Germany would never escalate, the Parliament on the afternoon of October 26 gave a formidable support to the chancellor just before she was to leave for the Brussels summit. It was very clear to all Europeans that the Bundestag was binding not only the chancellor's maneuvering room, but that of the European Council overall. This amounted to a problem for European democracy: financial strength and political leadership had given an edge to the German electorate over all the others.

## The Last EU Council for Papandreou

It was early in the morning on October 27 in Brussels when the Eurogroup leaders ended a ten-hour discussion and proudly announced a package consisting, as expected, of several connected parts: reducing Greece's debt to a sustainable level by a "voluntary" agreement with private creditors to accept the loss of one-half the value of the bonds; reaffirming that Greece was a unique case and that no other state would incur a default; recapitalizing Europe's banks to the tune of €106 billion to help them absorb the losses on Greek and other distressed debts;

and creating a €1.2 trillion firewall to prevent the spread of panic to still-solvent states, above all, Italy.

The communiqué opened with an acknowledgment that former commitments had been insufficient but without mentioning the involvement by the ECB in providing funds to support weak countries:

> Over the last three years, we have taken unprecedented steps to combat the effects of the worldwide financial crisis. . . . Further action is needed to restore confidence. That is why today we agree on a comprehensive set of additional measures reflecting our strong determination to do whatever is required to overcome the present difficulties and take the necessary steps for the completion of our economic and monetary union. We fully support the ECB in its action to maintain price stability in the euro area.[24]

A participant described the summit as an "extremely tense confrontation" between Merkel and Sarkozy "producing the only possible compromise." It was a game of two people, Merkel and Sarkozy. When Berlusconi tried to intervene he was even denied the right. The question boiled down to only one issue: what was acceptable to Merkel. The chancellor had made it more than clear that the only simple and effective solution—the involvement of the ECB—was not acceptable. In the design of the funds for the ailing countries, whose improvement was anxiously awaited by the markets, the leaders set out the reform of the EFSF, but—in compliance with Merkel's pledge to her parliament—no new money would be put up.

The two technical options for leveraging the resources of the EFSF were not exactly intuitive. The first option aimed at providing credit enhancement to new debt issued by member states, thus reducing their funding costs. This step would be in the form of a risk insurance to be offered to private investors as an option when buying bonds in the primary market. The second option was attracting resources from private and public financial institutions and investors, which could be arranged through funds known as "special purpose vehicles." This would enlarge the amount of resources available to extend loans for bank recapitalization and for buying bonds in the primary and secondary markets.[25] Actually, the feasibility of the EFSF schemes remained unclear.[26]

On the euro area's new economic governance, the leaders reinforced the coordination and surveillance of member states' policies.[27] On the issue of Greece, the most-expected decision regarded the anticipated losses by private investors, the Private Sector Involvement (PSI). According to the leaders, the PSI should secure the decline of the Greek debt-to-GDP ratio with an objective of reaching 120 percent by 2020: "To this end we invite Greece, private investors and all parties concerned to develop a voluntary bond exchange with a nominal discount of 50 percent on notional Greek debt held by private investors."[28] As a consequence of reinforcing PSI in the Greek case, the EU leaders had to reaffirm that the Greek solution was "exceptional and unique."[29]

Negotiation over the Greek package was a plain diplomatic disaster. By asking for very substantial losses of 50 percent from private investors, negotiators were setting a high level that completely discredited at least one of the two options for giving more power to the EFSF. As a matter of fact, the insurance option aimed at covering losses of private investors ranged from only 20 percent to 30 percent. Not only was the EFSF almost useless, but the leaders had demonstrated losses could be much higher than earlier envisaged. The Greek negotiations also took a dramatic political turn when the EU leaders asked to establish a permanent monitoring team based in Athens and formed of foreign officials hosted by each Greek ministry—a sort of bureaucratic occupation force that was expected to help improve the organization of public administration and to report on the implementation of the program. At that point Prime Minister George Papandreou threatened to walk away from the meeting. He did not follow through on the threat but vehemently explained to his colleagues that the agreement was unacceptable in many respects. The Greek premier felt that such a demand made his position untenable at home. The "monitoring on the ground" was a visible symptom of the loss of control that the Greeks had on any future policies, just when Greek citizens were expressing their discontent at the pain of austerity measures being imposed on them. The fact that Greece had to be kept out of the markets until 2020 meant also that external governance would last a decade.

Papandreou's political capital had already dried up, and he faced intense anger from voters who felt they had been squeezed to the breaking point by the austerity measures demanded by Greece's foreign lenders. Back in Athens just a few days later, on October 31, Papandreou announced he would submit the EU's program to a referendum vote. Basically, he thought he was handing back the ownership of the reforms to the Greeks and taking them away from foreign chancelleries. By doing this he thought he could recover legitimacy for his government. Papandreou said that the referendum would be a straight "yes" or "no" to adopting the €130 billion aid package. A "no" vote would unravel the deal hammered out by EU leaders and force Papandreou to resign. The referendum was to be held either in December or January, thus opening a phase of sheer uncertainty across the euro area.

## Not Even a Short-Lived Relief

Markets woke up early to the shortcomings of the latest euro zone deal. The tricks behind the leveraging of the EFSF were not credible, and the first reaction in China about investing in the "vehicle" attached to the EFSF was unconvincing due to a lack of details and to the fact that euro area countries were themselves not willing to provide the financial guarantees that they were asking of Beijing. The plans for banking recapitalization could easily backfire, triggering a credit crunch. Finally, the Greek PSI plan was in doubt now that George Papandreou had called for a referendum.

Rumors began to circulate about a forthcoming bad assessment on the Greek program by the EU-ECB-IMF troika. A failure in the program would push the Greek debt-to-GDP ratio above 180 percent. At that level, even private investor losses would become useless because even canceling the total value of the Greek debt in the hands of private investors would not be enough to bring it down to manageable levels. The level of public debt would remain unsustainable and the only option would then be a "hard default." It was a dramatic scenario. Once the troika acknowledged the debt unsustainability, Greek citizens would run to draw their deposits from the banks. Since all credit institutions in the country were cut off from any access to the interbank market, their only funding option would be the Bank of Greece, which for its part depended directly on the short-term loan program, known as Emergency Liquidity Assistance, of the European Central Bank. Loans under that program had to be approved by a two-thirds majority of the ECB Council and, at some stage, this majority could become difficult to achieve in the case of Greece. In such a circumstance, the Bank of Greece could do nothing but issue electronic money still denominated in euros but actually not accepted anywhere else than in Greece. De facto it would be the origin of a new currency and the beginning of the breakup of the euro. German finance minister Wolfgang Schäuble told Papandreou that if he insisted on calling the referendum, Berlin would not allow for the disbursement of the money.[30] Papandreou's position—already difficult—became untenable.

The prospect of a hard default seemed to be opening the way for Greece to exit the euro area. As a consequence of the emerging instability, Italian spreads over German bonds rose to historical highs since the euro zone membership, with ten-year yields trading between 6 percent and 7 percent. While the world stared at Athens, the existential crisis of the euro zone was playing out in Rome. The final blow to Italy's credibility came during Merkel and Sarkozy's closing press conference at the Eurosummit. Asked if they had confidence in Berlusconi's commitments, Sarkozy rolled his eyes, spread his arms, and started to grin ironically, looking for an accomplice. Merkel smiled, then resisted the temptation to say anything, but it was too late. The journalists burst into derisive laughter. Metaphorically, Sarkozy and Merkel had pulled the rug from under the feet of another colleague.

In order to deal with Papandreou, a meeting of the "Groupe de Francfort" with the Greek prime minister was convened prior to the Group of 20 meeting in Cannes. The group met four times on the sidelines of the G-20 meeting. In addition to Merkel and Sarkozy, Juncker, Barroso, Van Rompuy, and Lagarde huddled together before receiving Papandreou on the evening of November 3. The working dinner in the Palais des Festivals in Cannes was almost brutal. "We made Papandreou aware of the fact that his behavior is disloyal," said Juncker. "The euro group would like to have been informed about the intention to hold a referendum at the recent EU summit."[31] Papandreou was subjected to what amounted to an interrogation session. It was again made very clear to the Greek premier that should the majority of Greeks vote against the Brussels resolutions in a referendum, Athens would have to do without the transfer of billions in aid. The others announced to the Greek premier that the payment of the next €8 billion tranche of the first aid package, approved in early 2010, would be frozen and made dependent on a positive result of the referendum. Without EU aid, Greece would run out of money by Christmas at the latest. Papandreou was described as at the limit of his strength. Merkel and Sarkozy urged him to call off the referendum, or in case that was not possible, to bring it forward as much as possible and to hold it at the latest in one month. Finally, they said that the question was not just about the €130 billion rescue plan agreed after painstaking negotiations at the Brussels summit, but more importantly about Greece's continued membership of the euro zone. Papandreou caved in and announced to the press that the referendum was "a question of whether we want to remain in the euro zone." Papandreou understood he was politically finished. But more significant, the taboo on discussing the possible breakup of the euro zone had been violated.

### Belusconi Exit

Most of the G-20 negotiations on November 3 were actually devoted to how the euro zone, together with the International Monetary Fund, might be equipped to confront the dangers posed by Italy. In particular, EU leaders, in consultation with Barack Obama, discussed working more closely with the IMF on a fund that could step in to support Italy and Spain.

Tensions on the bond market showed that Italy was on the same downward path as Greece, Ireland, and Portugal. Interest rates on sovereign bonds were rising to 6.4 percent, perilously close to the mark that had triggered emergency Italian bond purchases by the European Central Bank in August. Analysts considered a rate of 7 percent to be the level at which many investors stop buying sovereign bonds and clearing houses start asking for higher margins, setting off automatic sales of the securities. On the morning of the G-20 meeting, German finance minister Schäuble and his French counterpart, François Baroin, tried to convince their Italian colleague, Giulio Tremonti, to implement additional austerity measures. The group reconvened at noon. This time U.S. Treasury secretary Geithner joined the meeting, and the trio demanded that Italy agree to allow both its reforms and its national budget to be monitored by the IMF, dependent on IMF funding. Tremonti preferred the involvement of the IMF, instead of the ECB, probably considering it a way to open his inevitable succession to Berlusconi, but the issue was not to be agreed upon without Berlusconi's direct involvement and the two Italian policymakers were almost not in speaking terms anymore.

The political capacity of Berlusconi was in question more than ever for two reasons. First, the two Italian fiscal packages approved during the summer amounted to chiefly raising taxes, damaging the weak growth of the economy. Second, his government was reported to be close to collapsing in an atmosphere marred by personal rivalry between Berlusconi and Tremonti and by extreme partisanship that undermined the credibility of any eventual parliamentary commitment that might be requested by the EFSF and ESM. Berlusconi suffered what an Italian chief negotiator defined as "an absolute loss of credibility: the problem is not that we cannot influence the talks, the other euro partners do not even listen to Berlusconi and Tremonti. They do not let them speak."[32] Berlusconi was isolated among the heads of state and government because of his peculiar lifestyle and his idiosyncratic view of what was, or was not, true.

Berlusconi has a quick mind but rarely studied the extensive paperwork prepared for him by Italian officials. In Cannes a more concrete issue had been the source of his troubles. After the EU leaders summit of October 27, Berlusconi had pledged to submit a new program of reforms at the G-20 summit. He renewed the commitment by telephone with Merkel on November 1, and he had been informed by the European Commission that he was expected to present a package of reforms approved by his government. Instead, an extraordinary meeting of Berlusconi's council of ministers in Rome the night ahead of the Cannes summit had produced nothing. After hearing Tremonti, the president of the republic, Giorgio Napolitano, had refused to sign the government's decree, which was judged inadequate. The European Commission had asked at least for a letter, addressed to Van Rompuy and Barroso, spelling out clearly the planned economic reforms. A first draft, prepared by Tremonti, had been sent back by the EU because it lacked a timeline for each reform. A second letter was accepted in Brussels but was considered far too generic because it lacked the details for each of the measures. Finally, Berlusconi was summoned to a private session in Cannes with Merkel and Sarkozy, who put him on the grill for hours. The two European leaders, incensed to see no concrete steps to ensure a return to balanced public accounts in 2013, accused him of having arrived in Cannes empty-handed.

Berlusconi was taken by surprise, for reasons that can be understood by reading two passages of the letter that he took to the partners:

> In 2014 we will have a budget surplus (cyclically adjusted) equal to 0.5 percent of GDP, a primary surplus equal to 5.7 percent of GDP and government debt of 112.6 percent of GDP. . . . As a consequence of the audit carried out by Eurostat, the deficit/GDP ratio, which was confirmed

as 4.6 percent for 2010, is virtually in line with that of Germany, revised from 3.3 percent to 4.3 percent. Furthermore, it should be noted that Eurostat has also corrected upwards the deficit/GDP ratio of France (from 7 percent to 7.1 percent), Spain (from 9.2 percent to 9.3 percent), Greece (from 10.5 percent to 10.6 percent), and Portugal (from 9.1 percent to 9.3 percent). In conclusion, in 2010 Italy—together with Germany—demonstrated by far the most virtuous conduct in terms of net borrowing in relation to GDP.

The Italian prime minister thought he had done more than enough, and surely more than the others.

In the evening, Merkel, Sarkozy, and Berlusconi met again. Surprisingly, President Obama participated in a part of the meeting. When they entered the room, Obama pulled Merkel aside for a private conversation. An open microphone caught his opening words: "I guess you guys have to be creative here." As a matter of fact, Merkel and Sarkozy put both political and financial pressures on the Italian premier. They suggested to him that Italy should resort to the new facilities available at the IMF, which could issue new credit lines quickly and without requiring significant conditions to countries with short-term liquidity problems, like Spain and Italy. The size of the credit line would be based on a country's share of IMF capital. Spain could expect a maximum of €23 billion in support, while Italy would qualify for €45 billion. These were not large amounts, given the need, but would be enough to enable the IMF to meddle in the Italian legislative procedures. In effect, Merkel and Sarkozy were arm twisting Berlusconi to carry out long delayed economic reforms and allow the IMF to monitor them. Sarkozy told Berlusconi that if he could not make a decision, his leadership was a problem for Europe as a whole.

It amounted to the final stage of the "waterboarding" sessions to which Berlusconi had been treated in the last months by his partners and by the markets. The old leader, who believed himself to be the best Italian political leader ever and one of the most authoritative in the world, was not able even to reply. He had not been briefed by Tremonti and felt like he had fallen into an ambush. He was shocked by the undiplomatic tone that Christine Lagarde used in offering that the IMF could open its Precautionary Lending Line to Italy, and so he declined the offer. At a later press conference, Berlusconi said, "Italy does not feel the crisis." He described the markets' sell-off of Italian bonds as "a temporary fashion," adding that "the restaurants are full, the planes are fully booked, and the hotel resorts are fully booked as well." Lagarde later issued a denial that she had made a loan offer, but a participant in the meeting said that, indeed, she had offered a €45 billion credit line. During the summit, Lagarde took a public stab at Berlusconi: "The problem that is at stake, and that was clearly identified both by the Italian authorities and its partners, is a lack of credibility of the measures that were announced."[33] The IMF chief added that an "Italian mission" would make its quarterly reports public and that she planned to visit Rome as part of the evaluation process. The addition of IMF monitors to those of the European Commission and of the ECB made the mission almost identical to the "troika" teams that had been conducting reviews of the euro zone's three bailed-out countries (Greece, Ireland, and Portugal). Italy objected to being considered "under surveillance." Berlusconi said that his country accepted only "advice" from the international institutions. In fact, Italy ended up being placed in the same monitoring "program" as the other countries, but without the financial assistance. Flying back from Cannes, Berlusconi understood he was hanging by a thread.

The insufficiency of Berlusconi's response to the European partners became evident on November 8 when the Italian government received a letter from Van Rompuy and Barroso asking thirty-nine detailed questions aimed at clarifying the imprecise commitments his government had made in its letter presented to the Eurosummit of October 26. In essence, the European officials were raising serious doubts about the credibility of the Berlusconi-Tremonti fiscal pledges. According to EU estimates, Italy would cut its fiscal budget so that its deficit was −2.4 percent of GDP instead of −1.6 percent in 2012 and −1.1 percent instead of +0.1 percent in 2013.[34] The balanced budget would be achieved only in 2014 instead of 2013, and the public debt would start to decline in 2013 instead of 2012.[35]

Later that night of November 8, in a meeting at Palazzo del Quirinale in Rome with President of the Republic Giorgio Napolitano, Berlusconi offered to resign within a few days of the approval of the proposed Stability Law.

*The End of the Euro*

While Berlusconi still mused about staying in power, he actually had run out of time: the next day dramatic movements in Italian bond yields took him and all European policymakers by surprise. Following the decision by a UK-based clearinghouse to raise margin requirements, Italian ten-year bonds lost 5 percent in value as yields soared to almost 600 basis points above the German Bund. Within minutes of the market opening, there was a fully fledged run on Italian government bonds. Yields jumped well past 7 percent before stabilizing just below 7.5 percent as a result of buying by the European Central Bank. This episode sparked concerns that a prolonged period of instability could end in a self-fulfilling funding crisis in the third-largest bond market in the world. Bond market tensions increased further. Spain issued ten-year bonds accepted by the markets at a shade below 7 percent on November 17. The price of euro-denominated interest rate swaps increased at an unprecedented speed showing that a credit risk was attached to all kinds of euro securities. For the first time in years capital flight was detected from the euro area into the dollar and else-where. The ultimate backstop, the European Central Bank, was still purchasing some government bonds, but in very low volumes. The Securities Market Program was evidently not working because the timid purchases were not strong enough to change the course of the bond prices. On the contrary they were grabbed by sellers as an opportunity to offload more bonds, and this was further depressing the prices.

Banks were in dire straits. The senior unsecured bond market was practically shut and the worst was that credit institutes needed to fund themselves urgently because in the first quarter of 2012, bank bonds for €230 billion were to be rolled over. Against this backdrop, the interbank market was not working and the whole banking system was about to stall.

Investors also started to offload sovereign bonds of the core countries, leaving the German Bund as virtually the only trusted AAA paper in the euro area. Yield spreads of Austrian and French bonds approached 200 basis points, taking the path that had seen Italy and Spain follow Greece, Portugal and Ireland. Even Dutch and Finnish yields broke away from those of German bonds, prompting a flight to safe assets outside the euro area. But on November 23, for the first time since the launch of the euro, an auction of German bonds failed to be underwritten by at least two-thirds of the offer.[36] It took intervention by the Bundesbank, doing exactly what it opposed at the European level—financing the state by purchasing its bonds on the primary market—to reduce the shock. But market investors were univocal in seeing that moment as a tipping point for the euro. The days of the common currency were counted.

## Settling the Politics of the Crisis

Under pressure from President Napolitano, the German chancellor, and the French president, Silvio Berlusconi finally capitulated and announced his resignation. On November 13 Napolitano asked Mario Monti, a highly regarded policymaker who had gained an outstanding reputation as former EU commissioner, to form a new non-partisan government.

Another political earthquake occurred in the same time period in Greece. When he returned to Athens after being pressured by EU leaders in Cannes, Papandreou had to cancel the referendum and finally give up the premiership. After days of difficult negotiations, on November 10 the main political parties reached an agreement on a transitional coalition government led by Lucas Papademos, the former vice president of the ECB. A statement from President Karolos Papoulias firmly stated that the priority of the new government would be to adopt and implement the October 26 agreement reached at the Eurosummit. Shortly after his nomination, Papademos addressed the nation on television and called on all citizens to participate in the process of adjusting the economy and implementing the aid program. The Greek hesitations about continuing along the European path were put aside.

Yet another transfer of power came on November 21, when the opposition came to power in Spain. In a landslide victory, the center-right People's Party won 186 of the 350 seats in Parliament, while the center-left Socialists, who had been governing since 2004, fell to 110 seats. By the end of November 2011, every one of the ailing countries had changed governments: Ireland, Portugal, and Spain through elections, and Greece and Italy through the combined pressures of the markets and European leaders. All of the new governments were committed from the start to honor the binding rules of the ECB and of the creditor countries. The common feature in all countries was that all new governments—elected or appointed, left-wing or right-wing—endorsed a strong pro-European stance. The new Italian and Greek prime ministers had impeccable credentials as economists, and Monti in particular had the quality to overturn the intellectual balance of powers in Europe. The political posture of distancing oneself from "sacrifice dictated by Europe" no longer had currency. For the moment, the broader sentiment seemed to be that all Europeans aspired to core-European institutions and to stability. Meanwhile, in Germany euro-skeptical parties were losing support, while more pro-European parties (including the Social Democrats and the Greens) were gaining support. In the polls, Merkel also was acknowledged as a strong leader because of her tough but pro-Europe stance. The first step of the political solution, the support of credible and pro-European governments, was secured.

### Another Summit, Another "Final" Solution

Exactly twenty years after the signature of the Maastricht Treaty, which had given birth to the project of a common currency, the EU leaders met in Brussels to mend the crisis of the euro. The decisions taken at the summit on December 8–9 were in line with the proposals for stricter fiscal discipline, as requested by Angela Merkel.[37] Conceding to the chancellor, the leaders also declined major reinforcements of the instruments they had previously created to backstop the crisis. No progress was made on the proposals for the common issuance of bonds or for giving bank status to the ESM. The leaders did agree to bring forward the introduction of the ESM to July 2012, compared to earlier plans for July 2013. But they left for future discussion the issue of whether the €500 billion maximum amount of ESM resources would be in addition to, or a replacement for, the €440 billion available to the EFSF. Although they left unclear the total amount of the available resources for the two facilities, the leaders did agree to make an assessment in March 2012 of the upper ceiling of the combined EFSF and ESM funding, and they decided to impose an overall ceiling of €500 billion for the targeted final effective lending capacity of the ESM.[38]

In a second element, the leaders decided that the euro area and other EU member states "will aim to make available additional resources of up to €200 billion to the IMF." The leaders hoped that the commitment would convince other non-European countries (apparently, China among others) to add up to an equivalent amount to the IMF resources. All in all, the firepower could come close to the threshold of €1 trillion necessary to support Italy and Spain throughout 2012 and 2013.

One major difference from the previous German strategy was the revocation of the private sector involvement (PSI), the steep debt write-downs imposed on Greece's creditors and potentially on every future subscriber of euro area bonds. That had been the famous mistake taken in Deauville in October 2010 by Merkel and Sarkozy, and insisted on by Merkel ever since. As Van Rompuy noted in his statement after the council meeting, "To put it more bluntly, our first approach to PSI, which had a very negative effect on debt markets, is now officially over."[39]

Finally, when British prime minister David Cameron refused to go along with his colleagues in agreeing to changes in the EU treaty, the other leaders decided to put the "new fiscal compact" for the euro zone in an "international agreement," to be signed by March 2012, probably by most of the twenty-seven member countries except the United Kingdom.[40]

The fiscal regime designed by the summit was the equivalent of a German dream. First of all, the annual structural budget deficit could not exceed 0.5 percent of nominal GDP.[41] The rule of a balanced budget was also to be introduced in member states' national primary legislation, that is at the constitutional or equivalent level. The rule should also contain an automatic correction mechanism to be triggered in the event of deviation and could be defined by each member state on the basis of principles proposed by the European Commission. The member states recognized, as requested by Merkel, the jurisdiction of the European Court of Justice to verify the adoption of this rule at each national level. The European Commission assumed a stronger role in setting a calendar for fiscal convergence and strengthening its surveillance on the implementation. Member states with deficits exeeding the limit would be asked to submit to the commission and the council for approval an economic partnership program detailing the necessary structural reforms to ensure an effectively durable correction of excessive deficits. The new rules also include automatic sanctions—which could be halted only by an unlikely vote of a "qualified majority" of the euro area countries. More than the ineffective fines of the past, the new sanctions would take the form of policy measures to correct the deficits monitored by the European Commission and the council. In effect, this was the famous transfer of sovereignty implied in the plan of fiscal union evoked by Chancellor Merkel.

As a compensation for the fiscal straitjacketing, there was nothing concrete: no larger EFSF-ESM, no mutualization of debts, no eurobonds.

## The ECB and the Wall of Money

The euro zone's adoption of this severe fiscal medicine cannot be understood without taking into account that another part of the solution was in Frankfurt. With the passing of the weeks it was clear that the ECB Securities Market Program (SMP) was not working. Purchasing daily €1 billion of bonds was useless. It actually invited investors to sell the bonds and keep the yields stable at very high levels. Draghi could not convince part of the ECB council to act boldly and to take the markets by surprise, and instead the bank acted timidly and predictably. The alternative to buying bonds came with a decision made in Frankfurt on December 8—just before the EU leaders gathered in Brussels. At the end of the monthly meeting of the ECB Governing Council, Draghi announced a move toward the most extensive enlargement of credit that had ever been made in the euro zone. During his follow-up press conference, Draghi disappointed the markets by denying that the ECB could engage in a radical increase in its program of purchases of government bonds. He reiterated that the ECB would never do anything against the EU treaty, or even against the spirit of the treaty.

This statement was the consequence of a harsh—Draghi called it "lively"—confrontation within the ECB Council that culminated in the threatened scenario raised by the German members that the bank could be taken before the German Constitutional Court and probably shot for high treason. At the same time, however, Draghi announced a program of unprecedented liquidity for the banks of the euro area. The ECB was ready to finance all the banks through a full allotment of credit, lowering dramatically the quality of collaterals (the assets that the bank have to deliver as a guarantee for the liquidity they receive). Each bank could receive whatever amount of liquidity it needed at a cost of only 1 percent and for an unusually long period of three years. The ECB agreed to take onto its balance sheet the risk of the collateral in the expectation that banks would deliver credit to the economy, thereby helping restart consumption and investments and, ultimately, purchases of the Italian and Spanish government bonds that were yielding more than 6 percent yearly (and therefore providing a high profit in the three years at practically no risk if the euro area was credibly avoiding a default).[42]

In order to understand the radical nature of the ECB's decision, it suffices to recall that the collateral securities that a bank might hand over to the ECB sometimes had no market, for instance, the unguaranteed securities issued by the same banks; hence, banks could obtain them at zero price and then deliver them to the ECB. Low-quality securities, for instance Greek sovereign bonds or Spanish mortgage loans, could thus be given new life, exactly in the same way that the U.S. Federal Reserve did in 2008 with its "quantitative easing" programs that salvaged billions of dollars in toxic subprime assets held by the American financial system. The experience of the Fed credit easing was very encouraging since, in the end, the Fed recorded a surplus in the value of its portfolio.

Under the ECB program, the banks could receive the liquidity directly from their national central banks, which could set even lower levels of quality for the collateral. The risk in this case was transferred directly to the national central banks—not to the ECB—and ultimately to the national governments, consistent with the evident fiscal nature of the intervention. In the event of a bad outcome, the national taxpayers would be called on to refinance the capital of the central bank. National central banks were particularly inclined to receive government bonds as guarantees, thus reviving interest in that market and providing wide liquidity through which banks could purchase other government bonds.[43] Obviously, this operation entails what an economist calls a "risk correlation": if things go well, both states and banks are in a better situation, but if things turn badly, the risks are multiplied because banks hold more government bonds and the state guarantees the banks' securities. In order to limit this risk correlation, the European Banking Authority asked the banks to increase their capital. At an ECOFIN meeting on November 30, Andrea Enria, the head of the European Banking Authority, had tried to tackle the risk that the states-banks spiral could get out of control. He proposed to the finance ministers options for the mutualization of banks' guaranties in order to break the loop between national banks and national sovereign debt. Knowing that some governments were less than enthusiastic about pooling responsibilities, he proposed five different options graduated for their degree of mutualization. They were all turned down, even the last one, which was to all effects a false mutualization: it appeared to mutualize the guarantee, but had a hidden-to-the-public room for compensation that allowed states to redistribute the costs along national lines at a later stage.

With this miserable degree of cooperative spirit, the liquidity provision outlined by Draghi on December 8 was evidently one of the few options left. It was the same strategy that the central bank had used in May 2009 through the hidden "Grand Bargain" (described in chapter 7), which had led the banks of the euro area to purchase up to 60–70 percent of the new government debt issued the rest of that year and to segment the bond market along national lines. It was also a second-best solution relative to the direct purchase of bonds by the ECB, because it lacked the strength and clarity of a formal and direct commitment of the ECB to the ailing countries. However, it was the only powerful weapon formally compatible with the European treaty and with the rhetoric of the Bundesbank (and the German Constitutional Court).

Draghi put in action a whole package: the ECB had cut interest rates twice in a short time and would also activate the credit swap lines with the dollar that are crucial for some of the larger banks. Moreover, it would lower the minimum reserve ratio from 2 to 1 percent, freeing more than €100 billion of collateral that banks could use again. Draghi also considered the collateral eligibility rule as too demanding, so he revisited the criteria to allow even small banks the ability to access the facilities. In mid-December 523 banks of the euro area, an unexpectedly high number, tapped almost €500 billion from the ECB under the new arrangement. This wall of money could be used gradually, so a big part of it went back at the ECB deposit facility and therefore was not employed on the economy immediately, but set aside for the bank bonds rollover. The short-term government bond market immediately benefitted, unsecured bonds responded very positively after six month of dearth in new issuances. Meanwhile, the nuclear weapon of direct purchase of bonds remained in the ECB's arsenal in case of a further and extreme deterioration of the crisis. What was avoided was a disastrous credit crunch that would have been the final blow for the euro.

## 2013: The Cold Fusion

Back in Berlin, on December 13, Chancellor Merkel presented the outcome of the summit to the Bundestag as a historical achievement comparable to the signing of the Maastricht Treaty: "We are not only speaking of fiscal union, we have now started to create it. That was the goal and that is what we got."[44] According to the chancellor, the flaws in the Maastricht Treaty had been mended. The abusive rhetoric of fiscal union made the optimists see the train for the political integration of the United States of Europe starting its long and uncertain journey on that cloudy night in Berlin. Optimism is a visual defect that collapses the desired future into the present view, but Merkel had a different perspective: "We are now on the right path, but we cannot rely on a single-blow solution." It would not be a matter of weeks or months, Merkel acknowledged, saying "the process will last for years."

Merkel had laid out the route. In her view, the euro area had an ambitious political horizon in the form of a fiscal union, and the short-term emergency on the financial markets had found an unlimited backstop through the European system of central banks. The markets were given a free hand to choose how to allocate the resources in the euro area, but just enough uncertainty was left so that investors could pile pressure on the countries in need of fiscal adjustment. In 2013 all the pieces of the puzzle should go in the right place. Each state would have a constitutional constraint to ensure a balanced budget; without fiscal margins of maneuver, all countries would have had to resort to structural reforms. The euro area would be fiscally "sterilized" and modernized; the average debt-to-GDP ratio of the euro area would decline permanently in the future; and less than three months after the Italian budget law posted a zero-deficit in 2013, Merkel would be able to run her electoral campaign at home announcing that all other peoples had decided to adopt the German virtues. Unfortunately, such political equations rarely work in practice.

Markets were not diffident to the euro per se, but to the political solidarity behind it. The euro area had no overall deficit of capital, but savings-rich citizens in the northern countries were no longer willing to invest their capital in the savings-strapped states in the south. The market feared that this difficult cohabitation—just like in an unhappy marriage—would end in a divorce. Mistrust could be defeated only with a credible promise of a shared and common destiny, but Merkel's sterilized fiscal union could not convince the markets that in case of sickness or disgrace one partner would help the other.

Far from being dispersed by the string of "comprehensive solutions" designed by the leaders in their seemingly endless meetings, the general lack of confidence in fact had been transmitted to the economy. Growth was falling steeply in most of the euro area. Firms were withholding investments, unemployment was on the rise, and cross-effects between trading partners were worsening the situation. The economic policies dictated by the European agreements were not helping. The prospect of a steep recession included an even more severe scenario in which fiscal policies—cutting public expenditures or reducing the available income of households through higher taxes—worsened the contraction of the economy. Such policies could even have negative effects on the level of debt relative to the GDP and thus become self-defeating, just as had happened in Greece.

Italy demonstrated the danger of this policy. According to the announced fiscal measures, Italy was expected to implement a fiscal contraction of more than 5 percent of GDP between 2011 and 2012. This fiscal tightening was to have an estimated direct negative effect of 2.6 percent on growth. If the analogy with Greece were to hold—recession and decline in trade across Europe prevent Italy from benefiting from a stronger external demand—then deflation would produce second-round effects further damaging the economy and potentially bringing it to decline by even more. Then, fiscal austerity would have to be tightened again to achieve the balanced budget, triggering more negative growth, and so on.

The game-changer came at the beginning of 2012 with structural reforms implemented under the new Italian prime minister, Mario Monti, including pension and labor reforms plus a range of market liberalizations, which led to a decline in the spread on Italian bonds by more than 200 points. As in Merkel's vision, Italy, Ireland, Portugal, Spain, and even Greece—deprived of margins needed to manipulate their fiscal policy—were all catching up rapidly with the kind of structural reforms already applied in the rest of euro area. All of the five countries were increasing the flexibility of their economies, in what will amount to the most visible convergence of policies ever seen in Europe. Nevertheless, as the disastrous worsening of the Greek economy demonstrated, this painful exercise of reforms and fiscal restriction had only one chance of success: a permanent reduction in the level of their interest rates. The experience of those countries already receiving assistance did not speak in favor of this eventuality, however. Market expectations—and therefore the level of interest rates—are ultimately influenced by how willing member countries are to backstop the ailing countries through fiscal solidarity or through unlimited support from the ECB. But the more the crisis story was told as being the responsibility of a few countries, the more difficult it was to justify solidarity or even let savings continue to flow across the euro area.

The ECB intervention had avoided a collapse, but it would probably need to be doubled or tripled in 2012 to have effects on the economy and on the interest rate spreads. Without that, the situation experienced by the weaker countries would be untenable: they were already enacting the strictest fiscal retrenchment and had the tightest monetary conditions while also reshuffling economic and social structures. A deep recession seemed inescapable, with risks of a spiraling crisis and popular unrest.

Unfortunately, the characterization of the crisis as a conflict between profligate countries and virtuous creditors further weakened an already deteriorated argument for helping ailing countries. For all the talk about fiscal union, the fear of creating moral hazard—concern that the debtors would not address core problems after receiving financial help—was killing all rescue plans. In fact, more than three years after the beginning of this story, it was evident that Europeans had acknowledged that the euro's survival had become an existential reason for them to take action. But, divided and trapped in multiple cages of national narratives, Europe was still suffering a crisis of trust, unable to speak to—and of—herself.

# Epilogue: Toward the Political Union

## The Fear of the End

Telling an endless story can be useful only if the end eventually depends on the story itself. Since its beginning, the narrative of the crisis has been mainly made up of fears and recriminations. Accordingly, all the countermeasures have aimed primarily to build a system so that each country would stand on its own. But at the beginning of 2012, the crisis is far from over and we are finally understanding that it requires common financial capacities and stronger political integration. This is the kind of integration that finds no narrative when national governments dominate the scene. Imagine if the amazingly complex and obscure negotiations described in these pages had happened in public, in front of the common parliament. The language would be different; the analysis of the causes and of the remedies would also be different. Then probably we would all speak of the strenuous efforts of seventeen interdependent countries to help and understand each other.

Not only was the institutional framework underlying the monetary union weak, but as described in the prologue, national politics had lived through the first ten years of the euro pretending that not much had changed. Governments resorted to tricks and stratagems to adapt to the monetary union and forced political discourse into national cages. For a long time, hostage to their own national rhetoric and perspectives, European leaders did not even understand the consequences for politics of the financial crisis and the need for a collective response to it.

In 2008 the lack of a common response to the banking crisis endangered the stability of the states, undermining the basis of European prosperity. Just one

year later, after the revelations in Greece made clear the seriousness of problems in the euro zone periphery, government bonds of advanced economies had
become risky and, metaphorically, states ceased to be immortal.

In 2010 European politics failed to provide conclusive answers to the unprecedented need for credibility posed by the risk of defaults of the states. The quality of the European response was not adequate to the size of the challenge. It
was necessary to use an unconventional weapon of mass construction: solidarity.
The crisis demanded the pooling of political responsibility to build reciprocal
trust, with all the necessary vigor and rigor, and deploying aid while sharing sovereignty to dismantle the risk of abuses by national politics. But Europe, in the
hands of the monopolists of national powers, was not yet ready to act decisively.

Rightly or wrongly, the language of the financial markets is shared by the
geopolitical world surrounding the euro zone. It is a language that enables only
short-term conveniences to prevail and implies great skepticism about the long-
term political commitment to Europe. Instead of developing the political answer
to this skepticism by building trust, Europe, under the pressure of markets, has
elevated mistrust and the fear of moral hazard to the level of organizing principles.
At the end of 2010, by the Deauville suicidal admission that euro area countries
were all exposed to default, the governments worsened the fears of the markets.

Since that moment, the drivers of the crisis have been the fury and the fears
of financial markets, which have dictated the timing and the content of policy
decisions on a totally unprecedented scale. The logic of finance is extreme and
unrelenting. In times of strong financial tensions, the logic of the market runs
against the logic of correct long-term policy initiatives. Fiscal tightening, for
instance, can be self-defeating if markets are very concerned about the short term
because it makes the deficit decline but debt may actually increase. So interest
rates rise instead of going down, worsening the fiscal position of the country. The
same happens if markets focus on short-term growth, fearing that a recession may
cause governments to give up their fiscal consolidation efforts. The overwhelming
power of the markets can come close to precipitating the very catastrophes the
markets fear. A lapse of faith or a less-than-innocent nihilist rhetoric can disrupt
the underlying balance of the states on which democracy and citizens' lives rest.

At the end of November 2011 the euro appeared to be in its last days. Even
Germany faced troubles selling bonds denominated in euros. For the first time
capital was leaving the area, the bank markets stalled, and a panic run seemed at
hand. The eventual breakup of the euro had not been ruled out. Based on the
political responses of the euro area leaders, nobody could feel entirely sure of the
currencies that in ten years would be used to repay the public debts: would it
still be the euro, and under what conditions? Or a new drachma? Lire or francs?
Finally, a run on the weaker countries' banks could happen even by accident. The
world's most financially integrated region would be ripped apart. Capital would

be hastily repatriated. The European internal market would break into national pieces, and immediately the same would happen to the European Union itself. Defaults and mass poverty would be followed by capital controls, protectionism, and the deterioration of democracy.

The mechanics of a breakup show that it cannot happen in an orderly fashion once it concerns large and financially integrated countries. Although there is an explicit provision to opt out of the EU, the treaty also includes an explicit provision that the adoption of the euro is irrevocable, so the only way for a country to leave the euro zone would be by requesting a treaty amendment to create an opt-out clause.[1] This almost certainly would lead to a painfully long negotiation, leaving the country involved at the mercy of disruptive events: national depositors would withdraw their money from the banks and move it abroad, and banks and the state would inevitably default. Firms would be bankrupted and citizens, especially the least privileged, would become dramatically poorer. Politics would be under such pressure that the well-ordered conditions of democracy would be put in danger.[2] If the economic costs are mind-boggling, the political costs would be too severe and long lasting to quantify.

## The Current Solution: Limited Trust and Repatriation

After risking the collapse again in November 2011, the euro area took the road of building "limited trust": making sure that each country was able to stand on its own. Three steps were necessary. First, national political credibility was restored in all the critical countries, most remarkably in Italy where Mario Monti needed just a few weeks to prove his expertise in domestic policymaking and become an intellectual keystone in the group of euro leaders.

Second, the ECB had the capacity to stabilize the infection and even tame the crisis. Although it offered sizable incentives to the investors, Mario Draghi's central bank left it to them to decide whether the individual euro countries deserved credit. What came into place was a system of restored political credibility, facilitated by a common institution, but only to the extent that the recovery of the credibility was acknowledged by the markets.

The third element was the fiscal compact inspired by Angela Merkel: a set of fiscal rules that had to be enshrined in a new European treaty. The fiscal compact was a profound change in Europe's politics because it shifted a substantial degree of fiscal sovereignty from the national to the European level, basically subtracting from the governments the greatest part of their fiscal policy discretion. The goal was to enact rules that would ensure stable budgets starting in 2015, so that each country could stand on its own feet while markets were being assuaged by the European stability mechanisms.

By these three steps it was possible that countries of the euro area could go back to trusting each other—or, more appropriately, could stop fearing each other. But we deceive ourselves if we believe that a crisis like the one we have seen can be overcome without changing the core of the problem: the contradiction of national politics in an interdependent world. Without a mutualization of fiscal and banking policies, the result of the ECB-solution and of the fiscal compact would be only an extensive repatriation of capital, leading to renewed national segmentation of the European economy.

At the end of 2011 the single European banking market did not exist anymore. Once it was clear that banks were still backed up by national states only (without common European guaranties) in case of difficulty, credit institutions retrenched into their national markets. The larger European financial groups started to divide their businesses along the lines of national markets, with French banks, for instance, dealing only with French customers and French securities and so on. Inevitably, the segmentation extended from the banking system to the financial system at large and particularly so for the government bonds that ended up more and more in national portfolios.

In what might be seen as a rearguard conception of national responsibilities, the repatriation of debt could be theorized as one exit strategy from the crisis. At the beginning of 2011, 52 percent of Italian public debt, for instance, was in the hands of nonresident investors, but that share fell to around 38 percent at the end of the same year. Of the latter figure, the Italian Treasury estimated that 18 percent was in the "steady hands" of reliable nonresident investors unlikely to panic at the first sign of trouble. This meant that 20 percent was held by fickle foreign investors—not too much higher than the estimated 12–14 percent for the United States, which was considered a reason for the stability of the comparably high American public debt. The repatriation of debt would also solve, or at least reduce, one of the problems behind the crisis: the pressure of global finance on national politics.

But what would remain of Europe after such a massive repatriation of capital? Not much. Single countries would return to being closed economic systems as in the 1970s, but with all the problems of a monetary union: a national economy using a "foreign" currency—just like emerging countries and without the ability to make adjustments with a national monetary policy, which would remain in the hands of the euro zone. The economic adjustments would rest entirely on domestic prices and wages, with the determinant of success being the net savings in each country. So, surplus countries would see asset prices increase, followed by wages and inflation, while deficit countries would suffer deflation. The two parallel processes would finally adjust the balance of payments in the most painful way, leading to recriminations that would justifiably put in question the rationale of the European Union, its fiscal straitjackets, its monetary inefficiencies, and so on—again bringing the European Union, not only the euro area, to a breakup.

Behind the repatriation of capital is the idea that each country has to stand on its own. But, apart for the obvious logics of fiscal stability, the idea that in a monetary union all countries do not have to depend on each other and that all have to behave the same way is deeply flawed. An economically integrated area draws strength from the specialization of its members, not from their similarities. Inevitably, productivity cannot be equal in a large area where some sectors produce high technology and others specialize in tourism or agriculture. As in any integrated area—the United States or Germany itself—productivity differs from one region to the other, and so do trade and fiscal balances. To pretend that this is different for Europe is to misunderstand the functioning of areas that are integrated. It is also a tragic political and even philosophical mistake to allow identity to prevail over integration.

## The Political Union: Solidarity and Responsibility

Eventually the permanent solution to the crisis will be a matter of integrating politics from the national states into the new sphere of interdependency revealed by the financial crisis. The events have shown that the euro area cannot survive without deeper integration. In 2012 the European countries started deepening the governance of the euro area through the new fiscal rules. A new European treaty will remove some of the discretion that governments use in managing their balances.

Shifting sovereignty to the center, the revised treaty will be a first step toward a fiscal union. Once the risk of transforming a fiscal union into a transferunion is dispelled, common governance and common issuance of debt could be realized. The framework for fiscal rigor would be complemented with some form of fiscal risk sharing, which would prevent economic dislocation in one country from developing into a disruptive crisis for the entire euro area. The logical means of doing this is through eurobonds, once fiscal discipline is secured. In order to get there one cannot have separate national fiscal authorities that spend and tax on their own, creating liabilities that might spread to the other countries; in other words, the past cycle cannot be repeated. As a result, fiscal federalism and political union will also have to become a reality.

All this will require political courage. This is not a matter of "investing" more or less money in the European project, but primarily one of calling things by their real names. First of all, the euro area leaders have achieved much more than they are willing to admit in spite of the challenges they have faced since 2008. In indirect form, they built some of the economic pillars of fiscal union and they began adhering to practices of political federalism. Many economic measures used during the crisis have a federal nature, including the borrowing capacity of the European Commission and the European Investment Bank. The balance sheet of the European system of central banks is an indirect mechanism of redistributing risks within the euro area, as is the ECB's collateral policy, which allows the central bank to take risks backed by the ultimate guarantee from member states. Even if the design of the two emergency funds—the European Financial Stability Facility (EFSF) and the European Stability Mechanism (ESM)—is intergovernmental rather than supranational, elements in the structure of the funds suggest they will be able to use their capital as a common resource. The coordination of debt issuances of the seventeen countries is a form of common debt management and could provide the basis for eurobonds in the future. The decision to provide loans to Greece, Portugal, and Ireland at below-market rates also represents a fiscal transfer dictated by the principle of federal solidarity. The economic interdependency of the euro area has never been as clear as in 2011, when even Germany had to slash its expected growth for 2012 by two-thirds as a consequence of the unresolved tensions in the euro area.

Greece remains the most serious case and is reeling under a severe squeeze of domestic demand. Greece is likely to require ten years to accomplish its painful adjustment, but it will be able to do it with the assistance of partners in a major demonstration of shared sovereignty. In the meantime, the other countries that are most in need of support—Ireland, Portugal, Spain, and Italy—are all implementing reforms that had never even been conceived until 2008. Remaining the most open economic area in the world, Europe is a powerful "convergence machine" that will facilitate the reintegration of those countries. The amazing degree of political interdependency has caused the change of governments in all those countries. The political change is often interpreted as a fruit of emergency; however, there is probably no greater testimony to the powerful political convergence under way across Europe. Even under unprecedented stress, the bulk of public opinion shares the commitments of their new governments to adopting the exigent standards demanded by other societies.

At least for the moment, bipartisan support is the rule in all national parliaments called on to comply with the conditions requested by the European institutions in exchange for financial assistance. De facto the traditional left-right national cleavages are less meaningful now than the conditions dictated by the national-European interdependency, and a new non-national left-right dimension sooner or later will emerge to revitalize our concepts of politics. National parliaments have even reneged on their own votes, as in the case of Slovakia or Finland, to respect the will of the majority of the other Europeans. All future national elections may be decided on the issues related to European integration, and apparently the most pro-European parties have the strongest backing by their citizens. The policies of national governments have been determined extensively at the European level, and the degree of common surveillance is now unprecedented. The letters from the ECB to various prime ministers setting the conditions for assistance to the national governments—and asking explicitly for the support of large parliamentarian majorities—show the feasibility of a common government.

Acknowledging that the euro area is already a new political entity is indispensable to solving the crisis permanently through a combination of solidarity and mutual responsibility. But then, national narratives must be honest. Germany must acknowledge that it has been the big beneficiary of the euro and that it can keep on being so in the future, but only at the cost of mutualizing the European policies. Germany, having based its economic model on exporting to the rest of the euro area, while importing from outside the euro area, must make a commitment that is purely a consequence of the degree of integration of the European economies, with all their inevitable and potentially beneficial differences. The smaller countries in the north and in the south have up to now profited from great economic openness and need now to dismiss the fiction that their political microcosms have remained intact.

As far as the culture of political integration is concerned, France is probably the most problematic country, and she must acknowledge the principle of a European sovereignty also in terms of her fiscal or industrial policies. Italy, the second industrial powerhouse in the continent, must follow up the severe fiscal adjustment by encouraging modern institutions in a law-abiding society. Finally, the periphery needs to be helped with multiyear programs that provide the sense of restoring trust within the European family. All these commitments have an inherently political nature. And this is exactly how it should be. National politics cannot pretend that not much has changed as a result of the European integration, or people will start to lose faith in the familiar concept of democracy. The response to the crisis has to come from a change in national politics, simply because—as explained in the prologue of this book—the real causes of the crisis rest there. Otherwise, being hostage of their own national rhetoric, European leaders may still be able to get things better, but only in the worst possible way.

In the age of globalization, the solution of the crisis—of any crisis, even one well beyond Europe—is solidarity hand-in-hand with mutual responsibility. To be enacted, both solidarity and mutual responsibility need the states to pool their sovereignty as tightly as never in the past. Europe has been the world's most advanced experiment in sharing power and responsibility among different peoples. Bashing Europe has become the new conformism of all xenophobic spirits, but if Europe's experiment fails, the world might never be able to dispel its fears in the globalized age.

Washington
January 2012

# Notes

## Chapter 1

1. Johann Wolfgang von Goethe, "Zahme Xenien, Bürgerpflicht." The proverb is commonly used in daily German and was repeated publicly in May 2011 by German finance minister Wolfgang Schäuble in the context of the sovereign debt crisis.

2. Interview with an anonymous source at the U.S. Treasury.

3. Christine Lagarde, French finance minister, keynote address at the annual meeting of the Institute of International Finance, Washington, October 11, 2008.

4. Nicolas Sarkozy, president of France, speech to the United Nations General Assembly, September 23, 2008 (www.un.org/en/ga/63/generaldebate/pdf/france-fr.pdf).

5. Ranked twelfth according to the *Financial Times* and sixth according to *Business Week*.

6. Reuters, "Le lien franco-allemand nécessaire face à la crise, juge Sarkozy," October 11, 2008.

7. Patrick Honohan, governor of the Irish Central Bank, "The Banking Crisis in Ireland. Regulatory and Financial Stability Policy 2003–2008," a report to the minister for finance, May 31, 2010.

8. Tommaso Padoa-Schioppa, Italian finance minister, document Prot. 1122/R, November 26, 2007.

9. European Union, "Report on Financial Crisis Management," April 17, 2001, Brussels (http://consilium.europa.eu/uedocs/cmsUpload/Brouwer%20Report%20on%20Financial%20Crisis%20Management.pdf).

10. Peer Steinbrück, *Unterm Strich* (Hamburg: Hoffman und Campe, 2010), p. 194.

11. BIS (Bank for International Settlements), *80th Annual Report* (Basel, June 2010).

12. As reported in Financial Services Authority (United Kingdom), *The Turner Review: A Regulatory Response to the Global Banking Crisis* (London: March 2009), p. 36.

13. Morris Goldstein and Nicolas Veron, "Too Big to Fail: The Transatlantic Debate," Working Paper 11-2 (Washington: Peterson Institute for International Economics, January 2011) (www.iadb.org/intal/intalcdi/PE/2011/07335.pdf).

14. Interview with a source at the German finance ministry.

15. "There was no viable alternative to intervention in support of HRE. The insolvency of a banking group of this size just two weeks after the collapse of Lehman Brothers would have triggered a chain reaction, the cost of which would have been several times higher than that which the German government might incur from its guarantees." Deutsche Bundesbank, *Financial Stability Review 2009* (Frankfurt: November 2009), p. 33 (www.bundesbank.de/download/volkswirtschaft/finanzstabilitaetsberichte/finanz stabilitaetsbericht2009.en.pdf).

16. "Zusammenfassung der Gespräche zur Stützung der Hypo Real Estate Gruppe (HRE) vom 26.09.2008– 28.09.2008, im Frankfurter Dienstsitz der BaFin [Summary of the discussions for the support of the Hypo Real Estate (HRE) from 26.09.2008– 28.09.2008, in the Frankfurt office of BaFin]," confidential document, Bonn, October 9, 2008, BaFin Bankenaufsicht.

17. Deutsche Bundesbank, *Financial Stability Review 2009,* p. 32.

18. Deutscher Bundestag, DrS 16/14000, Beschlussempfehlung und Bericht des 2. Untersuchungsausschusses.

19. According to a European Central Bank working paper, "This shift accounts for much of the spread increase for EU country government bonds relative to German or U.S. Treasury benchmarks. Coefficients for deficit differentials are 3–4 times higher and for debt differentials 7–8 times higher during the crisis period than earlier." Ludger Schuknecht, Jürgen von Hagen, and Guido Wolswijk, "Government Bond Risk Premiums in the EU Revisited: The Impact of the Financial Crisis," Working Paper 1152 (Frankfurt: European Central Bank, January 2010), p. 6.

20. Ibid, p. 5.

21. Steinbrück writes of "collective mistrust" in *Unterm Strich,* p. 201.

## Chapter 2

1. Daniel Gros and Stefano Micossi, "A Call for a European Financial Stability Fund," October 30, 2008 (www.VoxEU.org), and "The Cost of Non-Europe?" (Brussels: Centre for European Policy Studies, October 7, 2008) (www.ceps.eu/book/cost-non-europe).

2. That difficulty was the main reason why so many economists had failed to understand the mechanisms that produced the global crisis. It had been particularly clear in the case of the International Monetary Fund, which had made embarrassing forecasting mistakes that year, but also with the ECB.

3. Inflation actually touched 4 percent, but interest rate policy is expected to anticipate the peaks, not to react when they have been reached.

4. This technique is the so-called symmetric corridor approach.

5. Paul Mercier and Francesco Papadia, eds., *The Concrete Euro: Implementing Monetary Policy in the Euro Area* (Oxford: Oxford University Press, 2011), p. 235.

6. Willem Buiter, "The Central Bank as Market Maker of Last Resort 1," Maverecon Blog, August 12, 2007 (http://maverecon.blogspot.com/2007/08/central-bank-as-market-maker-of-last.html).

7. While "only" a few hundred banks participated actively in the weekly auctions, several thousand banks have access to the ECB, and its collateral policy was among the most liberal. The U.S. Federal Reserve also changed later to a broader approach.

8. Jacques de Larosière and others, "Report of the High-Level Group on Financial Supervision in the EU" (Brussels: European Commission, February 2009) (http://ec.europa.eu/internal_market/finances/docs/de_larosiere_report_en.pdf).

9. European Commission, "European Financial Integration Report" (Brussels: 2006, 2007).

10. European Central Bank, "EU Banking Structures" (Frankfurt, 2008).

11. A good description is provided by Jean Pisani-Ferry and Andrè Sapir, "Banking Crisis Management in the EU: An Interim Assessment" (cepr.org/meets/wkcn/9/977/papers/PisaniFerrySapir.pdf).

12. De Larosière and others, "Report of the High-Level Group on Financial Supervision in the EU," p. 41, para. 159.

13. For a bank, a liquidity crisis means uncertainty about whether expected payments will flow in regularly from other banks, clients will withdraw deposits, or securities will suffer heavy discounts or become illiquid. If a bank faces a liquidity shock and cannot refinance in the unsecured interbank market or in normal central bank operations (because it has run out of eligible collateral), then it will need the so-called ELA (emergency liquidity assistance) from the central bank. ELA is typically granted only at high penalty rates, control rights, or a larger than usual collateralization.

14. This led famously into troubles a former Italian central banker, Antonio Fazio, who otherwise had seen very acutely the dangers behind the foreign financial practices he was keeping away from his country.

15. The main exceptions to this trend were within groupings of small neighboring countries (such as the Benelux countries or Scandinavia), and the privatization of the banking sectors of central and eastern European countries.

16. Financial nationalism is deeply intertwined with other forms of distortion of the EU Single Market. Special tax regimes in Ireland, Austria, and in many smaller regional tax havens often are connected to the United Kingdom, but not exclusively. Practically every EU country has a fiscal enclave (Monaco, San Marino, Andorra, Gibraltar, Cyprus, Liechtenstein, Antilles, and even the Vatican State in some regards).

17. Peer Steinbrück, "'Ich fühlte mich getäuscht' [I felt I had been fooled]; Das Krisen-Tagebuch des Peer Steinbrück," *Der Spiegel*, nr 37/2010.

18. Christian Schmieder, Christoph Memmel, and Ingrid Stein, "Relationship Lending: Empirical Evidence for Germany," Discussion Paper Series 2: Banking and Financial Studies (Frankfurt: Deutsche Bundesbank Research Center, 2007), p. 14.

19. Oliver Vins, "How Politics Influence State-Owned Banks—The Case of German Savings Banks," Working paper 191 (Frankfurt: Goethe Universitaet, November 2008).

20. Deutsche Bundesbank, "Bundesbank Bulletin 21" (Frankfurt: November 2009), p. 61.

21. Vins, "How Politics Influence State-Owned Banks."

22. A colorful and detailed account of the recent German banking abuses can be found in Leo Mueller, *Bank-Räuber: Wie kriminelle Manager und unfähige Politiker uns in den Ruin treiben* (Berlin: Econ Verlag, 2010).

23. See detailed tables on preliminary locational and consolidated banking statistics at end June 2011, published by the Monetary and Economic Department, Bank for International Settlements, October 2011 (www.bis.org/statistics/provbstats.pdf#page=7).

24. *U.S. Securities and Exchange Commission v. Goldman Sachs & Co. and Fabrice Tourre,* April 15, 2010 (www.sec.gov/litigation/complaints/2010/comp21489.pdf).

25. Steinbrück, "Ich fühlte mich getäuscht."

26. Deutsche Bundesbank, *Financial Stability Report 2009* (Frankfurt, November 2009), p. 32.

27. Steinbrück, "Ich fühlte mich getäuscht."

28. European Central Bank, *Monthly Bulletin,* Frankfurt, July 2009, p. 70: "Although all countries have announced broad-based bank rescue packages, investors have differentiated between countries mainly on the basis of other, more country-specific factors. In particular, the literature on the determinants of long-term bond yields provides evidence that a country's macroeconomic and fiscal fundamentals affect investors' perceptions of its creditworthiness and that this is likely to influence developments in government bond markets."

## Chapter 3

1. An interesting and revealing description is given in Gordon Brown, *Beyond the Crash: Overcoming the First Crisis of Globalisation* (London: Simon and Schuster, 2010).

2. Ibid.

3. Bank of England, "Annual Report 2008," London, box 4.

4. European Central Bank, *Financial Stability Review* (Frankfurt, June 2009), p. 113. Such perceptions can be considered somewhat irrational if the aim of a bank nationalization is to protect bondholders and mitigate the risk of systemic failures.

5. The suggestion apparently was inspired by José Luis Zapatero, who wanted to react to Spain's exclusion from the earlier summit of the four major European countries.

6. Franco-German bilateral meetings were named after the village where Gerhard Schroeder and Jacques Chirac had reconciled their views after strong confrontations over the Nice Treaty on EU governance.

7. The plan adopted on October 12, 2008, included commitments to recapitalize the banks, to ensure their liquidity, and to offer government guarantees in order to resume activity in the interbank market. The principles expressed by the statement were intended to ensure sufficient liquidity to the financial institutions and facilitate the refinancing of struggling banks, to provide financial institutions with the capital resources to enable them to continue to finance the economy, to provide sufficient recapitalization of distressed banks, to ensure sufficient flexibility in the implementation of accounting rules given the exceptional circumstances, and to strengthen cooperation among European countries.

8. Ackermann would later release a statement saying that he would be ashamed if he had to resort to the state for help. The statement caused a furious reaction at the Chancellery. Ackermann was de facto throwing a stigma on the other banks that would need to ask for the state's support, weakening the whole package.

9. Martin Schulz, a very influential German MP, during a private lunch asked Barroso to reshuffle the commission and remove McCreevy. "The Commission has not listened to our requests for initiative," said the president of the EU Parliament, Hans-Gert Pöttering, considered close to the German chancellor. Barroso responded by enlisting Jacques de Larosiere, the former IMF general manager, to redesign the banking regulation, effectively sidelining McCreevy.

10. The article corresponds to the Article 87 of the Maastricht Treaty. I use the term "treaty" to refer to the consolidated two core functional treaties that lay out how the EU operates: the Treaty on European Union (TEU) and the Treaty on the Functioning of the European Union (TFEU).

11. On October 15, the ECB expanded its list of assets eligible for use as collateral in its credit operations and increased the provision of longer-term liquidity by fully meeting banks' demand for liquidity at maturities of three and six months; the list of eligible assets was subsequently tightened up allegedly because some Spanish banks were gaming the system, providing low-quality collaterals in credit operations with the ECB.

12. Nicolas Sarkozy, president of France, speech before the European Parliament, October 21, 2008 (www.ambafrance-uk.org/President-Sarkozy-s-speech-before.html).

13. According to French daily *Le Monde,* Sarkozy deemed the commission led by José Manuel Barroso hostage to the great baronies presiding over competition policy, the Stability and Growth Pact, and the internal market while being incapable of taking political initiatives. Arnaud Leparmentier, "Union Européenne Avant Le Conseil Européen; Sarkozy parie sur Londres et Moscou pour imposer sa vision," *Le Monde,* December 11, 2008.

14. "Jousting Egos: Germany and France Compete for Role of Financial Savior," *Der Spiegel,* October 29, 2008 (www.spiegel.de/international/europe/0,1518,587067,00.html).

15. Ibid.

16. Sheryl Gay Stolberg, "Leaders Move toward Meetings on Economic Crisis," *New York Times,* October 18, 2008.

17. Ibid.

18. Ibid.

19. Argentina, Australia, Brazil, Canada, China, France, Germany, India, Indonesia, Italy, Japan, Mexico, Russia, Saudi Arabia, South Africa, South Korea, Turkey, the United Kingdom, the United States, and the European Union.

20. Wen Jiabao, premier of China, "Chair's Statement of the Seventh Asia-Europe Meeting," Beijing, October 24–25, 2008 (www.fmprc.gov.cn/eng/wjdt/2649/t575942.htm).

21. Wen Jiabao, premier of China, "Together, We Will Overcome Challenges and Achieve Win-Win Progress," address at the Seventh Asia-Europe Meeting, October 25, 2008 (www.asem7.cn/misc/2008-10/25/content_57461.htm).

22. Nicolas Sarkozy, president of France, alongside M. Gordon Brown, prime minister of the United Kingdom of Great Britain and Northern Ireland, Statement at Versailles, October 28, 2008 (http://ambafrance-us.org/spip.php?article1160).

23. For the text of the "Agreed Language," see www.europa-eu-un.org/articles/en/article_8284_en.htm.

24. "Declaration: Summit On Financial Markets and the World Economy," Washington, November 15, 2008 (www.g20.org/Documents/g20_summit_declaration.pdf).

25. Leparmentier, "Union Européenne Avant Le Conseil Européen."

26. The pound slid from 1.2898 (on October 13) to 1.0446 (on December 22) against the dollar.

27. The relevant effect of the depreciation of the pound on the economy of the euro area is described in Directorate General for Economic and Financial Affairs, "Quarterly Report on the Euro Area," European Commission, Brussels, March 2009, p. 13.

## Chapter 4

1. The decisions of the EU Council and of ECOFIN (Economics and Financial Affairs Council) were taken under the Italian presidency of the EU.

2. Then chancellor Gerhard Schroeder did use the fiscal leeway to implement important reforms.

3. Some fiscal cost may have been necessary to pay for pension reform or for encouraging labor to be more flexible.

4. The European Commission publishes a yearly report: "European Economy—Public Finance in the EMU."

5. There is no crowding-out effect because higher demand is accommodated by a perfectly elastic money supply.

6. This situation is inefficient because marginal costs in the economy are moved away from their efficient level and changes in the net asset position may not reflect underlying preferences, wealth, and technology. During the five years leading up to monetary union, the nominal long-term interest fell by more than 5 percentage points in Italy, Portugal, and Spain, compared with an average decline of around 3 percentage points for the euro area as a whole. At the same time, the development of the single European capital market helped expand the availability of capital for euro area countries. Once currency risk is removed, and given the bank's portfolio dynamics of increasing diversification, country-specific risk was often overlooked or even seen as an opportunity for slightly higher yields.

7. Javier Suarez, "The Spanish Crisis: Background and Policy Challenges," DP 7909 (London: Center for Economic Policy Research, July 2010) (www.cepr.org/pubs/new-dps/dplist.asp?dpno=7909).

8. OECD current account balances for 2001–08 (www.oecd-ilibrary.org/trade/current-account-balance-of-payments_20743920-table5).

9. Analyses are documented in OECD, "Economic Survey on the Euro Area" (Paris: 2009 and 2010).

10. European Commission, "Communication from the Commission to the European Council: A European Economic Recovery Plan," Brussels, November 26, 2008 (http://eur-lex.europa.eu/LexUriServ/LexUriServ.do?uri=COM:2008:0800:FIN:EN:PDF).

11. Ibid.

12. "CDU-Bundesparteitag Mit dem Charme einer schwäbischen Hausfrau," *Frankfurter Allgemeine Zeitung,* December 1, 2008.

13. Hans-Werner Sinn, "Why Does Angela Merkel Hesitate?" Project Syndicate, December 29, 2008 (www.project-syndicate.org/commentary/sinn23/English).

14. The SPD was still haunted by the memory of the 1982 collapse of the SPD-led Schmidt government as a consequence of generous fiscal spending programs. Similarly, an attempt at revamping a Keynesian style tax-and-spend policy ended Oskar Lafontaine's term as finance minister after only five months in March 1999. Lafontaine's successor, Hans Eichel, regarded maintaining fiscal credibility as a key priority. By 2008 SPD finance minister Steinbrück's advocacy of conservative fiscal policy was additionally bolstered by his support for the pro-market "Agenda 2010."

15. Merkel was also resistant because a German fiscal stimulus was already in the cards as a result of two rulings by the German Constitutional Court on tax exemption on health spending and on the commuter tax allowance. With the federal government accounting for only 40 percent of the combined public sector—and even less in terms of investment spending—it relies heavily on the local authorities to implement its fiscal policy.

16. A signal that Deutsche Bank was seriously worried came on December 17, when it stunned the markets by announcing that it was not going to redeem €1 billion of callable bonds at the first opportunity. The debt would not mature until 2014, but it had a call date of January 2009, meaning the bank had a right to pay it back as early as the following month. It is a long-time industry practice for banks to redeem such bonds on the earliest possible date, as proof of the soundness of their balance sheets. Analysts said Deutsche Bank was the first major player to break the tradition, raising some awkward questions about the German bank's financial position. Actually, a small Italian bank had done the same just a few months earlier.

17. Margaret Heckel, *So regiert die Kanzlerin* [*So Governed the Chancellor*] (Munich: Piper Verlag, June 2009) (www.piper-verlag.de/sachbuch/buch.php?id=15745).

18. International Monetary Fund, "The Size of the Fiscal Expansion: An Analysis for the Largest Countries," Washington, February 1, 2009 (www.imf.org/external/np/pp/eng/2009/020109.pdf).

## Chapter 5

1. The International Monetary Fund (IMF) calculates that the share of U.S. sovereign debt held by private nonresident investors declined from 19 percent in 2000 to 12 percent in 2009 and 14 percent in 2011. See Carlos Cottarelli, director of the IMF fiscal affairs department, "Challenges of Budgtary and Financial Crisis in Europe," speech at the London School of Economics and Political Science, November 18, 2011 (www.imf.org/external/np/speeches/2011/pdfs/111811.pdf).

2. According to the IMF, monetary integration encouraged larger cross-border financial exposures. In the banking sector, the share of interbank loans to banks within the euro area increased from 15 percent in the late 1990s to 25 percent in the late 2000s, and doubled from 10 percent to 20 percent for interbank loans to banks in the EU but outside the euro area. In addition, home-country bias for investment funds' allocations of equity and debt securities declined significantly.

3. Lorenzo Bini Smaghi, European Central Bank, speech at the Goldman Sachs Global Macro Conference—Asia 2011, Hong Kong, February 22, 2011 (www.ecb.int/press/key/date/2011/html/sp110222.en.html).

4. Ibid.

5. Bank for International Settlements, "Quarterly Review," Basel, March 2009.

6. Ibid.

7. Ashoka Mody, "From Bear Stearns to Anglo Irish: How Eurozone Sovereign Spreads Related to Financial Sector Vulnerability," European Department Working Paper (Washington: IMF, May 1, 2009). Uncertainty showed in elevated levels of implied volatility as well as price/earnings ratios, which were extremely low by the standards of the past two decades.

8. IMF, *Global Financial Stability Report 2009* (Washington: 2009).

9. ECB, *Monthly Bulletin,* Frankfurt, July 2009, table 2 (www.ecb.int/pub/pdf/mobu/mb200907en.pdf).

10. The stock of money does not change even though the value of the money does.

11. Statistically it is possible to detect a correlation between the divergence of bond yields in the euro area and the generic perception of risk in the global markets.

12. The Eurosystem is directly affected by the services that rating agencies provide. Article 18(1), second indent, of the Statute of the European System of Central Banks and of the European Central Bank (ESCB Statute) stipulates that the ECB and the national central banks may "conduct credit operations with credit institutions and other market participants, with lending being based on adequate collateral." In the assessment of the credit standards of eligible assets, the Eurosystem takes into account, among other things, credit assessments deriving from different sources, including credit rating agencies that are defined as "external credit assessment institutions."

13. Rabah Arezki, Bertrand Candelon, and Amadou N. R. Sy1, "Sovereign Rating News and Financial Markets Spillovers: Evidence from the European Debt Crisis" (Washington, DC: IMF, March 2011), p. 8 (www.imf.org/external/pubs/ft/wp/2011/wp1168.pdf).

14. "Ft Alphaville" blog, *Financial Times,* January 19, 2009 (http://ftalphaville.ft.com/).

15. The BIS "Bulletin" for March 2009 noted that issuing government debt was increasingly difficult as long as the supply of government debt was rising. Moreover, growing volumes of corporate issuance and government-guaranteed bank debt meant that governments were bound to face increasing competition for investors.

16. Committee for European Securities Regulators, "CESR's Report to the European Commission on the Compliance of Credit Rating Agencies with the IOSCO Code: The Role of Credit Rating Agencies in Structured Finance" (Paris: May 2008) (www.esma.

europa.eu/system/files/CESR_08_277.pdf). In November 2008 the commission presented its formal proposal for a regulation, and in March 2009 the final text was submitted to the ECOFIN Council and, subsequently, to the European Parliament for adoption.

17. "On the Secret Committee to Save the Euro, a Dangerous Divide," *Wall Street Journal,* September 24, 2010.

18. The European Commission has a standing facility, underwritten by each of the EU's twenty-seven member states, which it can use to issue debt in the market. The standing authorization of total issuance was increased in 2008 from €12 billion to €25 billion. It was this facility that was used for the co-financing of the IMF programs for Hungary and Latvia. However, in Brussels it was clear that this facility was de facto earmarked for co-financing programs with EU members outside the euro zone.

## Chapter 6

1. In 1997, the finance minister of the French government led by Lionel Jospin was Dominique Strauss-Kahn, who later became managing director of the International Monetary Fund.

2. "Paris s'inquiète de la fragilité de la zone euro [Paris worried by euro zone fragility]," *Le Monde,* February 1, 2009.

3. "Un ministre français, 'si on s'en tient à la lettre des traités, on va dans le mur [A French minister: if we stick to the letter of the treaties, we go to the wall],'" *Le Monde,* February 1, 2009.

4. Author interview.

5. Ibid.

6. "A Test for Europe's Common Currency Support for Wobbly Euro Economies," *Frankfurter Allgemeine Zeitung,* February 20, 2009, translated in *Der Spiegel,* February 20, 2009 (www.spiegel.de/international/europe/0,1518,608985,00.html).

7. Ibid.

8. Ibid.

9. Author interview.

10. The provisions of the treaty establishing the European Community and the Stability and Growth Pact were intended to ensure sound fiscal policies and to support the Eurosystem's independent monetary policy, which aims to maintain price stability. Such provisions thereby promote a smooth functioning of the Economic and Monetary Union (EMU), in which a single monetary policy coexists with national fiscal policies. Article 101 of the treaty prohibits the provision by the Eurosystem of overdraft facilities in favor of community institutions or bodies, governments, and other public entities, as well as the direct purchase by the Eurosystem of debt instruments issued by such entities. This provision is intended to sever the direct link between monetary policy and fiscal policy and, in particular, to prohibit the monetary financing of government deficits. Article 102 of the treaty prohibits measures establishing privileged access by community institutions or bodies, governments, and other public entities to financial institutions, unless this is based on prudential considerations. According to Article 103 of the treaty, neither should the European Union be liable for or assume the commitments of governments or public

entities, nor should a member state be liable for or assume the commitments of another member state. This so-called no-bailout clause is intended to ensure that member states remain ultimately liable for their own borrowing. The most basic rule of fiscal policy, enshrined in Article 104 and the secondary legislation of the Stability and Growth Pact, is that member states should avoid excessive government deficits in excess of 3 percent of GDP. A general government debt-to-GDP ratio above 60 percent is excessive unless the debt ratio diminishes sufficiently and approaches the reference value at a satisfactory pace. When an excessive deficit is deemed to exist, the member state concerned is subject to an "excessive deficit" procedure to be enforced by the European Commission.

11. Goldman Sachs, "European Weekly Analyst," Issue 09/08, February 26, 2009, p. 4.

12. "Schleswig-Holstein quasi bankrupt," *Bild Zeitung*, February 24, 2009.

13. Interview, EU-Kommissar Verheugen, "Weltmeister in riskanten Bankgeschäften [World champions in risky banking business]," *Sueddeutsche Zeitung*, May 18, 2009.

14. "A darkened outlook for Germany's banks," *Financial Times*, June 10, 2009, p. 7.

15. International Monetary Fund, *Global Financial Stability Report: Navigating the Financial Challenges Ahead*, October 2009 (www.imf.org/External/Pubs/FT/GFSR/2009/02/index.htm). The IMF report was based on the assumption of a major collapse in eastern Europe that would send the banking systems of many western European countries down the drain, primarily Austria, Germany, Sweden, and Italy. This assumption proved wrong, but only because of aid interventions by the European Investment Bank, which lamented the delay and reluctance of other European institutions and of national governments.

16. Reuters news report, November 5, 2009.

17. *The Telegraph* added that EU banks had roughly $1.4 trillion of exposure to eastern Europe, and that EU corporate debts were 95 percent of GDP, compared with 50 percent in the United States.

18. "Bilanz des Schreckens [Balance of terror]," *Sueddeutsche Zeitung*, April 24, 2009.

19. Particularly affected were Hypo Real Estate, several Landesbanken, and Commerzbank. According to the BaFin, Commerzbank alone was holding securities and loans worth €101 billion affected by the financial crisis.

20. European Commission Directorate-General for Economic and Financial Affairs, "Surveillance of Intra-Euro-Area Competitiveness and Imbalances," May 2010 (http://ec.europa.eu/economy_finance/publications/european_economy/2010/ee1_en.htm).

21. Jacques de Larosière and others, "The High-Level Group on Financial Supervision in the EU," Brussels, February 25, 2009. The De Larosière report deserves a great deal of appraisal, but that goes beyond the scope of these pages.

22. Bundesbank, *Financial Stability Review 47* (Frankfurt: November 2009). On stability in the German banking system, the report notes, "The foundation for a new start was laid initially by the direct effects of the measures taken in Germany—above all, extensive provision of liquidity, guarantees for private savings deposits by central government, and the injection of capital into credit institutions as well as guarantees for bank bonds by the Financial Market Stabilisation Fund [Sonderfonds Finanzmarktstabilisierung or SoFFin]. The banks are now benefiting increasingly from the indirect effects of an improvement in the economic situation. For the time being, this has broken the feared

vicious circle of a weakened financial system and a cooling of the real economy. The collective burdens of stabilisation are nonetheless apparent in central banks' bloated balance sheets and prolonged higher government debt. In addition, there is the risk of future negative incentives if the financing behaviour of market participants increasingly involves anticipating the possibility of shifting losses on to the state."

23. Ibid.

## Chapter 7

1. After the crisis involving BNP Paribas on August 9, 2007 (see chapter 2), on August 22 a first supplementary longer-term refinancing operation was announced. Four months later, on December 12, 2007, central banks announced a coordinated action, and on December 17 the ECB announced an extraordinary two-week tender for its main refinancing operation. On October 8, 2008, the ECB announced a fixed-rate tender procedure with full allotment and narrowing of the "corridor" (the symmetric range between deposit and lending facilities).

2. After October 2008 there were six further cuts: November 6, 2008, by 0.50 percent; December 4, 2008, by 0.75 percent; January 15, 2009, by 0.5 percent; March 5, 2009, by 0.5 percent; April 2, 2009, 0.25 percent; and May 7, 2009, by 0.25 percent. The policy rate was at 1 percent as of May 2009, higher than in the United States and in Japan where it was at zero, but the abundant liquidity provision also had brought the overnight rate toward zero in the euro area.

3. The excess liquidity showed very clearly in the level of the interbank rates, which sank close to the lowest level of the deposit facility.

4. Bank for International Settlements, "Annual Report" (Basel: 2009).

5. Jean-Claude Trichet, president of the ECB, "The Financial Crisis and Our Response So Far," keynote address at the Chatham House Global Financial Forum, New York, April 27, 2009.

6. Ibid.

7. ECB, *Monthly Bulletin,* Frankfurt, March 2009 (www.ecb.int/pub/pdf/mobu/mb200903en.pdf).

8. The preoccupation of the Europeans with Wall Street's hazard was eloquently described by ECB president Jean-Claude Trichet in a visit to New York in April 2009 and a speech on April 27, 2009, given at the Chatham House Global Financial Forum: "The crisis, which originated within a few blocks from here," Trichet announced, "has swept across the globe." See Trichet, "The Financial Crisis and Our Response So Far."

9. European Council, "Presidency Conclusions," 7880/1/09 REV1 (Brussels, March 20, 2009), par. 5; Jacques de Larosière and others, *Report of the High-Level Group on Financial Supervision in the EU* (Brussels: EC, February 2009) (http://ec.europa.eu/internal_market/finances/docs/de_larosiere_report_en.pdf&sa=U&ei=hZ7WToim Hsnb0QHjrMGhAg&ved=0CA8QFjAA&usg=AFQjCNGmd6NpdiGqOCnjSu9s TwoJwdvS3g).

10. De Larosière and others, *Report of the High-Level Group on Financial Supervision in the EU.*

11. Emporiki was preparing for a particularly sharp fall in deposits—a problem facing many Greek banks.

12. Goldman Sachs Global Economics, Commodities and Strategy Research, *European Weekly Analyst,* March 19, 2009.

13. "Summers Backs State Action," *Financial Times,* March 9, 2009.

14. Alan Beattie, "The Gap of Twenty," *Financial Times,* March 14, 2009 (www.ft.com/intl/cms/s/0/cddc22d4-1005-11de-a8ae-0000779fd2ac.html#axzz1hNCUIZ2B).

15. Peter Ludlow, "The Spring Council of March 2009," Briefing Note 7.1 (Brussels: Eurocomment), p. 10.

16. Ibid.

17. European Council, "Presidency Conclusions" (Brussels: March 19–20, 2009), par. 7 (www.consilium.europa.eu/uedocs/cms_data/docs/pressdata/en/ec/106809.pdf).

18. Ludlow, The Spring Council of March 2009."

19. *Europäische Union muss geschlossen handeln* [European Union must act united], March 19, 2009.

20. These quotes from Merkel at the G-20 meeting in London are taken from newspaper reports and from the helpful and insightful reconstruction provided by Margaret Heckel in *So regiert die Kanzlerin* (Munich: Piper Verlag, 2009).

21. www.spiegel.de/politik/ausland/0,1518,617092,00.html.

22. G-20 Final Communique: "London Summit—Leaders' Statement," April 2, 2009 (www.g20.org/Documents/g20_communique_020409.pdf).

23. There are differences in the way the two institutions computed the results. While the IMF used a top-down approach, setting a macro framework first, the CEBS results are based on a bottom-up approach, bank-by-bank and obviously state-by-state. Furthermore, differences in accounting standards reduce the comparability of the studies.

24. Jean-Claude Trichet, president of the ECB, Lucas Papademos, vice president of the ECB, "Introductory Statement with Q&A," European Central Bank, Luxembourg, July 2, 2009 (www.ecb.int/press/pressconf/2009/html/is090702.en.html).

25. Economic and Financial Affairs Council, "Statement by Ministers and Governors on the EU-wide Stress Test" (Brussels: October, 1, 2009) (www.se2009.eu/polopoly_fs/1.17427!menu/standard/file/Statement%20by%20Informal%20Ecofin%20on%20EU%20stress%20test%20TC.pdf).

26. ECB, "Editorial," *Monthly Bulletin,* Frankfurt, September 2009 (www.ecb.int/pub/pdf/mobu/mb200909en.pdf).

27. ECB, "Editorial," *Monthly Bulletin,* Frankfurt, November 2009, p. 6 (www.ecb.int/pub/pdf/mobu/mb200911en.pdf).

28. Jean-Claude Trichet, ECB president, "Introductory Statement," ECB press conference (Frankfurt: September 3, 2009) (www.ecb.int/press/pressconf/2009/html/is090903.en.html).

29. The liquidity provision by the ECB had begun in the summer 2007, but it became systemic just after the Lehman failure when banks had to resort to ECB financing for survival since the interbank money market had dried up completely. An example of the different conditions can be taken from October 6, 2008, when the ECB offered banks a normal financing operation of approximately €40 billion, but the banks asked

for more than €250 billion at a rate of 4.60 percent. Of these, at least €200 billion was redeposited by the banks at the ECB at an interest rate of 4.25 percent. Banks were taking a deadweight loss in a deal that would go on for months: the uncertainty of banks forcing them to borrow in excess at the only financial window still working—no matter the cost—in order to have resources available in the event of a deeper trust crisis. One year later things were completely different since banks could get money from the ECB at a very cheap rate of 1 percent.

30. Author's estimates.

31. According to Citigroup's European analysts, the share of ECB liquidity relative to total bank assets rose from a quite stable average of 2 percent before the crisis to close to 10 percent in Greece and from 2 percent to 6 percent in the case of Ireland. In the case of Spain the change was smaller but still significant, from around 1 percent before the crisis to 2.5–3.0 percent since October 2008.

## Chapter 8

1. Joschka Fischer, "From Confederacy to Federation: Thoughts on the Finality of European Integration," Humboldt University, Berlin, May 12, 2000 (whi-berlin.de/documents/fischer.pdf).

2. Chancellor Angela Merkel, "Humboldt-Rede zu Europa," May 27, 2009 (www.hu-berlin.de/pr/medien/aktuell/reden/standardseite/humboldt-rede_merkel).

3. The Rome Treaty setting up the European Community and the Maastricht Treaty establishing the European Union and European Monetary Union were merged into one document dubbed the "Treaty on the Functioning of the EU." This merger implied that all policies falling under EU competence—such as the single market, economic policy, taxation, home affairs, and agriculture—would be governed by one document.

4. The president will be selected by a qualified majority of the European Council for two-and-one-half years and will represent the European Union in international affairs and be responsible for calling the meetings of the European Council, scheduled to convene four times a year (instead of twice previously).

5. This position combines the posts of the high representative of common foreign and security policy—representing the EU versus non-European countries—and the EU commissioner for foreign affairs in charge of relations with the EU neighbor countries.

6. The European Commission will have the principal right to initiate legislation. Any rights of the EU Council will be narrowly confined. The president of the European commission will be appointed by majority vote of the EU Parliament for a five-year term, but preselected by the European Council. The president will have the right to select commissioners from several candidates presented by national governments.

7. With the Lisbon Treaty, the EU Parliament was to have full legislative powers, together with the EU Council, in most of the areas that fall under EU governance. There would be 92 policies that would fall in the legislative powers of the Parliament instead of the previous 35. Most important is the extension of its powers to agriculture, which covers more than 45 percent of the EU budget, and cooperation in home and justice.

8. The European Court of Justice will serve as the final instance on EU law. Below it will sit a European high court, which will serve as a court of first instance to citizens, EU member states, and public institutions. Some policy fields may be delegated to specialized courts. This structure had been inherited from the Nice Treaty, but powers of the high court and the specialized courts are enhanced.

9. Bundesverfassungsgericht (Federal Constitutional Court of Germany), 2 BvE 2/08 vom 30.6.2009, Ruling of the Constitutional Court, paragraphs 256–57 (www. bverfg.de/entscheidungen/es20090630_2bve000208.html).

10. T. M. Robinson, ed., *Heraclitus: Fragments, A Text and Translation with a Commentary by T. M. Robinson* (University of Toronto Press, 1987).

11. Christian Tomuschat, "The Ruling of the German Constitutional Court on the Treaty of Lisbon," *German Law Journal* 10 (2009): 1259–62.

12. Joachim Jahn, "Vereinigte Staaten von Europa wird es nicht geben [There Will Be No United States of Europe]," Interview with Paul Kirchhof, *Frankfurter Allgemeine Zeitung,* June 30, 2009.

13. Bundesverfassungsgericht (Federal Constitutional Court of Germany) BVerfG, 2 BvE 2/08 vom 30.6.2009, Paragraph-Nr. (296), (www.bverfg.de/entscheidungen/ es20090630_2bve000208.html).

14. Ibid.

15. Bundesverfassungsgericht: BVerfG, 2 BvE 2/08, June 30, 2009, paragraphs 270–72 and 273–89 (www.bverfg.de/entscheidungen/es20090630_2bve000208.html).

16. Bundesverfassungsgericht: BVerfG, 2 BvE 2/08, June 30, paragraphs 284–85 (www.bverfg.de/entscheidungen/es20090630_2bve000208.html).

17. The ruling acknowledged openness toward Europe as one of the cornerstones of the German constitutional system. The constitutional mandate to realize a united Europe, which follows from Article 23.1 of the Basic Law and its Preamble, means with regard to the German constitutional bodies that participation in European integration is not left to their political discretion. The Basic Law seeks European integration and an international peaceful order. Therefore, not only the principle of openness toward international law (*Völkerrechtsfreundlichkeit*), but also the principle of openness toward European law (*Europarechtsfreundlichkeit*) applies, according to the court.

18. Constitutional Court: English version of the press statement. Article 2.c (www. bundesverfassungsgericht.de/pressemitteilungen/bvg09-072en.html).

19. Joachim Jahn, "Vereinigte Staaten von Europa wird es nicht geben [There Will Be No United States of Europe]," Interview with Paul Kirchhof, *Frankfurter Allgemeine Zeitung,* June 30, 2009.

20. Thomas Petersen, Institut für Demoskopie Allensbach, "Der Kampf Europas mit der Gleichgültigkeit [Europe's fight against indifference]," *Frankfurter Allgemeine Zeitung,* May 21, 2008, p. 5.

21. Der Bundeswahlleiter (www.bundeswahlleiter.de/de/bundestagswahlen/ BTW_BUND_09/ergebnisse/landesergebnisse/).

22. The phrase "ideological ballast" was used by Willy Brandt in 1976 in his book *Begegnungen und Einsichten,* where he explained the background analysis behind the Godesberger Program, which took the SPD toward the social market economy.

*Chapter 9*

1. Treaty of the European Union (TEU), Article 4.3.

2. "Greek Socialists Ride Wave of Discontent," *Financial Times,* October 3, 2009.

3. "Back Down to Earth with a Bang," *Kathimerini,* March 3, 2010.

4. Charlemagne, "Empathy in Short Supply in Greece: Not a Simple Fable about Ants and Crickets," *The Economist,* March 8, 2010.

5. Ibid.

6. Gikas Hardouvelis, "Glueck im Unglueck," *Frankfurter Allgemeine Zeitung,* September 1, 2010, p. 7.

7. European Commission, "Commission Opinion on the existence of an excessive deficit in Greece," March 24, 2009 (ec.europa.eu/economy_finance/economic_governance/sgp/pdf/30_edps/104-05/2009-03-24_el_104-5_en.pdf).

8. Theodore Pelagidis and Michael Mitsopoulos, *Understanding the Crisis in Greece* (New York: Palgrave Macmillan, 2011).

9. Transparency International, *Corruption Perceptions Index 2010* (Berlin: 2010) p. 7 (www.transparency.org/publications/publications/cpi2010).

10. "Petty Bribery on the Rise: Poll Finds Use of 'Fakelakia' in Public, Private Sectors Rises 10 pct to 750 mln Euros," eKathimerini, February 18, 2009.

11. The recovery was still going on in 2011 (for about €260 million) as shown in http://europa.eu/rapid/pressReleasesAction.do?reference=IP/11/476&type=HTML.

12. By contrast, the economist Joseph Schumpeter argued that capitalism did not begin with the Industrial Revolution but in fourteenth-century Italy. In Venice and Florence the small city-state governments fostered the development of the earliest forms of capitalism.

13. Although Greece formally joined the European Exchange Rate Mechanism only in March 1998, it was suffering a balance-of-payments crisis in the mid-1980s, despite an extremely strong U.S. dollar, which eventually led to the Plaza Accord in July 1985.

14. European Commission, "Final Report on Greek Government Deficit and Debt Statistics," COM(2010), Brussels, January 8, 2010. The report mentioned unreliability of data, lack of respect for accounting rules, and timing of the notification; poor cooperation between the national services involved in the compilation of EDP figures and lack of independence of the National Statistical Service and of the General Accounting Office; an institutional setting and a public accounting system inappropriate for a correct reporting of EDP statistics, notably nontransparent or improperly documented bookkeeping; lack of accountability in the individual provision of figures used in EDP notification, such as, in some cases, absence of written documentation or certification; and unclear responsibility and/or lack of responsibility of the national services providing source data or compiling statistical data, with inappropriate adjustments to data, combined with unclear empowerment of officials responsible for the data.

15. "Wall St. Helped to Mask Debt Fueling Europe's Crisis," *New York Times,* February 13, 2010.

16. Athens News Agency, October 20, 2009.

17. European Commission, "Final recommendation for a council decision establishing whether effective action has been taken by Greece in response to the Council recommendation of April 27, 2009," SEC(2009) 1549, Brussels., November 11, 2009.

18. G. Hardouvelis, ed., *Sources of Growth: Can Greece follow the Irish example?* (in Greek) (Athens: Kerkyra Publications, 2006).

19. European Commission, "Euro area quarterly report," December 2009, p. 8.

20. "Revised Greek deficit figures cause outrage," Euobserver.com, October 20, 2009 (euobserver.com/19/28853).

21. In a poll by Politbarometer for the German public television (politbarometer. zdf.de) at the end of October 2009, 53 percent of survey participants were against tax cuts in 2011. In a less representative online survey by the German finance ministry, only 4 percent supported a further fiscal easing, while 89 percent preferred a budget consolidation.

## Chapter 10

1. An interesting analysis has been produced by Jacopo Carmassi and Stefano Micossi for the Center for European Policy Studies, "The Role of Politicians in Inciting Financial Markets to Attack the Euro Zone," Brussels, June 21, 2010 (www.ceps.be/book/role-politicians-inciting-financial-markets-attack-eurozone).

2. "Stark: 'Le banche aiutino Atene' [Banks must help Athens]," *Il Sole-24 Ore,* January 7, 2009.

3. The most eloquent statement of the case for calling in the IMF was made by two economists within the euro area, Jean Pisani-Ferry and André Sapir, "Greek Crisis: Lending Is Not Giving," Bruegel, Brussels (www.bruegel.org/publications/publication-detail/publication/394-greek-crisis-lending-is-not-giving/).

4. "Moody's Says Greece, Portugal May Face 'Slow Death,'" Bloomberg, January 13, 2010.

5. "Euro Weakens to Five-Month Low Versus Dollar on Greece Concerns," Bloomberg, January 20, 2010.

6. George Povropoulos "Greece will fix itself from inside the eurozone," *Financial Times,* January 22, 2010.

7. Allensbach-Analyse: "Vertrauensverlust für den Euro [Loss of trust in the Euro]," *Frankfurter Allgemeine Zeitung,* April 28, 2010.

8. Some "wisemen"—the economists acting as independent advisers to the government—have criticized excessive moderation in wages as a voluntary cut in the purchasing power of families.

9. The current account can also be interpreted as the net change in the foreign assets a country owns. A current account deficit implies that a country's indebtedness vis-à-vis the rest of the world increases. If net savings of the domestic private sector were to exceed the government deficit, that is, its demand for savings, the private sector would invest its excess savings abroad, implying a current account surplus and an increase in the net foreign investment position of that country.

10. This geographical effect even shows in regional proximity to Germany within the same national boundaries.

11. European Commission, "Recommendations for Greece," Brussels, February 3, 2010 (http://ec.europa.eu/economy_finance/articles/sgp/2010_02_03_sgp_en.htm).

## Chapter 11

1. Peter Garnham, Victor Mallet, and David Oakley, "Traders Make $8bn Bet against Euro," *Financial Times,* February 8, 2010.

2. Such an insurance contract against the default of five-year Greek bonds would cost around €400,000, twelve times as much as a CDS on German bonds. The build-up in net short positions represents more than 40,000 contracts traded against the euro, equivalent to $7.6 billion.

3. Susan Pulliam, Kate Kelly, and Carrick Mollenkamp, "Hedge Funds Try 'Career Trade' against Euro," *Wall Street Journal,* February 26, 2010.

4. Author's interviews with participants.

5. Pulliam, Kelly, and Mollenkamp, "Hedge Funds Try 'Career Trade' against Euro."

6. Ibid.

7. Sam Jones and Brooke Masters, "Hedge Funds Raise Bets against Euro," *Financial Times,* March 2, 2010.

8. Jean-Claude Trichet, president of the ECB, "Introductory statement with Q&A," European Central Bank, Frankfurt, February 4, 2010 (www.ecb.int/press/press conf/2010/html/is100204.en.html).

9. Meera Louis, "EU Finance Ministers Urged to Skirt Question of Greek Default," Bloomberg, February 9, 2010.

10. Ibid.

11. Holger Steltzner, "Die griechische Tragödie: Der letzte Anker darf nicht reißen [The Greek Tragedy, the last anchor must not tear]," *Frankfurter Allgemeine Zeitung,* February 10, 2010.

12. Oliver Santen, "Korruption! Ohne Schmiergeld läuft in Griechenland fast nichts mehr [Corruption! Almost nothing works in Greece without bribing]," *Bild Zeitung,* February 1, 2010.

13. Steltzner, "Die griechische Tragödie: Der letzte Anker darf nicht reißen."

14. Ibid.

15. Peter Ehrlich, Timo Pache, and Nikolai Fichtner, "Berlin will Griechenland retten [Berlin wants to save Greece]," *Financial Times Deutschland,* February 9, 2010.

16. Ralph Bollmann, "Das Comeback des Mannes im Rollstuhl [The comeback of the man in the wheelchair]," *Frankfurter Allgemeine Zeitung,* December 18, 2011.

17. "Eurogroup draft declaration on the Greek crisis," February 10, 2010. On file with author.

18. "Berlin Looks to Build Greek 'Firewall,'" *Financial Times,* February 9, 2010.

19. Peter Ludlow, "A View on Brussels: Van Rompuy saves the day," *Eurocomment Briefing Note* 7, no. 6 (February 2010).

20. Ibid.

21. A. Leparmentier and P. Ricard, "Les Européens s'engagent à soutenir la Grèce pour défendre l'euro [The Europeans are committed to supporting Greece to defend the euro]," *Le Monde,* February 12, 2010.

22. European Council, "Statement by the Heads of State or Government of the European Union," Brussels, February 11, 2010 (www.consilium.europa.eu/uedocs/cms_data/docs/pressdata/en/ec/112856.pdf).

23. Ibid.

24. Ibid. The reference to the euro member states was requested by Sarkozy as an acknowledgment of the new role of the heads of only the countries belonging to the monetary union.

25. Sebastian Kemnitzer, "Nicht ohne einen Haider [Not without a Haider]," *Stern,* September 8, 2010.

## Chapter 12

1. On the revenue side of the ledger, these include a hike in the value-added tax rate from 19 percent to 21 percent, further increases in taxes on fuel, tobacco, and alcohol, and a new tax on luxury goods. On the expenditure side, the highlights were a 30 percent reduction in public-sector bonuses (the so-called thirteenth and fourteenth salaries—two extra months' worth—given to workers as holiday pay), a 12 percent cut in allowances for civil servants, and a freeze on state-funded pensions.

2. Statement by the ECB's Governing Council on the additional measures of the Greek government, March 3, 2010 (www.ecb.int/press/pr/date/2010/html/pr100303.en.html).

3. "ECB vs IMF," *Market Sense,* Economics and FI/FX Research, UniCredit Group, Milan, March 4, 2010, p. 3 (www.research.unicreditgroup.eu).

4. Olivier Blanchard, Giovanni Dell'Ariccia, and Paolo Mauro, "Rethinking Macroeconomic Policy," IMF Staff Position Note SPN10/03, International Monetary Fund, Washington, February 12, 2010.

5. There were also more fundamental reasons for avoiding an IMF intervention. See Carlo Bastasin on the blog *Baseline scenario* (http://baselinescenario.com/2010/02/24/the-imf-cannot-help-greece/#more-6564).

6. For Greece the advantage of an IMF deal was that it took some of the political sting out of support operations. In the mid-1970s, for instance, when Italy needed international support, it could have concocted a deal with Germany, but the Germans preferred to see the IMF negotiating with Rome.

7. The analogy with the Bretton Woods era was stressed by Giancarlo Corsetti and Harold James in "Why Europe Needs Its Own IMF," *Financial Times,* March 8, 2010.

8. Wolfgang Schäuble, "Why Europe's Monetary Union Faces Its Biggest Crisis," *Financial Times,* March 11, 2010.

9. "EZB lehnt EU-Währungsfonds strikt ab [ECB rejects the EMF strictly]," *Handelsblatt,* March 8, 2010.

10. Holger Steltzner, "Ein Euro-Schuldenfonds [A Euro Debt Fund]," *Frankfurter Allgemeine Zeitung,* March 10, 2010.

11. Schäuble, "Why Europe's Monetary Union Faces Its Biggest Crisis."

12. Ibid.

13. G-20 Leaders Statement, Pittsburgh, September 24–25, 2009, p. 22, paragraph 2. But at the G-20 summit in Toronto on June 26–27, 2010, leaders reached contradictory conclusions, endorsing "growth friendly fiscal consolidation," in other words, reducing budget deficits while at the same time adopting policies on wages and other matters intended to spur economic growth.

14. C. Randall Henning, "Germany, EMU and the Politics of Global Macroeconomic Conflict" (Washington: Peterson Institute for International Economics, 2010).

15. Helmut Schmidt, "Die Bürokraten ausgetrickst [The bureaucrats tricked]," *Die Zeit*, August 24, 1990.

16. Wolfgang Schäuble, public statement at the Bundestag, March 16, 2010.

17. Wilhelm Hankel, Wilhelm Nölling, Karl Albrecht Schachtschneider, and Joachim Starbatty, "A Euro Exit Is the Only Way out for Greece," *Financial Times*, March 25, 2010.

18. Committee on Economic and Monetary Affairs, "Monetary Dialogue with Jean-Claude Trichet, president of the ECB," March 22, 2010 (www.europarl.europa.eu/document/activities/cont/201004/20100408ATT72328/20100408ATT72328EN.pdf).

19. "Statement by the Heads of State and Government of the Euro Area," Brussels, March 25, 2010 (www.consilium.europa.eu/uedocs/cms_data/docs/pressdata/en/ec/113563.pdf).

20. Ibid.

21. Markus Brauck, Markus Feldenkirchen, Ullrich Fichtner, Isabell Hülsen, Dirk Kurbjuweit, Martin U. Müller, Takis Würger, "Im Namen des Volkes [In the name of the people]," *Der Spiegel*, February 28, 2011.

## Chapter 13

1. The pressure would remain even after May. By December Athens was expected to need at least €16 billion. Fiscal plans for the years ahead were also uncertain, and the financing needs for redeeming the old debt would remain extraordinarily high until 2014, with around €30 billion to be refinanced every year.

2. "Greek Banks Ask for Rest of €28 bln Support Deal," Reuters, April 7, 2010.

3. "Statement on the Support to Greece by Euro Area Members States," Brussels, April 11, 2011 (www.consilium.europa.eu/uedocs/cms_data/docs/pressdata/en/ec/113686.pdf).

4. As of April 9, 2010, the market-rate yield on Greek government bonds of comparable maturity was 7.261 percent.

5. Yields on government bonds fell on Monday, April 12, by 54 basis points for the ten-year bond, 44 basis points for the five-year bond, and 88 basis points for the three-year bond.

6. Moody's Investors Service, "Moody's downgrades Greece's sovereign ratings to A3: on review for further possible downgrade," April 22, 2010 (www.moodys.com/research/Moodys-downgrades-Greeces-sovereign-ratings-to-A3-on-review-for--PR_198275).

7. International Monetary Fund, *Global Financial Stability Report*, Washington, April 2010.

8. "Saving the Euro," *Financial Times,* October 10, 2010.

9. Bundesverfassungsgericht [German Constitutional Court], "Motion by the Government to the Constitutional Court opposing the claim of unconstitutionality of aid to Greece," ruling of the Court, September 7, 2011, p. 14.

10. European Commission, Economic and Financial Affairs, "Euro area and IMF agreement on financial support program for Greece," May 3, 2010 (http://ec.europa.eu/economy_finance/articles/eu_economic_situation/2010-05-03-statement-commissioner-rehn-imf-on-greece_en.htm). The text of the agreement and additional details were contained in IMF, "Staff Report on Request for Stand-By Arrangement," May 9, 2010 (www.imf.org/external/pubs/ft/scr/2010/cr10110.pdf).

11. Comments by Herman Van Rompuy, president of the European Council, on Greece and solidarity in the Euro area, Brussels, May 5, 2010, PCE 83/10.

12. Kerin Hope, "Papandreou Says Greek Survival at Stake," *Financial Times,* April 30, 2010 (www.ft.com/intl/cms/s/0/7c9c940a-5445-11df-b75d-00144feab49a.html#axzz1jNonkZRp).

## Chapter 14

1. Enda Curran, "Greece Bailout by IMF, EU Judged Inadequate, Australian PM Says," Dow Jones Newswires, May 7, 2010.

2. Jonathan Stearns, "G-7 to Discuss Market Turmoil in Today's Greece Call, Japan's Tamaki Says," Bloomberg, May 7, 2010.

3. "ECB Pares Spanish, Italian Bond Purchases, AFME Says," Bloomberg, May 14, 2010. The quote is from Sander Schol, director of the Association for Financial Markets in Europe.

4. Marc Brost and Robert von Heusinger, "Interview with Jean-Claude Trichet, president of the European Central Bank," *Die Zeit,* July 23, 2007.

5. In terms of monetary policy, the major concern was that inflation expectations would be stoked by an incomplete sterilization of the money supply increased through the purchase of bonds or by the losses suffered by the ECB balance sheet (the bank would buy bonds that could lose value in the event of a default). Actually, the traditional stability of money demand in Europe tended to exclude the transmission of additional money supply to the price levels. Moreover, inflation expectations translate into actual inflation only when households and businesses consume or invest more, a very unlikely eventuality in this case considering that many countries were deflating wages through their austerity programs.

6. Commodity Futures Trading Commission and Security and Exchange Commission, "Findings Regarding the Market Events of May 6, 2010," Report of the staffs of the CFTC and SEC to the Joint Advisory Committee on Emergency Regulatory Issues (www.sec.gov/news/studies/2010/marketevents-report.pdf).

7. At 2:32 p.m., against a "backdrop of unusually high volatility and thinning liquidity," a mutual fund complex initiated a program to sell a total of 75,000 E-Mini S&P 500 contracts (valued at approximately $4.1 billion) as a hedge to an existing equity

position. This was an unusually large position and the computer algorithm the trader used to trade the position was set to "target an execution rate set to 9 percent of the trading volume calculated over the previous minute, but without regard to price or time."

8. The story of the May 6 decision is based on confidential talks with three participants.

9. Jean-Claude Trichet, president of the ECB, Lucas Papademos, vice president of the ECB, "Introductory statement with Q&A," European Central Bank, Lisbon, May 6, 2010 (www.ecb.int/press/pressconf/2010/html/is100506.en.html).

10. Stacy-Marie Ishmael, "Merkel's Calls for 'Orderly Insolvencies' Threaten More Disorder," *Financial Times* Alphaville blog, based on Bloomberg reports, May 4, 2010.

11. This was also triggered by a 4.1 percent drop in the euro the previous week, the biggest weekly decline since the aftermath of Lehman Brothers.

12. The statement was published by the president's office and later relaunched by press agencies. A version can be viewed at http://news.bbc.co.uk/2/hi/8663734.stm.

13. Fico's problem was, as usual, domestic: he was seeking reelection and was being pressed by the right-wing opposition Slovak Democratic and Christian Union party to refuse aid to Greece.

14. Moody's Investors Service, "Moody's Assesses Risk of Sovereign Contagion on Certain European Banking Systems," May 6, 2010 (www.moodys.com/research/Moodys-Assesses-Risk-of-Sovereign-Contagion-on-Certain-European-Banking--PR_198943).

15. Monetary Affairs Commissioner Olli Rehn described the criteria in a letter preliminary to the summit: "First, we need to reinforce the Stability and Growth Pact, both its preventive and corrective arms. We need a more systematic and rigorous preventive budgetary surveillance, so that cases like the Greek case will never happen again. Second, we must go beyond budgetary surveillance. We need to address macro-economic imbalances and divergences in competitiveness and, therefore, we need to reinforce both export competitiveness, which is urgently needed in many countries, and domestic demand where needed and possible. The third building block will be a crisis-resolution mechanism . . . with strong in-built conditionalities and also disincentives for its use."

16. Article 122.2: "Where a Member State is in difficulties or is seriously threatened with severe difficulties caused by natural disasters or exceptional occurrences beyond its control, the Council, on a proposal from the Commission, may grant, under certain conditions, Union financial assistance to the Member State concerned. The President of the Council shall inform the European Parliament of the decision taken."

17. Nelson D. Schwartz and Eric Dash, "Greek Debt Woes Ripple Outward, from Asia to U.S.," *New York Times,* May 9, 2010.

18. Ibid.

19. The White House, "Interview of the President by Sergey Brilev of Channel Rossiya, Russian Television," interview conducted on May 6, 2010, released on May 8, 2010 (www.whitehouse.gov/the-press-office/interview-president-sergey-brilev-channel-rossiya-russian-television).

20. I rely here on Peter Ludlow's description of Sarkozy's and Merkel's statements as reported in *Eurocomment Briefing Note* 8.1, 2010, integrated with other information.

21. Ibid.

22. Spanish prime minister José Luis Zapatero was reported by a British paper as revealing that Sarkozy had threatened to pull France out of the euro and break up the Franco-German axis unless Germany opened its purse. See "Nicolas Sarkozy Threatened Euro Withdrawal," *The Guardian,* May 14, 2010.

23. "Statement of the Heads of State or Government of the Euro Area," May 7, 2010 (http://ec.europa.eu/commission_2010-2014/president/news/speeches-statements/pdf/114295.pdf).

24. "Currency Union Teetering, 'Mr Euro' Is Forced to Act," *Wall Street Journal,* September 27, 2010.

25. Tony Barber, "Saving the Euro: Bound towards a Tense Future," *Financial Times,* October 13, 2010.

26. For the €60 billion to be provided by the European Commission, the legal basis of the mechanism was treaty Article 122.2, appealing to the "exceptional circumstances." Berlin thought it was too vague and feared it might be invoked in countless other circumstances, but eventually saw no other solution in the short term. The same article had been used in aiding the eastern European countries that faced balance-of-payment problems. A similar justification could be adopted now, and the size of the aid was indeed consistent with the current external problems of the periphery.

27. "Quand l'euro est devenu un problème américain [When the euro becomes an American problem]," *Le Monde,* May 16, 2010.

28. Extraordinary Council meeting, press release, May 9, 2010, p. 7 (www.consilium.europa.eu/uedocs/cms_data/docs/pressdata/en/ecofin/114324.pdf). The special purpose vehicle would be based on Article 352 of the European treaty, normally referred to as "the flexibility clause," enabling the council to adopt appropriate regulations unanimously (upon a proposal of the commission and approval by the European Parliament) for the realization of the broadly aimed objectives of the Union according to Article 3 of the treaty, even if the treaties do not provide for the necessary powers. Article 352 was problematic, however, because it had to be applied not to the EU as a whole but only to the Eurogroup, and Britain had already clearly said that it would not participate. Berlin required that the agreement be expressly subject to the requirements of national constitutions.

29. European Central Bank, "ECB decides on measures to address severe tensions in financial markets," ECB press release, May 10, 2010 (www.ecb.int/press/pr/date/2010/html/pr100510.en.html).

30. "Kaufprogramm birgt erhebliche Risiken [The purchasing program entails substantial risks]," interview with A. Weber, *Börsen-Zeitung,* May 11, 2010. The crucial passage is "The purchase of government bonds entails substantial risk as far as a policy oriented to the stability is concerned. For this reason, I am critical of this part of the decisions of the ECB-Council, even under the current exceptional circumstances."

31. The ECB Governing Council decided on the following measures, announced the following day: it would purchase public and private sector debt securities on the secondary markets under a Securities Markets Program, to ensure depth and liquidity in

dysfunctional market segments and so restore an effective monetary transmission mechanism, and it would conduct sterilizing operations to reabsorb the liquidity generated by the Securities Markets Program, thus ensuring that the monetary policy stance would not be affected.

32. "Internationale Konferenz in Berlin: Merkel zofft sich mit Freunden der Finanzindustrie [International conference in Berlin: Merkel quarrels with friends in the finance industry]," *Der Spiegel,* May 20, 2010.

33. "Deutsche Bank CEO Doubts Greece Can Repay Debt," Reuters, May 13, 2010.

## Chapter 15

1. "Laudatio der Bundeskanzlerin der Bundesrepublik Deutschland, Dr. Angela Merkel [Laudatory speech by the Federal Chancellor of the Federal Republic of Germany, Dr. Angela Merkel]," May 13, 2010 (original text in German; translation by the author) (www.karlspreis.de/preistraeger/2010/laudatio_der_bundeskanzlerin.html).

2. Ibid.

3. "Statement of the Heads of State or Government of the Euro Area," May 7, 2010, pp. 2–3 (http://ec.europa.eu/commission_2010-2014/president/news/speeches-statements/pdf/114295.pdf).

4. On most of the pillars sketched in the May 7 Eurogroup meeting, there were relatively positive signals. Spain and Portugal had followed the requests of the Eurogroup with further fiscal consolidation. In a matter of weeks they were followed by meaningful fiscal actions in most other euro area countries, Germany, France, and Italy included. Germany led the group with a strong rhetoric about the largest fiscal austerity intervention in its history. This drew heavy accusations from Washington and a public bickering between U.S. Treasury secretary Timothy Geithner and German finance minister Wolfgang Schäuble. But the package was more a long-term commitment to the new fiscal limits inscribed into the constitution than a frontloaded barrage to fiscal slippages.

5. Proposals include ensuring consistent accounting, aligning national fiscal rules with treaty obligations, switching to multi-annual budgetary planning, and ensuring that the whole system of government finances is covered by the fiscal framework (http://ec.europa.eu/economy_finance/articles/euro/2010-06-30-enhancing_economic_policy_coordination_en.htm).

6. Given the recognition that private-sector imbalances typically translate into some degree of public sector imbalances, the commission wanted to develop a detailed "scorecard" for the private sector as well, including competitiveness indicators and current accounts. If imbalances were perceived to be of a serious nature, the corrective arm of the mechanism would kick in and the member state would be placed in an "excessive imbalances position." This would lead to the issuance of detailed policy recommendations and regular reporting from the member state to the ECOFIN Council and the Eurogroup. Citing Article 126 of the European treaty, the commission also proposed a vast array of sanctions.

7. Lorenzo Bini Smaghi, member of the Executive Board of the ECB, "The Challenges Facing the Euro Area," speech at the Official Monetary and Financial Institutions

Forum meeting, Abu Dhabi, November 1, 2010 (www.ecb.int/press/key/date/2010/html/sp101101.en.html).

8. European Council, "Conclusions of the European Council," June 17, 2010, paragraph 14, p. 6 (http://ec.europa.eu/eu2020/pdf/council_conclusion_17_june_en.pdf).

9. Alan Beattie, "IMF Calls for More 'Stress-Test' Openness," *Financial Times,* July 21, 2010.

10. One of the participants in the meeting at the Bundesbank said, "we can thank God that we have Weber." Weber still promoted publication of results, at least partly, but did not want to leave the control over the stress tests to the CEBS, the committee of European banking supervisors (although the Bundesbank is an influential member of this committee). Weber had changed his position, as he had supported full transparency in June. He risked being at odds with the EU political leaders and thus reducing his chances of succeeding Trichet as president of the ECB (www.eurointelligence.com/article/browse/17/article/so-much-for-the-stress-test-axel-weber-wants-to-impose-conditions-that-render-them-a-farce.html?tx_ttnews[backPid]=743&cHash=a155d677cdb7088824d7a93fbfe536d0).

11. European Banking Authority, "2010 EU Wide Stress Testing" (www.eba.europa.eu/EuWideStressTesting.aspx).

12. "Europe's Bank Stress Tests Minimized Debt Risk," *Wall Street Journal,* September 7, 2010.

13. Adrian Blundell-Wignall and Patrick Slovik "The EU Stress Test and Sovereign Debt Exposures," OECD Working Papers on Finance, Insurance and Private Pensions 4 (Paris: OECD Financial Affairs Division, August 2010) (www.oecd.org/dataoecd/17/57/45820698.pdf).

14. Ibid, p. 6.

15. Klaus Regling and Max Watson, *A Preliminary Report on the Sources of Ireland's Banking Crisis,* Ministry of Finance, Republic of Ireland, May 2010 (www.bankinginquiry.gov.ie/Preliminary%20Report%20into%20Ireland%27s%20Banking%20Crisis%2031%20May%202010.pdf).

16. "Ireland: A Crunch Period," *Economics Special,* Economics & FI/FX Research, UniCredit Group, Milan, September 20, 2010.

17. International Monetary Fund, "Ireland: 2010 Article IV Consultation: Staff Report and Public Information Notice on the Executive Board Discussion," July 13, 2010.

18. "Ireland's Crash—after the Race," *The Economist,* February 17, 2011.

19. Ibid.

20. Ibid.

21. Regling and Watson, *A Preliminary Report on the Sources of Ireland's Banking Crisis.*

22. "Dell Shifting Production to Poland from Ireland," *New York Times,* August 1, 2009 (www.nytimes.com/2009/01/08/business/worldbusiness/08iht-08dell.19188945.html).

23. "Europe on the Brink—As Ireland Flails, Europe Lurches Across the Rubicon," *Wall Street Journal,* December 27, 2010.

## Chapter 16

1. Herman Van Rompuy, president of the European Council, "Remarks following the last meeting of the task force on economic governance," European Council, Luxembourg, October 18, 2010 (http://consilium.europa.eu/uedocs/cms_data/docs/pressdata/en/ecofin/117154.pdf).

2. Van Rompuy had discussed with Merkel the possibility of adopting a Schengen-type solution, a reinforced cooperation among willing countries, but the chancellor ruled it out on grounds that decisions concerning economic governance had to be taken by all twenty-seven EU members and not by an inner group. Some aspects, first of all tougher sanctions, could hardly be imposed without changing the EU treaties.

3. Discussions between the two sides continued until the weekend of October 16–17, when Schäuble's and Lagarde's staffs worked in a bilateral meeting sheltered from publicity. They elaborated an understanding that the two governments wanted to present together, as they had done in developing a joint working paper before the July European Council meeting.

4. "EU Faces Moment of Truth on Budget Reform—Rehn," Reuters, October 18, 2010.

5. Task Force on Economic Governance, "Strengthening Economic Governance in the EU," European Council, Brussels, October 21, 2010 (www.consilium.europa.eu/uedocs/cms_data/docs/pressdata/en/ec/117236.pdf).

6. Ibid., p. 1. The language regarding "all relevant factors" was requested by Italy, which was disproportionally hit by the provision although it had been remarkably careful during the crisis.

7. Further specifications for the automaticity of sanctions were specified in paragraph 24 and 25 of the text, p. 7.

8. Ibid., p. 2.

9. Ibid., p. 12.

10. "Franco-German Declaration: Statement for the France-Germany-Russia Summit—Deauville," October 18, 2010 (www.elysee.fr/president/root/bank_objects/Franco-german_declaration.pdf).

11. "Tremonti: "Habemus novum pactum" Accordo sulla stabilità dell'economia Ue [We have a new pact, agreement on EU economic stability]," Repubblica, October 19, 2010.

12. Charles Forelle, David Gauthier-Villars, Brian Blackstone, and David Enrich, "Europe on the Brink: As Ireland Flails, Europe Lurches across the Rubicon," Wall Street Journal, December 27, 2010.

13. European Council, Conclusions, October 28–29, 2010, p. 2 (http://consilium.europa.eu/uedocs/cms_data/docs/pressdata/en/ec/117496.pdf).

14. Peter Ludlow, Eurocomment, Briefing Note 8.3, p. 21.

15. European Council, Conclusions, October 28–29, 2010, p. 2.

16. Ludlow, Eurocomment, Briefing Note 8.3, p. 21.

17. Jean-Claude Trichet, president of the ECB, and Vítor Constâncio, vice-president of the ECB, "Introductory statement with Q&A," European Central Bank, Frankfurt, November 4, 2010 (www.ecb.int/press/pressconf/2010/html/is101104.en.html).

18. The Irish government's official forecast for growth between 2010 and 2014 was for positive and increasing rates (0.25 percent, 1.75 percent, 3.25 percent, 3.0 percent, 2.75 percent).

19. "Statement by the Finance ministers of France, Germany, Italy, Spain, and Britain at the Group of 20 meeting in South Korea, November 12, 2010."

20. Marcus Walker and Charles Forelle, "In Euro's Hour of Need, Aide Gets 'Madame Non' to Say Yes," *Wall Street Journal,* April 14, 2011.

21. Peter Spiegel and David Oakley, "Irish Contagion Hits Wider Eurozone," *Financial Times,* November 12, 2010.

22. Bank for International Settlements (BIS), "Quarterly Review," Basel, December 2010.

23. *The Economist* on February 17, 2011, titled its report about Ireland as "After the Race—Once among the richest people in Europe, the Irish have been laid low by a banking collapse and the euro zone's debt crisis."

24. "German Stance May Push Nations towards Bankruptcy – Greek PM," Reuters, November 15, 2010.

25. Patrick Jenkins, Sharlene Goff, and John Murray Brown, "Dublin Feels Pressure on Rescue Package," *Financial Times,* November 17, 2010.

26. Richard Tomlinson and Sandrine Rastello, "Strauss-Kahn Bailouts Give IMF Chief Popularity over Sarkozy," Bloomberg News, January 26, 2011.

27. BIS, "Quarterly Review."

28. The figures from the BIS cover the banks' exposure to other countries through lending to banks, companies, and governments.

29. Aaron Kirchfeld and Patrick Donahue, "Merkel Defies Deutsche Bank as Ackermann Frets Bonds," Bloomberg News, January 28, 2011 (www.bloomberg.com/news/2011-01-27/merkel-defies-deutsche-bank-as-ackermann-frets-over-sinking-bonds-in-davos.html).

30. "Statement by the Eurogroup," November 28, 2010 (http://consilium.europa.eu/uedocs/cms_data/docs/pressdata/en/ecofin/118050.pdf).

31. Ibid., p. 2.

32. Ibid.

33. The maturity curve of Irish bonds showed no difference in its rising trend around 2013 when there should have been one, since—given the EFSF—Irish bonds were protected until 2013, and unprotected thereafter. Investors were, in fact, convinced that Irish bonds would be unsafe much earlier than in 2013.

34. Jean-Claude Trichet, president of the ECB, "Introductory Statement at Quarterly Hearing before the Committee on Economic and Monetary Affairs of the European Parliament," Brussels, November 30, 2010 (www.ecb.int/press/key/date/2010/html/sp101130.en.html).

35. European Central Bank, "ECB announces details of refinancing operations with settlement from 19 January to 12 April 2011," Frankfurt, December 2, 2010 (www.ecb.int/press/pr/date/2010/html/pr101202_1.en.html).

36. Tommaso Padoa-Schioppa, "Break the vicious circle and restore confidence," letter to Prime Minister George Papandreou, December 2, 2010.

37. European Council, Conclusions, December 16–17, 2010, p. 5 (www.consilium. europa.eu/uedocs/cms_data/docs/pressdata/en/ec/118578.pdf).

38. Ibid., Annex III: Statement by the Heads of State or Government of the Euro Area and the EU Institutions, p. 11.

39. European Commission, Economic and Financial Affairs Council, "Quotes" (http://ec.europa.eu/economy_finance/emu10/quotes_kohl_en.htm).


## Chapter 17

1. Jean-Claude Trichet, president of the ECB, and Vítor Constâncio, vice-president of the ECB, "Introductory statement to the press conference (with Q&A)," European Central Bank, Frankfurt, January 13, 2011 (www.ecb.int/press/pressconf/2011/html/ is110113.en.html).

2. The summit was still going on when, in the morning of December 17, 2010, Moody's Investors Service announced that it had cut Ireland's credit rating five levels and that further downgrades were possible as the Irish government struggled to contain losses in the country's banking system. The news came as a shock. Irish lawmakers on December 15 had voted to accept an €85 billion aid package. But Moody's said that confidence in Irish banks "evaporated" in the run-up to the bailout.

3. Monetary unions are prone to what economists call "externalities" (effects on one party that might be caused or influenced by another party) because interconnections of the banking systems make it almost impossible to isolate the financial problems in any one country.

4. Carlo Cottarelli, Lorenzo Forni, Jan Gottschalk, and Paolo Mauro, "Default in Today's Advanced Economies: Unnecessary, Undesirable, and Unlikely," International Monetary Fund, September 1, 2010.

5. In most advanced economies, the main problem is the primary deficit rather than the interest bill. As a result, the needed adjustment would not be much affected by debt restructuring, even with a sizable haircut. IMF economists calculated the effect of a 50 percent haircut—exceptionally large by historical standards—on the primary budget adjustment needed to stabilize the debt-to-GDP ratio. Such a haircut would shave off half a percentage point of GDP on average in the most advanced countries considered by the exercise, and 2.7 percentage points for Greece, lowering the needed adjustment from a massive 14.1 percent to a still-large 11.4 percent of GDP.

6. Lorenzo Bini Smaghi, "Europe Cannot Default Its Way Back to Health," *Financial Times*, December 17, 2010.

7. In a speech in Bruges on November 2, 2010, Angela Merkel even argued that the often-claimed distinction between the Community method and intergovernmentalism was a dangerous anachronism. "Speech by Federal Chancellor Angela Merkel at the opening ceremony of the 61st academic year of the College of Europe," November 2, 2010 (www.bundeskanzlerin.de/nn_704298/Content/EN/Reden/2010/2010-11-02-merkel-bruegge.html). Merkel coined the term "Union Methode" to characterize the rejuvenation of the centrality of member states. The decision to set up the EFSF in May

2010 was inevitably going in the direction of intergovernmentalism because the EFSF had no juridicial personality and its debts were accounted national debts.

8. Leo Tolstoy, *War and Peace,* Book 9, chapter 10.

9. Legislative Observatory European Parliament, "2011/2071(INI)—12/01/2011 Non-legislative basic document" (www.europarl.europa.eu/oeil/popups/summary. do?id=1148725&t=e).

10. Nicolaus Blome, "Kanzlerin macht jetzt erstmals massiv Werbung: Wird Bundesbank-Chef Weber der nächste Mr. Euro? [For the first time, the chancellor steps in hugely for him: will Bundesbank boss Weber be the next Mr. Euro?]," *Bild Zeitung,* January 15, 2011.

11. The good performance of Axel Weber, in November 2010, at the German Embassy in Paris before a string of French politicians and economists was not enough to allay concerns.

12. Jean-Philippe Lacour, Karl de Meyer, and Dominique Seux, "Conflit Paris-Berlin en vue sur la succession de Trichet [Conflict between Paris and Berlin for Trichet's succession]," *Les Echos BCE,* January 18, 2011, p. 8.

13. Ignazio Angeloni, "Quale banchiere per l'Europa in crisi [What kind of banker for Europe in the crisis]," Italianieuropei, March 2011.

14. Ibid.

15. "Euro-Zone: Merkel schmiedet Plan für gemeinsame Wirtschaftsregierung [Eurozone: Merkel forges plan for common economic government], *Der Spiegel,* January 29, 2011.

16. "Franco-German 'Pact for Competitiveness' Hits Immediate Opposition," EuObserver.com, February 2, 2011.

17. EurActiv Spain (the Spanish branch of the "EurActiv" networked websites— www.euractiv.es) reported that Prime Minister Zapatero endorsed Merkel's plan, despite tense relations with the conservative German leader at the height of the euro zone crisis in 2010. In return, Merkel praised a landmark agreement signed by Spain's Socialist government, trade unions, and employers on pension reform and employment, saying it was politically helpful to achieve such reforms by consensus.

18. Irwin Stelzer, "Europe's Not Playing Ball with Merkel," *Wall Street Journal,* February 7, 2011.

19. Nikolaus Blome, "Bundesbank-Krise: Wie gefährlich ist Webers Abgang für Merkel? [Bundesbank-crisis: how dangerous is Weber's exit for Merkel?]," *Bild Zeitung,* February 10, 2011.

20. *Die Zeit* interview with Jean-Claude Trichet, president of the European Central Bank, conducted by Mark Schieritz and Uwe Jean Heuser, February 16, 2011 (www.ecb. int/press/key/date/2011/html/sp110216.en.html).

21. The Germans insisted that they could not move on this point until they were satisfied that Portugal, which might well require EFSF help in the near future, had done enough to satisfy the Commission-ECB team, which had been looking into the situation during the past few weeks.

22. As Jacob F. Kierkegaard, of the Peterson Institute for International Economics, observed: "The broader message is clear. Recipient countries will have to do what the AAA-rated countries want to qualify for lower lending rates." A very useful analysis on this point was published by Kirkegaard in the "Real Time Series," edited by Steve Weisman at www.piie.com/realtime/?p=2082.

23. Although every government agreed that loans could be made only on the basis of a "debt sustainability analysis" and that they would be subject to "strict conditionality," Germany and Finland asked to attach a unanimity clause to the decisions on delivering a loan. In both cases, the principal reason was their obligations to their national parliaments.

24. Author interview.

25. Author sources.

26. European Commission, "Quarterly Report on the Euro Area," vol. 10.1—2011 (http://ec.europa.eu/economy_finance/publications/qr_euro_area/2011/pdf/qrea1_en.pdf).

27. Europe 2020 was the EU's growth strategy for the coming decade with the aim of delivering high levels of employment, productivity, and social cohesion. Concretely, the EU set five ambitious objectives—on employment, innovation, education, social inclusion, and climate/energy—to be reached by 2020. Each member state was to adopt its own national targets in each of these areas. Concrete actions at EU and national levels would underpin the strategy.

28. This system was composed of the European Systemic Risk Board (ESRB); the three European Supervisory Authorities (European Banking Authority, European Insurance and Occupational Pensions Authority, European Securities and Markets Authority); the Joint Committee of the European Supervisory Authorities; and the competent or supervisory authorities in the member states.

29. Six non-euro area member states decided to join the pact: Bulgaria, Denmark, Latvia, Lithuania, Poland, and Romania. Details can be found at European Commission, "Background on the Euro-Plus Pact," Information Prepared for the European Council, December 9, 2011 (http://ec.europa.eu/europe2020/pdf/euro_plus_pact_background_december_2011_en.pdf).

30. European Council, Conclusions, March 24–25, 2011 (www.consilium.europa.eu/uedocs/cms_data/docs/pressdata/en/ec/120296.pdf).

31. European Commission, "Euro Area Quarterly Report, April 2010." A decision taken by mutual agreement is a decision taken by unanimity of the Member States participating in the vote; abstentions do not prevent the decision from being adopted.

32. In line with the IMF, debt is considered sustainable when a borrower is expected to be able to continue servicing its debts without an unrealistically large correction to its income and expenditure. This judgment determines the availability and the appropriate scale of financing.

33. On the third point, Trichet specified: "The new macroeconomic surveillance framework, as amended by the Council, does not yet provide a clear focus on the euro area countries with large current account deficits, significant losses of competitiveness

and high levels of public and private debt, as well as any other vulnerabilities challenging our economic and monetary union. As regards fiscal surveillance, ambitious benchmarks are needed when establishing an excessive deficit. The scope for considering 'any relevant factors' in case of an excessive deficit should be clearly reduced. The adjustment path towards a country's medium-term budgetary objective also needs more ambition. In this context, the annual improvement in the structural balance should be significantly higher than 0.5 percent of GDP when a country's government debt exceeds the reference value of 60 percent of GDP, otherwise there are fiscal sustainability risks."

34. Jean-Claude Trichet, president of the ECB, "Reforming EMU: Time for Bold Decisions," speech at the conference "What Future for the Euro?"of the Group of the Progressive Alliance of Socialists and Democrats in the European Parliament, Frankfurt, March 18, 2011 (www.ecb.int/press/key/date/2011/html/sp110318_1.esn.html.)

*Chapter 18*

1. An interesting policy brief on the nature of the European project was published in the summer by Deutsche Bank Research with a strong and unusually skeptical assessment of the future of European integration and a clear suggestion to scale it down; see Thomas Mayer, "The Political Economics of the Euro," Deutsche Bank Research, Frankfurt, July 1, 2011.

2. Achieved through a reduction of the Postbank holdings; see Deutsche Bank, "Quarterly Financial Report, June 2011."

3. International Monetary Fund (IMF), "Euro Area Policies, Staff Report," Washington, July 2011, p. 14.

4. On April 12, for instance, the Group of Twenty's Financial Stability Board sent an alarm on the riskiness of exchange-traded funds synthetic products without mentioning which bank was under observation. In the following weeks it appeared that especially one large French bank, Société Generale, was exposed to a peculiarly dangerous version of the "counterparty risk" implicit in the product, being its own counterparty.

5. IMF, "Global Financial Stability Report," Washington, April 2011, p. 12.

6. Ibid., p. 13.

7. Amagerbanken A/S, the insolvent Danish lender seized by the government, was the first European bank to be rescued under new regulations designed to ensure that senior bondholders suffer losses in a bailout, as reported by Bloomberg, "Amagerbanken Senior Bondholders to Suffer Losses," February 7, 2011.

8. IMF, "Global Financial Stability Report," p. 14.

9. Ibid., p. 16.

10. A. Blundell-Wignall and P. Slovik, "The EU Stress Test and Sovereign Debt Exposures," OECD Working Papers on Finance, Insurance and Private Pensions 4, OECD Financial Affairs Division, August 2010, p. 7 (www.oecd.org/dataoecd/17/57/4582 0698.pdf).

11. Such exposures are defined as an exposure above 5 percent of Tier 1 capital.

12. IMF, "Greece: Third Review under the Stand-By Arrangement," March 14, 2011, p. 6.

13. Ibid., pp. 9–10.

14. George Papaconstantinou, "Give Greece Time to Prove It Can Do the Job," *Financial Times,* June 27, 2011.

15. Some of the most influential bankers and lawyers had developed a double or triple role: they were buying and selling on the market, advising the governments, and shaping public opinion through an array of consultant-economists who published their allegedly independent assessments on the crisis on media worldwide.

16. IMF, "Greece: Third Review under the Stand-By Arrangement," p. 22: "The aim should be to begin implementing medium-term policy reforms during the second half of 2011. Staff believes that doing so is critical to the sustainability of the program."

17. Bob Traa, senior resident representative in Athens, "Achieving Sustainable Economic Reforms in Greece in 2011 and Beyond," IMF, Athens, June 7, 2011.

18. "Darum kriechen die Griechen nie aus der Krise [That's why the Greeks will never get out of the crisis]," *Bild Zeitung,* May 13, 2011.

19. Papacostantinou, "Give Greece Time to Prove It Can Do the Job."

20. Traa, "Achieving Sustainable Economic Reforms in Greece in 2011 and Beyond."

21. Final election results provided by the Ministry of Justice of Finland (http://192.49.229.35/E2011/e/tulos/tulos_kokomaa.html).

22. A major role was played by the tsunami-caused March 11, 2011, nuclear accident at Fukushima in Japan, which put the wind in the sails of the environmentalists. The Green Party became the main party in a coalition with the Social Democratic Party and nominated the first Green president of a Land in German history.

23. "Fehler nicht auf die Notenbanken abwaelzen [Do not unload the mistakes on the central banks]," *Frankfurter Allgemeine Zeitung,* May 26, 2011.

24. Plenum der Ökonomen (www.wiso.uni-hamburg.de/lucke/?p=581).

25. Paul de Grauwe, "Only a More Active ECB Can Solve the Euro Crisis," Policy Brief 250 (Brussels: Center for European Policy Studies, August 2011).

26. European Central Bank, (European System of Central Banks) Statute article 18.1-18.2 (www.ecb.int/ecb/legal/1341/1343/html/index.en.html/).

27. Christian Reiermann, "Alles immer nur schlimmer [Everything always worse]," *Der Spiegel,* August 29, 2011.

28. Evangelos Venizelos, "The Greek Debt Crisis: Prospects and Opportunities," speech at the Peterson Institute for International Economics, Washington, July 25, 2011.

29. IMF, "Euro Area Policies: 2011 Article IV Consultation—Staff Report; Public Information Notice on the Executive Board Discussion," Washington, July 2011, p. 11.

30. Ibid., p. 12.

31. *Der Spiegel* reported that even an exit of Greece from the euro area had been considered. The German magazine had originally broken the story. See "Schäuble bereitet sich auf Griechenland-Pleite vor [Schäuble prepares for Greece default]," *Der Spiegel,* July 3, 2011, p. 25.

32. "Trichet: ECB Would Reject Greek Bonds as Collateral," Reuters, July 17, 2011.

33. The total amount of the second loan to Greece was estimated between €80 and €90 billion (€25 to €30 billion by the banks and €20 billion by the IMF, on top of the EFSF lending €40 billion).

34. Author's sources. At the end of March 2011, the credits of the Bundesbank toward the rest of the euro area amounted to €330 billion, double the level of the end of 2009. They were equivalent to the overall external debt position of Portugal, Ireland, Greece, and Spain. The ECB itself held roughly €40 billion of Greek securities in its portfolio. Furthermore, the credits of the national central banks against commercial banks in their countries were huge, equivalent to 54 percent of GDP in Ireland, 38 percent in Greece, and 23 percent in Portugal. A default on the debt in the periphery was likely to shake the solidity of the monetary institutions.

35. The basis for a Greek soft restructuring was already on the table. In March, the Eurogroup changed the terms of credit to Athens by extending the maximum maturity of the loans from three years to seven-and-one-half years. The IMF had considered switching the assistance status for Greece from a Stand-by Agreement to an Extended Fund Facility, with the repayment profile stretching up to ten years. "Voluntary" involvement of private creditors could go in the same direction. Extending the maturity of the bonds coming due before 2014–15 would release resources for roughly €30 billion from the existing program.

36. Council of the European Union, Conclusions, June 23, 2001, paragraph 16, p. 6 (www.consilium.europa.eu/uedocs/cms_data/docs/pressdata/en/ec/123075.pdf).

37. Ibid., paragraph 9, p. 5.

38. The credibility of the EU package was put in question by a request advanced by the Finnish government during the EU Council. The Finnish Parliament was going to approve the loan to Greece only if it included collateral guarantees. The Helsinki finance minister hinted, in terms that struck a bellicose note, that Greece had a lot of property, real estate, and islands to sell.

39. Moody's Investors Service, "Moody's Downgrades Portugal to Ba2 with a Negative Outlook from Baa1," July 5, 2011 (www.moodys.com/research/Moodys-down grades-Portugal-to-Ba2-with-a-negative-outlook-from--PR_222043).

40. Jennifer Hughes, Ralph Atkins, and Michael MacKenzie, "Moody's Warns of Second Rescue for Portugal," *Financial Times,* July 5, 2011.

41. Tracy Alloway, "Why Here? Why Now? Why This Particular Euro Zone Peripheral?" *Financial Times,* Alphaville blog, July 27, 2010.

42. I will follow Norberto Bobbio's definition of the European ideology in Norberto Bobbio, "Teoria generale della Politica" (Turin: Einaudi, 1999).

43. The *Financial Times* ("Il Risorgimento, May 18, 2011) commented: "The country's political gridlock has long been the obstacle to economic reform. However this stasis has reached its nadir under Mr. Berlusconi. Despite styling himself as a dynamic friend of business, the prime minister has diverted scarce parliamentary time from structural reforms to his rabid crusade against the judiciary. . . . The result is that as France and Germany continue their recovery from the economic crisis, Italy is stagnating. Recent figures showed that the economy grew at a measly 0.1 per cent in the first quarter of

2011. Foreign investment is falling; one in four youths is unemployed; government debt has hit €1,800 billion."

44. The reason for the backloading was that in April the budget law (as written in the Documento di Economia e Finanza) had already accomplished a triennial structural fiscal adjustment of 0.8 percent of GDP a year, stronger than requested by the Stability and Growth Pact (0.5 percent) and based on growth forecasts lower than those of consensus.

45. Berlusconi wanted to avoid a €500,000 penalty imposed in connection with the bribery of a judge years earlier.

46. Vítor Constâncio, vice president, European Central Bank, speech at Milano Bocconi University, October 10, 2011.

47. "Debt Contagion Threatens Italy," *New York Times*, July 12, 2011, citing an estimate by Barclays Bank.

48. Chancellor Merkel's press conference in Berlin, July 11, 2011.

49. Statement by the Eurogroup, July 11, 2011 (www.consilium.europa.eu/uedocs/cms_data/docs/pressdata/en/ecofin/123601.pdf).

50. "Chancellor Merkel's Dangerous Lack of Passion for Europe," *Der Spiegel*, July 18, 2011.

51. Author interview.

52. The EWG is composed of high-level officials of the finance ministries of the euro area, the European Commission, and the ECB.

53. The generosity to the banks must be put in context of the stress tests: market participants were very concerned about sovereign exposures of the banks after the European Banking Authority identified capital shortfalls in eight of ninety major banks and recommended capital raising for another sixteen banks.

54. The schedule as reported in "Europe Takes Step Closer to Economic Government," *Der Spiegel*, July 25, 2011, pp. 19–21.

55. Peter Ludlow, "The Meeting of the Euro area Heads of State and Government on 21 July—Preliminary Evaluation," Eurocomment, Brussels, p. 11.

56. European Council, "Statement by the Heads of State or Government of the Euro Area and EU Institutions," Brussels, July 21, 2011 (www.consilium.europa.eu/uedocs/cms_data/docs/pressdata/en/ec/123978.pdf). At point 3 the statement reads: "We have decided to lengthen the maturity of future EFSF loans to Greece to the maximum extent possible from the current 7.5 years to a minimum of 15 years and up to 30 years with a grace period of 10 years. In this context, we will provide EFSF loans at lending rates equivalent to those of the Balance of Payments facility (currently approx. 3.5 percent), close to, without going below, the EFSF funding cost."

57. In a note to the text, the Council added: "Taking into account the cost of credit enhancement for the period 2011–14. In addition, a debt buy-back program will contribute to €12.6 billion euro, bringing the total to €50 billion euro. For the period 2011–2019, the total net contribution of the private sector involvement is estimated at €106 billion euro."

58. Ibid., paragraph 8, p. 2.

59. Ibid., paragraph 10, p. 3.

60. Ibid., paragraph 16, p. 4.

## Chapter 19

1. "The Man Who Screwed an Entire Country: The Berlusconi Era Will Haunt Italy for Years to Come," *The Economist,* June 9, 2011.

2. The text of the letter was published on September 29, 2011, by the newspaper *Corriere Della Sera* (www.corriere.it/economia/11_settembre_29/trichet_draghi_inglese_304a5f1e-ea59-11e0-ae06-4da866778017.shtml).

3. Draghi had described the forthcoming letter and its contents in a phone call to the prime minister. Draghi explained the logic of the letter, adding that since Italy was not part of an assistance program, necessarily it had to deal directly with the ECB. But according to press reports quoting Tremonti when he received the final version of the letter, "Berlusconi actually went rabid."

4. Italian poet Alessandro Manzoni described it in the nineteenth century: "How often you have watched the Alps longing for a friendly banner." Manzoni, "Marzo 1821 [March 1821]."

5. In the jargon of Brussels, it was a "recommendation of recommendation."

6. European Council, Recommendation of July 12, 2011, on the National Reform Program 2011 of Italy and delivering a Council opinion on the updated Stability Program of Italy, 2011–14 (2011/C 215/02).

7. Jean-Claude Trichet, president of the ECB, and Vítor Constâncio, vice-president of the ECB, "Introductory statement to the press conference (with Q&A)," European Central Bank, Frankfurt, August 4, 2011 (www.ecb.int/press/pressconf/2011/html/is110804.en.html).

8. Author's sources.

9. European Central Bank, "Statement by the President of the ECB," Frankfurt, August 7, 2011 (www.ecb.int/press/pr/date/2011/html/pr110807.en.html).

10. Ibid.

11. "Franco-German Statement on the Euro Zone Debt Crisis," Reuters, August 7, 2011.

12. Bank for International Settlements, "Quarterly Review," Basel, September 2011, p. 10.

13. European Central Bank, Statistics (www.ecb.int/stats/html/index.en.html/).

14. Schäuble's interview in *Der Spiegel,* quoted in English in Peggy Hollinger, Chris Bryant, and Quentin Peel, "Germany and France Rule Out Eurobonds," *Financial Times,* August 14, 2011.

15. "Joint letter from Nicolas Sarkozy, president of the Republic, and Angela Merkel, chancellor of Germany, to Herman Van Rompuy, president of the European Council," August 16, 2011 (www.ambafrance-uk.org/French-and-German-leaders-defend).

16. As stated in the letter in ibid., Merkel and Sarkozy launched the proposal of an "enhanced cooperation" (a procedure that allows EU countries to advance without the participation of all twenty-seven countries) to reinforce fiscal and economic discipline.

> Building on their commitments under the Euro Plus Pact, all Member States of the euro area will incorporate a balanced budget fiscal rule into their national legislation by summer 2012. . . . All Member States of the euro area should confirm

without delay their resolve to swiftly implement the European recommendations for fiscal consolidation and structural reforms, especially as regards labour-market, competition in services and pensions policy, and adapt appropriately their draft budget.

17. On September 2, Spain issued five-year bonds at a yield of 4.49 percent, 38 basis points lower than in the previous auction, after the political parties had agreed on a constitutional deficit limit proposal.

18. Kati Pohjanpaio, "Finland Gets Collateral Deal With Greece," Bloomberg, August 17, 2011 (www.bloomberg.com/news/2011-08-17/finland-gets).

19. Bundesverfassungsgericht (German Federal Constitutional Court), "Constitutional complaints lodged against aid measures for Greece and against the euro rescue package," press release, September 7, 2011 (www.bundesverfassungsgericht.de/de/en/press/bvg11-055en.html).

20. "Interview with W. Schäuble," *Frankfurter Allgemeine Zeitung*, September 22, 2011, p. 8.

21. Abigail Moses and John Glover, "German, French Bond Risk Climb to Records on Economic Slowdown Concerns," Bloomberg, September 22, 2011.

22. Data from Bloomberg and Standard & Poor's.

23. Paul de Grauwe, "The Governance of a Fragile Euro Zone," Working Document 346 (Brussels: Center for European Policy Studies, May 2011).

24. International Monetary Fund data on public finance from 1996 to 2008; data on projected deficits from the country's fiscal programs presented to the EU Commission.

25. Vítor Constâncio, vice-president of the European Central Bank, "Contagion and the European Debt Crisis," keynote lecture at the Bocconi University/Intesa Sanpaolo conference on "Bank Competitiveness in the Post-crisis World," Milan, October 10, 2011 (www.ecb.int/press/key/date/2011/html/sp111010.en.html).

26. Ludger Schuknecht, Philippe Moutot, Philipp Rother, and Jürgen Stark, "The Stability and Growth Pact: Crisis and Reform," Occasional Paper 129 (Frankfurt: European Central Bank, September 22, 2011).

27. Jens Weidmann, "Die Krise als Herausforderung fuer die Waehrungsunion [The crisis as a challenge for the Monetary Union]," speech, Cologne, September 13, 2011. He added, "Monetary policy in a monetary union therefore differs crucially from a purely national monetary policy, such as in the United States or the United Kingdom, where there is no danger of having to shunt risks resulting from unsound public finances between the taxpayers of different countries in order to avoid jeopardizing financial stability."

28. Daniel Gros and Thomas Mayer, "Refinancing the EFSF via the ECB," Center for European Policy Studies Commentary (Brussels: August 18, 2011) (www.ceps.be/).

29. Weidmann, "Die Krise als Herausforderung fuer die Waehrungsunion."

30. Ibid.

31. Quentin Peel, "Germany and the Euro Zone: Besieged in Berlin," *Financial Times*, September 26, 2011.

32. Based on the growth estimates of the Italian treasury ministry in the "Nota di aggiustamento del Documento di Economia e Finanza," September 22, 2011.

33. Mario Draghi, "L'Italia e l'economia internazionale, 1861–2011 [Italy and the international economy, 1861–2011]" (Rome: Banca d'Italia, October 12, 2011).

## Chapter 20

1. "Schuldenschnitt für Griechenland immer wahrscheinlicher [A cut on Greek debt more and more likely]," *Der Spiegel,* October 12, 2011 (www.spiegel.de/wirtschaft/soziales/0,1518,791459,00.html).

2. Irving Fisher, "The Debt-Deflation Theory of Great Depressions," *Econometrica* 4, no. 1 (1933): 337–57. A reprint may be found at http://fraser.stlouisfed.org/docs/meltzer/fisdeb33.pdf.

3. Bank for International Settlements (BIS), "Quarterly Review," Basel, December 2011, graph 1, right-hand panel.

4. Italy's two-year credit default swap premiums rose above the ten-year premiums, a typical sign of the fears of default in the coming months.

5. International Monetary Fund, "Consolidated Spillover Report—Implications from the Analysis of the Systemic-5," July 11, 2011. The report observed that only the United States, among the major economic areas of the world, could have a systemic contagion effect at the global level (www.imf.org/external/pp/longres.aspx?id=4584).

6. BIS, "Quarterly Review," p. 11.

7. Once more, the fragmentation of banking regulation played against the solution of the crisis: northern European bank supervisors amplified the interest rate differentials on loans to firms in southern Europe by setting limits to the exposure of their banks; see BIS, "Quarterly Review," p. 11.

8. European Banking Authority (EBA), "2011 EU-wide Stress Test Aggregate Report" (http://stress-test.eba.europa.eu/pdf/EBA_ST_2011_Summary_Report_v6.pdf).

9. EBA, "Results of the 2011 EBA EU-Wide Stress Test: Summary" (http://stress-test.eba.europa.eu/pdf/bank/BE004.pdf).

10. Christine Lagarde, managing director, International Monetary Fund, "Global Risks Are Rising, but There Is a Path to Recovery," speech, Jackson Hole, Wyo., August 27, 2011.

11. The Basel Committee, one of the most important technical authorities in world banking regulation, decided also to take into account the losses in market value on sovereign bonds for the calculation of the prudential capital. The decision was opposed by the central banks in the periphery, but the Spanish and Italian governors were put in minority by their colleagues. While the market value depends on the current market price, the historical value is the value of the asset when it was purchased.

12. David Enrich and Laura Stevens, "Old Debts Dog Europe's Banks," *Wall Street Journal,* November 7, 2011. According to a report of a Swiss bank, "sixteen top European banks were holding a total of about €386 billion ($532 billion) of potentially suspect credit-market and real-estate assets," instruments like "collateralized debt obligations" and "leveraged loans." That was more than the €339 billion of Greek, Irish,

Italian, Portuguese, and Spanish government debt that those same banks were holding at the end of last year, according to European "stress test" data. European banks, on average, had only halved their stockpiles of the legacy assets since 2007, the analysis found. Meanwhile, the top three U.S. banks—Bank of America, Citigroup, and J. P. Morgan Chase—had slashed such assets by well over 80 percent over a similar period. Four French banks trimmed theirs by less than 30 percent. Deutsche Bank's exposure to toxic assets was estimated to be more than 150 percent of its tangible equity. To avoid the losses of marking down the value of the tossic assets, or to raise capital, the German, British, and French banks cut government bonds of the periphery by around €65 billion, or 14 percent of the total, in the twelve months before September 2011.

13. A further blow to the flagging confidence of investors came in mid-October when, following more than a year of difficult negotiations, the European Parliament agreed to ban the so-called naked credit default swaps (CDS) on sovereign debt in an attempt to curb what German and French policymakers, in particular, saw as hedge fund bets on the sovereign crisis. Italy and Spain again were opposed to a ban on naked CDS, fearing that it would spook investors unable to buy a hedge on their securities, and add further pressure to the countries' borrowing costs. They were right; the consequence was an immediate increase in borrowing costs in the periphery, aggravating the crisis in its worst phase.

14. "Herbstgutachten der Wirtschaftsweisen [Autumn report of the wisemen for the economy]," October 2011 (www.sachverstaendigenrat-wirtschaft.de/). The "wisemen for the economy" is formally known as Der Sachverständigenrat zur Begutachtung der gesamtwirtschaftlichen Entwicklung [Council of the experts for the assessment of the economic development] and is headquartered in Wiesbaden, Germany.

15. At an ECOFIN meeting on September 16 in Wroclaw, Poland, U.S. Treasury secretary Timothy Geithner lashed out at his European colleagues. Europeans were shocked by what they thought was a display of impudence against the backdrop of what they considered failures of the U.S. economic management for many years. German and Austrian ministers hit back at Geithner.

16. "U.S. Secretary Geithner on the Need to Work Closely with the ECB," Reuters, September 24, 2011.

17. "Merkel, Sarkozy Promise New Crisis Package, Offer No Details," Reuters, October 9, 2011.

18. Mario Draghi, president of the European Central Bank, "Continuity, Consistency and Credibility," introductory remarks at the 21st Frankfurt European Banking Congress, "The Big Shift," November 18, 2011 (www.ecb.int/press/key/date/2011/html/sp111118.en.html).

19. "Angriff auf die Bundesbank—Jetzt sollen unsere Gold-Reserven geopfert werden [Attack on the Bundesbank—now we are asked to sacrifice our gold reserves]," *Bild Zeitung*, November 5, 2011.

20. Interview with Helmut Schmidt, "Im Herzen sind die Bundesbanker Reaktionäre [In their hearts the Bundesbankers are reactionary]," *Die Zeit*, July 7, 2010.

21. Mario Draghi, "Intervento alla Giornata Mondiale del Risparmio del 2011," speech, Associazione di Fondazioni e di Casse di Risparmio Spa, Rome, October 26, 2011.

22. Meeting account based on author's sources.

23. Peter Ludlow, of Eurocomment, described the transatlantic talk in his newsletters "A Tale of Five Summits" and "Reflections on the Euro Crisis at the end of November 2011."

24. European Council, "Euro Summit Statement," October 26, 2011 (www.consilium. europa.eu/uedocs/cms_Data/docs/pressdata/en/ec/125644.pdf).

25. The EFSF would have the flexibility to use these options simultaneously, deploying them depending on the specific objective pursued and on market circumstances. The leverage effect of each option would vary, depending on their specific features and market conditions, but could be up to four or five. In addition, further enhancement of the EFSF resources could be achieved by cooperating even more closely with the IMF. The Eurogroup, the European Commission, and the EFSF were to work on all possible options.

26. In particular, the success of the proposed special purpose vehicles depended on the extent to which investors were willing to finance the sovereign debt of vulnerable countries at yields that did not threaten debt sustainability. The issue of recapitalizing the banking system had been handled by the EU Council just before the beginning of the Eurogroup, so the EU Council communiqué only mentioned that an agreement had been found to encourage an increase in capital for a total of €106 billion. Banks had a deadline of June 2012 to raise their "core" capital ratios to 9 percent.

27. There were three main issues. First was reinforcing national fiscal frameworks by basing national budgets on independent growth forecasts and introducing national legislation to establish rules on structural balanced budgets, preferably at the constitutional level or equivalent. The second matter involved enhancing fiscal monitoring and, by allowing the European Commission and the Council to examine and comment on national draft budgets, monitoring implementation and suggesting amendments. The third was a commitment to stick to the recommendations of the commission regarding the implementation of the Stability and Growth Pact.

28. European Council, "Euro Summit Statement," October 26, 2011, paragraph 12, p. 4. "The euro zone Member States would contribute to the PSI package up to €30 billion. On that basis, the official sector stands ready to provide additional program financing of up to €100 billion until 2014, including the required recapitalization of Greek banks." The leaders added that they welcomed the "decision by the Eurogroup on the disbursement of the sixth tranche of the EU-IMF support program."

29. Ibid., paragraph 16, p. 5.

30. Noah Barkin and Erik Kirschbaum, "The Maverick behind Merkel," Reuters Special Report, December 14, 2011 (www.reuters.com/article/2011/12/14/us-europe-merkel-schaeuble-idUSTRE7BD0IU20111214).

31. Stefan Simons, "Tough Words—Merkel and Sarkozy Halt Payments to Athens," *Der Spiegel,* November 3, 2011.

32. Author's sources.

33. International Monetary Fund, Transcript of a Press Briefing with Christine Lagarde, Cannes, France Friday, November 4, 2011.

34. European Council/European Commission, "Request for Clarifications on the Letter from PM Silvio Berlusconi to the President of the European Council and the President of the European Commission," November 8, 2011.

35. The EU fiscal forecasts were based on growth estimates revised in October that were lower than those of the Italian government: for 2011, 0.5 percent (instead of 0.7 percent); for 2012, 0.1 percent (instead of 0.6 percent); and for 2013, 0.7 percent (instead of 0.9 percent).

36. A German bond auction on November 23 was poorly subscribed, raising just 65 percent of the target amount after the yields were marketed at a 200-year low.

37. Council of the European Union, "Statement by the Euro Area Heads of State or Government, Brussels, December 9, 2011" (www.consilium.europa.eu/uedocs/cms_data/docs/pressdata/en/ec/126658.pdf).

38. In that respect, it remained open that the EFSF might still be able to put in place new programs up to the middle of 2013 (its original end-date), so that the two facilities together might be able to employ a higher amount of resources in that critical period. The EFSF role was eventually limited to raising the money (mostly from private sources) to fund bailouts for the three small euro area countries under assistance.

39. European Council, "Remarks by Herman Van Rompuy, President of the European Council, Following the First Session of the European Council," Brussels, December 9, 2011 (www.consilium.europa.eu/uedocs/cms_data/docs/pressdata/en/ec/126657. pdf). As for PSI, the new agreement called for the ESM to "strictly adhere to the well-established IMF principles and practices," which means that investors in the euro area debt will be subject to the threat of a haircut no more than any other sovereign debt in the world.

40. Council of the European Union, "Statement by the Euro Area Heads of State or Government, Brussels, December 9, 2011," paragraph 16, p. 8.

41. Economists know that the definition of structural deficit is controversial, but it is also a necessary tool to avoid procyclical effects, that is, to avoid cutting deficits too much during a recession.

42. Mario Draghi, president of the European Central Bank, and Vítor Constâncio, vice president of the European Central Bank, "Introductory Statement to the Press Conference (with Q&A)," European Central Bank, Frankfurt, December 8, 2011 (www.ecb. int/press/pressconf/2011/html/is111208.en.html).

43. An analogous mechanism could be valid for securities issued by the banks, and the Italian government quickly took the opportunity to back them with state guarantees.

44. Angela Merkel, "Government's Statement by Chancellor Merkel: Europe Will Emerge Stronger from the Crisis," Regierungserklärung von Bundeskanzlerin Angela Merkel zu den Ergebnissen des Europäischen Rats am 8. und 9. Dezember in Brüssel [Government statement by Federal Chancellor Angela Merkel about the results of the December 8–9 EU Council in Brussels], December 14, 2011 (www.bundeskanzlerin. de/Content/EN/Artikel/__2011/12/2011-12-14-er-bk-regierungserklaerung__en.html).

## Epilogue

1. European Treaty Articles 4(2), 118, and 123(4).

2. The disorder and the dire political consequences would worsen in the case of an expulsion from the euro area. This option is also not consistent with the treaty

and would require an amendment through unanimous consent from all twenty-seven countries of the European Union, including the expelled country. Although a number of potential sanctions and remedies consistent with the treaty can be imposed on an "errant state"—one example is Articles 7(2) and (3), which allow the council to suspend some of a member states' rights (including its voting rights in the council) for a "serious and persistent breach by a Member State of the principles mentioned in Article 6(1)" of the EU treaty—the spirit of the treaty is to correct wrongdoing rather than expel the errant country.

# Index

395